Path from Puebla

Significant Documents
of the
Latin American Bishops since 1979

Edward Cleary, OP
Editor

Phillip Berryman
Translator

Secretariat
Bishops' Committee for the Church in Latin America
National Conference of Catholic Bishops

In its 1987 planning document, the NCCB Committee for the Church in Latin America was authorized to prepare a publication to commemorate the tenth and twentieth anniversaries, respectively, of the Second and Third General Conferences of the Episcopal Council of Latin America (CELAM). This present volume brings together significant documents of national episcopal conferences or regional groupings of bishops in Latin America issued since the Third General Conference held in Puebla, Mexico, in 1979. *Path from Puebla: Significant Documents of the Latin American Bishops since 1979* has been reviewed and approved by Monsignor David M. Gallivan, Executive Director of the NCCB Secretariat for Latin America, and is authorized for publication by the undersigned.

Monsignor Daniel F. Hoye
General Secretary
June 19, 1988   NCCB/USCC

ISBN 1–55586–225–X

Excerpts from *Documents of Vatican II*, Walter M. Abbott, SJ, general editor, copyright © 1966, America Press, Inc., 106 West 56th Street, New York, N.Y. are reprinted with permission. All rights reserved.

Contents

IV. Economic Life

V. Critical National or Regional Issues

A. Land

B. Refugees

C. Drug Addiction and Trafficking

VI. Transnational Issues

A. Central America

Document Index according to Countries and Regions

Southern Andes, Peru
Witnesses to the Resurrection (1987)

Uruguay
Solidarity and Hope (1983)
Pastoral Reflections on the Present Situation (1986)

Venezuela
The Church Speaks for the Unemployed (1986)
They Will Build Their Houses and Live in Them (1987)

Central America, Panama, and Mexico

Costa Rica
United in Hope (1981)

El Salvador
Called to Be Artisans of Peace (1984)

Guatemala
Massacre of Peasants (1982)
To Construct Peace (1984)
Guidelines for Charismatic Renewal (1986)

Honduras
Statement on War, Dialogue, and Reconciliation (1983)

Nicaragua
Christian Commitment for a New Nicaragua (1979)
Eucharist: Fount of Unity (1986)

Panama
Ecumenism: Objectives, Attainments, and Flaws (1984)

(with Central America)
Message to Our People (1984)

(with Central America
and the United States)
Joint Statement by Central American and U.S. Bishops (1987)

Mexico
At the Service of the Human Community: An Ethical Consideration of the International Debt (1987)

Southern Pacific Coast, Mexico

Statement on the Refugee Situation (1982)

The Gospel and Temporal Goods (1985)

Caribbean

Antilles

True Freedom and Development in the Caribbean (1982)

Cuba

National Encounter of the Cuban Church (1986)

External Debt and the New International Economic Order (1986)

Christmas Message (1987)

Dominican Republic

Message to the Dominican People (1985)

Haiti

Priorities and Changes (1986)

Christmas Message (1987)

Puerto Rico

The Political Situation of the Country (1983)

Peace among Human Beings (1984)

Abbreviations Used in
Path from Puebla

AA   *Apostolicam Actuositatem* ("On the Apostolate of the Laity"). Decree of the Second Vatican Council (Rome 1965).

AAS   *Acta Apostolicae Sedis* ("Acts of the Apostolic See"). Periodical published at Vatican City as the official record of papal statements (Rome, 1909-).

AG   *Ad Gentes* ("On the Missionary Activity of the Church"). Decree of the Second Vatican Council (1965).

CELAM   Episcopal Council of Latin America.

EN   *Evangelii Nuntiandi* ("On Evangelization in the Modern World"). Apostolic Exhortation of Pope Paul VI (1975).

GS   *Gaudium et Spes* ("Pastoral Constitution on the Church in the Modern World"). Second Vatican Council (Rome, 7 December 1965).

JP   *Justice and Peace in a New Caribbean*. Pastoral Letter of the Catholic Bishops of the Antilles (1975).

LAB   The Latin American Bureau. Office established by the National Catholic Welfare Conference (now NCCB/ USCC) to deal with Latin American affairs; forerunner of the present Secretariat.

LE   *Laborem Exercens* ("On Human Work"). Encyclical of Pope John Paul II (1981).

LG   *Lumen Gentium* ("Dogmatic Constitution on the Church"). Second Vatican Council (Rome, 21 November 1964).

MM   *Mater et Magistra* ("Mother and Teacher") Encyclical of Pope John XXIII (1961).

Medellín *The Church in the Present-Day Transformation of Latin America in the Light of the Council.* Conclusions of the Second General Conference of Latin American Bishops (Medellín, 1968).

Message *World Day of Peace Message* (1983). Message of Peace given by Pope John Paul II.

NCCB National Conference of Catholic Bishops (USA).

OA *Octogesima Adveniens* ("On the Eightieth Anniversary of *Rerum Novarum*"). Apostolic Letter of Pope Paul VI (1974).

OAP *Opening Address at Puebla.* Pope John Paul II (Puebla, 1979).

OT *Optatam Totius* ("On Priestly Formation"). Decree of the Second Vatican Council (1965).

PAVLA The Papal Volunteers for Latin America.

PC *Perfectae Caritatis* ("On the Appropriate Renewal of the Religious Life"). Decree of the Second Vatican Council (1965).

PO *Presbyterorum Ordinis* ("On the Ministry and Life of Priests"). Decree of the Second Vatican Council (7 December 1965).

PP *Populorum Progressio* ("On the Development of Peoples"). Encyclical of Pope Paul VI (1967).

Puebla *Evangelization at Present and in the Future of Latin America.* Conclusions of the Third General Conference of Latin American Bishops (Puebla, 1979).

QA *Quadragesimo Anno.* ("On Reconstructing the Social Order"). Encyclical of Pope Pius XI (1931).

RH *Redemptor Hominis* ("Redeemer of Man"). Encyclical of Pope John Paul II (1979).

RN *Rerum Novarum* ("On the Condition of Labor"). Encyclical of Pope Leo XIII (1891).

USCC United States Catholic Conference.

Another Anniversary

This volume has been produced in commemoration of the twentieth and tenth anniversaries, respectively, of the Latin American Bishops' Assemblies at Medellín and Puebla. However, American Catholics should commemorate another significant date: in November 1959, North American and Latin American bishops met at Georgetown University in Washington, D.C. There, at the behest of the Vatican, they discussed what, for the Church in the United States, evolved into a five-point program of assistance for the Church in Latin America: (1) the involvement of American diocesan priests in missionary work in Latin America; (2) the establishment of U.S. diocesan missions in Latin America; (3) the creation of a group of lay missionaries; (4) the recruitment of missionaries for Latin America from religious communities in the United States; and (5) the establishment of a national fund for the Church in Latin America.

As we approach the five hundredth anniversary of evangelization in the Americas, thirty years would seem to be a small piece of history to review. Such a review is useful, however, because it is in this period that a serious institutional relationship has come to exist between the Church in the United States and the Church in Latin America. (Latin America is the imprecise label we will use for Mexico, Central America and Panama, the Caribbean Islands—regardless of language—and the continent of South America.)

While political and canonical relationships had taken place since the sixteenth century (Florida and much of the Southwest belonged to the ecclesiastical provinces of Cuba and Mexico until they became possessions of the United States), a truly ecclesial and collegial relationship began only in the years immediately preceding the Second Vatican Council.

Providentially, the dialogue continued formally and informally at the Council. Assistance programs were designed with the unmistakable influences of conciliar thinking. The relationship between the Church of the United States and that of Latin America has deepened in these thirty years, and both have benefited immensely.

A convenient way to study this relationship is to examine the activities of the office created by the U.S. bishops, through which they have dealt with the Church in Latin America. Shortly after the Georgetown meeting, the National Catholic Welfare Conference (now the National Conference of Catholic Bishops and the United States Catholic Conference) created the Latin American Bureau (LAB). Briefly, its purpose was to address the issues of (1) missionary personnel; (2) the education of U.S. Catholics in the Latin American reality; (3) and financial assistance. These really summarize the five-point program discussed since the Georgetown meeting. In subsequent reorganizations of the NCCB/USCC, the Latin American Bureau became the Division for Latin America, and, finally in 1974, it received its present name: the Secretariat for Latin America (SLA).

In the United States, there had been an enthusiastic reception of the call of Pope John XXIII who, in 1963, asked not only for financial and material assistance for Latin America, but even 10 percent (a tithe) of the priests and religious of the Church in the United States. At the same time, great social upheavals, beginning with the Cuban Revolution in 1959, placed Latin America in the geopolitical spotlight. There was sudden interest in this heretofore little known part of the world. There was an insatiable thirst for information, especially among Catholics who had heard and wished to respond to the pope's plea. There was enthusiastic willingness on the part of many to serve as missionaries in Latin America, as well as a commitment of financial aid from Catholics in the United States, through their bishops. We can describe the response of the United States under the three headings suggested above: missionary personnel, education of U.S. Catholics, and financial assistance.

Missionary Personnel

In 1960, there were 2,405 U.S. missionaries in Latin America. Had the Church in the United States responded literally to John XXIII's plea for a tithe of U.S. clergy and religious, 23,000 more would have eventually joined them. However, in 1968, the peak year, only 4,589 American missionaries ministered in Latin America. At this writing, there are 2,906 missionaries (including 231 lay persons) from our country serving there.

The Latin American Bureau encouraged dioceses and religious communities to recruit clergy, religious, and laity in the early sixties, but training and placement of these missionaries proved difficult to coordinate. Bishops and religious superiors from the United States made arrangements with individual dioceses in Latin America missions, with little study or coordination, sometimes causing heavy concentration of foreign personnel in certain areas.

In 1966, there were seventy-five U.S. diocesan missions. Presently, there are about half that number. While diocesan priests still serve in Latin America, it is now more common for them to join traditional U.S. missionary groups as associates for a fixed period of time.

In the mid-1960s, the LAB created and trained a number of lay missionaries called the Papal Volunteers for Latin America (PAVLA). The concept of lay missionaries was a revolutionary one. In spite of the fact that lay men and women now comprise the fastest growing segment of today's U.S. church personnel abroad, the PAVLA experiment ended in 1971. Today, lay persons may join the lay associate programs of many missionary groups. Several dioceses, such as Cleveland, Denver, and soon, Chicago, are also involving lay men and women in their programs.

Numerically, our missionary representation in Latin America is just about the same as in 1960, and half as many as in 1968. This does not mean, however, that John XXIII's plea has gone unheeded. Thousands of American priests, religious, and laity have given the most productive years of their lives to the Church in Latin America. There have been and continue to be excellent experiences. Perhaps some positive examples will illustrate this.

The San Miguelito Mission in Panama, originally sponsored and staffed by priests of the Archdiocese of Chicago, became in the 1960s, a paradigm for the many Latin American pastoral workers and U.S. missionaries arriving in Latin America. Now, years later, its indelible marks are still clearly recognizable in the pastoral history of Latin America: *pastoral de conjunto* (poorly translated as "team ministry"), lay involvement in ministry, and evangelization through smaller groupings of neighbors. The San Miguelito experience was an important moment in Latin American church history.

A lesser known example is that of the missionary team from the Diocese of Jefferson City (Missouri) in the Dioceses of Puno and Ica (Peru). Since 1962, priests, religious, and laity from this small diocese have maintained a successful and mutually enriching ecclesial relationship. From the beginning, these American missionaries have completely assimilated themselves into the life of the diocese, assuming its priorities, never building "a church apart," or an "American island." Missouri Catholics feel that they are part of a missionary experience in Peru and are surprisingly familiar with the Peruvian reality through a highly successful diocesan mission exchange and education program.

Guatemalan *campesinos* (peasants) still gather to pray in the room where their pastor, Fr. Stanley Rother, of the Diocese of Oklahoma City, was murdered in 1981. In death, he joins many native catechists and "Delegates of the Word" who made the supreme sacrifice out of love for the gospel. Fr. Rother's room has become a Guatemalan shrine.

More than 180 communities of men and women religious from the United States still labor in Latin America. The Congregation of the Holy Cross, for example, arrived in Chile many years ago and soon found themselves administering a private school for the affluent. Since then, St. George's College has produced many fine politicians, socially committed professionals, and Chilean priests who have ministered among the poor. These priests and brothers also minister in some of Santiago's poorest neighborhoods. They have suffered harassment and persecution because of their consistent option for the poor. They have now established an independent Chilean province with a good number of Chilean members.

The Franciscans of the Holy Name Province became involved in Bolivia in the mid-1950s, and within a few years, they began a mission in Peru. Those who remain are now members of the local province and are outnumbered by the indigenous members of the Peru-Bolivia Province.

When lay woman Jean Donovan, Maryknoll Sisters Ita Ford and Maura Clarke, and Ursuline Sister Dorothy Kazel—all of the Diocese of Cleveland's Mission in El Salvador—were murdered on December 2, 1981, they joined hundreds of thousands of Central American victims of the fratricidal wars in that region.

These are but a few of the many examples of American church men and woman who have mingled their lives, and sometimes their deaths, with those of their Latin American brothers and sisters. While U.S. missionaries are now fewer, the number of young Latin American men and women replacing them is most encouraging. Today, more than in earlier years, it is quite common for U.S. missionaries and Latin American clergy, religious, and lay ministers to work, pray, and live together. Since the CELAM assemblies at Medellín and Puebla, the Latin American Church, from the base communities to the hierarchy, has opted for the poor. This option has not been lost on young people. Thousands of sons and daughters of the poor have considered religious and priestly vocations. These young people, among the most committed Christians in their countries, also point to the example of foreign missionaries as crucial in their vocational choices.

Certainly, American missionaries have made mistakes. The examples of the attempted reproduction of U.S. parishes, institutions, and worship styles are many and sad. We often created little "oases" in the desert. With well-meaning but insensitive displays of resources, we appeared more generous and effective than national clergy and religious who did not solve problems and build as quickly as the foreigners. We learned, often too late and with no little pain, that the only effective way to "be Church" was to do so in a truly local, incarnate way, in dialogue with our brothers and sisters in ministry, with respect for the culture of the people we served, and under the leadership of the diocesan bishop and conference of bishops.

This writer went as a missionary to Latin America in the mid-1960s and participated in some of the above " sins." As I travel through

Latin America today, I meet missionaries more mature in years and in spirituality, much more comfortable working within local ecclesial structures and means.

In the early 1960s, there was an effort, through the LAB, to coordinate recruitment and training of missionaries from dioceses and religious communities in the United States. Soon, however, these tasks fell to the individual sending groups, in coordination with the receiving missionary regions. While a better organized program would have seemed more desirable to some, it was not to be. The bishops of the United States sponsored programs for PAVLA at The Catholic University of America in Washington, D.C., and courses for clergy, religious, and laity at The Catholic University of Puerto Rico in Ponce. Today, there are training courses in several centers, conducted by missionary-sending groups. The bishops of the United States, through the Secretariat for Latin America, sponsor one such program: the Latin American Program at the Mexican American Cultural Center in San Antonio, Texas. Participants in this program receive courses in missiology, social analysis, and inculturation at the center. They also spend nearly a month with families and communities in central and northern Mexico. The program takes place annually from August to November.

In spite of diminished numbers, a U.S. missionary presence in Latin America would seem to be a permanent part of our future, just as a Latin American presence will be an unmistakable part of the future of the North American Church. An unexpected but welcome dividend for the Church in our country are the many hundreds of returned missionaries who are engaged in "reverse mission." They have provided credible personal knowledge of events and policies in the countries where they formerly worked. They have become effective ministers within the burgeoning Hispanic Catholic community in the United States. They have introduced uniquely Latin American concepts into the mainstream of U.S. Catholic pastoral life. Most important, they have given to their brothers and sisters in ministry much needed witness of evangelical poverty and healthy social involvement. Some observers would say that this concept of "reverse mission" may well be the most significant result of our experiences in Latin America.

Education of U.S. Catholics

The Latin American Bureau was originally assigned the task of educating U.S. Catholics in the realities of Latin America. When we recall the social, pastoral, and theological effervescence in Latin America during the 1960s and 1970s, this was an exciting challenge. The LAB organized the Catholic Inter-American Cooperation Program (CI-

COP), part of which involved an annual—and very successful—inter-American conference. Leading religious and political figures, social scientists, and educators came together from all over Latin and North America. These gatherings attracted hundreds of participants, and the written proceedings were widely disseminated. The bishops' Latin American office supported publications such as *LADOC, Noticias Aliadas, Latinamerica Press,* and *Latin America Calls.* The first three widely respected publications were local Latin American initiatives, funded by the U.S. bishops' allocations program. Today, they are fully independent and self-supporting.

The Secretariat for Latin America has been less involved in formal educational efforts but has made several significant contributions. Since the mid-1960s, it has partially funded the annual Inter-American Bishops' Meeting. Part of the process that led to the pastoral letter *Economic Justice For All* was an important consultation between U.S. and Latin American bishops, partially funded by U.S. Catholics through the SLA. In 1987, when the bishops of the United States wished to update their position on the situation of Central America, they arranged a consultation with Central American bishops in Costa Rica. The SLA provided funding for this meeting. This present volume is another example of the desire of the U.S. bishops to provide ongoing education for American Catholics with regard to the life of the Latin American Church. Occasional seminars focusing on Latin American topics are also funded from the National Collection for the Church in Latin America. Many important Latin American church documents, beginning with the conclusions of the CELAM assemblies at Medellín and Puebla, have been translated and disseminated by this office. The SLA has coordinated important contacts between U.S. bishops and North American missionaries in Latin America. These contacts have been crucial to our bishops' understanding of Latin American issues.

In this section, we have attempted to describe how Catholics in the United States, through the SLA, have contributed to a better understanding of Latin American issues within our own country.

Financial Assistance

The coordination of a missionary effort and the education of Catholics in the United States on Latin American issues are only two of the historical mandates of the NCCB Committee for the Church in Latin America. Indeed, time, events, and reorganization have made them its least time-consuming tasks. By far, the major concerns of the committee are presently the collection and distribution of funds for pastoral projects in Latin America. Each year since 1966, the National Collection for the Church in Latin America typically has been taken place on the last weekend of January. In 1987, the collection raised $3,496,355; the collected funds grows each year by about $200,000. In that same year, 317 specific projects of a pastoral nature were supported in virtually every Latin American country. While 1988 figures are not yet available, it appears that more than 350 projects will receive partial funding. Since its beginning, the NCCB Committee for the Church in Latin America has supported more than 3,600 separate pastoral projects, with a total of nearly $42 million. While this may seem a rather modest sum, in view of the tremendous financial resources of our country, it should be remembered that there are in the United States many private Catholic foundations, Catholic dioceses, and other official church agencies that also independently channel many millions of dollars annually into the Latin American Church. An informal 1986 study by this office determined that in 1986, in addition to SLA funds and private Catholic foundation grants, nearly $25 million was channeled from U.S. Catholics to the Church in Latin America. These funds went to development projects, local efforts of missionaries, gifts to Latin American church agencies and personnel, and so forth.

It may be useful to outline the criteria and the process by which the NCCB Committee for the Church in Latin America (comprised of seven U.S. bishops) authorizes financial assistance for projects of the Latin American Church. First, the criteria and some examples.

From the beginning, the Committee for the Church in Latin America, under the leadership of Richard Cardinal Cushing (Boston) and Bishop James A. McNulty (Buffalo), rejected a paternalistic role. Input was sought from leaders of the Latin American Church. A group of Latin American bishops, headed by the visionary Chilean, Bishop Manuel Larraín, joined U.S. counterparts in drawing up the criteria that (with minor adjustments) still guide the committee in apportioning the funds collected annually.

The committee assists church projects, especially those related to the application of the conclusions of the Second Vatican Council; the Second General Assembly of the Latin American Bishops at Medellín, Colombia; and the Third General Assembly at Puebla, Mexico. Particular priority is given to pastoral programs and to pilot projects that will provide the basis for effective planning for the Church in Latin America.

Since the inception of the U.S. bishops' fund for the Church in Latin America in 1959, certain basic principles were taken into consideration when establishing criteria for financial aid. With their brother bishops in Latin America, the U.S. bishops recognize that programs should be designed to aid the Latin American Church in the development of local responses to local challenges. All economic aid from outside is, by nature, exceptional and transitory.

The object of the fund is to initiate programs, not to maintain them.

Applicants must supply from local sources about one-third of the cost of a project for which funding is requested. Most projects are funded for only twelve months.

The committee wishes to assist in the development of local church leadership. Therefore, among its priorities are projects of formation of lay leadership, preparation of evangelizers, catechists, and permanent deacons. In recent years, the fastest growing project category deals with the formation of seminarians and religious. In 1987, $759,300 in grants were approved for the formation of young men and women pursuing religious and priestly vocations. Several grants have been made to the Latin American Organization of Seminaries (OSLAM) in order to better prepare seminary formation teams.

Since pastoral planning is so important in Latin America, the committee is most supportive of serious studies and surveys of a socio-religious nature in local settings in Latin America. Many of the research projects of the respected Centro Bellarmino in Santiago (Chile) have been partially sponsored by the committee. The Episcopal Conference of Panama recently did an in-depth study, with committee support, of the phenomenon of the growth of religious sects. The highly specialized task of translating the Holy Scriptures into Papiamentu, the indigenous language of the Netherlands Antilles, is also a committee-sponsored endeavor. Especially useful to the Brazilian Church is the research provided by the Center for Religious Statistics and Social Investigation (CERIS). SLA has supported several of its projects over the years.

There are many other significant Latin American church initiatives that have been supported by U.S. Catholics through the annual collection for the Church in Latin America: the formation of Honduras' "Delegates of the Word" in the late 1960s (extended since then throughout Central America); the highly successful "Symposium of the Haitian Church" in 1986; several important courses and congresses for leaders of Brazil's many *comunidades de base* (basic ecclesial communities).

Latin America's bishops, religious, clergy, and laity have been most creative and active in the past thirty years. The Church in the United States, by the design of its bishops and the generosity of its members, has been most supportive.

Now to explain the process by which grants are made. Petitioners can be lay persons, clergy, religious, bishops, groupings of bishops— anyone who exercises some recognized pastoral function. They make contact with the committee through the Secretariat for Latin America. If, after initial correspondence or conversation, it seems that a project fits within the committee's guidelines (outlined above), the petitioner is given a simple form on which he or she will describe the project, giving a clear idea of its proposed budget and the expected results.

Each project must be reviewed and approved by the local diocesan bishop, the national episcopal conference, or CELAM (depending on its scope). The endorsement of the diocesan bishop or of the episcopal conference is sought in order to ensure that the project is in line with local pastoral priorities.

The seven members of the NCCB Committee for the Church in Latin America meet twice each year, usually in May and November, to review the projects and allocate the funds. Two to three months prior to each meeting, the committee members must thoroughly study materials relating to the projects that will be discussed. That is why petitioners are advised that it may take from eight to twelve months to receive a final reply from the committee.

Conclusion

By reviewing the past and present activities of the committee for the Church in Latin America and its secretariat, we have sketched some important aspects of collaboration between the Church in our country and the Church in Latin America since 1959. The information shared here should not make U.S. Catholics complacent. Rather, our purpose is to point out some of the concrete and creative ways in which they, with and through the NCCB/USCC, have accompanied the Church in Latin America for these past thirty years. Our hope is that what has been shared in these pages will encourage North American readers to exercise even more informed solidarity and greater financial generosity with our sister churches to the south through the annual Collection for the Church in Latin America. An equally important hope is that U.S. Catholics will acquire and study NCCB/USCC documents relating to the Church in Latin America (available through the USCC Office of Publishing Services). Present socioeconomic realities there, as well as the policies of our own government, demand that we maintain and increase our respectful participation in pastoral life in that part of the world.

With God's grace, with the continued creativity of the Latin American Church, with the conscientious generosity and commitment of Catholics of the North and South, the next 500 years of evangelization in the Americas can only yield a richer harvest.

Monsignor David M. Gallivan
Executive Director
Secretariat, Bishops' Committee for
the Church in Latin America

Medellín and Puebla
from a
U.S. Perspective

Rationale for This Publication

The Committee for the Church in Latin America of the National Conference of Catholic Bishops decided to co-publish the documents in this book in order to fulfill, in part, its functions to assist in the education of the U.S. Church on the Church in Latin America. The committee, through its Secretariat for Latin America, sponsors many projects and programs of an evangelistic and pastoral nature throughout Latin America. The committee members have seen fit to publish papers from their sister episcopal conferences that have inspired these projects and programs. Many of these documents have never been available in English and have never been published *en bloc*, even in Spanish.

We entered the project also out of solidarity with our brother bishops in Latin America, who have been courageously faithful to the prophethic mission to preach the good news and to denounce injustices and violence that take away from the vision of the kingdom of Christ. For a proper appreciation of the role of the Church in a part of the world beset by political and social turmoil, these documents are invaluable to the Church in the United States.

Because our country is so much and so often the source of Latin America's ills, it is imperative that we know the response of the Church there and discover avenues that could lead us in influencing our governmental and economic institutions that have a bearing on the people of Latin America.

The Church in Latin America, through its bishops' statements, has raised moral and justice issues of universal scope. Principles of our teaching tradition on morality and social justice are applied to concrete and specific situations in these statements. They are a reminder that the teachings of the Church's principles on such matters are not irrelevant to the late twentieth century but, on the contrary, are very much on target and at the cutting edge of contemporary issues. The

Church does have something of paramount importance to say on issues of justice, peace, human dignity, and political and social reform. These papers remind us that the Church not only has a right to speak on such issues but also has a serious duty to do so.

In speaking out, the Latin American bishops have at least indirectly spoken to us, the bishops of the United States. Their pronouncements are a frequent inspiration that provides impetus for our own prophetic statements. Their courage gives us courage; their hope gives us hope; and their perspective sharpens our own. This writer is convinced that both the Medellín and Puebla conferences were a strong influence in our decisions to speak out on peace and economic justice issues.

Historical Overview of Medellín and Puebla

To have a clear picture of the substance of the documents of the Second and Third Conferences of Latin American Bishops, we have to consider the historical contexts of both Medellín and Puebla. The first conference was held in Rio de Janeiro in 1955. It was the first time that Latin American bishops had come together in Latin America in modern times. A previous meeting had been held in Rome in 1899. At Rio de Janeiro, the structures of CELAM (*Consejo Episcopal Latinoamericano*) were set up and these, in turn, were instrumental in establishing the relationship among the local churches and among the leaders of those churches, which led to the cohesion expressed at Medellín and Puebla.

Medellín and Its Historical Context

Medellín was held in 1968, a year of confrontation that was approaching the culmination of a decade of strife and turmoil in many parts of the world. This had been especially true in Latin America. To capture the scene, one only has to cite a few examples: Fidel Castro took over Cuba in 1959; the short-lived "Revolution in Freedom" under Eduardo Frei in Chile occurred in the mid-1960s; the Tupamaro Movement in Uruguay began in 1964; Camilo Torres, priest-guerrilla in Colombia, was killed in 1966; in 1962, a communist guerrilla army was organized in Venezuela; a student revolt was mercilessly shot down in Mexico in 1968, a scarce month or so after Medellín.[1]

Medellín confronted head-on the historical situation in which Latin America found itself in 1968. The conference fathers observed the

---

[1] See Parada, *Crónica de Medellín,* pp. 117–165.

happenings around them as signs of the times that must be interpreted in the light of revelation and church teaching, particularly that of Vatican II (*Gaudium et Spes*) and of papal pronouncements such as John XXIII's *Pacem in Terris* and Paul VI's *Populorum Progressio*. The title of the Medellín documents reveals its intent: *The Church in the Present-Day Transformation of Latin America in the Light of the Council*. Challenged by Pope Paul VI, who opened the conference, and led by a distinguished honor roll of ecclesiastics such as Eduardo Pironio, Pablo Munoz Vega, Leonidas Proano, Raul Silva, Juan Landazuri, and Helder Camara, Medellín became a singular prophetic moment in which the Church in Latin America began to identify itself with the poor.[2] This prophetic thrust would have both heroic and tragic consequences, as we have witnessed in almost every country in Latin America. There have been victories for the oppressed people of certain countries, victories shared by the Church because of its courageous involvement. But there has also been a terrible price the Church has paid for that involvement, such as the horrible death of Archbishop Romero in El Salvador and the violent deaths of other bishops, numerous priests, religious, and lay leaders.[3] Medellín began a pastoral thrust that would involve the Church in matters of justice in a real and credible way. Evangelization and justice came to be seen as substantially the same work.

While Medellín does not mention the theology of liberation as such, one can see its influence throughout the documents. Each section follows the analytical process of "see, judge, and act." The facts are given first; these are then seen in the light of revelation and church dogma; and finally, pastoral recommendations are made. Themes that run throughout the documents are social sin and the poor (2.1.7.); unjust structures that are responsible for oppressed people (1.2.); "institutionalized violence" as description of the situation of injustice that violates fundamental rights (2.16.); promotion of the human dimension of life; fidelity to God and fidelity to the human person; need for a profound conversation and for authentic liberation (1.2.3.); and conscientization (1.3.17.). The theology of liberation created new theological categories such as theology from the perspective of the poor, a liberation spirituality based on popular religiosity, a reading of Sacred Scriptures from the standpoint of the poor. New methodologies of making theology were suggested, experienced, and developed. The experience of making theology was extended to *campesinos* (peasant farm workers) and residents of *favelas* and *barrios* (shanty towns).

---

[2] Cf. Penny Lernoux in *Puebla and Beyond*, p. 11.
[3] Cf. ibid., p. 18.

Comunidades eclesiales de base (base Christian communities) became the instrument that popularized these themes and approaches to pastoral life and the means whereby Medellín reached the masses.

Puebla and Its Significance

When the conference at Puebla was convoked, first by John Paul I, then, after his sudden death in 1978, by John Paul II, some felt that Medellín had gone too far in its social thrust, which some considered too liberal. For many of the participants at Puebla, here was an opportunity to balance Medellín and perhaps even retract some of what had been said in 1968.[4]

The preliminary consultative document for Puebla, *Evangelization at Present and in the Future of Latin America,* issued in 1977, articulated a view of Latin America different from that which formed the background to Medellín. Latin America's social problems were seen as a natural outgrowth of the transition from an agrarian to an urban-industrial society. The basic assumption of the text reflected the theory of development.[5] The text was criticized as weak and superficial and as a denial of Medellín. The document was effective, however, in setting off intense debate that prepared bishops and other concerned people for the conference.

Pope John Paul II opened the conference in Puebla at the Seminario Palafoxiano. He told the bishops to exercise their principal duty of pastors and to be "teachers of truth—not a human or rational truth, but God's truth, which is the principle of authentic liberation."[6] He went on to subdivide this liberating truth into three aspects: the truth about Christ, about the mission of the Church, and about human beings. He was pointing out that a solid Christology is the basis to a well-founded ecclesiology and the anthropology that the Church has to offer humankind.[7] The pope urged the bishops to be signs and builders of unity and defenders and promoters of human dignity.[8]

The pope's message included both a warning and encouragement. He warned against the depicting of Jesus as a political activist involved in a class struggle:[9] a peoples' Church, born of the people pitted against

---

[4] Cf. ibid., pp. 20–25.
[5] Cf. ibid., pp. 23–24.
[6] John Paul II, "Opening Address at the Puebla Conference" in *Puebla and Beyond*, p. 58.
[7] Cf. Virgilio Elizondo in *Puebla and Beyond*, p. 49.
[8] Cf. John Paul II, "Opening Address," pp. 64–69.
[9] Cf. ibid., p. 60.

the "institutionalized" or "official Church,"[10] reducing the salvation of Jesus Christ to political, economic, and social liberation.[11] At the same time, John Paul II spoke about serving the poor. Moises Sandoval offers a good summary:

> . . . the needy and marginalized (i.e., all those whose lives reflect the suffering countenance of the Lord). He spoke about proclaiming the complete truth about human beings: "human beings are not pawns of economic or political processes, . . . instead these processes are geared toward human beings and subject to them" (I.9). He called for the advancement of human liberation, asking that the Church's voice "when the growing affluence of a few people parallels the growing poverty of the masses" (III.4). He emphasized that "there is a social mortgage on all private property" (III.4). He spoke of the "sometimes massive increase in violations of human rights in many parts of the world . . . the right to be born; the right to life; and right to responsible procreation; the right to work; the right to peace, freedom, and social justice; and the right to participate in making decisions that affect people and nations" (III.5).[12]

The meeting in Puebla was held in a spirit of tension and fear.[13] Peripheral debates held outside the official meetings provided forums for heated and exciting debates.[14] The outcome was a series of compromises that both conservative and more liberal participants appeared to accept.

It has been said that the Puebla document is ambiguous, with elements that please both conservatives and progressives.[15] The fears that the *comunidades de base*, liberation theology and its theologians would be condemned did not materialize, but then neither was there condemnation of oppressive regimes.

The central theological doctrine of the Puebla document contains God's plan of salvation, manifested in Christ, who on his death and resurrection offers Latin America its authentic liberation. The Church is both the sign and extension of the risen Lord's presence and must consider the Latin American people as part of a divine plan not merely from the determinist, psychological, economical, and statistical points of view (cf. 307–315). The work of the Church is evangelization, which must necessarily lead to liberation and human promotions (cf. 470ff).

Thus, Puebla did not turn the Church away from the prophetic

---

[10] Cf. ibid., p. 3.
[11] Cf. ibid., p. 2.
[12] Moíses Sandoval in *Puebla and Beyond*, p. 34.
[13] Cf. ibid., pp. 34–36.
[14] Cf. ibid., pp. 38–39.
[15] Cf. ibid., p. 41.

message of Medellín, rather, it reinforced it and restated its themes, with stronger language in some places. The document is an affirmation of the work of the Church among the poor and oppressed.

The bishops of Puebla call for a "civilization of love" and, in this way, seek to promote a nonviolent approach to the resolution of social problems, even though these are due to a permanent violence of structures against the poor and the powerless (cf. 486). The significance of Puebla was expressed well by Dom Helder Camara: "As bishops, we have not betrayed our people, but on the contrary, with divine grace, have been able to carry forward the strength of Medellín."[16]

The pastoral-theological themes of Puebla can apply wherever the Church exercises her mission. In other words, there is a universal dimension to the themes, sometimes eloquently presented in the Puebla document. The central themes of liberation, communion, and participation are intertwined with more traditional theological themes of the incarnate and redeeming God (Christology); the missionary and servant Church (ecclesiology); and Christian anthropology. What Puebla did—and Medellín before it—was to reflect theologically on Latin America's social reality. Theological themes are reread, as it were, from the real world that Latin America lives in this latter part of the twentieth century. These, in turn, provide the Church with the bases for pastoral planning and pastoral action.

Some of the themes are as follows:

1. *The Church and kingdom vis à vis the world.* The aim of the Church's social teaching is always "the promotion and integral liberation of human beings in terms of both their earthly and their transcendent dimensions. It is a contribution to the ultimate and definitive kingdom" (475).

2. *The dignity of the human person.* "Every attack on human dignity is simultaneously an attack on God himself, whose image the human being is. Thus, evangelization in Latin America demands that the Church voice a clear message about the dignity of the human being" (306).

3. *Social justice as liberation.* The Puebla document applies its concepts of communion participation and liberation to the notion and mission of justice: "The love of God, which is the root of our dignity, necessarily becomes loving communion with other human beings and fraternal participation. For us today, it must become first and foremost a labor of justice on behalf of the oppressed (cf. Lk 4:18), an effort of liberation for those who are most in need of it" (327).

4. *Charity (agape) as a wellspring of justice.* The document, in its ex-

---

[16] Ibid.

planation of the commandment of love, calls for a "civilization of love" based on the gospel. "Christian love goes beyond the categories of all regimes and systems because it entails the insuperable power of the Paschal Mystery, the words of the sufferings of the cross and the signal pledges of victory and resurrection. . . . The civilization of love repudiates violence, egotism, wastefulness, exploitation, and moral follies" (*Message to the Peoples of Latin America*, no. 8).

5. *Poverty as a theological concept.* Puebla devotes an entire chapter to "A Preferential Option for the Poor." In this chapter, Puebla presents one of the most challenging aspects of its message. Christ himself is the starting point of this reflection: "He established solidarity with [human beings] and took up the situation in which they find themselves—in his birth and in his life, and particularly in his passion and death where poverty found its maximum expression" (1141).

6. *The Church as servant.* There is a clear emphasis in the document of the Church as servant. In its section on "The Truth about the Church," the people of God are to be both sign and service of communion people. "All those who make up the people of God . . . are servants of the gospel . . . as the servant of the gospel, the Church serves both God and human beings" (271).

7. *Young people as a preferential option.* Young people receive the second preferential option after that of the poor. The young, while being objects of evangelization, are also subjects of it: "In the Church, young people come to feel that they are a new people: the people of the Beatitudes, with no security but Christ, with the heart of the poor; a contemplative people with an attitude of evangelical listening and discernment; builders of peace and the bearers of joy and a complete liberation project, aimed principally at their fellow young people" (1184).

8. *Prophetic role of bishops.* The bishops at Puebla commit themselves to making every effort to promote justice and to defend the dignity and the rights of the human person and to make clear through their lives and attitudes that their preference is to evangelize and serve the poor (cf. 706–707).

9. *The spirituality of popular Catholicism, especially devotion to Mary.* The section on "Evangelization and the People's Religiosity" (see 444ff) is one of the most original in the Puebla document. The treatment given to the people's religiosity is a very complete analysis of its advantages and shortcomings in the area of evangelization. The challenge of Puebla on evangelization agents is to elaborate a "pedagogy of evangelization," which demands that these agents love the people and be close to them, but they be prudent, firm, constant, and audacious. This section is one of those areas in which Puebla moved

beyond Medellín, which did not give as much prominence to the people's religiosity.

Influence of the Church in Latin America on the Church in the United States

Hispanics in the United States

The post Medellín-Puebla spirit of the Church in Latin America is being felt in the United States, especially in the Hispanic communities. Pastoral agents in this country who deal with Hispanics to a great extent have been touched to a greater or lesser degree by the pastoral life in Latin America. Pastoral experts from Latin America have been invited to the United States and have taught in the various regional pastoral institutes that have been set up around the country. One of these is the Mexican American Cultural Center (MACC) in San Antonio, Texas, which has been, to a great extent, a "pastoral bridge" between Latin America and the United States, particularly in the Southwest. Members of the Hispanic priests' association, P.A.D.R.E.S., and members of the Hispanic religious sisters' national organization, HERMANAS, enrolled in classes at the Instituto Pastoral de Latinoamerica (IPLA) in Quito, Ecuador. These IPLA graduates returned to the United States and were instrumental in making the message of Medellín known; one such graduate, Rev. Arturo Tafoya, went on to become bishop of Pueblo, Colorado.

Rev. Virgilio Elizondo, eminent Hispanic theologian, writer, and founder of MACC, accompanied Archbishop Robert Lucey of San Antonio to the international meeting of catechists held at Medellín immediately after the Latin American bishops' conference. It was upon his return to San Antonio that the idea of MACC was born and brought to fruition. MACC has become the model of other pastoral centers around the country that address Hispanic pastoral and social issues.

At MACC that idea of *"El Comite de Religiosos Hispanos en el Ministerio"* (CORHIM) surfaced. CORHIM addressed the particular spiritual needs of Hispanic religious men and women, in a style borrowed from the *Confederacion Latinoamericana de Religiosos* (CLAR). This process took place in a three-week period, marked by intensive theological reflection on the life of Hispanic religious in the light of U.S. ecclesial and social reality.

The influence of Medellín and Puebla has also been felt by writers and publications. Of special note is Orbis, the book publishing department of Maryknoll. Periodicals such as *Sojourners* and the publications of the Center of Concern and MACC reflect Medellín and Puebla. In Spanish, *El Visitante Dominical* has followed the same spirit. The books and other writings of Rev. Virgilio Elizondo are prime examples of the Latin American Church's influence in this country.

The Commission for Church History in Latin America (CEHILA) organized a U.S. chapter in 1976. The first attempt to write a history of the Hispanic Church in the United States was begun by this group; it was published in 1983, with the title *Fronteras* (a MACC publication). The book is reflective of the CEHILA approach to history, which is looked upon from the perspective of the poor. CEHILA-USA continues to meet annually to develop the history of the Hispanic Church in the United States.

In the area of liturgy, one can readily see the influence of the post Medellín-Puebla Latin American Church. Most of the Spanish-speaking Catholics in the United States are led in prayer by means of liturgical texts brought to this country from Latin America, particularly from Mexico and Colombia. The most popular lectionary in Spanish was developed by the Northeast Pastoral Center and is taken from the translation of the Scriptures as found in *La Biblia Latinoamericana*. The notes, both exegetical and explanatory, are imbued with the concepts and insights peculiar to Medellín, Puebla, and Latin America theology. Much of the music sung in Spanish liturgies here has its origins in Latin America. The variety of Hispanic cultures is manifest in the various rhythms and beats of the music in churches in this country; it is relatively easy to distinguish what is Mexican, Andean, Caribbean, and Central American. The various instruments used in liturgies here reflect the variety of musical expression throughout Latin America. But what is particularly interesting to note is that the theological theme that recurs in Latin American hymnology is a clear thrust toward freedom from all kinds of sin and oppression.

As in Latin America, the Church in the United States among Hispanics is seen to be more and more involved in works of justice. Like their Latin American brothers and sisters, Hispanics in the United States are generally poor and live on the margins of society. Injustices arising from discrimination and prejudice are prevalent among Hispanic peoples in the United States, and the cry for justice among them has been heard and heeded by the U.S. Church at every level. There remains, however, a reluctance on the part of some church leaders to adopt too quickly and to embrace too much the themes of liberation from Latin America.

The three *Encuentros* (National Hispanic Pastoral Meetings) that have been held in 1972, 1977, and 1985, have all emphasized involvement in the area of social justice among the Hispanics of the United States. It is at the *Encuentros* that a direct influence is seen from the

Medellín-Puebla spirit. The processes involved, the language and spirit of the *Encuentros* reflect a definite Latin American approach. Such recurrent themes in the *Encuentros* as *el pueblo; educación integral; evangelización y justicia social; pastoral de conjunto; comunidades eclesiales de base* echo the ideals and aspirations of Medellín and Puebla. The Third *Encuentro* (1985) emphasized the "prophetic" mission of Hispanics in the United States. As a minority group, Hispanics saw themselves as having the prophetic duty to challenge, from their unique perspective, the dominant society. This prophetic posture that Hispanics attempted to embrace at the Third *Encuentro* is in the same vein as the Medellín-Puebla counterparts.

The same concern for social justice is found in the U.S. bishops' pastoral letter *The Hispanic Presence: Challenge and Commitment* (1983). There are strong statements regarding migrants, social justice and social actions, prejudice and racism, and *comunidades eclesiales de base*. In *Hispanic Presence*, the U.S. bishops point out that Hispanics are "as yet an untapped resource as a cultural bridge between North and South in the Americas." They also state that "the Church in the United States has much to learn from the Latin American pastoral experience; it is fortunate to have in the Hispanic presence a precious human link to that experience" (12.0.).

Many of the pastoral movements among Hispanic church communities have received their impetus from the post Medellín-Puebla thrust. The obvious examples in this regard are the *comunidades eclesiales de base*. While they have not taken on a strong hold in this country, where they are present, they are a good model of "making Church" in our communities. The *comunidades* have received official approval and encouragement in the conclusions of the various *Encuentros*, in the U.S. bishops' pastoral letter on Hispanics, and in the *National Pastoral Plan for Hispanic Ministry* approved in 1987. The *comunidades* movement offers one of the best responses to the threat of Protestant sectarian proselytism.

Another movement that, to some extent, has been influenced by the Latin American Church is the charismatic renewal. It has provided the opportunity for a more free-flowing and informal expression of faith among those who feel inclined to express their faith in that way. Many members of the Hispanic community have been introduced to the reading of and praying with Scripture because of the charismatic renewal. In many instances, the social justice dimension is brought into the prayer reflection dynamics of the charismatic movement.

The whole concept of evangelization, that is, of reaching out to the unchurched, has been very helpful to the Church in the United States in identifying its role with regard to Hispanics. Evangelization programs have been brought to this country from Latin America and continue to be successful in attracting Hispanics back to the Church. Evangelization was the overall theme of the Second *Encuentro* (1977), and the concept continues to provide a challenge for the Church.

Prophetic Role of the U.S. Bishops

It has already been stated above that the bishops of Latin America have inspired greatly the teaching role of the U.S. bishops in matters regarding social justice and peace. The limited exchanges among the bishops of North America and South America have had some bearing on this. But, possibly, the most important reason is the missionary connection between the U.S. bishops and Latin America. The direct connection that some bishops, dioceses, and local parishes have had with Latin America has been through the missionaries that these have sent to Latin America. Upon their return, missionaries have brought with them the concerns of Medellín and Puebla, as well as their pastoral thrust. These missionaries' letters and missionary magazines have done much to educate the average American Catholic about the situation in Latin America. Among those who have been educated about the heroic life of the Church in Latin America have been the U.S. bishops themselves, especially those who have missions in that part of the world. Direct connections are maintained through visits to the areas where they have missionaries. These visits have left an indelible mark on these bishops and have led to strong convictions on the role of the Church in Latin America.

Some of U.S. bishops have had their own martyrs in Latin America; U.S. missionaries have suffered persecution, torture, and even death for the sake of the gospel and for the sake of the poor. These persecutions and deaths have committed the Church in the United States to Latin America in a real and dramatic way. Because blood has been shed, many bishops feel that the Church in the United States has an enormous stake in the future of the Church in Latin America.

The teaching role of the U.S. bishops on matters regarding justice and peace have been definitely enhanced by the example of the heroic teaching on the part of Latin American bishops at Medellín and Puebla. The U.S. bishops have appropriated their own preferential option for the poor of their country and for the poor of the world. They too have stressed a nonviolent approach to institutionalized structures of oppression and injustice.

From the advantage of the NCCB Committee for the Church in Latin America, we can report with satisfaction that our Latin American bishops are excited and affirming of the U.S. bishops' statements on peace and economic justice. The same praise that we have reserved for the documents of Medellín and Puebla are now coming back to us because of our own statements. It is, therefore, with pleasure and joy that we offer these documents for the instruction, challenge, and inspiration of Catholics in the United States.

Most Rev. Ricardo Ramirez, CSB
Bishop of Las Cruces
Chairman
Bishops' Committee for the Church
in Latin America, 1985–88

Bibliography

Eagleson, John and Philip Scharper, eds. *Puebla and Beyond*. Documentation and Commentary. Maryknoll, N.Y.: Orbis books, 1979.

National Conference of Catholic Bishops. *The Hispanic Presence: Challenge and Commitment*. Pastoral Letter on Hispanic Ministry. Washington, D.C.: USCC Office of Publishing and Promotion Services, 1983.

———. *National Pastoral Plan for Hispanic Ministry*. Washington, D.C.: USCC Office of Publishing and Promotion Services, 1988.

Parada, Dr. Hernan. *Crónica de Medellín*. Bogota, Colombia: Indo-American Press Service, 1975.

Sandoval, Moíses, ed. *Fronteras: A History of the Latin American Church in the USA since 1513*. San Antonio, Tex.: Mexican American Cultural Center, 1983.

Second General Conference of Latin American Bishops. *The Church in the Present-day Transformation of Latin America in the Light of the Council*. Vol. I, "Addresses." Vol. II, "Conclusions." Washington, D.C.: USCC Division for Latin America, 1973.

Secretariat for Hispanic Affairs, NCCB/USCC. *Prophetic Voices: The Document on the Process of the III Encuentro Nacional Hispano de Pastoral*. Washington, D.C.: USCC Office of Publishing and Promotion Services, 1986.

Segunda Conferencia General del Episcopado Latinoamericano. *La Iglesia en la Actual Transformación de América Latina a la Luz del Concilio*. I: Ponencias. II: Conclusiones. Bogotá, Colombia: CELAM, 1968.

Tercera Conferencia General del Episcopado Latinoamericano. *La Evangelización en el Presente y en el Futuro de América Latina*. Documento de Consulta a las Conferencias Episcopales. Consejo Episcopal Latinoamericano: CELAM, 1978.

———. *La Evangelización en el Presente y el Futuro de América Latina*. Puebla. Consejo Episcopal Latinoamericano: CELAM, 1979.

Path from Puebla
Criteria and Major Themes

When Dom Luciano Mendes was asked about the Church's involvement in land struggles, he could hardly stop in his response. Finally, he apologized to his audience at the University of Notre Dame. "Really," he said, "I am not the only one preoccupied by this issue. When I was with Pope John Paul recently, the first thing he asked me was, 'How is the land reform going?'" I replied, "Not very well." He said, "Then you must ask President Sarney, why."

As president and former general secretary of the Brazilian Bishops' Conference, Mendes has come in contract with many church workers involved in helping to obtain land or land titles for peasant farmers, sharecroppers, or landless farm families. Further, as auxiliary bishop of São Paulo, Mendes spent much of his time on the street, becoming acutely ware of the problems of families without land or homes.

Frances O'Gorman, another Brazilian working closely with grass-roots organizations, told the same audience the cost of the Church's involvement: "When the base Christian community leaders come together for our annual national meeting, we display a large cross with many—now hundreds—of names of Christians killed in these struggles. Last year, we tacked up part of the bloody shirt of Father Josimo as well" (Tavares, a beloved advocate for the poor).

Some issues, such as land reform and the Church's involvement in the question, are so clearly major concerns of the Latin American Church that we need spend only a brief time in justifying their inclusion in this compilation. Other issues will need lengthier explanation of their importance for the Latin American Church. It is hoped that understanding the issues, evident or not, will show what the Latin American Church confronts, often with implications for readers in the United States.

In this section, I wish to explain why the various works were selected for this volume and what themes became evident in the pastoral communications.

Criteria for Selection

To begin, the criteria for inclusion in this volume should be shown. These criteria were discussed with staff members of the NCCB Secretariat for Latin America and other advisers. We agreed that we would not select letters, homilies, or statements of individual bishops. This decision follows the original intention and mandate to present documents representative of bishops' conferences or regional groups of bishops.

First, we sought pastoral writings that were seen as being of special importance by the the writers of each document: the statement or pastoral letter was not a routine statement—something said to summarize a yearly or semiannual meeting—but, rather, was written and published with urgency. The documents often gave internal signs: a tone of urgency, a dramatic reaction to a situation, a need to communicate, or a special occasion for teaching. Second, the local Church saw the statement or letter as important and special. These letters received attention, oftentimes positive, sometimes negative. Third, persons in other countries often looked upon these communications as important and special. They commented on their appearance and reprinted them. Fourth, we looked for statements or letters that had relevance to situations in other Latin American countries or that would be of special interest to other national churches that had been keeping up with difficult situations, such as the churches in Cuba. Finally, we gave preference to selecting pastoral writings from as many episcopal conferences as possible, to show the range of the Latin American bishops' concerns.

Many persons aided in the formation of the above criteria and especially in the selection of specific pastoral writings. This aid came directly through numerous letters and conversations with officials at the National Conference of Catholic Bishops and the Pontifical Commission on Justice and Peace, with fellow social scientists observing the Latin American Church, and, above all, with Latin American church leaders and grass-roots representatives. Indirect assistance came from the selection of pastoral writings, displayed as important, by the Latin American Bishops' Council (CELAM) in its *Boletin*, the National Conference of Catholic Bishops (USA), and the Vatican in *L'Osservatore Romano* (various editions, especially Spanish).

Other sources also highlighted what editors considered to be noteworthy documents coming from Latin American bishops. These documentation sources are too numerous to be named, but the more important cannot be passed by without acknowledgment: *LADOC (Latin America Documentation); SEDOC (Servicio de Documentaco);* and *La Documentation Catholique* and the documentary sections of *Paginas, Revista Eclesiastica Brasileira, Mensaje, Criteria, Sic,* and *Iglesias.*

These selections were checked against the internal testimony of the bishops' conferences themselves. Sometimes, in later statements, the conferences refer to earlier letters that they thought of as specially important; or the introductory remarks reveal an estimate of the document's worth, as when Archbishop Bernardino Pinera, president of the Chilean Bishops' Conference, said of the *Pastoral Orientations, 1986–1989,* that "among many recent documents, this is one of the best conceived and one whose reading should prove beneficial and agreeable."

Setting the Stage

After the Latin American bishops met at the Third General Conference at Puebla (1979), Archbishop John Quinn of San Francisco reported on the conference to the bishops of the United States. That the assembled bishops would be interested in what he had to say about the Latin American Church surprised some observers. That the president of the National Conference of Catholic Bishops would receive a standing ovation for his report increased their amazement.

Three high-ranking bishops from the United states attended the Puebla Conference; not one assisted at or was invited to the prior general conference at Medellín (1968). Before the Second Vatican Council—say in 1960—probably not one bishop in the United States could name five of his counterparts in Latin America. Nineteen years later, Archbishop Quinn reported to his fellow bishops: "The bonds between our conference and the episcopal conferences of Latin America have been strong, continual, and substantial."

Archbishop Quinn continued: "At Puebla, the directions set at Medellín were decisively reaffirmed by a conscious and broadly supported decision of the Latin American bishops. Puebla served only to strengthen the conviction of Medellín that the dominant social characteristic of Latin America is the widespread oppression of the majority of peoples of those nations. The mechanism of oppression is located in social structures that benefit a very few at the expense of the majority. The oppression of the many by a minority of powerful and entrenched local government and private interests—particularly, when the oppressors and the oppressed are both Catholics—can only be described as a sign against the Creator and a desecration of the human person.

"In this context and with the guidance and urging of four popes from Pius XII to John Paul II, the Church in Latin America both at Medellín and at Puebla has made the decisive choice to find in and through the poor the first imperative of evangelization. This option, so in keeping with the gospel, must, of course, be understood in the perspective of that other gospel imperative: the mission of the Church is universal, for everyone, rich or poor. It involves a preferential but not exclusive love for the poor."

Such is the context for watching further developments in the Church in Latin America after the Puebla Conference. The Latin American Church did not have a benchmark general conference in 1988 or 1989, by which to measure its evolution. Instead, it has been necessary to follow the statements and pastoral letters of individual national conferences. That is the intent of this book, to trace the path from Puebla.

The Church and Major Developments of the Decade

In terms of general direction, we suggest that the Church has continued on the same path it was on from Medellín through Puebla. Increasingly, understanding of issues becomes more detailed and plans more proficient. Option for the poor and resistance to oppression continued through the repeated efforts of episcopal conferences. This orientation was affirmed even in countries where to do so increasingly alienated the Church from the holders of national power and by national churches often depicted as conservative.

The first remarkable aspect of the Latin American Church that strikes outsiders is the spiritual renewal that marked the Church in the 1970s and is even more evident in the 1980s. Millions of Catholics relate to the Church through small Christian communities. Therein, they pray together on a regular basis, read and reflect on Scriptures (a practice unusual for Latin American Catholics twenty years ago), and attempt to live out their lives in conformity with their newly developing faith. A Peruvian observer said, "There is a conviction in all these communities that members cannot be faithful to the Lord if they are not involved in and committed to the life of the people—their problems, suffering, struggles, and hope."

One of the fruits evident in this renewal also impresses outsiders: seminary walls in many parts of Latin American, including countries with the most repressive environments, can hardly contain young men who wish to enter the priesthood. Conflict and tension also followed in the same path as this awakening. The questions of what it meant to be Christian or what it meant to be Church centered the discussion and acted as background for some of the pastoral writings of the bishops, as on charismatic renewal in Guatemala or unity among the elements of the so-called popular church and the formal church in Nicaragua.

A second major development during the decade has been the intensification of efforts of Protestant groups and numerous cults and new religious movements to gain converts in Latin America. Where one Protestant chapel could be found in Huehuentenango, Guatemala, a decade ago, now more than thirty chapels have been built. The example repeats itself all over Latin America. Nine hundred religious churches and groups—other than Catholic—are registered in

Argentina alone. The Catholic Church's response has not been so much a reaction against this movement as intensified action and a call to itself to better planning and more extensive evangelization.

Third, a great change of the decade marked the political and social environments of many countries of Central and South America: militaries retreated, if not all the way to the barracks, at least from the presidential palaces. And democratization began. The Church in most of these countries reacted positively to the change, welcoming a return to the norm of democratic politics.

Several cautions apply here. First, Central America, with the exception of Costa Rica, does not have a tradition of democratic rule. So, for many Central Americans, including the bishops, democracy is not a reality that has been experienced. Hence, cautious optimism, rather than unconditional enthusiasm, has often been expressed about "democracy." Second, democracy seldom means the full range of citizens' rights and privileges that is available in North Atlantic countries. Hence, governments often do not provide effective police investigations or juridical justice, which means continuing concern of the bishops about their flock and themselves. Third, and most important, departing military governments sometimes dictated new national constitutions, largely on their own terms. Or, they set up the rules of the game for those who would follow them into power—new presidents and congresses. The episcopal conferences found themselves having to comment on these constitutions and rules of the game, to safeguard just claims of citizens.

No issue became more complex and painful for new governments and the churches than the prosecution of military leaders who were implicated in imprisonment without legal procedure, torture, and murders of hundreds of thousands of citizens. Thus, the churches of Argentina, Brazil, and Chile at the request of many citizens, especially aggrieved parties, found themselves as partners in a difficult national debate.

Rather than discuss "democratization" (which could presume more reality than exists), some social scientists have turned to talking about the process that is taking place in many Latin American countries as regimes are in transition. The bishops, too, do not often talk about a return to or establishment of democracy.

Another major development—one centered in Central America but radiating out to affect other Latin American nations and Spain—has been the involvement of outside countries, especially the United States and the Soviet Union, in Nicaragua and surrounding territories.

A fifth trend developing in the 1980s has been the greater impoverishment of people in the lower and lower middle strata of society. The costs of development were especially borne by them in the 1970s. Now the costs of recession increased their burden, as markets declined and prices rose. Millions found themselves without full-time employment or land. Many fled, ringing the cities of Latin America with slums or adding to the refugee camps in other countries. External debts were being called in by banks in creditor nations, and Latin American countries were forced into austere measures that most deeply affected the lives of the already poor.

No wonder, then, that the Latin American churches found themselves forced to react in their pastoral writings to the changes in the environment that greatly affected their mission to building a society ruled by justice and love, participation and dignity.

Major Themes of Pastoral Concerns

No attempt was made to begin the search for noteworthy pastoral writings with specific categories in mind. For a year and a half, the search was carried on using only the criteria mentioned above. Only at the end of the search was the effort made to summarize themes in bishops' statements. The following attempt to select according to the main thrust of pastoral writings, recognizing that overlapping of themes inevitably occurs in some documents.

1. Renewal and Ecumenism

Reactions to the Puebla Conference

As they departed from the Puebla Conference, Brazilian bishops sent a message to their people, affirming the directions the conference had taken, especially that of a preferential option for the poor and the social transformation of the region. They also called attention to the necessity of affirming indigenous cultures and popular religiosity. Above all, with the fathers of the conference and Pope John Paul II, who opened the conference, they wished to proclaim Jesus as the center of the life of the Church.

The Ecuadorian bishops, upon returning from the conference, began a lengthy process to implement the conclusions in their country. This work of collaboration between priests, sisters, and lay people resulted in the selection of eight objectives for pastoral work on the national and local levels. These objectives reflect many of the themes of Puebla: evangelization (making Christ better known), work among the poor, lay participation, and formation of small communities.

These and other conferences would show the influence of Puebla in many ways, especially in the manner and content of their arguments, as in the Church's right to comment on the political order; the commitment to denounce the causes of poverty; and the desire to join with persons of good will to uproot poverty and to create a more just and humane world. The spirit of Puebla appears to spread throughout whole pastoral statements, as in planning documents to be mentioned below.

Pastoral and Spiritual Renewal

A number of pastors convinced themselves through experience and immersion that basic Christian communities should serve as major instruments in the renewal of their churches. The Brazilian church, now in it third decade of observing, modifying, and empowering the small communities, reaffirmed this strategy for the coming years. They see these communities as a new way of being Church, one that they believe will also be a ferment in the renovation of Brazilian society.

The Colombian church chose to emphasize the renovation of parishes. In a massive project over several years, involving many priests, sisters, brothers, and lay persons, the Colombian bishops attempted to recast the parish at a time "when profound change and radical transformation are affecting its very life and mission." They call for a renewal of priestly identity and intensified efforts at prayer; sacramental bond with the bishop; becoming servants of the Word, especially to the poor; systematic training of lay persons; and a general need for conversion and a recovery of values. They also take note of communities without priests and thank the religious and lay apostles who work in them.

Throughout Latin America, the charismatic or Pentecostal movement has spread like wildfire. The number of Catholics participating in the groups rises into the hundreds of thousands. As if to match the phenomenal growth of non-Catholic religions in Guatemala, Catholic charismatics have also mushroomed at an accelerated pace. In the face of this relatively new phenomenon, the Guatemalan bishops reflected on various aspects of the movement and gave guidelines for its participation in the renewal of the Church.

National Pastoral Planning and Orientations

Pastoral planning has become an important enterprise in the Latin American Church. Only recently and gradually did national churches gain enough coherence and unity to form national bishops' conferences. This process began in the early 1950s in Brazil and continued in the 1960s.

The national churches, still living largely in the colonial manner, began to take stock of their weaknesses in terms of resources, especially human ones, after World War II when Latin America became increasingly incorporated into the transnational world system, including religious organizations. Under the inspiration of the Holy See, and with new resources, including a huge missionary influx, Latin American churches could begin planning how to use the new resources. That their resources were limited was an additional reason to plan for their effective use. Further, competition from the political left, and especially from Protestants and new religious movements, added urgency to deployment of personnel and strategies to be used. For example, the poor and the young were special targets of pastoral action, and base Christian communities were often favored pastoral instruments.

Poorer countries, especially, found pastoral planning useful and necessary. In their *Pastoral Plan, 1986–1991,* the Bolivian bishops built on rudimentary planning attempts in the early 1970s and more experienced vision and planning of the mid-1980s. They formed their vision of the Church in the world as that of beginning to build up the kingdom of God.

The Chilean bishops, as too the Brazilian bishops, have had considerable experience acting as a national church organization. They also have been doing pastoral planning for a longer period of time than most other episcopal conferences. The Chilean bishops center their vision around Christ, as Servant of Life—a role the Church wishes to continue, albeit in a nondemocratic environment.

While the Chilean and Bolivian churches offer noteworthy examples of using planning to allow God better to renew them, no Latin American church appears to offer the dramatic touch to planning that the Cuban church does. Beaten down by political and economic discrimination, practicing Catholics came to number only about 200,000 in a population of nearly 10 million. Yet, many recent observers, including John Cardinal O'Connor of New York, have witnessed a vibrant Church and an unfamiliar and extensive interest in religion among the larger Cuban population. Cuban bishops have pointed to the process of involvement of many Cuban Catholics in planning for the future of the Church in Cuba as part of this renewal.

Relations with Other Religions

Perhaps, no issue has become as complex and difficult as relations with other religions. Ten years ago, many described this area of concern as "ecumenism" (as at Puebla), but no longer. Many of the religious groups that have come to Latin America, beginning in the late–1970s and continuing into the 1980s, have no interest in dialogue or cooperation with the Catholic Church (or historical Protestant ones). Many newcomers are hostile to convinced Catholics and hope to supplant their Church. The bishops of Panama, one of the historical crossroads and interchanges for Latin America, took on the hard task of sifting through the differences among Protestants, cults, and new religious movements. They pointed toward practical conclusions, as well.

2. The Political Order

Regime Transition/Democratization

In the 1980s, six South American nations returned from military rule to a political order tending toward democratization. The churches in three Southern Zone countries were much involved in publicly seeking changes in repressive environments as regime changes became foreseeable or in helping to guide national political actors through difficult transitional periods. The Argentine bishops spoke to the nation and to the military, especially, through pastoral letters, such as *Church and National Community* (1981) and *Way of Reconciliation* (1982), before the military left office in 1983. In Brazil, the transitional period was longer, and the Brazilian bishops made many detailed comments on changes to be effected in the political order after full military rule. They especially attempted to modify aspects of the new constitution in a pastoral letter (too detailed and specific to Brazil to be included here). In Uruguay, the path to regime change from military rule was a lengthy, unstable, and tiresome process of quarrels and disputes. The Uruguayan bishops, at various times, especially in their pastoral letter *Solidarity and Hope* (1983), attempted to point out suffering evident in the country and the moral issues involved in the social and economic organization of their country. After Mario Sanguinetti took office as president in 1985, he and fellow Uruguayans still faced the dilemma of what stance to take on military personnel who were involved in repression of their people. In *Pastoral Reflections on the Present Situation* (1986), the Uruguayan bishops rejoiced in the new state of law that returned to Uruguay and offered moral considerations on the issue of whether closure should be offered on prosecution of the military.

Political change in the Andean countries of Peru, Bolivia, and Ecuador focused less on the consequences of military rule and more on general stability of the countries and the necessity of rebuilding fragile economic structures hard hit by changes in the world economic markets, especially of minerals and petroleum, and in forging coalitions among political actors, allowing consensus enough for governments to rule. Bolivia's bishops became masters in this enterprise. On a number of occasions, they played the role of ultimate conciliators between the government and groups such as students, teachers, miners, and other organized labor groups. In *National Convergence* (1984), the Bolivian bishops addressed the extremely divisive situation in which the country had found itself: labor unions had disrupted the country; the military threatened takeovers; demands were made for early elections; and serious threats were made of civil war. The nation had arrived at what one observer called "a near flash point." The bishops intervened—as they were to do several more times—to negotiate a solution.

In Central America, the civilian presidents of Guatemala and El Salvador found themselves in situations much more tightly controlled by the military, even after the military left the presidential palace. The episcopal conferences of Guatemala, in *To Construct Peace*, and of El Salvador, in *Called to Be Artisans of Peace*, made elaborate statements about the political order for which they hoped the principles of peace and reconciliation, along with justice, would be of major concern to all citizens, as well as to the newly elected officials.

A much more drastic change in regime seemed to be called for in the toppling of two long-entrenched dictatorships in Nicaragua and Haiti. In Haiti, little change at all occurred, as the system left by Duvalier largely continued. The Haitian church, which had taken an active stand in the departure of Duvalier, issued many statements, first of hope and encouragement, as in *Priorities and Changes* (1986), and then of arriving at a critical impasses in its *Christmas Message* (1987), in the face of manipulation and intimidation by the forces left by Duvalier.

In Nicaragua, change did occur dramatically but not in the direction in which the episcopal conference thought it was pointing in *Christian Commitment for a New Nicaragua* (1979). Many more statements from the conference would be issued in ensuing years, each increasingly critical of the performance of the Sandinist government. Then, the conference issued another landmark document *Eucharist: Fount of Unity* (1986), calling for a new attempt at reconciliation of differences and (for the first time) a formal rejection of financial aid to the Contras.

Appeals for Dialogue and Participation under Military Rule

The Chilean bishops continued, through years of military dictatorship, to act as "the voice of those who cannot speak." In *The Rebirth of Chile* (1982), the bishops described the various crises into which the nation had fallen, pleaded for a Christian solution to the crises, and called for a return to full democracy. Five years later in *Lent and National Life* (1987), on the eve of the pope's visit, the bishops again argued the case of participation by the Chilean people in the structuring of national political life.

In the other South American military dictatorship, President Stroessner, faced with return to civilian government among four of his neighbors, began to allow for a degree of liberalization. The

Paraguayan bishops, in *A Call for National Dialogue* (1986), took a bold step in calling for an enlarged political process that would embrace various political parties, including several that had been listed as illegal.

Appeals for the End of Repression

In societies dominated by repressive or restrictive political and social environments, the Church was virtually the only institution allowed some freedom of expression. During two of the worst periods of repression, bishops' conferences spoke as a cry from the heart in *I Am Jesus, Whom You Persecute* (Chile, 1980) and in *Massacre of Peasants* (Guatemala, 1982). Both conferences spoke out again about human rights violations, including murder, on a number of occasions. Episcopal conferences in El Salvador, Haiti, Paraguay, and Nicaragua joined them in documenting and protesting repression, restriction, and expulsion.

Difficult National Situations

In the 1980s, many Latin Americans countries found themselves faced with increasingly grave social and political problems. As the Ecuadorian bishops said in *Building a Society with Dignity and Morality* (1985): "When entire groups of human beings lack the conditions of life adequate for the diginity of a human being, in the countryside or slums, in childhood or old age, we feel compelled to speak." They and other bishops' conferences delved into issues such as public morality and corruption, presence and forms of violence, exploitation of petroleum and other national resources, and distribution of land. Dominican bishops, in a *Message to the Dominican People,* voiced similar concerns. Even Costa Rica, highly regarded for its democratic practices and economic stability, found itself at least temporarily but severely buffeted by a faltering economy that affected some Costa Ricans much more than others. In *United in Hope* (1981), the bishops reflected on the situation in the light of Christianity and called for greater justice, sharing, and sensitivity. The Puerto Rican bishops faced a vexing problem in the question of the "status" of the island in *The Political Situation of the Country* (1983). They attempted to put forth ethical and moral considerations in a debate that they regarded as too rhetorical and overly heated.

3. Development and Liberation

The non-Spanish-speaking churches of the Caribbean region have grouped themselves together in the Antilles Episcopal Conference.

The conference has expressed itself in several noteworthy pastoral writings. In 1982, they took up the complex and extensive issue facing the region: socioeconomic and human development. Their lengthy and careful considerations in *True Freedom and Development in the Caribbean* anticipate much of the discussion that would later center on the Caribbean Initiative and similar proposals to speed development in a volatile region.

Many Latin American bishops prefer to speak of similar problems in terms of liberation rather than development. The theology that undergirds that term has undergone serious scrutiny by theologians and especially by the Vatican's Congregation for the Doctrine of Faith in *Instruction on Certain Aspects of the Theology of Liberation* (1984) and in *Instruction on Christian Freedom and Liberation* (1986). The Peruvian bishops' conference took careful note of the instructions and responded formally to the 1984 instruction in *Liberation and the Gospel* (1984).

The bishops of the Southern Andean region of Peru applied the ideas of liberation and kingdom to the situation of their people in a remote and underpriviledged part of the nation, through several pastoral communications, especially *Witnesses to the Resurrection* (1987).

4. Economic Life

Many of the crises in national life, mentioned above, arise especially from economic causes. To say economic is also to say human causes and individual decisions; so say the bishops of the Southern Pacific region of Mexico. In *The Gospel and Temporal Goods* (1985), they address their pastoral reflections to middle- and upper-class Christians, raising questions about the use of temporal goods and the responsibility to the poor.

In the 1980s, most Latin American countries suffered severe declines in their economies, with major negative effects on the masses of the poor. Three of the most serious specific issues have been unemployment, inadequate housing, and external debt. The Venezuelan bishops took up the the question of growing unemployment and underemployment, seeking solidarity with the unemployed and making concrete suggestions. The following year, the Venezuelan bishops addressed a vexing problem, which is worldwide: inadequate housing. They estimate that one-third of their population suffers acutely from overcrowding, lack of security and public services, and unsanitary conditions.

One of the first pastoral statements dealing at length with external debt as a religious and moral problem came from the Cuban bishops. They were invited to participate in an international meeting on the topic in Havana. Bishop Adolfo Rodriguez, president of the Cuban

Bishops' Conference, presented his views on the subject, which were subsequently adopted by the whole conference and published as their statement, *External Debt and the New International Economic Order*. Mexico suffers greatly from an $80 billion debt. The Mexican bishops note the extent of the suffering this has caused and discuss the moral and ethical issues involved in *At the Service of the Human Community: An Ethical Consideration of the International Debt*.

5. Critical National or Regional Issues

As mentioned in the beginning of this section, the Brazilian bishops have had an abiding interest in the struggles over land, both farming land and urban land for housing. Pastoral statements by individual bishops and by the conference of bishops over the last twenty years would fill a large book. Two of their most salient statements are *The Church and the Problem of Land* (1980) and *The Use of Urban Land and Pastoral Action* (1982). In a similar way, for some years, the Paraguayan bishops have been following closely the struggles of peasant farmers, colonists, and native Indian groups as they attempt to obtain land or land titles. The bishops carefully laid out many of the issues in *The Paraguayan Peasant and the Land* (1983). In the Amazonian region of Peru, the bishops have spoken forcefully about colonizers and outsiders who have exploited the resources of the area and moved on, ignoring the rights of native communities. The bishops have acted as advocates for land titles as well.

In terms of issues, the struggle over land occupies center stage in the concerns of many national churches. Bishops in Chile, Peru, Guatemala, El Salvador, and Haiti, to name the more obvious examples, have ardently taken up the issue. The depth of concern noted by Archbishop Mendes at Notre Dame is matched in the statements of many other bishops' conferences in Latin America. The struggle over land may be the major social concern of the Latin American Church of the 1990s.

The problem of housing relates closely to the issue of land. The bishops of Venezuela, who a year previously had called special attention to the acute problem of unemployment, turned to address another problem that affected perhaps the majority of the people of their country: inadequate housing. Large-scale migration from farming areas and from other countries to cities in Venezuela left millions with inadequate housing. More than inconvenience occurs, as stress, lack of security, and unsanitary conditions abound. Such conditions prevail in much of Latin America.

Economic flux and political repression and unrest have lead many Latin Americans to flee their native lands. One of the greatest concentrations of refugees can be found in southern Mexico. The bishops in the region expressed their brotherly concern and sensitivity for refugees in the *Statement on the Refugee Situation,* calling attention to the refugees' plight and seeking assistance for them.

Finally, a problem of ever-growing proportions has been that of drug trafficking and drug addiction. At the center of much of the drug trade, Colombia has been experiencing increasing terror and threat to public order. The Colombian Bishops' Conference recognized with alarm the extent of the problem and some of its consequences in its pastoral *Statement on Drug Addiction and Drug Trafficking* (1984).

6. Transnational Issues

Central America

One of the great issues of the decade for Latin America has been the war in Nicaragua, which involved neighboring Central American countries as well. The Nicaraguan armed struggle was much more than conflict among Nicaraguans or even just Central Americans. The United States, the Soviet Union, Cuba, Argentina, Israel, and other countries contributed greatly to the internationalization of the conflict.

Among the first to call attention to the international character of the Nicaraguan war and the dangers of its spreading much more widely were the Honduran bishops. Their statement *On War, Dialogue, and Reconciliation* (1983) described the dangerous situation and reaffirmed the stand the bishops had taken against the war in an earlier pastoral message of 1982.

The Regional Conference of Bishops of Central America and Panama acknowledged "the fratricidal struggles and the threat of overall conflagration in Central America" in *Message to Our People* (1986). The leadership of this conference (SEDAC) later met with five delegates from the National Conference of Catholic Bishops (USA). Together they issued the *Joint Statement by Central American and U.S. Bishops* (1987). They concentrated their attention on two issues: the policy of the United States toward Central America and undocumented refugees and emigrants from the region, now residing in the United States. They called for resolving conflicts by political—not military—means and unanimously affirmed that the United States should give clear priority to economic aid for development over military aid.

World Peace and Nuclear Arms

The bishops of Puerto Rico asserted the Church's right to ethical and moral guidance on the questions of nuclear arms and world peace. They reviewed the Church's recent teaching about nuclear armaments and the arms race. More specific, the bishops' ethical-moral preoccupation led them to question the potential for international war in Puerto Rico and the Caribbean. They focused on the high degree of social and military vulnerability and, conversely, on the potential role of peacemaking for the island.

Conclusion

The agenda of concerns set forth by the bishops of Latin America represents a major shift over time in the role the bishops play in Latin America. The volume and weight of pastoral communications on the political order and socioeconomic problems of their countries show a Church concerned with the well-being of the peoples of their countries in the here and now. Theirs is not an other-worldly religion. Nor is Latin American Catholicism, as expressed by its bishops, neutral; they have chosen, by and large, to take sides with the poor, sometimes having to struggle against sluggish or insensitive governments or entrenched interests, both national and international.

Much more so than in the past, the bishops have taken a wider view of Church than their own dioceses. The formation of national bishops' conferences over the last thirty years has educated Latin American bishops and helped to give them a vision of Church that also reaches beyond national boundaries.

Great diversity exists among bishops' conferences. But in common, they have settled on evangelization and spiritual renewal as the heart of their enterprise. They have typically adopted a three-step methodology of describing the worldly and spiritual situation in which the Church lives, of reflecting on the situation in the light of Christianity, and of setting forth objectives for implementation. They take for granted that they have a mandate to offer ethical and moral guidance, especially in a region that is predominately Catholic, and they have often entered into debates on national and international issues that affect their people.

Lastly, many believe that the Latin American bishops are speaking to the people of the United States and to their government. The bishops' concern for the poor reaches into consideration of the international economic order, of which the United States is one of its centers. Economic and political decisions made in the White House, in the Congress, by multinational corporations, and by many other transnational (legal and illegal) actors in the United States affect Latin America. The Latin American bishops respond to these decisions as they increasingly see the effects of these choices in the lives of their people.

Rev. Edward L. Cleary, OP
Editor

Brazil
The Message of Puebla
(1979)

The Brazilian Church, the largest Catholic Church in the world, has an active bishops' conference. Since the early 1950s, the Brazilian episcopal conference has been a leading force in the renewal of the Latin American Church. Thus, it was with special significance that the Brazilian bishops, unlike many other Latin American bishops' conferences, issued a statement at the end of the Puebla Conference (Third General Conference of the Latin American Bishops Council, 1979).

In their statement, the Brazilian bishops point out the important role the Catholic Church played in Latin America from the Medellín Conference (1968) to the one at Puebla. In the future, the Church's preferential option for the poor will be amplified to promote the social transformation of Latin America.

During the period from Medellín to Puebla, the Church has been remarkably present at the center of our age. The option for the poor made in Colombia has been broadened in a Church that is ever more committed to the gospel and to the social transformation of the continent, and which reflects the contradictions of development and new expectations for the decade of the 1980s.

1. As a Christian region, Latin America, through the voice of the Church, is increasingly taking on everything that is latent in the affirmation of its own native culture, as it confronts a kind of modernization that tends to take away people's own characteristics. The Church emphasizes the role of popular religiosity as a deep lode of the identity of our peoples, who increasingly face the threat of seeing their own original structures uprooted.

2. Above all else, Puebla is the word of Pope John Paul II and of the pastors of our region, joyfully proclaiming the content of Catholic faith. Puebla presents to the people of our hemisphere the truth about Jesus Christ, about the Church, and about human beings. In the light of God's design, every human person is called to recognize that Christ confers on him or her the dignity of being a child of God and a brother or sister of all human beings. It is the role of the Church to announce this fresh news, with new vigor through witness and and through the word. That is what evangelizing is about. Latin America has the mission of showing the world that reconciliation through forgiveness and through love is possible.

3. The Latin American Church is rediscovering credibility for its message in the ability of Christians to live their faith in more brotherly and sisterly communities, in which each one through inner conversion strives to overcome individualism, to become liberated from structures of injustice and sin, to seek communion with one's brothers and sisters through service, and in solidarity to take on the responsibility for promoting justice on our continent.

4. By defending a dynamic vision of the relationship between the hierarchy and the other members of the community, at the Puebla, the Church has especially reinforced the connection between, and integration of, the ministries of bishops, priests, and deacons. It has reaffirmed the need to live in a radical fashion the consecrated life within the vocation of particular churches, by encouraging commitment to the poor so as to be able to have a presence in those places where there is a greater need for evangelization.

5. The Puebla document is especially insistent on the activity of lay people, whose role is essentially to give witness to temporal structures. In this area, the priority goes to action for justice in the defense of human beings against all kinds of marginalization and domination in our age. Indeed, such tasks lead also to being active in political parties or in functions of public life, which assume that a democratic state has already been achieved.

6. As the voice of unvoiced injustices, today the Church is increasingly the voice of the whole community, which is generally crushed by the controlling structures of the overorganized society of our age: a society that leaves less and less space for intermediate communities and for legitimate social pluralism; a society of programs that increasingly leaves space for creativity only in countercultures and in spontaneous vital associations, especially in base communities. Puebla also wants to reinforce the renewing impulse of the family in the fractured society of our age.

7. In a context of ever wider gaps and greater inequalities, the Church is becoming aware that to speak of the people and of the poor is not necessarily the same as speaking to the people and to the poor. Thus, as it emerges from Puebla, the Church is to be ever more a Church of witness and service, as it continues its teaching and ministering.

8. At Medellín, the yearning for liberation translated into pastoral terms the hope for a kind of development and an improvement in the social condition of the whole region within this very generation.

The shocks, contradictions, and reversals of the great changes expected at mid-century only reinforce at the end of the 1970s the fact that Christians find in the message of communion and participation a continuing hope. Communion is the ongoing witness of the Church alongside all those groups of the powerless, those who have been left out of the scant currents of progress during this decade. That explains the presence of the episcopacy, the very symbol of the neighbor, due to the enormity of the marginality and the new silences within our peoples. The bishops will participate in an effort to improve, at each moment, this picture of affliction and despair, with ongoing innovative services, in immediate actions that will not leave help and improvement for the peoples of the region up to the vagaries of change in social systems and a prolonged wait that has already been too long for Latin America. That also explains the priority of commitment to the poor and to youth.

9. Thus, Puebla embodies the teaching activity of the Church, the declaration and defense of the individual and social rights of the person, along with the denunciation of the spiral of institutionalized violence—both subversive and repressive. It is issuing a warning even now about new rights of the person in the ever more controlled society of the future, vis-a-vis emerging control mechanisms and widening gaps between nations, and between rich and poor within countries.

10. Defending the ideal of a legitimate integration of Latin America, the bishops at Puebla are becoming aware of the new challenges of international society, of the economic, political, social, and cultural self-determination of the peoples of the hemisphere. The hierarchy calls for the right to a worldwide balanced life in common, not only among nations but between nations and giant companies, which urgently need a code of conduct. The bishops especially proclaim the Christian requirements of a new international order: that it not be Malthusian; that it take into account the basic needs of humankind; that it embody a legitimate pluralism; that it be capable of applying, in a social manner, the products of excess production and disarmament to development and to making our common store of technology widely available. The Church recognizes the gospel dimension of the legion of those who are uprooted by the structures of our day, from migrants to political refugees. There is an urgent need for political society on our continent to increase the number of migratory laborers received; to prize the right of asylum, which is a genuinely Latin American institution; and to make amnesty the sign of Christian reconciliation for our age, making it less one of confrontation and ever more one of hope.

Ecuador
The Ecuadorian Church and Puebla
(1980)

The bishops here apply the documents of the Puebla Conference to the evangelization of Ecuador. The Ecuadorian Church was one of the most ambitious in attempting consciously to implement the Conference of Latin American Bishops at Puebla.

In a lengthy process that was intended to educate and involve many lay and religious leaders, consultations were held at the grass roots thoughout the country. The work of collaboration and cooperation can be seen in the choice of objectives selected for implementation in Ecuador. These objectives include evangelization, especially among the poor; formation of base communities; and greater lay participation. In part, one of the objectives chosen, priestly vocations, may be well on the way to fulfillment as seminaries in Ecuador receive more and more candidates for the priesthood.

Foreword

This document of the Ecuadorian Church contains its overall proposal for evangelization, drawn up after the Conference of the Latin American Bishops in Puebla de los Angeles. It is the fruit of prayer and of joint study and reflection carried out by the bishops, together with their people, which the bishops' conference then unanimously approved and now promulgates in order that it may be put into action.

After the Puebla Assembly, the Ecuadorian bishops made great efforts to spread awareness of the magnificent pastoral document that had been approved there, to encourage its study, and to apply it specifically to our circumstances. This aim has been accomplished in three stages, lasting over a year.

1. The objective of the first stage, carried out July 8–13, 1979, involving 190 delegates from all ecclesiastical jurisdictions and representing the major Catholic institutions of our country, was to "study the Puebla document and to prepare leaders for a nationwide study." During this first stage, not only did the assembly delve deeply into the rich body of pastoral and doctrinal guidelines found in the Puebla document, but in addition, the team of experts, who were to offer guidance and advice for the work of study and reflection in different church jurisdictions, was set up.

2. The purpose of the second stage, which was carried out in the dioceses and ecclesiastical jurisdictions at different times, as circumstances and opportunity permitted, was to have all pastoral agents study the Puebla document and have all the different groups in the Church reflect on it so as to make concrete applications in accordance with the priorities of the Puebla Conference and the specific needs and requirements of the pastoral situation in the various dioceses and missionary jurisdictions. This stage produced fruit in the form of the very worthwhile contributions sent to the secretariat of the bishops' conference in preparation for the national assembly, which was to elaborate a final document on the basis of this rich material.

3. Thus, in May of this year, an assembly made up of bishops, priests, brothers, sisters, and lay people, totaling 130 participants, prepared the document for applying these fundamental points and directives. Following a decision of that assembly, a special commission, which was chosen from among the participants, was selected to draw up the final version of the document, and the request was made that it be published as soon as the bishops had given their approval.

The commission carried out its assigned task with utter fidelity, and the text was sent to all assembly participants to examine and send in the revisions they believed necessary.

4. Finally, the Bishops' Conference of Ecuador celebrated its plenary assembly in the city of Ibarra, July 21–24, in order to make the document its own and to provide final ratification. Present with the bishops was a select delegation from the Ecuadorian Conference of Religious and some priests who were there as experts. They examined and inserted the revisions sent by members of the assembly after familiarizing themselves with the text of the drafting commission. The bishops' conference then proceeded to give its official approval to the document that we now present.

At Puebla, the Ecuadorian bishops advocated dedicating the document of this great conference as an homage to the Blessed Virgin Mary, "the star of evangelization." Today, the bishops' conference dedicates to her its overall proposal for evangelization for the present and the future of our dear Ecuador.

Quito
September 8, 1980
Feast of the Nativity of Our Lady

OBJECTIVES

1. To take up both now and in the future the task of liberating evangelization, which is carried out through the activity of the Spirit, preferentially among the poor, out of the poor, and together with the poor, making God present in his son Jesus Christ, who journeys with them and in them reveals his face.

2. To promote and defend the dignity of the human person and, as Christians, in the light of the message of Christ, to assume our responsibility in the building of a just and human society.

3. To work to form ecclesial communities that will make possible a broad common experience of the Church, as family and people of God, and as expression of the preferential option for the poor.

4. To encourage the participation of lay people in the Church's evangelizing mission and, toward that end, to make effective the diversity of lay ministries so as to serve the life and growth of the ecclesial community and the building of a just and family-spirited society.

5. To take on and to purify the religiosity of our people, from within the context of their own culture, so that it may come to live and express through its own signs, symbols, and language, the faith that identifies it as a believing people, committed to the process of liberating evangelization.

6. To strengthen the particular (diocesan) church as a center of communion and pastoral planning, so as to build the unity of the Church in Ecuador for the sake of evangelization.

7. To foment the missionary spirit so that the members of the people of God may put their good will to work and thus collaborate in evangelizing action and specifically missionary activity, both in our nation and worldwide.

8. To aid in the discovery, discernment, and maturation of vocations to the ministerial priesthood and to the consecrated life as service in the Church. To train and update pastoral agents in the process of transformation for the sake of building the kingdom.

Brazil
Basic Christian Communities
(1982)

In its pastoral planning and innovations, the Brazilan Church has emphasized the formation and proliferation of base Christian communities. These have been conceived of as groups (twenty to forty persons, usually adults) who gather together on a regular basis. The members read a biblical selection (often from the Sunday readings), reflect on its meaning for their lives, and seek an application in their lives.

Not even God knows how numerous these participants are. Moderate estimates place the number between one and two million persons. Uncontrolled growth, simplistic biblical interpretations, and other dangers threaten unity and orthodoxy. But the Brazilian experience, now in its third decade, has been far more positive than negative. The bishops have noted life where little existed.

Introduction

1.   In our country today, basic Christian communities (= BCCs) are one of the most dynamic expressions of the life of the Church, and for various reasons, they are arousing interest in other sectors of society.
2.   We can make our own the words of the bishops at Puebla: "In 1968, base-level ecclesial communities were just coming into being. Over the past ten years, they have multiplied and matured. . . . In communion with their bishops, . . they have become centers of evangelization and driving forces for liberation and development" (*Puebla*, 96).
3.   In our country, the BCCs, which are specifically ecclesial in nature, have arisen from within the institutional Church and have become "a new way of being Church." It can be said that it is around them that the Church's pastoral and evangelizing activity is taking shape, and that will be even more the case in the future.

43

4.   As an element of internal renewal and a new way for the Church to be present to the world, they are clearly irreversible, if not in the details of the way they are structured, at least in their driving spirit.
5.   As pastors become aware of the life of the Church in our society, we want to look at them with affection; to be attentive and listen to them; to try to examine their life, which is so closely connected to the ongoing history of the people in which they are present; and to seek to discover the way to the future opening up before them.
6.   This document is limited in breadth and scope. We do not intend to take up here all aspects of the organization, life, and creativity of BCCs, nor are we going to go into the differences between various kinds of communities.

BCCs will have other opportunities to express their experience, the obstacles they encounter, and the hopes they treasure. Hence, in this document, we simply want to reflect on the path followed by BCCs in the light of the documents of the Church, to make explicit their ecclesial nature, and to take up some emerging problems that require further elucidation.

In doing this, we intend to provide a service for all communities that remain faithful to their origins and to help the whole Church in Brazil to understand better the wealth of this gift of the Spirit.

I. Basic Christian Communities in Brazil
Origins and Journey

7.   BCCs have not arisen by spontaneous generation, nor merely as the fruit of a pastoral decision. They are the result of the convergence of pastoral discoveries and conversions that involve the whole Church— people of God, pastors and faithful—in which the Spirit is at work unceasingly.
8.   As far back as 1962, our Emergency Plan stated: "There is an urgent need to give vitality and dynamism to our parishes in order to turn them into apt instruments for responding to the pressing demands of the situation in which we are living." One of the ways proposed for this purpose was to make the parish "a community of faith, of worship, and of charity" so that it might become "ferment within the human community."
9.   One of the recommendations was to "identify natural communities and to begin to work on the basis of the reality they present. In these communities which are open to evangelization, the dynamic elements will help awaken and form leaders of new communities. Lay people have a very decisive role in these communities" (*Emergency Plan*, 5.5).

"It should be noted that it is preferable to win over pagan or indifferent communities in urban centers by getting into natural communities. The most sure way is evangelization starting from life problems" (ibid., 5.6).

10. In these statements was already to be found the germ of some of the constitutive traits of what would become the basic Christian community.

11. Vatican Council II, which was eminently pastoral, had a great impact on the Church. Its major key ideas provided the theological basis for the intuition, which was already being felt in practice, that pastoral renewal should take place on the basis of the renewal of community life, and that the community should become an instrument of evangelization.

12. In their emergence, BCCs have been nourished by key ideas, among which we can point out the following:

- The Church as people of God, in which "to each person the manifestation of the Spirit is given for the common good" (1 Cor 12:7).

- The Church as "sacrament or sign of intimate union with God, and of the unity of all mankind" (*Lumen Gentium* [= LG], 1); in other words, as deep communion between persons becomes visible in the participating and responsible community.

- The irreplaceable task of lay people and their specific mission in the Church and in the world (cf. LG, 76ff.; *Apostolicam Actuositatem* [= AA]).

- The function of the Church, which journeys together with all of humankind, experiences with the world the same earthly lot, and is "a leaven and a kind of soul for human society" (*Gaudium et Spes* [= GS], 40). Human history and salvation history mesh together.

As they read the Bible, BCCs are in a privileged position to rediscover the liberating aspect of salvation history. They see their own journey prefigured in the Exodus of the people of Israel and raised to a new level in the experience of the paschal mystery of Jesus Christ. They take on their struggle for justice as an embodiment of prophecy in today's society. They also rediscover the experience of the brotherliness and sisterliness of the early communities, who came together in prayer and the breaking of bread, shared their goods, and lived united with a single heart and a single soul (Acts 2:4).

13. The *Plan for Joint Pastoral Action* (*Plan Pastoral de Conjunto 1966– 1970* [= PPC]) of the Brazilian Bishops' Conference, whose objective was to create the means and conditions to enable the Church in Brazil to adjust to the Vatican II image of the Church, stated: "The Church is and and always will be a community. In it there will always be present and active the ministry of the Word, liturgical life, and especially Eucharist, missionary action, the development of the faith of all the members of God's people, the presence of God in human development, and the visible organization of the ecclesiastical community itself" (PPC, p. 27).

14.   The territorial spread and population density of the parish are obstacles to experiencing community. Hence, the Plan says: "It has become urgent that within the parish territory there be awakened and encouraged base communities, in which Christians will not be anonymous persons, but will feel welcomed and responsible and will become an integral part of those communities, in communion of life in Christ and with all their brothers and sisters" (PPC, pp. 38–39).

15.   In this statement, there were initial traces of two ideas that were later to become the coordinates of pastoral action in Brazil and throughout Latin America: *communion* and *participation*.

16.   Pointing to the initial experiences of BCCs, Medellín (1968) provided various pastoral reasons for developing them, fully taking on the council's ecclesiology in the pastoral options it proposed. "At its own level, the base Christian community should take on responsibility for the wealth and expansion of the faith, as well as for worship, which is the expression of that faith. The base community is therefore the initial cell from which the Church is built up, the focal point for evangelization, and at present a primary factor in human formation and development" (*Medellín,* 15, III.10).

17.   Echoing the council, which asserted "the right of all people to human civilization, proper to the dignity of the person, without any discrimination of sex, nation, religion, or social condition," it is Medellín's particular credit that it heard the cry rising out of inhuman situations on our continent and it officially gave that cry a place in the Church.

18.   In their final message to the people of Latin America, the bishops say: "In the light of the faith that we profess as believers, we are striving to discover God's Plan in the 'signs of our times.' It is our interpretation that the aspirations and cries of Latin America are signs revealing the direction of the divine Plan operating in the redeeming love of Christ, which is the basis for these aspirations within the consciousness of a brotherly and sisterly solidarity."

19.   In the successive pastoral plans issued by our Conference of Bishops, BCCs gained increasing attention until they were made "priorities" in the third and fourth two-year plans.

20.   When dealing with evangelization in today's world, the 1974 Synod of Bishops reflected on the experiences of BCCs, which to some extent are occurring everywhere. On the basis of the results of the Synod, Pope Paul VI wrote the apostolic exhortation *On Evangelization in the Modern World* (*Evangelii Nuntiandi* [= EN]). After laying out the

new dimensions of evangelization in our age, the Holy Father, as it were, officially recognized BCCs by indicating to them the conditions for being the site and means for evangelization.

21. In their journey, our BCCs have been able to take as their basis these clear and sure guidelines in *Evangelii Nuntiandi* and to take advantage of all the reflection found in studies and documents produced by the Conference of Bishops, as well as of the many and varied meetings of BCCs themselves.

22. Along with Puebla, we can testify that "in small communities, particularly those that are better organized, people grow in their experience of new interpersonal relationships in the faith, in deeper exploration of God's Word, in fuller participation in the Eucharist, in communion with the pastors of the local Church, and in greater commitment to justice within the social milieu that surrounds them" (*Puebla*, 640).

23. Looking back over the steps taken during these twenty years, we do not find it rash to say that, taking their inspiration from the council's teachings, our BCCs have become instruments for building the kingdom and making concrete the hopes of our people.

II. The Ecclesial Nature of BCCs

24. During his pastoral journey through Brazil, the Holy Father gave the bishops a message for the leaders of base communities. In this message, the Holy Father reaffirms his confidence in BCCs, and he devotes particular attention to their ecclesial nature.

25. "Among the dimensions of base Christian communities, I believe it is useful to call attention to that dimension which most clearly defines them and without which their identity would vanish: their ecclesial nature. I stress this ecclesial nature because it is already explicit in the term used for such communities, especially in Latin America (*comunidades eclesiais de base*, grass-roots ecclesial communities). Being ecclesial is what stamps their originality and their way of existing and operating. And the "base" in question is specifically ecclesial in nature and not merely sociological or of some other nature" (*Message to Base Community Leaders*, 3).

26. As we look toward the BCCs with a good deal of joy and hope, we bishops would also like to call to mind this aspect with special emphasis, conscious that in so doing we are safeguarding their deep vitality.

27. "A sensitive attention and a serious courageous effort to maintain the ecclesial dimension of these communities in all its purity is an eminent service both to the communities themselves and to the Church: to the communities because it keeps them within their ecclesial identity and protects their freedom, effectiveness, and their very survival; to the Church, because only those communities that authentically live their ecclesial inspiration without dependencies of any other sort will serve their essential mission of evangelization. Such attention and such effort are a sacred duty for Peter's successor because of his 'concern for all the Churches' (cf. 2 Cor 11:28). They are also the duty of each bishop in his diocese and of the bishops, united in collegiality, within a nation. They are also the duty of those who have some responsibility in the communities themselves" (*Message*, 4).

28.   The characteristic notes of a true ecclesial community have been spelled out by Pope Paul VI in *On Evangelization in the Modern World* (EN, 58). Pope John Paul II reminds us of his main points: "This ecclesial nature is expressed in the community's sincere and loyal ties to its legitimate pastors, its faithful adherence to the aims of the Church, its complete openness to other communities and to the larger community of the universal Church, an openness that will shun any sectarian temptation" (*Message*, 5).

29.   At Puebla, the bishops of Latin America asked, "When can a small community be considered an authentic base-level ecclesial community?" and answered:

30.   "As a community, the [BCC] brings together families, adults and young people, in an intimate interpersonal relationship grounded in the faith. As an ecclesial reality, it is a community of faith, hope, and charity. It celebrates the Word of God and takes its nourishment from the Eucharist, the culmination of all the sacraments. It fleshes out the Word of God in life through solidarity and commitment to the new commandment of the Lord; and through the service of approved coordinators, it makes present and operative the mission of the Church and its visible communion with the legitimate pastors. It is a base-level community because it is composed of relatively few members as a permanent body, like a cell of the larger community" (*Puebla*, 641).

31.   The BCCs that have maintained these basic characteristics have also experienced great vitality. Such vitality will be in direct proportion to the intensity of the ecclesial dimension lived in the communal practice of the people of God, and especially of those who are most poor and humble. Faithful to the essential conditions that define them as Church, BCCs have demonstrated great richness and creativity in their manner of being and living the vocation of the Church present in the world.

32.   They are aware that they have been called and nourished by the Word, upon which they reflect under the impulse of the Spirit for the sake of personal and social conversion.

33.   They pay attention to the overall situation, act upon it, and seek to change it when circumstances so demand. Underlying this activity to change the situation is the conviction that God also speaks to us through events and calls us to build a society along the lines of the divine design.

34. These communities are connected to one another, to the parish, to the particular Church of which they form a part, and to the universal Church, and they maintain a sincere communion with their pastors.

35. They advance in their awareness of their missionary duty. They evangelize by seeking "to convert, solely through the divine power of the Message [the Church] proclaims, both the personal and collective consciences of people, the activities in which they engage, and the lives and concrete milieu which are theirs" (EN, 18).

36. They celebrate everyday events as signs of God's presence, finding both the root and summit of their experience as brothers and sisters in the Eucharist.

37. They express their charity through service: mutual service among themselves and service to the larger human communities in which they are set as ferment, sign, and commitment to the liberation of every human and all humans.

38. Whatever be the route chosen to set them up, they strive to reproduce the mystery of the Church in their own life. Hence, the BCCs in Brazil strive to be communities of faith and worship, sacrament of the saving presence of God in the history of human beings.

39. *Lumen Gentium* says: "This Church of Christ is truly present in all legitimate local congregations of the faithful which, united with their pastors, are themselves called churches in the New Testament. For in their own locality these are the new people called by God, in the Holy Spirit and in much fullness (cf. 1 Thes 1:5). In them the faithful are gathered together by the preaching of the gospel of Christ, and the mystery of the Lord's Supper is celebrated. . . . [In them] there is manifested a symbol of that charity and 'unity of the Mystical Body, without which there can be no salvation.' In these communities, though frequently small and poor, or living far from one another, Christ is present. By virtue of Him the one, holy, catholic, and apostolic Church gathers together" (26).

40. As living cells of the Church, BCCs as a whole, have been a ferment of spirit and community and community life in the various spheres of ecclesial life. They have made a powerful contribution to parish renewal and to the renewal of various pastoral processes, along the lines of growing communion and participation. In many places, pastoral work with groups is used as a stage prior to the setting up of BCCs. In BCCs, vocational work and new ministries receive a new impulse and a very specific field in which to develop. In their life and practice, BCCs have found surprising ways to carry out incarnate kinds of evangelization, catechesis, and liturgy, very much connected to the Word of God. In their "hunger and thirst for justice," they have found routes to a concrete practice of ecumenism. Moreover, they develop a participatory intercommunication and a growing critical sense toward the massifying tendencies of the media. In their continual effort to act, reflect, and celebrate, BCCs are an educational alternative for those who are seeking a new society in which individualism, competition, and profit will give way to justice and brotherhood and sisterhood.

41.　All of this heightens the responsibility of all those priests, religious, and lay people who exercise leadership roles at different levels in BCCs. It demands of them both a deep fidelity to the Church and great openness to new ways of concretizing in practice the BCCs' community and missionary dimensions. Quoting the Holy Father's message, we would issue a reminder that the leader of the base community, "much more than a teacher is a witness: the community has a right to receive from that person the persuasive example of Christian life, of operative and radiating faith, of transcendent hope, of selfless love. May that person be, moreover, one who believes in prayer and who prays" (*Message*, 12).

42.　Along the way, the fidelity of the BCCs is continually put to the test in our society, which is ever more pluralistic and marked by conflicts. The urgency of certain vital problems and the temptation of simplistic solutions are risks to which the communities must be alert. In the next section, we want to reflect on some aspects that we believe are important so that on their journey, the BCCs not lose their way but, on the contrary, go resolutely forward and become more fruitful.

III. Some Particular Aspects of BCC Pastoral Work

BCCs and the Poor

43.　From their beginnings, BCCs have flourished more among simple and poor populations. This is so for several reasons. Initially, BCCs took root particularly among scattered populations in the rural interior of the country. The fact that there was no resident pastor meant that lay people were quicker to take on ministries and to place the power of the Church within the community of brothers and sisters. Thus, priests and religious shifted to becoming the ones who developed local leadership, leaving lay people more space. BCCs also flourished intensely on the outskirts of large cities. In those areas, there is less experience of the centralizing tendency of the traditional parish structure since urban growth is a recent phenomenon and has encountered a Church with a new community and missionary awareness.

44.   However, the most important aspect about the coming together of BCCs and the poor and simple people is its deep gospel meaning. In the Bible, the privileged position of the poor is a manifestation of the mercy of God, who takes on the defense of those who are helpless because their cause is just.

45.   In addition, the poor live more fully the values of brotherliness and sisterliness, mutual aid, and service, which are key characteristics in this new way of being Church. They also remain more open and available for the things of God in terms of their time and interests.

46.   Moreover, the simplicity of BCCs, both in their size and structure, and in their language, life, and atmosphere, are closer to the spontaneous and simple way they live. That has made the BCCs the place where simple, illiterate, and poor people become very much a part of the Church as participating and active members. In parish structures, the poor have generally stayed more at a distance, more as the objects rather than the agents of evangelization, more the beneficiaries than those responsible for the different services.

47.   All these reasons explain why at Puebla the bishops could say: "The [BCCs] embody the Church's preferential love for the common people. In them, their religiosity is expressed, valued, and purified; and they are given a concrete opportunity to share in the task of the Church and to work committedly for the transformation of the world" (*Puebla*, 643).

48.   Nevertheless, it would not be correct to conclude that BCCs are possible only among the poor classes. It would be even worse to conceive of two churches, irreducibly opposed: a church of the poor in BCCs, and another church of the middle or rich classes in the parish and other organizations.

49.   It would be a disfiguration of the very nature of BCCs to isolate them within the Church or to make a sociological meaning their primary and constitutive element. Recalling the words of Pope Paul VI in *Evangelii Nuntiandi,* we repeat that we must avoid "the very real danger of [these communities] becoming isolated within themselves, then of believing themselves to be the only authentic Church of Christ, and hence of condemning other ecclesial communities" (EN, 58).

50.   Hence, BCCs are to work together "for the benefit of the bigger communities, especially the individual Churches," and thus be "a hope for the universal Church . . ." (EN, 58).

51.   What is basic in BCCs is proposed as the ideal for all Christians. All are called to live in brotherly and sisterly communion in an intense way and to integrate faith and ongoing history, starting from their overall situation and concrete life. In this sense, BCC pastoral work poses a gospel challenge to traditional parish work, and to those church groups and movements that, in their style and language, are closer to people who belong to other social classes.

52.   BCCs are especially promising and suggestive with regard to a redefinition of urban pastoral work, which is more and more urgent. As Puebla says: "In particular, we must explore how these small communities, which are flourishing mainly in rural areas and urban peripheries, can be adapted to the pastoral care of the big cities on our continent" (*Puebla*, 648).

53.   This will certainly not be done at the expense of the space that the poor and simple have won in the Church in their BCCs nor by simply retracing their path. It will be the fruit of a brotherly/sisterly spirit search on the part of the whole Church. The point of convergence for this search is obviously a more evangelical life, one that is able to collaborate toward building a more just and family-spirited society: "United in a [BCC] and nurturing their adherence to Christ, Christians strive for a more evangelical way of life amid the people, work together to challenge the egotistical and consumeristic roots of society, and make explicit their vocation to communion with God and their fellow humans. Thus, they offer a valid and worthwhile point of departure for building up a new society, 'the civilization of love'" (*Puebla*, 642).

54.   BCCs are thus evangelizers of the world: "Every ecclesial community in Latin America should strive to serve our continent as an example of the way of living together in which freedom and solidarity are successfully combined; in which authority is exercised in the spirit of the Good Shepherd; in which a different attitude toward wealth is lived out; in which efforts are made to establish participatory forms of organization and structure that are capable of paving the way for a more humane type of society; and, most important of all, in which it is unmistakably clear that any merely human form of communion, devoid of radical communion with God in Jesus Christ, is incapable of sustaining itself and is fated to end up turning against humanity" (*Puebla*, 273).

BCCs and the Sociopolitical Dimension of Evangelization

55.   Step by step, the journey of the BCCs has made more explicit the Church's evangelizing mission. From the outset, they have sought to take on the whole of life, thus overcoming disincarnate spiritualism. The effort of the small rural communities in the beginning to create more human living conditions was a good reflection of the awareness the Church had during the council period that evangelization is relevant to the vast underdeveloped areas of the world.

56.   Thus, on a small and local scale, BCCs reflected the process of coming to awareness present within all pastoral work that the Church is an agent of development and human formation. Medellín sees BCCs as "the initial cell by which the Church is built up, the focal point for evangelization, at present, a primary factor in human formation and development" (*Medellín*, 15.10).

57.   The effort by BCCs today to struggle for justice and the integral liberation of human beings reflects a more precise analysis of social reality, seen as the fruit of unjust structures and the oppression of the poor. Here also, BCCs reflect the awareness of the Church in terms of its evangelizing mission. "Action on behalf of justice and participation in the transformation of the world fully appear to us as a constitutive dimension of the preaching of the gospel, or, in other words, of the Church's mission for the redemption of the human race and its liberation from every oppressive situation" (*Synod on Justice in the World*, 6; also EN, 30–31).

58.   "It is well known in what terms numerous bishops from all the continents spoke of this at the last Synod, especially the bishops from the Third World, with a pastoral accent resonant with the voice of the millions of sons and daughters of the Church who make up those peoples. Peoples, as we know, engaged with all their energy in the effort and struggle to overcome everything which condemns them to remain on the margin of life: famine, chronic disease, illiteracy, poverty, injustices in international relations and especially in commercial exchanges, situations of economic and cultural neocolonialism, sometimes as cruel as the old political colonialism. The Church, as the bishops repeated, has the duty to proclaim the liberation of millions of human beings, many of whom are her own children—the duty of assisting the birth of this liberation, of giving witness to it, of ensuring that it is complete. This is not foreign to evangelization" (EN, 30).

59.   "Between evangelization and human advancement—development and liberation—there are in fact profound links. These include links of an anthropological order, because the [human being] who is to be evangelized is not an abstract being but is subject to social and economic questions. They also include links in the theological order, since one cannot dissociate the plan of creation from the plan of Redemption. The latter plan touches the very concrete situations of injustice to be combated and of justice to be restored. They include links of the eminently evangelical order, which is that of charity: how in fact can one proclaim the new commandment without promoting in justice and in peace the true, authentic [human] advancement . . .? We ourselves have taken care to point this out, by recalling that it is impossible to accept 'that in evangelization one could or should ignore the importance of the problems so much discussed today, concerning justice, liberation, development, and peace in the world. This would be to forget the lesson that comes to us from the Gospel concerning love of our neighbor who is suffering and in need'" (EN, 31).

60.   "The same voices which during the Synod touched on this burning theme with zeal, intelligence, and courage have, to our great joy,

furnished the enlightening principles for a proper understanding of the importance and profound meaning of liberation, such as it was proclaimed and achieved by Jesus of Nazareth and such as it is preached by the Church" (ibid.).

61.   The presence of the Church in the social sphere becomes complete only through concrete activity, as Pope Paul VI says: "In the social sphere, the Church has always wished to assume a double function: first to enlighten minds . . . and second, to take part in action and to spread, with real care for service and effectiveness, the energies of the Gospel" (*Octogesima Adveniens* [= OA], 48).

62.   The Church is also aware that the preaching of the gospel has a political dimension. "The Church's mission is to evangelize and is eminently pastoral in nature. Nevertheless, that mission in no way leads it to overlook the country's social and political problems, insofar as those problems always have a prominent ethical dimension" (*Reflexão cristã sobre a conjuntura política* [*Christian Reflection on the Political Situation*] Permanent Commission of the Conference of Bishops, 1981, no. 2). "The Church is not the one to interpret partisan aspirations nor to mediate between political factions. However, that does not mean that it is apolitical. It knows that in practice any claim to be apolitical means a political stance of tacit complicity with a given configuration of political power, whatever it may be" (ibid., no. 6).

63.   Hence, the sociopolitical dimension present in the activity of BCCs is, in itself, the same dimension that should be present in other church communities and agencies for evangelization. The new element brought by BCCs has been the fact that, within the Church, they provide a space in which the humble folk themselves can share in the evangelization of society through the struggle for justice. In this sense, BCCs have proven to be a privileged site for education for justice and an instrument of liberation.

64.   However, both BCCs and other church communities need to be alert so that this kind of activity, which faith demands, may maintain fidelity to the faith itself, in both content and method.

65.   There is always room for deepening the full scope of the kind of liberation being sought. We must overcome continually the temptation of those who would "reduce [the Church's] mission to the dimensions of a simply temporal project. They would reduce her aims to a man-centered goal; the salvation, of which she is the messenger, would be reduced to material well-being. Her activity, forgetful of all spiritual and religious preoccupation, would become initiatives of the political or social order. But if this were so, the Church would lose her fundamental meaning. Her message of liberation would no longer have any originality and would easily be open to monopolization and manipulation by ideological systems and political parties" (EN, 32).

66.   The BCC would also lose its identity if its ideal of liberation were not the full liberation of human beings in Christ. Hence, BCCs must always be alert in their self-examination so as to discover whether their life and activity are being guided by the totality of the demands of faith, or whether their activity is being consumed by undertakings of a social nature.

67.   Concern for deepening the word, for education in the faith, for conversion of heart, for the celebration of the sacraments, and for prayer must become part of the life of the community and inspire all its social and political action for the sake of the common good.

68.   On this point, our message is intended more directly for coordinators and pastoral agents for the communities. The people themselves in the communities will not always come to the point of distinguishing God and salvation in Jesus Christ from their overall struggle and journey. It is the role of pastoral agents, who have been more highly trained, to be vigilant with their gospel-inspired love, so that alien ideologies and political manipulation do not disfigure the community. We must always go back to the ecclesial roots of the community. These roots will provide continually "the inspiration of faith, the motivation of fraternal love, a social teaching which the true Christian cannot ignore and which he must make the foundation of his wisdom and of his experience in order to translate it concretely into forms of action, participation, and commitment" (EN, 38).

69.   Let no one find in these words any doubt or reservation about the activity of Christians and of BCCs in the social and political realm. On the contrary, their purpose is to provide motivation for such activity and safeguard its inner strength, which will be ever more vigorous to the extent it is truly evangelical.

BCCs, the Common Struggle for Justice, and the Popular Movements

70.   The kingdom of God is broader than the visible Church and its primary content is everything that is the fruit of truth, justice, and love wherever that may occur. Similarly, the kingdom is brought about through the working of the Spirit in Christians, but also through every person of good will. By the same token, the BCC—the small local Church—cannot claim to have a monopoly on the kingdom of God for, and within, the environment where it exists and acts.

71.   As Church, the BCC is sign and instrument of the kingdom: It is that tiny portion of the people where God's word is expressly received and celebrated in the sacraments, signs of faith, especially in the Eucharist.

72.   Thus, the practice of justice is not enough to make one a member of a BCC. Something more is required: that practice must become explicit in the person and the work of Christ. Similarly, it is not enough for a BCC to further the values of the kingdom. In order for it to be true to what it is, that activity must be related constantly and explicitly to the person and mission of Jesus Christ, Son of God, and his paschal mystery, through which the establishment of God's kingdom has been initiated within humankind. The whole life of BCCs must be aimed toward the kingdom of God, but firmly rooted in the celebration and deepening of faith.

73.   In announcing and furthering the values of the kingdom, BCC members, and the BCC itself, will find themselves together with persons and groups who are struggling for the same, or similar, values, but who do not share the same faith or who are members of other churches. The promotion of justice and the dignity of the human person is a privileged area for brotherly and sisterly collaboration among Christian churches and between them and all people of good will. While maintaining their own identity, BCCs should be open to joint reflection and action in everything that can benefit the human person.

74.   The problem becomes more sensitive when it is a question of collaboration with ideological groups that are closed in on themselves, and especially with groups that explicitly reject faith and openness to God. Without denying the values that such groups might have, it is always necessary to distinguish the possibility of collaboration and at what level it might take place. While BCCs can work in specific projects alongside some groups that are not explicitly Christian, in the case of other groups, such collaboration may sometimes go no further than being in agreement over certain valid objectives, yet always leaving it very clear that there is a deep split over conceptions of the world and of human beings and their destiny.

75.   Today, in practice, BCCs that bring together poor and simple people from outlying areas of cities and from rural areas must take a clear stance with regard to the popular movements that have emerged quite recently as the the people's instrument for struggle for a more just society. Many members and leaders of these movements belong to BCCs and had their consciences awakened in them. However, as a result of previous circumstances, people of good will who did not have faith took part in the development of BCCs, which, because they were Church, were the only place in which social action was tolerated.

76.   Without destroying the brotherly and sisterly bonds that have been created, and without nullifying the progress made, we must keep clear the distinction between BCCs and popular movements. The popular movements are social movements among the poorer classes, and their aims are liberation and the social and political development of the people. These are not church movements, nor are they dependent on the Church for their organization and activity, since they are fully independent of the Church. BCCs must become aware of this, so that they will not occupy a space that is not theirs and imprint a rhythm of ecclesial life on a secular movement. Moreover, BCCs would lose their identity if, in order to fit in with popular movements, they were to change their way of life and their explicit faith values.

77.   Bearing that in mind, it remains true that what the Church teaches about the presence and activity of Christians in the structure and organization of the world is fully valid for BCCs. In this sense, popular movements, neighborhood development efforts, the fields of work, and our common life are spheres to be fermented by BCCs, providing the energy and ferment of the gospel for the integral liberation of human beings.

BCCs and Lay Movements

78.   We are happy to note that BCCs have opened a new and fruitful space for the participation of lay people in the Church. This is the case not only because BCCs offer a more active participation due to their more human scale and their closeness to one's personal life, but also because they favor a new and more diversified distribution of the various ecclesial services and ministries. This greater participation by lay people and the rise of new ministries are two fruits of major import within the life of the Church.

79.   This does not mean, however, that BCCs are a new lay movement. BCCs are not a movement; they are a new way of being Church. The BCC is the primary cell of the larger body of the Church or, as Medellín puts it, "the initial cell from which the Church is built up." As Church, the BCC has the basic characteristics that Christ wanted to give to the ecclesial community. The BCC is a new way of bringing about that ecclesial community that is the Body of Christ. Hence, the pastoral or hierarchical ministry is part of the BCC. The bishop and priest are not on the outside; they are not mere advisors or fellow journeyers. Their presence, even when it is not constant, has a special and unique meaning since they make present Christ the head, as they do in any ecclesial community.

80.   Therefore, for BCCs, it is not enough that they remain united to their bishops and priests like any Christian movement. BCCs are cells of the ecclesial body, and, therefore, they have bonds of a closer nature in the way they relate to the pastors who head the churches in the name of the Lord. This does not do away with the proper autonomy of BCCs in the unfolding of their own life and mission, but it entails special demands for ecclesial coresponsibility and communion.

81.   At the same time, it must be emphasized that BCCs offer special conditions in which lay people can grow and become adult members of a church community, without handing over their vocation and role to the hierarchy. Likewise, BCCs offer ministers better conditions for exercising their service without nullifying the creativity, initiative, and participation of lay people. That is why BCCs have always been, and are regarded as, an excellent way to achieve the ideal of ecclesial community.

82.   In the BCC, the whole community has a real opportunity to take on its mission, and the various vocations and ministries work together for their own edification and continuing vitality. In this manner, far from being able to dispense with the hierarchical ministry, BCCs require a ministry that is more available, more dedicated, and trained for helping faith to grow, for celebrating the sacraments in a vital way, and for journeying with the community in communion with the other communities in the particular church [diocese] in fidelity to their vocation as Church.

Coordination and Ultimate Responsibility Within BCCs

83.   We repeat what the bishops said at Puebla: "As pastors, we are determined to promote, guide, and accompany the [BCCs] in the spirit of the Medellín Conference . . . and the guidelines set forth by *Evangelii Nuntiandi*. . . . We will also foster the discovery and gradual training of animators for these communities" (*Puebla*, 648). We are more and more convinced of the immense wealth that BCCs can bring to our churches in Brazil and to the revitalization of evangelizing activity. In our dioceses, we experience a great deal of joy when we enter into more direct contact with BCCs on pastoral visits and efforts in the task of evangelization. We also note that this joy is shared by the whole people, which desires to live in intimate communion with its pastors. If now and again there are problems, that is no special property of BCCs; it can happen with any other church community as well. Such problems are signs of a community that is still imperfect and requires greater conversion on the part of all. But BCC pastoral work is always an integral part of our pastoral work, and very often it is even a priority area.

84.   In recent years, some churches have begun to promote interecclesial meetings between base communities, bringing together communities from several dioceses. Participants from these meetings have subsequently organized meetings on a national level, asking one particular church to serve as host. Preparation for these meetings consists of diocesan and regional meetings, which choose representatives for the national meetings.

85.   One very positive aspect of these meetings is the fact that they energize, deepen, and support the spirit of the communities which, for their part, provide a witness of vitality and zeal for the gospel to the whole Church. Moreover, there have always been bishops taking part in these national meetings.

86.   Nevertheless, there are certain other aspects, which, at this point in a journey that is already long and rich, now require more thought and guidance so as to prevent damage to ecclesial communion. It is essential that the general coordination of each meeting be accepted by the regional body or diocese that is acting as host. Similarly, the coordination of preparatory regional and diocesan meetings ought to be accepted officially by those dioceses and regional bodies with the approval of the bishops of the dioceses or regions. After all, the coordination of pastoral works is an aspect of episcopal ministry and should be exercised in deep communion with the bishop and under his ultimate responsibility.

87.   The intention here is not in any way to lessen active participation by members of the communities, but is rather to safeguard the full ecclesial character of the meetings. In fact, it often happens that an apparently more spontaneous kind of coordination can jeopardize important ecclesial aspects, which these meetings should maintain.

88.   It is the role of the bishops to watch over the journey of the churches entrusted to them and to guarantee to Christians themselves the authenticity of efforts undertaken by the Church or in the name of the Church. We want to take on our mission ever more in the spirit of brotherly and sisterly service, and we know that we can rely on the spirit of faith in our communities.

BCCs: Object of Interest and Misunderstanding

89.   During the last few years, BCCs have begun to attract the attention of different sectors in the Church and in society. They have become an object of research and study by theologians and of reporting in the media. Such media attention makes it quite clear how certain groups and institutions outside the Church are interested in BCCs.

90.   All this is a sign of the increasing importance of BCCs. Theological studies shed light, and they help to understand this new reality, but they should not be confused with the life of the communities. BCCs, in turn, have made a significant contribution toward the elaboration of the more original lines of our own theological and pastoral thinking. The fact that BCCs and theological thinking are traveling together could mean a continual revitalization of evangelizing action.

91.   The interest in BCCs on the part of institutions and groups outside the Church seems to have another and quite different meaning. There, what one often finds is complete disinformation and a desire to manipulate, when the aim is not simply to use BCCs as a target for more general attacks on the Church.

92.   In fact, what is being questioned is the very mission of the

Church. What is being repudiated are not simply the BCCs in themselves, but rather the whole process of evangelization when it turns toward a prophetic critique of injustice, and when it strives to build a more family-spirited society. BCCs, in a simple but effective way, are able to practice more intensely the demands of the Church's social teaching. They make commitment to the poor visible. Their very existence and activity are denunciations of the social iniquity that robs the poor of their chances and their say in things. If BCCs suffer persecution, it is for the sake of the Church and the gospel and, thus, they are the heirs mentioned in the Beatitudes.

93.   The words of the Lord apply to BCCs: "Do not live in fear little flock. It has pleased your Father to give you the kingdom" (Lk 12:32). The Spirit of fortitude will be their strength in contradiction, and their pastors will be ever at their side, supporting and confirming their journey.

94.   As we conclude these thoughts, we want to give thanks to God for the gift that BCCs constitute for the life of the Church in Brazil; for the union existing between our brothers and sisters and their pastors; and for the hope that this new way of being Church is going to continue to be more and more a leaven of renewal in our society.

Permanent Council
Bishops' Council of Brazil
Brasilia
November 23–26, 1982

Colombia
Renewal of the Parish
(1982)

The Colombian bishops wished to emphasize the renovation of parish life as a major step in the renewal of the Church in Colombia. Five years of preparation and consultation were spent as part of the process of education and involvement by parish members.

The bishops see parishes as central to the lives of Catholics, "accompanying persons and families throughout their lives, through educating and helping them grow in the faith and acting as a center of coordination and motivation of communities, groups, and movements. For the celebration of the Eucharist and other sacraments, the parish makes present the universal Church."

The bishops believe that pastors and parish workers "have been sent especially to the poorest and most needy in the parish," stating the preferential option for the poor, emphasized at the Medellín and Puebla Conferences. The bishops also take for granted the existence of communities without priests, expressing special thanks to women and men religious and lay workers who act as community leaders.

1. Salutation

Beloved Priests, Religious, and Faithful:

We bishops of Colombia, meeting in our XXXVIII Plenary Assembly, in order to seek the renewal of the parish, a community of the baptized of which you are all members, send you our fraternal greeting and the blessings of God our Father and of Jesus Christ the Lord.

2. Gratitude to Pastors, Priests, and Other Pastoral Agents

Over the centuries, the wealth of the gospel and the light of Christian faith have come down to us in the context of a parish community.

The virtues that emanate from the gospel, stamping our country unmistakably as a Christian nation, have grown and remain in the parish despite many obstacles and risks. We will be ever mindful of and always grateful to all those who throughout the history of Colombia have carried out and are carrying out this plan of salvation and, particularly, to the self-sacrificing priests—secular and religious—who sometimes with unlimited fidelity and generosity have surrendered their lives to the service of parochial ministry.

3. Prior Tasks for Parish Renewal

This plenary assembly has gathered for the purpose of facing the challenges that the present evolution of the world and history present to the parish community and seeks to find paths toward authentic renewal and the vital growth of that community.

The first step in this effort has been made by those very communities, presided over by their pastors, who at the local level and then at a national conference of pastors, as fruit of their work, magnificently cleared the way and provided us with a solid basis for our pastoral reflections in this assembly. May our grateful word as pastors and brothers go out to all of them.

4. Commitment to Parish Renewal

In its very being, the parish, to some extent, carries out all the functions of the Church since it accompanies persons and families throughout their lives in the education and growth of their faith and is the center that provides coordination and leadership for communities, groups, and movements. In addition, through the celebration of the Eucharist and other sacraments, it makes present more clearly the Church as a whole (cf. *Puebla*, 644). Hence, today, when profound change and radical transformation are affecting its very life and mission, the parish more than ever requires complete commitment on the part of all its members—priests, religious, and lay people—in order to preserve its identity, renew it, and spur it to act.

5. The Priest, Model of the Flock

This commitment and this shared responsibility, beloved priests, lead us to repeat Paul's words to Timothy: "For this reason, I remind you to stir into flame the gift of God bestowed when my hands were laid on you. The Spirit God has given us is no cowardly spirit, but rather one that makes us strong, loving, and wise" (2 Tm 1:6–8). A primary task is the renewal of our priestly identity, which, within the limits of our flesh, obliges us always to be ministers of Christ and dispensers of the mysteries of God, "totally dedicated to the work for which the Lord has raised [us] up" (*Presbyterorum Ordinis* [= PO], 3).

Once more, we invite you to seek unceasingly the holiness that is impossible unless we intensify our time devoted to prayer. Intimate union with Our Lord will make you true models of the flock.

6. Sacramental Bond with the Bishop

Your priestly service must bear the seal of authenticity provided by the permanent sacramental bond with your bishop, whose indispensable and immediate collaborators you are, and whom you make present in the parish community. Common fraternal life is both a treasure and a condition for exercising your ministry effectively, and it leads you, thereby, to embody with your brother priests a genuine priestly community, one that enables you to share the concerns, delights, and sufferings of the ministry.

7. Servants of the Word, Sent Especially to the Poor

Constituted to serve human beings in the things that refer to God, you must keep, as the primary and fundamental effort in your ministry and proclamation, the celebration and embodiment of the divine Word of which you are servants and heralds. While you are in debt to all in the ministry of evangelization, without any reservation or exclusion, be mindful that together with Christ you have been sent especially to the poorest and most needy in your parishes (cf. Lk 4:18; Is 61:1), whom you ought to serve with joyful unconcern, through the witness of a simple and austere life.

8. Trainers of Lay People

We will never be able to say that our parishes are true Christian communities and dynamic signs of salvation in Christ, unless there is at our side an active laity, conscious of itself and of its mission in the Church (cf. *Ad Gentes* [= AG], 21). It is therefore urgent that there be systematic training of lay people in different age groups and reflecting their varying situation in society, especially within families, so that they may be led at each moment to accept their proper responsibilities and their Christian commitment in today's world.

In this work of yours as pastors, the noblest and most important in the priestly life, we want to assure you of our unceasing concern and our resolute support since you are our constant presence within parish communities.

9. Deacons, Servants of the Word and of Charity

Standing alongside the priest, because they participate in the Sacrament of Orders, are permanent deacons, to whom we likewise address our word of greeting, blessing, and gratitude, and whom we urge to continue to aid in the building of the parish community with their service of the Word, of the Eucharist, and of charity in the different ministries.

10. Religious, Treasure for the Parish, Due to Their Charisms

Religious, both men and women, have always been present in this work of building the parish community, aiding through the witness of their life and the proclamation of the Word, in response to their own particular charisms.

We now address you, beloved religious, to thank you for your evangelizing activity and to ask you to make ever more present within the parish community the treasure of your charisms and to make your collaboration in pastoral activity ever more closely integrated.

11. The Faithful, Those Who Are to Restore Christian Values

Finally, our message as pastors goes out to all faithful Catholics who, in their different groups, comprise the parishes of our Church.

With the Apostle Paul, we can say "You . . . are my joy and my crown" (Phil 4:1). Indeed, you have kept the faith you received from your elders, expressed in love for God and for neighbor, in embodying Christian virtues, and in expressions of popular piety.

12. Urgent Need for Conversion and Recovery of Values

Nevertheless, with just as much truth and pastoral concern as we stated in a recent document, we must say that the mystery of evil is also present and operating in many ways in our communities.

Disregard for life and for the human person; flagrant injustice; the shattering of the moral law and the loose habits that thereby result; and family breakup, among other evils, are the great challenges facing our parish communities.

It is your task to join with your pastors in a decisive action in order to recover Christian values. The first step in that direction is one's own personal conversion.

13. *Witnesses and Apostles*

We exhort you to rekindle the power of your baptism, which commits you to be faithful witnesses to the gospel through your life and activity, and to be active members of the Church in order to effect the Christian transformation of our society for which we yearn.

To those who work more closely with priests in lay ministries and apostolic groups to build the kingdom of God, we offer our warm word of affection and gratitude.

14. *Communities without a Priest*

We want to express special appreciation to you who are leaders of parish communities without your own pastor, due to the lack of priests. To you religious and lay apostles who offer your service of charity to these communities, we offer our word of encouragement. Your service to the community places you in the same historic context as that of the early communities. May the grace of our Lord be with you.

You, the faithful of such communities, may be certain of our pastoral concern for you. Pray the Lord of the harvest to send laborers to serve your parishes.

15. *Renewal and Practice of Faith*

To those who have given up religious practices, and to those who have not yet made a faith decision, we also address our greetings as brothers, with the hope of the happy moment of return and of the generous acceptance of the Lord in your hearts.

Divine grace; the enlightenment of the Holy Spirit; the motherly protection of Mary, Our Lady; the patronage of St. John Mary Vianney, the model for pastors; and the generous joint effort of priests, religious, and lay people provide us with the firm assurance and the joyful confidence that the work of this plenary assembly, whose conclusions will be published at the appropriate time, will lead our churches along the sure paths of a genuine renewal, of which this assembly seeks to be only the resolute and happy beginning.

> Mario Revollo Bravo
> Archbishop of Pamplona
> President of the Bishops' Conference

Fabio Betancur Tirado
Auxiliary Bishop of Medellín
Secretary of the XXXVIII Plenary Assembly

Leonardo Gómez Serna
Prelate of Bertrania
Secretary of the XXXVIII Plenary Assembly

Guatemala
Guidelines for Charismatic Renewal
(1986)

The charismatic or Pentecostal renewal among Catholics (and Protestants) has been growing rapidly in Guatemala and other parts of Latin America. The Guatemalan bishops studied and reflected on what was taking place and on what theological grounding there should be for the movement.

The instruction treats the theology of charisms, a Christ-centered spirituality, the Spirit in the Church, and Vatican II. Included here are sections six and seven, "Fruits and Risks of the Movement."

6. Fruits of the Charismatic Renewal

6.1. In many circles where the renewal is present, the fruits of the action of the Holy Spirit are beginning to be visibly present. For many people, the call received in baptism to be disciples is something real, an invitation to become engaged in a personal relationship with Jesus and with the Holy Spirit through whom we have access to the Father—all in consonance with the intent of Vatican II (cf. *Optatam Totius* [= OT], 8).

6.2. There are also countless cases of witness from priests whose lives, once touched by this personal level of faith, have undergone a deep conversion of the heart. They have redirected their lives toward God and have, thereby, experienced an inexpressible joy in their priestly lives, a greater interiorization of the celebration of the holy Eucharist, and a rediscovery of the value of sacramental penance.

6.2.1. Out of this experience, there has emerged a new depth of personal prayer and an "attentive and devout" recitation of the Liturgy of the Hours. They have rediscovered the importance of the cross as the center of life, that cross that remains in the heart of the apostle even after the glory of the resurrection and the outpouring of the Holy Spirit.

6.2.2. An intimate relationship with the Persons of the Most Holy Trinity has led to a new growth in love toward all members of the human family. Apostolic celibacy is lived at deeper levels of surrender and total self-giving. This transformation in the life of priests has also taken place in the lives of sisters who, through the action of the Holy Spirit, have rediscovered the original features of the charisms of their founders and what is specific about their religious families. This has contributed to the good of the Church, which is enriched and unified with the manifold variety of charisms and the different forms of life under vows, while, at the same time, religious have radically reoriented their lives toward "the one thing necessary."

6.3. For many lay people, belonging to the renewal has enabled them to discover the person of Jesus Christ, the value of their baptism, and their proper and irreplaceable role in the Church. For them, the renewal has been a response to the need they have experienced for spirituality, for joyful prayer, community prayer, prayer of praise.

6.3.1. The renewal has aroused in almost all its members a very great love for sacred Scripture and an eagerness to read it constantly and to penetrate deeply into its teachings.

6.3.2. In many people, participating in the movement has enkindled a sincere zeal for the apostolate, and they proclaim to others the marvels of the Lord and of his Spirit.

In summary, we could say that the renewal is helping many people to find the meaning and importance of their relationship with God in their lives. It is a great help for reestablishing a strong sense of the absoluteness of God as Lord but, at the same time, a sense that God is very much united to us through his Son and the Holy Spirit.

6.4. The genuine renewal is a constant invitation to place more trust in God and to demonstrate openly our faith in the face of an intellectualistic secularism that characterizes industrial and consumer society.

6.4.1. The renewal has provided groups with the experience of the power of the Holy Spirit, who energized the early Church, arousing faith in circles as hostile as those that the very first Christians encountered.

6.5. These are the precious fruits of the charismatic renewal, in the presence of which we cannot but recognize the activity of the Holy Spirit. Indeed, this movement, like many other movements that have arisen within the church community, is producing fruits of genuine conversion and is furnishing the Body of Christ with new vitality.

7. Risks of the Charismatic Movement

7.1. In pointing out the risks we discover in the charismatic renewal, we want to draw attention to two things:

7.1.1. We cannot attribute to a genuine renewal in the Spirit the faults that are due to poor guidance from leaders or carelessness on the part of pastors.

7.1.2. The deviations we find in the charismatic renewal are not much more disturbing than those that occur in other movements, confraternities, congregations, or extremist groups.

7.2. It is especially important to point out the danger of falling into true aberrations, unless the movement is well known and understood. Consequently, it has been necessary to exercise a great deal of vigilance over its activities. Normally, other groups in the Church do not require such extreme concern. Experience shows that where there does not exist an almost extreme care over charismatic groups, they easily go off track, something that does not occur with other movements.

7.2.1. The charismatic renewal generally promotes an exclusive or peculiar kind of prayer, but it cannot be said that this is essential to a renewal in the Spirit. For the point is not a method of prayer, but a deepening in the life of prayer through the action of the Holy Spirit, who comes to our aid and helps us to pray in a filial manner, deep within our hearts, hidden away in our rooms, where our father sees us (cf. Mt 6:6).

7.2.2. Ignoring this point has led to a grave problem, creating excessively exclusive attitudes and behavior and causing certain valid kinds of prayer, such as vocal prayer, the rosary, and so forth, to be abandoned (and sometimes disrespected).

7.2.3. In some places, taking part in a liturgy of a "charismatic" nature is a condition for taking part in the Eucharist. Such conditions do not reflect a mature faith, which is the immediate fruit of life in the Spirit.

7.2.4. It is almost never made clear that the outpouring of the Holy Spirit comes from Christ's sacrifice on the cross, which is transmitted to us by means of the sacraments. Consequently, the sacraments should be prominent in the charismatic renewal as privileged divine actions of the outpouring of the Spirit, especially the holy Eucharist, the reception of which augments the life of the Holy Spirit within us.

7.2.5. We must make a similar observation about the sacrament of reconciliation. By its very institution, we know that the Lord has intended to connect it to an outpouring of the Spirit (cf. Jn 20:22–23). Prayers of spiritual healing can never replace the action of Christ, proper to the sacrament of reconciliation. Unfortunately, in many cases members of the renewal have abandoned this sacrament because they consider it superfluous in view of what they take to be a prayer of spiritual healing.

7.2.6. In some circles, there is an attempt to replace the magisterium of the Church with what is assumed to be the direct magisterium of the Spirit. The mission of the Holy Spirit is not to replace the legitimate magisterium of the Church, but to deepen it, internalize it, make it better understood. Therefore, the irreplaceable magisterium must be reaffirmed more than ever.

7.2.7. There is a danger of taking what is secondary and external as what is essential to the renewal. In this sense, certain forms of prayer are regarded as privileged and almost made exclusive—raising one's hands, applause, Protestant-style hymns, and so forth—to the extent of falling into the vice being combatted: being tied to stereotyped forms of prayer. People demand a spontaneous kind of prayer, and they end up praying almost exclusively in the "charismatic" manner.

7.2.8. The so-called baptism in the Spirit, an ambiguous term, has created a great deal of confusion over something essential to our faith. It seems to diminish the importance of sacramental baptism, which in fact is the only baptism in water and in the Holy Spirit. This terminology would also seem to leave no room for the sacrament of confirmation, whose outpouring of the Holy Spirit and gifts cannot be put on the same level as a mere imposition of hands by a charismatic group.

7.2.9. In certain groups—either left on their own or poorly advised—there has been created a false sense of independence, expressed in attitudes of self-sufficiency and a false idea of the ministerial priesthood. Consequently, they dispense with the guidance of priests on the grounds that they are spiritually mature. Such attitudes not only run contrary to the Church's teaching, but they also create division in parish communities.

7.3. Many groups overemphasize emotion and feeling in spiritual experience. When that happens, it is easy to fall into a great deal of subjectivism and into a kind of illuminism, both of which are very dangerous. It would seem that there is an attempt to substitute emotional experience for solid doctrine, and there is a tendency to forget that one's depth of faith in Jesus Christ is tested precisely when the emotions supporting it are absent.

Another attitude that can lead off track or at least to ambiguity is the so-called prayer of healing. However, the Church's teaching on care and prayer for the sick must be clarified.

7.4.1. Certainly, Jesus himself identifies with the sick person and makes eternal salvation or condemnation depend on aid given to the sick (cf. Mt 25:39–46). One of the works of mercy in the Church has been, is, and will be, visiting, caring for, and praying for the sick.

7.4.2. During his ministry, Jesus himself had a special place in his heart for the sick, and many of his miracles were healings of all kinds of illnesses (cf. Mt 4:23–26, 9:1–7, 15:9–31; Mk 1:32–35, 7:31–37, 8:22ff. and *passim*). Hence, it should come as no surprise that Christ has instituted the sacrament of the anointing of the sick (cf. Jas 5:13–16). Through the centuries, the Church has administered zealously this sacrament. The Christian community has direct experience of its saving effects of physical and spiritual healing.

7.4.3.   We Christians believe and trust in the promises of Jesus when he often told us that "everything we ask the Father in his name, he would grant us," and that we should ask in order receive and knock so that it may be opened to us (cf. Mt 7:7–9). Prayer for health, both spiritual and physical, certainly may be part of this prayer of petition, based on trust and faith in Christ Jesus.

7.4.4.   It is very consoling for us to observe in many members of the renewal apostolic interest in this work of mercy, which is essential to the following of Christ. This apostolate of prayer for the sick belongs to the whole community and is not the exclusive responsibility of sacred ministers, even though the administration of the sacrament of the anointing of the sick is reserved to them.

7.4.5.   In charismatic renewal groups, there are often huge assemblies especially organized to pray for the sick. Such assemblies should be under the responsibility of a priest, authorized for that occasion by the bishop to assure that everything will unfold according to the spirit of our Catholic tradition for the greater glory of God and for the good of the sick who, with faith, come forward to receive the healing power of Jesus in his Church.

7.4.6.   With regard to "exorcism," in the proper sense, the norms laid down by the *Code of Canon Law* (c. 1172) are in effect. Before undertaking an exorcism, any priest must obtain proper permission from his bishop. In this area, there have been reports of some irregularities, which must be avoided.

With the best of good will and faith, and out of a great desire to aid needy people, some have made mistakes because they were not trained adequately for this ministry. We must point out that with regard to exorcism, Catholic and Protestant traditions follow very different procedures.

With regard to prayer for people who are emotionally disturbed or who show symptoms that are difficult to diagnose, it should be reserved for people who have enough discernment and proper training. That will avoid scandals and make it possible to give proper attention to sick people who have placed their trust in the prayer of faith of their brothers and sisters.

Bolivia
Pastoral Plan 1986–1991
(1986)

In a country where Catholic church resources are scarce, pastoral planning becomes urgent as a means to employ well these resources. Several dioceses have been engaged in planning for many years. The national bishops' conference has attempted to plan at the national level since 1973.

Pastoral planners in Bolivia have assumed a holistic approach: lay leaders, priests, sisters, and bishops have all been a part of the effort. In many ways, the impetus for and the "guarantee" of successful strategies and implementation have come from lay leaders. Through two or three decades of formal and informal education, many lay catechists and base Christian community participants have assumed leadership positions.

Lay leadership is reflected in specific objectives of the Plan. The empowerment given lay persons in Bolivia also has led to a notable increase in seminarians (objective 5). Although not yet enough to supply all its needs or to replace the large number of foreign missionaries, the number of seminarians is beginning to exceed space available in the seminaries.

During recent decades, pastoral agents have pointed constantly to the need for "coordinated pastoral work"* for the Church in Bolivia. Some particular churches [dioceses] have already acquired the sustained experience with pastoral planning that makes "coordinated pastoral work" possible, while others are taking steps to achieve it.

The Bishops' Conference of Bolivia has been in touch with this

---

* *Pastoral de conjunto:* There is no satisfactory single translation for this expression, which has been used in the Latin American Church since the 1960s. It refers to the idea of an overall pastoral planning and coordinated pastoral work, involving pastoral agents on the diocesan or even national level. Here it will be translated as "coordinated pastoral work."

concern for twenty years through dialogue, constant encouragement, and the promulgation of documents on *Pastoral Focus* (1973, 1975, 1986), *Pastoral Options* (1983), and *Pastoral Guidelines* (1980, 1986), which were intended to serve on the national level as the foundations for the various diocesan plans, and also for the *Common Pastoral Path* in order to stimulate and guide pastoral activity.

Pastoral Focus

This is a planning tool intended to provide guidance for a common reading of the overall situation in society in order to obtain a pastoral diagnosis: what is missing in that situation; and the potential for realistic development for use in our present pastoral activity, as expressed in the *Pastoral Focus*. Priorities are drawn from this diagnosis, and they are made specific in objectives, plans, and programs of pastoral activity.

Pastoral Guidelines

These define pastoral priorities on the national level and should be taken into account in all diocesan plans.

Common Pastoral Path

This is an agreement reached by the bishops, as members of the Bolivian Bishops' Conference, to make an effort to stimulate and guide pastoral work in all the churches along the lines of a local adaptation of a model published by the bishops' conference. The most important aspects of the *Common Pastoral Path* are laid out here.

National and Diocesan Plans and Programs

The fact that these instruments—the *Pastoral Focus*, the *Pastoral Guidelines*, and the *Pastoral Path*—exist makes it possible for the services of the bishops' conference and the diocesan plans to mesh together and energize a continually improving "coordinated pastoral work." This joint pastoral work, while paying attention to the particular features of each diocesan church, at the same time allows for the exercise of episcopal collegiality and communion among different local churches.

Included in this booklet are previous versions of the *Pastoral Focus* and *Pastoral Options*, which have been incorporated into the present *Pastoral Focus* and *Pastoral Guidelines*.

The purpose of publishing them is to be of service to pastoral agents in all ecclesiastical jurisdictions at a time in which each particular church [diocese] is being asked to work out the instruments for a coordinated pastoral work, utilizing the plans and adaptations of the *Common Pastoral Path*.

Pastoral Focus

0. Introduction

0.1.   On the basis of the present concerns of the bishops, pastoral agents, and the faithful and of dialogue among them, keeping a relationship with the *Pastoral Focus* of 1976, in communion with the churches of Latin America and of the Universal Church, we believe we must offer some enlightenment and some guidance that may provide, as it were, the ecclesial atmosphere for facilitating the planning and programming of pastoral activity more adequately.

0.2.   These are only some guidelines, which it is important to take into account, in order that the Church in Bolivia, in its concern for communion and evangelization, may have some of the more important reference points for the life of our local churches in the painful reality of our country. It is, as it were, the horizon that orients our knowledge and interpretation of the situation; provides the rationale for our planning; and expresses our will to be faithful to Christ and to our people. This is what we call simply, the *Pastoral Focus*.

1. Building the Kingdom of God in Ecclesial Communion

1.1.   As he began his public life, Jesus announced the presence of the kingdom of God as good news (cf. Mk 1:14–15; Mt 4:17) and as the principle of new life and of new hope for humankind.

1.2.   This announcement of the kingdom of God expresses the calling of the Church in all its pastoral action.

1.3.   The kingdom of God assumes that he is the center of life, of human beings, of their history and of all creation.

The kingdom of God puts us into relationship with the God who is great, good, close to human beings and present in the world; who has his "secrets" (cf. 1 Cor 2:11–12) for humankind and for the world; he communicates those secrets and wants to see them realized.

1.4.   For God, to reign means to make all human beings his children, capable of recognizing that they are brothers and sisters and living as such, and of coming to the point where all peoples live in communion, transforming all creation into God's dwelling (cf. Eph 1:5,9–12), until God is all in all (cf. 1 Cor 15:28). This is the great news that changes the whole of life.

1.5.   God is gradually bringing about this kingdom in us personally and with us through history, until it finds its fullness in the eternal glory of Christ, in which all will joyfully share. All human beings are invited to contribute to building it.

1.6.   Building this kingdom entails a concrete challenge to our Church in Bolivia, given the particular moment in which we live and the very characteristics of the kingdom.

It is a kingdom of truth. To build it is to seek and live the truth, banishing lying, deceit, alienation. . . .

It is a kingdom of freedom. To build it is to become free and to create environments and structures that respect and favor the true freedom of the children of God.

It is a kingdom of brotherhood and sisterhood. To build it is to accept universal communion, solidarity among all human beings, mercy and reconciliation, demolishing all barriers, such as those of race, language, ideologies, religions, regional differences. . . .

It is a kingdom of justice. To build it is to establish just relationships among ourselves and within all spheres of our society, struggling against oppression, corruption, exploitation. . . .

That is how this kingdom is and manifests itself as a kingdom of life and of love.

1.7.   It is precisely the importance of the kingdom and the serious obstacles hindering its arrival in our midst that prompt us to propose as the pastoral horizon for our churches the building of the kingdom in ecclesial communion.

2. Christ, Builder of the Kingdom

2.1.   In order that the kingdom may arrive in its full dimensions, and in all its depth, God has sent us his Son, who from the beginning identified himself fully with the will of the Father.

2.2.   Jesus announced this kingdom as arriving and already present; the kingdom was the core of his preaching (cf. Mt 4:23; 9:35).

2.3.   Jesus revealed it as a small seed, but one containing life-giving power (cf. Mk 4:26–34) like wheat, which at harvest time is separated from weeds (cf. Mt 13:24–30); like the treasure and the pearl, which are worth sacrificing everything (cf. Mt 13:44–46). He manifested it through miracles, signs of the presence of the kingdom, which dispels evil, suffering, and death, the fruit of sin.

2.4.   Jesus embodied the kingdom in his own life, climaxing in his death and in resurrection. Accepting his death in filial surrender to the Father, he destroyed the power of death in human beings. God the Father exalted him, raised him up, made him Lord of history and of the new humanity, so that he might pour forth his spirit over all human beings (cf. Acts 2:17). In Jesus, he manifested his kingdom; that is why we see it "shining resplendently on the visage of the risen Jesus . . ." (*Puebla*, 197).

2.5.   In Jesus, we all have access to the kingdom. However, there is no other way but that followed by Jesus, the way that leads us to change our life, to free ourselves from the kingdom of evil (hatred, selfishness, violence, lying, whatever causes suffering, whatever causes death), the way that leads us specifically to die with Jesus in order to share in his triumph and be transferred to the kingdom of the beloved Son (cf. Col 1:13) where we also are children of God in dignity and freedom. Along this way, Mary, Virgin and Mother, the first disciple, the Sorrowing One, and Assumed One, "shines forth on earth, until the day of the Lord shall come . . . as a sign of sure hope and solace for the pilgrim people of God" (LG, 68).

3. The Church, Servant of the Kingdom

3.1.   Jesus entrusts to his apostles his own mission, which announces and makes real the good news of the kingdom, and for that purpose, he pours forth his Spirit over them (cf. Acts 2:4). Thus, is the Church constituted as the new people of God, whose Head is Christ (cf. Col 1:18). The members are those who are vitally linked to him through faith and conversion and, thus, give personal and community witness to the kingdom.

3.2.   The Spirit is ever prompting them to live the mystery of the Church, which is essentially a mystery of communion. They live this mystery in attentiveness to the Word of God, a common life as brothers and sisters, the breaking of the bread, and prayer (cf. Acts 2:42). This life in communion and participation leads to "great apostolic influence" (cf. *Perfectae Caritatis* [= PC]).

3.3.   Through the gift of life that they share, all feel responsible for the growth and greater vitality of the community that they are building, each according to his or her particular vocation, and the gifts that the Spirit bestows for the good of all (cf. 1 Cor 12:7). Some of them, bishops, priests, and deacons, are especially ordered to a more radical service of the kingdom and of communion among all. Others, those in religious life, by means of the vows that consecrate them to follow Jesus more closely, manifest that the eternal kingdom has already broken into this life and is drawing all to its fullness (LG, 42, 44). But the communion of all believers who live, celebrate, and share their faith in Jesus the Lord is the primary way of serving the kingdom. It is already its manifestation. It is gospel.

3.4.   Hence, all are called to announce this gospel of the kingdom. Indeed, the whole Church, in its persons, as well as institutions and organizations, exists to evangelize.

3.5.   Evangelizers must be attentive to discover and sow the seeds of the kingdom in each person and human situation and to respect and favor its growth. They bring the values of the kingdom and its demands for conversion and transformation to all human beings and to all peoples; to all dimensions of human life: personal, cultural, social, political, and religious, striving to enable all persons to reach the liberty that enables them to live with the dignity of children of God.

3.6.   Evangelizers are to have the spirit of the poor (cf. Mt 5:3), in order to seek actively the kingdom and its justice (cf. Mt 6:33), to be willing to start out from what is small, to bear trials, privation, and persecution. By such means, God wants to teach them, "in a deeper way, the value, importance, and centrality of the cross of Christ" (1985 Synod of Bishops, *Final Report*). Evangelizers experience that it is the poor and humble who receive the revelation of the kingdom (cf. Mt 11:25), and with Jesus, they give thanks to the Father. This very experience explains his preference for the poor (cf. Lk 4:18; 6:20) and shows us what direction our evangelization should take.

3.7.   By proclaiming the gospel, evangelizers cause the Church to be born and grow out of the poor and humble. They will show a great deal of respect for, and dedication to, the small groups and communities of the faithful who are hungering for God's Word, who pray, celebrate, and share their faith, aid one another to change their lives and their environment, concerned for the poverty and sufferings of their brothers and sisters. These small groups are conducive to allowing the Word to penetrate into the human heart, to be assimilated into the people's culture, to apply its transforming power to the structures of life.

Today, from this perspective, we find in basic Christian communities one of the privileged sites for evangelization and the growth of the kingdom.

In this manner, our parishes and the particular church, united around its bishop, are being revitalized. This particular church manifests the visible face of the universal Church.

Conclusion

Our pastoral focus sets us in motion toward building the kingdom in ecclesial communion. Our Bolivian situation makes us feel the urgency of this service. It is our ardent desire that this kingdom of

God come into our midst, to our people, and to all creation, which groans in expectation.

Pastoral Guidelines 1986–1991

Overall Objective

To evangelize Bolivians in an holistic manner in their concrete situation so that together we may build up the kingdom of God, as Church of Christ in communion with God and with our brothers and sisters out of the gospel option for the poor.

Specific Objectives

1. To build unity, as a sign of the kingdom, through the long and difficult way of dialogue.
2. To assume our country's diversity of cultures in order to evangelize them.
3. To develop, guide, and accompany basic Christian communities as a privileged site of evangelization.
4. To aid the laity, and especially the family and youth, to take on their identity and their mission within the Church and in the world, as builders of human society.
5. To intensify the promotion of vocations, in a way appropriate to the social and cultural situation of our country and to the birthplaces of those in training. To arouse and promote the spread of essential nonordained ministries and evangelization on the basis of the Church's expressions of community life.

Common Pastoral Path

The plenary assembly of the bishops' conference, meeting in Cochabamba in October 1985, voted to draw up and carry out a *Common Pastoral Path* [*Camino Pastoral Unido*] to serve as the vehicle for evangelization and church renewal in this period of the celebration of 500 years of evangelization in Latin America.This *Path* will serve as an instrument for

- renewing the Bolivian Church within the framework of Vatican II, Medellín, Puebla, and the *Pastoral Focus* in order to celebrate 500 years of evangelization in Latin America;

- preparing the Bolivian Church to welcome with renewed evangelizing energy Pope John Paul II, who will visit Bolivia during the years envisioned by our plan;

- encouraging all pastoral forces now operating in local churches to become ever more united and to coordinate a genuinely co-ordinated pastoral work;
- coordinating the efforts of the commissions of the bishops' conference to provide leadership and stimulus for the tasks of evangelization of the local churches;
- mobilizing all pastoral agents toward a renewed impulse of evangelization;
- contributing to the formation of a laity ever more committed and responsible; and
- setting in motion an ongoing gradual process of organic renewal of the life of the local churches.

Major Pastoral Themes of the Common Pastoral Path

The Gift of Faith
(Building the Kingdom of God: Evangelization)
Pastoral Aspects:
1. Training evangelizers for the kingdom of God: popular religiosity, family, youth

The Bond of Charity
(Building the Kingdom of God: The Church—Communion)
Pastoral Aspects:
2. Forming small groups in which the Church is experienced and particularly, basic Christian communities
3. Parish renewal

The Hope of Universal Communion
(Building the Kingdom of God)
Pastoral Aspects:
4. Renewal of pastoral work in specific milieux
5. Attention to missionary situations within our country
6. Taking on, in a responsible manner at the level of the local church, the Universal Church's mission to the nations.

Period for Carrying Out the Common Pastoral Path

There will be a nine-year preparation period for the celebration of the 500-year anniversary of the evangelization of Latin America.

It is clear that this *Path* of renewal will not end with the next nine years of effort. All of us wish to set in motion a new evangelization of our Church for the year 2000 and beyond.

Those Included in the Commitment of the Common Pastoral Path

+ All pastoral agents, at the site of their normal work;
+ Lay people as genuine pastoral agents;
+ The whole pastoral structure at the level of BCCs and local churches;
+ Small pastoral teams (national and local) for the programming, leadership, coordination, and evaluation of the *Path*.

What the Path Requires

This *Path* basically requires a programming of pastoral work. This entails

1. Study of the 1986 *Pastoral Focus* and the 1986 *Pastoral Guidelines* approved by the bishops to clarify and provide orientation for the whole *Path*;
2. Analysis of the overall situation in society and the Church;
3. Setting priorities in pastoral work;
4. Setting up a harmonious process for dealing with and renewing the various aspects of pastoral activity;
5. Creatively discovering the most appropriate activities for each pastoral aspect of the *Path*;
6. Evaluating the advance of the process so as to reaffirm it continually in order that it reach its objectives.

Proposal for a Logical Model and the Possibilities for Adapting the Path

As a contribution by the Subsecretariat of Pastoral Coordination of the Bolivian Bishops' Conference, we here propose a planning model for the *Common Pastoral Path*, divided logically into years for taking up the pastoral aspects of the *Path*.

Each year represents a stage in which the emphasis is placed on one part of the *Path* that is to be developed throughout the renewal process.

This proposed model notwithstanding, each local church may modify the development sequence of the *Path* if the local situation so demands.

It must be emphasized that the renewal of each aspect of pastoral activity must continue to broaden and aid the renewal of other aspects.

It is also obvious that the more the local churches coordinate the elements of the *Path* they carry out year by year, the more it will be possible to carry out common initiatives on the national level with the aid of planning tools used in common.

Finally, it is well to emphasize that all efforts to plan and carry out the *Path* should be understood as a joint carrying out of the 1986 *Pastoral Focus* and *Pastoral Guidelines* approved by the assembly of bishops to guide and illuminate the life of the Bolivian church.

Planning Model of the Common Pastoral Path

Stages of the Process

Stage One: Preparation
                      (Building the Kingdom of God: Evangelization)
                      The Gift of Faith
            +   Convocation
1986   +   Consciousness-raising
1987   +   Leadership Training
1988   +   Evangelization of the Family, Youth and Popular
                      Religiosity

Stage Two: Ecclesial Communion
                      (Building the Kingdom of God: The Church—
                      Communion)
                      The Bond of Charity
1989   +   Basic Christian Communities
1990   +   Parish Renewal

Stage Three: Mission and Apostolate
                      (Building the Kingdom of God)
                      The Hope of Universal Communion
1991   +   Pastoral Work in Specific Milieux
1992   +   Missionary Situations within the Country
1993   +   Opening to Our Mission "to the Nations"

Note: The schedule of years is simply a proposal, which each local church may modify in its planning for the *Common Pastoral Path*.

Chile

Church, Servant of Life
Pastoral Guidelines
1986–1989
(1985)

In contrast to pastoral letters that had to deal with unpleasant aspects of a repressive social environment, this pastoral communication concentrates on planning positively for the future. The plan builds on a previous three-year plan and a lengthy evaluation of that plan.

Pastoral planning in Latin America is remarkable in several regards. For one, planning is assumed to be a national enterprise for all dioceses and vicariates. The level of generalization is such that the orientations will be useful for various localities or groups. However, the bishops did not seek uniformity, but rather a "community of spirituality" and theological grounding.

Pastoral planning in Chile has become increasingly simple and concrete. Instead of long lists of goals, activities, and agents, typical of the 1960s and 1970s, the bishops in 1985 chose only three pastoral directions: option for the poor, reconciliation in truth, and pastoral formation. The section that appears here represents the heart of the bishops' meditation on their plan.

Pastoral Guidelines

Our call to opt for life is an all-embracing call. It touches all levels of human existence and is the fruit of vital attachment to Christ.

It is a creative proposition. The attitude of one who would seek to restore life where death dwells is not enough for us. The Lord calls us to something much more exciting: he asks that we devise imaginative answers that can go far beyond the devastation of war. For that purpose, we can rely on his light and the power of his Spirit.

We bishops of Chile, meeting to discern the challenges that lie ahead of us, think our option for life must find expression in three pastoral lines, that is, three leading ideas present in our pastoral activity:

preferential option for the poor; reconciliation in truth; and formation of persons.

1. Preferential Option for the Poor

In continuity with the official teaching of the Church and with the *Pastoral Guidelines 1982–1985,* we want to invite the Church to opt for the "style of Jesus" (cf. no. 34). We repeat that to opt for the poor is not to make a social-class option. It means putting into practice that manner that God's preferential love has taken in history. It is the new and original way the Lord has of calling all human beings to salvation.

From the weakness of the blood shed by Abel, God cries out for the salvation of anyone who tends toward the path of Cain and liberates that person from the murder instinct. Out of Abraham's advanced age and Sara's barrenness, he brings forth a people more numerous than the stars in the sky. This is the God who hears the cry of the people and marches at the head of their liberating exploits. In order to unify the people in their dispersion, God raises up a king who is weak and small as David. In the fullness of time, God looks at Mary, the humble daughter of Nazareth, and pours out his tenderness on her and takes flesh in her womb and is born in the most remote place on the outskirts of Bethlehem. Out of that situation, he announces salvation to his people, liberation to captives and the Lord's time of grace. That is the source of the immense strength of his weakness.

Scandalizing many, the Messiah-King becomes the most vulnerable of all humans. And in order to occupy the first place in creation, he literally occupies the last place within humanity. He becomes slave and servant. He takes on the wounds of humanity and bears the weight of all our weaknesses. And from the infinite weakness of the cross, he rises up over the world so as to draw to himself whatever the power of sin has scattered.

By its very nature, the preferential option for the poor cannot be exclusive. But neither can it be watered down. It always invites, never excludes. But it also demands. Jesus is very clear when he demands detachment from the goods of this earth and good administration of the talents one has received. And the perfection of the following of Christ leads the saints to get rid of their possessions and give the proceeds to the poor. Thus dispossessed of our very selves, we will be quick to follow the footsteps of the Lord, who though he was rich became poor in order to enrich us with his poverty.

In continuity with *Pastoral Options 1982–1985,* we declare that the preferential option for the poor has three complementary aspects that demand one another:

a) For a Christian, it is essential to live with the style of Jesus.

Around this spirituality are organized the various aspects of our preferential love for the poor. This life style is a reflection of the Sermon on the Mount and especially of the Beatitudes. This is the salt and the ferment we are called to bring to the personal and social common life of human beings. Thus, we will be signs of the kingdom in a world inclined toward power and wealth.

b) Second, we are called to serve the poor. This is a permanent call of the Church, starting with the first community in Jerusalem. It "is the privileged, though not the exclusive, gauge of our following of Christ" (cf. Acts 2:44–45; 4:32–35). In our land, this means a call to promote a huge outpouring of solidarity so as to guarantee bread, shelter, health, dignity, and respect for each of its inhabitants.

c) Finally, the preferential option invites us to look at life from the viewpoint of the poor. That means seeing it from where the Lord took his place in order to grant us salvation. His life teaches us that this perspective is the most generous, the most universal. This attitude leads us to listen carefully to the cries of the suffering people, to support their initiatives in solidarity, and to respect the organizations that the people set up in order to meet their basic needs.

Seen in this manner, the preferential option has a deep coherence and beauty that unquestionably leads us to rediscover what is best in our humanity. It leads us to see human beings in themselves, in the greatness of their own dignity. This greatness becomes clear when we put aside the false glitter of titles and powers that so disfigure it. One is never more a person than when recognizing one's own weakness, one's own indigence. Then we learn to ask for help, to share life, and to cry out to God to be our Savior. That is when we begin to live humanly.

Taking into account the challenges posed by the situation of our country, the preferential option for the poor includes the gospel commitment to struggle for the promotion and defense of human rights. That is the case not only because they are laid out in the Universal Declaration of the United Nations. Our commitment is prior: We believe they are written in the human heart and that Jesus has ratified them more deeply by promulgating the law of love. It is out of our faith in Jesus that we defend human rights, and if we want them to be respected in their totality, it is because Jesus Christ has come to liberate all corners of human existence.

Our adherence to the cause of life means that, among human rights, we give priority to those that guarantee the essentials of life. The integrity of persons; respect for their freedom; access to work, to bread, to education, to housing, and to health care have a special place among human rights in the eyes of the Church. On the other hand, our preferential option for the poor, leads us to promote in a special way the rights of the poor, including their freedom to organize and their social welfare and security.

In order to put this preferential option into practice, we pray that all may receive the grace of having a tender heart and deep feelings of mercy. The poor deserve priority attention, "whatever may be the moral or personal situation in which they find themselves" (*Puebla*, 1142), because they were the ones to whom Jesus first addressed his mission, and that is the decisive argument for our bias toward the poor.

2. Reconciliation in Truth

Attentive to the God of Life, we bishops feel that this God entrusts to us the mission of reconciling. Because we have so much in common, we Chileans are called to be "a people of brothers and sisters." If, however, we live in a tense and polarized country, that is because we we have not managed to eliminate the practice of violence. In the cry that rises out of the wounds of our people, we see how urgently those of us who make up the Church are called to be those instruments of reconciliation in truth, in justice, in freedom, in love that Chile needs today.

Our view would be partial if we limited ourselves to social conflict. It would also be superficial. Thanks to the gift of faith, we know that the roots of reconciliation are found in the human heart, for it is from there that the breaking away from God, which has disfigured creation as a whole, proceeds. In the origins of human life is the tendency to self-deification. That is why human beings seek to pursue their lives behind God's back. Adam and Babel symbolize this tragedy that affects humankind. And the consequence of this self-deification is the break between man and woman—a break with one's own flesh—and hardship in subduing the earth and bearing one's children. And even more tragic, the difficulty of loving oneself as God loves each one. Breaking away from God has led us to deface creation and to build a world in which languages are jumbled.

Nevertheless, sin has not been able to destroy creation. Our divine origin is stronger than sin, which is only a virus that strikes us but cannot overcome the basic texture of our life—even less so after the coming of Our Lord Jesus Christ to liberate us from the clutches of the evil one and to teach us the path of sonship and daughterhood. Thanks to God, there is in the human heart "a nostalgia" for reconciliation "without limitation and on all levels" of life. This power of the Spirit impels us to take the road away from sin. Accepting God as Savior of our lives, we want to be reconciled with ourselves and with our brothers and sisters, with our families, with our people and our history. We want to be reconciled with all creation, which groans under the servitude to which it has been subjected by our manipulation.

"The Church finds itself facing human beings wounded by sin and affected in the inmost part of their being, but at the same time moved toward an irrepressible desire to be liberated from sin" (*Penance and Reconciliation*, 23). And it has been sent for these human beings and for the world as a "sign and instrument of intimate union with God, and of the unity of all mankind" (LG, 1).

Reconciliation is not something tactical or sporadic. It is the Church's permanent mission, and it becomes more urgent in the situation of our country. But the roots of reconciliation are found in the mystery and life of our Lord Jesus Christ. He reconciled in his own person peoples who, because of sin, were in conflict, and he made his apostles "ambassadors" of reconciliation so that they would go to tell individuals and peoples to allow themselves to be reconciled by God (cf. Col 1:18–20). Nailed to the cross, he slew enmity, and risen from among the dead, he was made Head of the new world that had been reconciled through him.

So important to the Church is reconciliation that one of the seven sacraments that reflect its life and inmost nature is precisely the sacrament of penance or reconciliation. The history of this sacrament tells us of the process that must be carried out if reconciliation is to be true. That is, it tells us of the way to conversion (penance) that leads to reconciliation and to peace with God and our brothers and sisters.

This sacrament teaches us that "reconciliation is not a mere forgetting of the fault on the part of the one offended. It also demands, on the part of the offender, acknowledgment of guilt; reparation, as far as possible, for the damage caused; and the humble reception of the pardon of God and of the brother or sister, with the sincere purpose not to repeat the offenses" (*Reconciliation in Truth*, 5).

The sacrament of reconciliation teaches us that this penitential process is carried out in the light of the mercy of God, who offers his forgiveness to humans. It is precisely the power of God's love that moves the sinner to acknowledge his or her sin and to travel the road of conversion. In this process, the priest occupies a fundamental place. His ministry forms part of the sacrament of reconciliation, and his attitude ought to be a transparent sign of the Merciful Father who returns the repentant sinner to life.

So rich is the current *Ritual of Penance* that we urge priests to go back to study the "General Observations" found there and to celebrate this sacrament in the ways the Church presently provides. This is the best pedagogy of reconciliation that we can offer our communities. That is what is taught in the history of the Church and the lives of the saints, who, transformed by the grace of this sacrament, have achieved the gift of a reconciled heart.

Without this spirit and this practice, we would not be able to advance with fidelity along the pastoral path of the coming years. Each task should be imbued with this purpose. Each Christian and member of the Church should further it. We cannot forget that in order to really be a reconciling Church we must also be a reconciled Church—that is, a Church that recognizes its own sin, grows in the practice of discernment, and propels a current of communion and participation so as to allow itself to be built according to God's will.

We want a Church that may be a permanent place of encounter and reconciliation. A Church that dialogues and invites dialogue. A Church that, from within itself, gives testimony that it is possible for opposed positions to meet in a climate of freedom and family feeling, calmly and loyally. A Church whose greatest characteristic may be the quality of its love.

To call to reconciliation, therefore, means responding to something urgent for the Church and for our country. It is to respond to the deep appeals of the Spirit, who dwells in our heart. But it is also to set out along a path of joy, of life, of peace in the Lord. Through the experience of Jesus, we also know that reconciliation is only attained on the cross. But through this same experience, we are certain that when we take the step of reconciliation, we obtain the fruit of resurrection. That resurrection is satisfaction over the evil repaired, the joy of coming together again, the deep humanity found in "making peace" and returning to live in the family spirit that had been lost.

3. Formation of Persons

Putting into practice the preferential option for the poor and undertaking the path to reconciliation are demands that the Lord places on his Church. We bishops believe that he asks of us a third commitment with equal emphasis: the formation of persons whose first option is Jesus Christ and the gospel.

A people cannot develop without persons of deep and well-rooted convictions nor without small communities in which life is treasured and shared. Both Church and country need men and women prepared to offer the best of themselves for others. In this field, the Church can make a specific contribution, one that is vital and enriching. That is why we insist on the formation of persons through whose lives will shine the originating experience of Jesus, the contagious power of the Spirit, the creative criteria of the God of Life. This is part of our essential mission, and we have always sought to respond to it faithfully through our parishes, movements, and schools, and through preaching, catechesis, liturgy, and the practice of charity.

3.1. Content of Formation

The Church is called to form a "new person" on this earth. A person open to God and to humans, who breaks with all forms of individualism and strives to live fully the adventure of brotherhood and sisterhood. A person whose formation embraces the totality of his or her life. The Beatitudes provide the basis for this formation. They are the best expression of the "new law." According to this law, nothing human can be foreign to us, since in everything human there is a place for God, which we must make present. Hence, the spiritual, the doctrinal, the social, the occupational, the political, and the cultural are dimensions of the human being that we must encompass with the wealth of our faith. If formation is to be truly holistic, we cannot separate the formation of persons from the heart of the small community or from the community of the Church. From Jesus, we have learned that disciples are formed in community.

Thinking of the formation we want to provide, we emphasize certain aspects:

a) We want a formation based on a personal and community experience of the God of Life. Saint Peter saw Jesus transfigured on the mountain; Saint Mary Magdalene received the grace of being forgiven; Saint Paul experienced his presence on the road to Damascus; Saint Francis kissed him in the leper; Saint Teresa became intimate with him through prayer. Without an originating experience of Jesus, formation goes on rootless.

b) We want to form disciples, that is, apprentices and servants of the kingdom. This means allowing the criteria of Jesus expressed in the living Word of the gospel to penetrate deeply within us. If we are attracted by experiencing him, then we will allow ourselves to be seduced by his kingdom. If we have a personal experience of the Lord, it is more likely that admiration for his person will flow through us, especially if we place formation in this perspective. The Master will be able to criticize and convert our criteria, which can easily be contaminated by prevailing ideologies and customs.

c) We want to form witnesses, that is, persons whose activity will be comprehended fully in the light of the incarnation and the resurrection of the Lord. If we opt for the poor, it is because that is how the Lord took flesh. If we want to reconcile, it is because that is what we learned at the foot of the cross. If we practice forgiveness, it is because we believe that even the dead arise. Witness is more than being kind or well behaved. It is living what Jesus lived and what can be understood fully from the perspective of Jesus.

d) We want to form persons who are deeply human. We are convinced that the gospel is the most fitting response to the deep desires of humankind, which have a spot in the heart of every human being.

This conviction has to be present throughout the course of our formation. According to God's plan, there cannot be any contradiction between the natural and the supernatural, between the criteria of the kingdom and human aspirations, between rationality and feeling (cf. Rom 7). Presenting the gospel as what it is—God's living response to humankind—leads us to traverse a path of deep integration of the human personality. Through the effect of grace operating within us, it enables us to go infinitely beyond our humanity.

e) We want to form people capable of celebrating. Every day we understand better this trait of human life. Joy, happiness, celebration are basic elements of the person and central aspects of the kingdom, which is not food and drink but justice and peace and joy in the Spirit. This demands a liturgical formation that may help us to experience the Lord in the sacraments of faith, to be festive over his living presence in our midst, and to celebrate, rather than "administer" the rites that are constitutive of human life. Signs, symbols, gestures, and words take on a contagious vitality when they are made fruitful by the Spirit in the heart of the celebration of faith.

f) We want to form convinced and convincing Christians. Persons who wholeheartedly cling to the God of Life and who, consequently, work untiringly to institute the culture of life. We do not want moralistic men and women, slaves to the law and to scruples. We want men and women shot through with the life of the Spirit, who makes them free to love and to serve, who tears away any attachment so that they may be able to take up the way of Jesus as a way of freedom. The best argument for their freedom will be that they love with the very love of the Lord.

g) We want missionary Christians. We fully take on what we asked in the *Pastoral Guidelines 1982–1985*. Those basic outlines remain completely in force. The Lord wants Christians who can take on their history and respond to the demands of the present moment; persons who work for the integral liberation of their people and who contribute to the transformation of the society in which we are living. We here add the content that emerges in these present guidelines: Christians who, in their mission, opt for the poor and who spare no effort to make reconciliation not simply an intention but a practice.

3.2. Means for Formation

This is not the moment to list all the means of formation the Church has available. The most essential means are those that the Lord has passed on to us: Witness, the Word, personal and community prayer, the sacraments of faith, the practice of charity, suffering accepted, self-denial, and entrusting oneself voluntarily. Means also include our institutions devoted to formation: educational establishments such as schools and universities; centers for pastoral training such as parishes, movements, Christian base communities, vicariates; tested experiences of formation such as retreats and spiritual exercises, workshops, vigils, and sharing sessions. All the wealth of the Church should be at the service of formation.

With regard to priorities, we think we have to concentrate our best efforts on the ongoing formation of apostolic personnel. Number one consideration must be given to those who are training for the priesthood and for religious life. We must seek to devise a way of accompanying pastoral agents who serve the Church with such abnegation. Those who carry out ministries of serving the community, whether official or unofficial, should receive preferential attention. For being faithful to the pastoral challenges laid out above, young people must be at the center of our concern.

Finally, we would like to summarize the direction we are indicating by saying that it is Christian persons and communities we want to form. We need Christians who are workers, Christians who are professionals, Christians who are pastoral agents. We must make Christian experience a noun and not just a qualifying adjective, a first name and not a surname, our first option and not just something to round out our life.

Cuba
National Encounter of the Cuban Church
(1986)

The greatest event in the Cuban Catholic Church since the revolution has been, by all accounts, the National Encounter (ENEC). Thousands of Catholics mobilized themselves in a multi-year endeavor to prepare for the Congress. They attended grass-roots meetings throughout the island. Bishops, priests, sisters, and lay participants carried forward the discussion at diocesan and national levels. Their efforts culminated in the Congress.

Throughout it all, Cuban Catholics struggled to tell the truth about themselves. The description of the Church was painful: less than 2 percent of Cubans regularly attended services; the Church could count on barely two hundred priests; and discrimination against active Catholics was still a fact of Cuban life.

Nonetheless, the exercise proved to be a cleansing and energizing one for the life of the Church in Cuba. In the opening address to the Congress, Bishop Adolfo Rodríguez Herrera, speaking in the name of the Cuban bishops, set the tone for the Congress.

Introduction

At a gathering of priests in 1979, in El Cobre, which was in fact dealing with the topic of hope, Bishop Ascárate made a proposal for a nationwide reflection process, which he himself called "tilting at windmills." No one could then imagine that such a quixotic idea would one day become a reality, and that that hesitant idea was to be the first spark of a vast spiritual blaze enveloping our whole Cuban Church, of which those of us who are gathered here today are a kind of proof. Indeed, from this point on, what was once mere thought is now a reality.

From that first moment, this ENEC* was something real. We are celebrating it here today, providentially during this International Year of Peace, twenty years after the Second Vatican Council, on the 50th anniversary of the canonical crowning of the Virgin of Charity of Cobre, at a time in which a cross given to us by the pope—a replica of the first cross planted on soil in the Americas in 1514—is being taken around our island and is here with us to preside over this assembly, and on the 133rd anniversary of the death of Father Varela, the Cuban of whom it has been said that as long as there is thinking in Cuba, people will think of the one who first taught us to think.

Gathered here are brothers and sisters from Pinar del Rio and from Havana, from Matanzas and from Cienfuegos-Santa Clara, from Camagüey, Holguín, and Santiago, in an unusual meeting, which is not bringing those from Pinar with those from Holguín, nor those from Santiago with those from Santa Clara, nor laity with priests, but simply bringing together Cuban Catholics, without any artificial divisions, who have brought something of their lives so as to seek together how the Church in Cuba can build communion with God and with the Cuban people of which we form part.

Behind every priest here, stand all the priests of Cuba who are not present; behind every sister here, stand all the sisters of Cuba who are not present; behind every lay person here—man or woman, young, adult, worker, peasant, professional person, student—stand all Cuban lay people. We represent them; we are accountable to them; without them, our presence here would be meaningless. It would mean even less outside them or against them: against their yearnings, their expectations, their opinions, their hopes, which we must not disappoint.

For a Church that has many problems, that has only 200 priests, scant means, poor resources, simple folk, the path over these five years of church reflection has been long, and it has not been easy. But despite its limitations, this Church has been able to bring about this truly historic event. It is a Church that cannot say to the Lord, and certainly not today, "Lord you have not given us anything," for this gathering is proof to us that he has given us the greatest miracle, the most mysterious and difficult mystery, what is called the "miracle of empty hands," the hands that can give even what they do not

---

* ENEC (*Encuentro Nacional Eclesial Cubano,* literally "National Encounter of the Cuban Church") was a national meeting of lay, clergy, and religious held in 1985 after years of preparation through parish and diocesan meetings. To a considerable extent, ENEC represented the first systematic grass-roots effort by the Catholic Church to come to terms with the changes wrought by the revolution, which started some twenty-five years earlier.

have. The first to be surprised by this convocation and by this *Working Document* has been the Church itself.

The Two Coordinates of ENEC

ENEC arose with two basic dreams in its heart. The first was a dream of being a faithful image of our Master, Jesus Christ, from whom the Church is inseparable since from him, it receives its essence and its existence and with them its mission, of whom it is the universal sacrament of salvation since it occupies his place without replacing him.

It also arose with the dream of better serving our Cuban people: serving their happiness, their national unity, their progress, their spiritual welfare. This is the people whose character and history, whose sacrifices and hopes, whose dangers and problems we share. This is the people to whom we as Christians have something to share that connects with the very roots of our identity as a nation, which is Christian, of mixed blood, island-bound, and Cuban.

Our intention is that these two attitudes—fidelity to Christ and fidelity to Cuba—be the two coordinates of our ENEC. At this inauguration, the bishops of Cuba, in whose name I am speaking and whose sentiments I am expressing, wish to encourage everyone, with sincere affection, to act in harmony with this intuition that is at the very root of ENEC.

ENEC as Celebration

During these five years, we have heard priests, sisters, and lay people repeat very insistently that ENEC should not be just one more meeting but, rather, a celebration of the Cuban Church. We are now in the midst of that celebration, in this feast that belongs to all Cubans, for history teaches us that when the Church is happy, whole peoples are also happy.

This is a celebration proclaiming its faith in Christ in whom we believe above anything else, more than in this very ENEC. In him, in his words and deeds, we want to seek together our stance as Church for the here and now. The aim of ENEC can be nothing but that of following the same path as Christ, which is always the same, but which has a thousand different ways of calling the Church to fulfill its mission in this world, experiencing all variations, even the most painful, until it comes to its fullness.

This is a celebration that proclaims our faith in the gospel as wonderful news for any human being, however vulnerable, since the gospel furnishes us with proof of the Father's love, as described in the parable of the merciful Father.

This is a celebration that proclaims what Pope Paul VI called, "faith in the human being and in the innate power of good," which is stronger than evil, as love is stronger than hatred, and as life is stronger than death.

This is a celebration that, with head held high, proclaims respect for our Christian identity, like the person in the gospel who finds the treasure of the gospel and is ready to lose everything else rather than lose that treasure.

Finally, this is a celebration that proclaims our faith in the Church, but not in the Church as abstract, theoretical, ideal, worldwide, made up of mere theological terms, but in a concrete, practical, real Church, which is called the Church of God in Cuba, whether beautiful or wrinkled, happy or distressed; both holy and sinful; perfect and also perfectible; therefore, a Church continually under judgment by the gospel and continually called to conversion and to holiness of life, to whose merits we all appeal every day when we say to the Lord, "Lord, look not at our sins but at the faith of your Church."

Key Aspects of ENEC

This is a Church seeking to be missionary, for otherwise it would be like a sect heading straight into phariseeism and would cease to be the Church; a Church seeking to be a sign of communion, for otherwise it would be like a Noah's Ark, with a pair from each species, and would cease to be the Church; a Church seeking to be incarnate, for otherwise it would be "opium of the people" and would cease to be the Church.

And if (as all our diocesan assemblies have intuited) our Church in Cuba wants to be missionary and wants to be a sign of communion, then the human Church must be the Church of openness; the Church of dialogue; the Church of participation; the Church with outstretched arms and open doors; the Church of forgiveness; the Church of service; the Church that "washes feet" like the Master (cf. Jn 13:5), that walks two miles with the person who asks one, that hands over its coat when asked for a shirt, and that offers the left cheek to one who strikes its right (cf. Mt 5:39); that is, the Church that in this life always comes forth with something unexpected: serenity, understanding, love.

In reading the *Working Document*, it seems to us that actually the effort in this ENEC is not to search for new criteria or new principles. The perennial ones are satisfactory for us, those that derive from the gospel and are the very same ones that emerge from the diocesan assemblies. Our effort is rather to seek how to apply them to our specific situation.

The point is to open to others the whole enormous experience of brotherliness and sisterliness, service, unity, solidarity, joy, hope against all hope that we have been living within the Church for twenty-seven years and to offer it to them, so that people may make use of this experience to the extent that their personal freedom may require.

When we read the major points made by our diocesan assemblies, we note that our Catholics simply have changed accents, emphasized aspects, renewed perspectives, read new signs, in a basic continuity with the past and with the gospel, in order to better fulfill our mission on this Cuban soil, which is the good soil of the gospel, where it is enough to sow the seed in order to watch it grow and flourish.

Our Christians opted for dialogue from the very beginning when dialogue was no more than a yearning. They opted for opening, when the doors seemed closed and the curtains drawn; they opted for evangelization, when in our pastoral work, we went no further than so-called silent witness; they opted for incarnation when it was said that religion cannot form good citizens because its supernatural character makes these citizens questionable in affairs of a natural character.

Therefore, no event prior to ENEC had to produce any abrupt change in the direction taken by the original options made by Cuban Catholics, just as no event subsequent to ENEC, whether adverse or favorable, should change this unanimous determination and this gospel intuition on the part of Cuban Catholics who said: "Opening, certainly! May it open new space for the Gospel"; "Dialogue, certainly! May it be sincere and realistic both externally and internally"; "Incarnation, certainly! May it not be like an abstract dogma"; "Evangelization, certainly! . . ." They also welcomed unrestricted respect for our Christian identity. If nothing had happened along the way to ENEC, such an event would have taken place exactly like this ENEC. Any sign, whether subsequent or prior, would do nothing but reformulate what is already formulated, and re-explicitate what is already explicit.

Some Assumptions

Before beginning our assembly, we bishops believe it would be a good idea to note or to clarify three points that, properly speaking, are not our own since they come from the same sentiments that were expressed in the diocesan assemblies:

1. The ENEC is not seeking a sparkling document, although there will be a document that will belong to the Church, and in that document, the Cuban Church wishes to formulate in writing its pastoral

approach. Nor is the purpose of ENEC to celebrate a fiesta, although it is a festive celebration of the Church.

The ENEC was born as a new spirit in our Church, and that spirit is more important than the papers and the celebration. The ENEC will really achieve its objective when this spirit permeates through to the heart of the Church, into its life, institutions, and persons. The ENEC is the lungs of the Cuban Church; the conscious awareness of the Cuban Church; the response of the Cuban Church to new needs, under the teaching inspiration of the Holy Spirit; this spirit is what will prevent our pastoral activity from being paralyzed, anarchic, or false, and that is the number one objective of this reflection.

Nor is there any need to say that ENEC will go down in history as a judgment, for that belongs only to God. It is not true that a person or an institution or a system can change the direction of another from outside through force or condemnation. We are still weighed down with the memory of the high price paid during periods when we sought to combat error through the Inquisition, and it did not work; then we did so by declaring *"anathema sit"* and it did not work; then by means of the Index, and it did not work; then by means of the Holy Office, and it did not work; finally, through apologetics, and it did not work either. We cannot ignore love for the sake of truth or effectiveness, and "love always triumphs over judgment" (Jas 2:13).

2.   The ENEC only marks an intermediate step and is also heading toward other intermediate steps, leading toward the goal that transcends us and transcends the Church. It is not a finish line, but a new beginning. It seeks to be prophetic, suggestive, and programmatic, looking out at long range. Therefore, the deep intuition of ENEC must be achieved within the patience of the Church, which ever waits, even in the night.

God does not provide everything in this life—nor does ENEC. Nothing in life is until today and from today; life is woven together step by step and so is ENEC. The ENEC cannot deal with everything, treat everything exhaustively, or solve everything. The only thing the ENEC can do is fulfill what the Lord taught: "Walk today's stretch of road today, and tomorrow's tomorrow, without trying to see the whole road."

A question lies implicitly before us: What will be the historic fate of the Cuban Church after the ENEC? Perhaps tomorrow, we will have the impression that nothing has happened, that the sun keeps rising the same as ever, and that everything remains the same. But it will not be the same: as in the blessing of the minister, as in the consecration of the Eucharist, where it seems that nothing has happened, but something has happened, indeed.

In this life, we can err by being too slow, but we can also err by being too hasty. This is the first ENEC. Why must it be the last? Cuban

Catholics have a reputation for being very generous, and it will always be easier to ask the generous to be patient than to ask the impatient to be generous.

3. If anyone here is worried about what kind of climate will prevail in this assembly, it is because such a person has forgotten many things. That person has forgotten the climate that prevailed in parish, vicariate, zone, and diocesan assemblies over a five-year period. That person has forgotten that we are Cubans, children of this people schooled in very liberal and tolerant traditions, always able to listen, always able to pay attention, always able to show respect.

Such a person has forgotten the human and spiritual quality of our Cuban priests, sisters, and lay people, of whom our Church feels very proud. They have shown their capability by elaborating this *Working Document*, which is the most ecclesial and yet the least clerical in our history.

There are many reasons that give us assurance ahead of time that we have not come here to hear our own voices, to see what we can get for ourselves, to make make rash trumpet blasts at this moment, which is not one for trumpet calls but for coherence, realism, and service.

Many eyes worldwide are trained on the Cuban Church which, at this moment, seems to be at the center of things. The fact is that Cuba, its Church, its State, its people, all of us share the opportunity and the responsibility for aiding the overall evolution of the world.

We trust in God, but we also trust in you. During these twenty-seven years, the Cuban Church has entrusted to the laity its most cherished and holy things, the things that the Church regards as of the greatest importance. It entrusted to you the Eucharist so you could take it to the sick; it entrusted to you the sacred Scriptures so you could read them in the assembly; it entrusted you with celebrations of the Word so you could lead them; it entrusted to you parish finances so you could take charge of administration. With the same confidence, the Cuban Church today entrusts to you its future, confident in your responsibility and seriousness, in your serenity and solidity, in your obedience and objectivity.

The Church proves its good will by allowing diversity in unity and equality in diversity, under its universal golden rule: *In certis unitas, in dubiis libertas, in omnibus charitas.* (In matters that are certain: unity; in matters that are doubtful: freedom; in all things: charity).

Reflection of the Heart

Brothers and Sisters: In this ENEC, we must think with our head but without smothering the reasons of the heart. We must do so first because the Lord taught us to see the essential, the deep things, with our heart, and he grieves when human beings think only with their heads: "There is none who thinks with his heart," says Isaiah. The second reason is that the language of the heart is easier for everyone to understand, and that is especially true of Cubans who are friendly, expressive, emotional, little given to revenge or resentment, who do not harbor things for a long time, as was reflected in the surveys in preparation for the ENEC.

No one will find in the *Working Document* the spirit of revenge, resentment, and recrimination, a desire to focus on wounds suffered, or the rigid discourse of the older son in the parable. Nor will such a person find coldblooded strategy or duplicity or selfish calculation or false compromises or arrogant style. Nor will there be found a striving to be lily-white angels, empty triumphalism, opportunistic adjustment, or the simplistic optimism of those who stuff cotton in their ears to keep from hearing of their own errors and to keep from knowing the errors of others.

The *Working Document* does not seek to give any further encouragement to the kind of fear that paralyzes, the kind of mistrust that weighs down, the kind of cowardice that masks, or the kind of attitude that inhibits. It does not fall into the error of reductionism in the area of faith, by putting faith to one side or having it challenge or compete with other ideologies as though faith were an experience that could be reduced to any other human experience.

Our ENEC has no aspirations to reconquer power or to salvage positions, favors, or privileges for the Church. The Church wants nothing else but the space it needs to carry out its mission and also to pronounce its ethical and moral—not political—judgment, even on problems that are not strictly religious but are human problems. That is not a privilege but a right and a service: the right of human beings to receive God's Word and to illuminate their whole lives with the light of this Word. In an open and friendly way, the Church wants to proclaim its faith to all human beings, even to those who consider it their enemy, for the Church does not want to feel like anyone's enemy. In sum, the Church hopes and expects that the faith will cease being a problem, a weakness, an ideological distraction in our country, and that the future will not look like the past.

In order to arrive at that point, the Church has no other way and no other language but the way and language of the heart.

The Hope of the Church

The Spirit is going to lead us over his ways, which are not our ways, toward imitating Jesus ever more faithfully and toward an ever closer communion with our Cuban people, with whom we share an amalgam of faith, culture, and race, and with whom we also share the good fortune of having been born here.

By our nature, we Cubans are able to build anything together. Together we are going to build this road of the Spirit, taking the credit for whatever goes well in our country, and when things go wrong, humbly asking ourselves what we can do to make them go right.

Open to the Spirit's unpredictability, the Cuban Church wants to be the Church of hope: remembering the past, living the present, and hoping toward the future.

We have a hope, and we want to offer words of hope to those who request them of us, to those who need them, to those whose gaze is fixed only on earthly things, thus limiting their human aspirations, and who feel that they are missing something. We have neither the very first nor the very last word, but we believe that there is a very first and very last word, and we hope in the One who has it, the Lord. Toward him we look with serene confidence toward the ever uncertain future. For we know that tomorrow before the sun rises, God's providence will have arisen over Cuba and over the whole world.

Panama
Ecumenism
Objectives, Attainments, and Flaws
(1984)

*Churches of evangelical Protestants and of new relig-
ious movements have sprung up in the Caribbean region
as mushrooms in a rain forest. One Catholic pastor, in
a not untypical example, told of fifty chapels of these
groups exisiting in his parish, when only one had been
there fifteen years ago.*
*In a long, thoughtful treatment of the larger issue of
ecumenism, the bishops of Panama also take up the problems of sects and sectarianism and of pseudo-Christian
groups and the ideological struggles they engender. Parts
three and four and the conclusion are presented here.*

Part Three: Sects and Sectarianism

New Phenomenon

26. The rapid spread of religious movements, commonly called *sects*,
in recent decades has created a new situation that demands the attention of the Catholic Church.

The phenomenon is not new in Panama, and it is occurring elsewhere
in Latin America, Europe, and Africa. Specifically, the evangelical
churches from the North have increased the number of their missionaries since 1953, and their missions have focused especially on
Latin America.

In our area, the spread of these religious groups has accelerated since
the 1950s, especially in popular circles, and even more intensively in
the past two decades.

How These Assemblies Act

27. They are usually called *Pentecostal* churches, *assemblies*, or *evangelical* groups. They can be observed in many poor neighborhoods

and in the Panamanian countryside with their familiar worship along-side someone's house or under tents.

They normally spread through personal contacts, by inviting neighbors and colleagues to their assemblies. There are also large and spectacular campaigns, advertised through the media, with well-known preachers from other countries invited.

Some Characteristics

28.   Simple people are dazzled by the celebration of Pentecostal assemblies.

Preaching is biblical and experiential, aimed at the personal problems of the individual: God is sought in order that he may respond to all needs.

Worship is very emotional, and all present take part. What is "awe-inspiring" or "miraculous" is given prominence. Although their religious services are quite long, they are very lively. All take part with acclamations, singing, weeping, and dancing. Sometimes, as the organizers expect, the Lord "manifests" himself, and one hears the gift of tongues. With long sermons aimed at the emotions of the believers, there is an effort to lead the congregation to surrender to Christ and to observe an impeccable morality.

There is a palpable sense of belonging among the believers. People know each other personally and there is a solidarity within the group. There is also an energetic missionary activity: a convert must bring the gospel to others.

Their Positive Aspects

29.   We recognize the positive aspects we find in these assemblies, which can help us put more vitality into our own pastoral work:

- the effort to proclaim the gospel of Jesus Christ as good news for human beings;
- worship that is experiential and participatory, although emotional, inward-turning, and perhaps somewhat individualistic;
- the yearning for God;
- the sense of brotherhood and sisterhood among the members; and
- active participation by the members.

Elements of Preaching

30.   An important element in preaching is the second coming of Christ: "We are now in the last days." Salvation refers mainly to the other life and is reserved for those who have accepted Christ. At his second coming, Christ will return to render justice to everyone and, therefore, no human effort is going to change the human situation. Thus, there is not much concern for social or political matters.

The true fruit of the new life is to separate oneself from the world, keeping oneself safe for the "Great Day." Only the members of the group are chosen by God, and there is contempt for other religious groups, primarily the historic churches, which are sometimes identified with the antichrist and are regarded as the work of the devil.

Some Groups Oppose Ecumenism

31.   Many of these groups reflect a sectarian spirit opposed to ecumenism. *Sectarianism* is an attitude that tends to absolutize one's own truth and condemn other groups or ecclesial communities as unfaithful. For such a mindset, any dialogue with other communities is superfluous and useless. The only ones saved are the members of one's own group.

Etymologically, the word *sect* designates those who follow a particular doctrine or master. Hence, the "sect" is the group that splits off from the broader tradition and from contact with other groups. Thus, the sect is hindered from understanding the complete truth, and it strives to present what it regards as its own truth.

Characteristics of Sectarianism

32.   In this sense, we may list the following characteristics of the sectarian attitude:

- *Reductionism* of the truth and the tendency to accentuate what is partial, that is, to take an aspect of the truth, absolutizing and accentuating disproportionately with respect to other aspects of revealed truth. This reductionism goes hand in hand with a free interpretation of the Bible.
- *Fundamentalism* by which certain biblical texts are interpreted literally without the proper connection to the whole of revelation. This gives people a false sense of security.
- *Exclusivism*, by which people consider themselves the only ones saved.
- *Escapism* or evasion of their commitment to the world. The fact that their message is reduced to their own group reflects an immature faith that uncritically reinforces the growing secularization of our society, in which religion is reduced to a matter of private life and does not intersect with social life. As a result of their unconcern for social commitment, the people are unable to work for justice and for a real participation in politics.

- *Rejection* of tradition and church authority, which leads to the atomization of Pentecostalism and continual splitting into new groups.
- *Proselytizing* vigorously toward members of other Christian communities, taking advantage of the religious ignorance and lack of identity of many Catholics so as to incorporate them into their groups.
- A *hostile and aggressive attitude* toward the historic churches making ecumenism very difficult as a way toward unity.

It is worth mentioning that sometimes there are groups or sects that are willing to dialogue, although that often depends on the attitude of the pastor who is leading them.

Witness of Faith, Yes; Proselytism, No

33. We want to deal with the proselytism of these groups. "*Proselytism* here means a way of acting not in accordance with the gospel spirit, insofar as unworthy means are used to draw people to one's community, for example, by taking advantage of their ignorance or poverty" (Ecumenical Directory, *Ad totam ecclesiam,* 28).

Giving witness is not the same as carrying out proselytizing activity:

> Giving witness with words and works is the essential mission and the responsibility of every Christian and of each church, for all are subject to the Lord's command. The purpose of witness is to persuade people to accept the supreme authority of Christ, to put their whole trust in him, to be at his service in love, in the communion of the Church.
>
> *Proselytism* is unjustified pressure or intimidation, or small gifts given openly or covertly, so as to bring about apparent conversion. Proselytism is the corruption of witness.
>
> When we place the success of our Church above the honor of Christ; when we are so dishonest as to compare the ideal of our own Church with the reality of another church; when we seek to have our own Church triumph by calumniating other churches; when we seek ourselves, whether personally or collectively, instead of loving the souls entrusted to us, we are debasing witness (Central Commission of II Assembly of World Council of Churches, cited in CELAM No. 52, *Elementos de Pastoral Ecuménica*).

These assemblies proselytize by generating a feeling of guilt and perdition, often artificially produced through psychological techniques, in order to then present Christ as the "only Savior."

Incompatible with the Ethics of Evangelization

34.   We must state that

the means, methods, and mindset of proselytism contradict the principles of an ethics of evangelization, since they do not respect the dignity of the human person, the rights and ecclesial worth of other groups or Christian denominations, nor the particular nature of the act of faith, as the human being's response to God's Word, in Jesus Christ, in freedom, truth, and charity (ibid., p. 99).

Psychological Techniques

35.   We draw attention to the psychological techniques used by some groups, which in a short period turn the follower into an individual with no willpower at the service of the religious leader. From the very beginning, these groups use strong pressure to nullify the personality of the new member. This pressure is applied through the following methods:

- The obsessive idea that the world is evil and condemned, and that the only chance for salvation is through the sect.
- The gradual suppression of all elements of personal freedom: elimination of close contact, cutting off all contacts with the real world, suppression of individual and free thinking, the imposition of an authoritarian discipline.
- Elimination of all personal responsibility by means of threats and punishments and the automatic acceptance of beliefs, or through long prayer and meditation sessions that induce altered states of consciousness.

An example of what such psychological pressure can produce is the mass suicides of the followers of the Reverend Jim Jones, which happened in the jungles of Guyana some years back. Psychological pressure can completely change the normal behavior of sect members.

Ideological and Political Factors

36.   Finally, we cannot ignore the political and ideological factor contributing to the spread of evangelical assemblies and sectarian groups in our region.

In early summer 1969, Nelson Rockefeller presented to President Nixon the evaluation of his special trip through Latin America. Rockefeller had come to the conclusion that it was very useful for United States policy to strengthen conservative sects, since, according to Rockefeller, the Catholic Church, given its commitment to the poor and its demand for a profound structural change, "has ceased to be a trustworthy ally for the United States and the guarantor of social stability on the continent" (Celestino Fernando, "Las Sectas," *Vida Nueva* No. 1381, p. 29).

Multiplication of Sects, Sign of Immaturity

37.   The phenomenon of the multiplication of sects of Christian origin, in Panama as elsewhere in the world, seems to be a sign of immaturity. It is a sign of immaturity on the part of the sects themselves which, notwithstanding their generous faith in Christ, do not manage to give much importance to his desire that we all be one in him; on the contrary, they contribute to making Christians even more divided. It is a sign of immaturity among Catholics, many of whom live a faith separated from life, and since they lack a deep knowledge of this faith, they seek a multitude of masters after their own desires out of a yearning for novelties, as Saint Paul said to Timothy with regard to some Christians of his own time (cf. 2 Tm 4:3; also Eph 4:14).

Attitude of Respect and of Clear Criticism

38.   As Church, we must maintain an attitude of respect toward the individuals who take part in these assemblies. Nevertheless, as we have emphasized above, this attitude assumes that Catholics have a clear awareness of their own faith and the ability to defend and explain it. When that is not the case, Catholics can easily become confused in the presence of any criticism, especially when it is done aggressively and in a proselytizing way, no matter how superficial and unfounded that criticism might be.

Part Four: Pseudo-Christian Sects and Their Ideological Struggle

Presenting Themselves as Christian When They Are Not

39.   Alongside Pentecostalism, other kinds of groups are spreading, taking advantage of confusion and often presenting themselves as Christians, even though in fact they are not. These are the Mormons, Jehovah's Witnesses, the Moon Sect and other similar groups. With them there is no room for ecumenical dialogue.

They make their approach, Bible in hand, but these sects see their own sacred books as more important. They deny the divinity of Jesus Christ and his resurrection. While Mormons and Jehovah's Witnesses are sects of a *millenarian* nature, the Moon Sect is *syncretistic* in nature. For example, there is an enormous gulf between the Christian faith received from the apostles and the beliefs of Mormons. For their part, the Jehovah's Witnesses recognize the Bible as God's Word, but their text is notoriously different from the one used by Christians and that enables them to draw conclusions that are different from, and even contrary to, those held by the rest of Christendom. In sum, these sects manipulate the Bible in order to prop up the doctrine found in their own books.

Along with Mormons, Jehovah's Witnesses are one of the most active sects in Latin America, and one that has caused the greatest confusion and harm not only to the faith of Catholics, but to that of Protestants as well.

40.   The Moon Sect is one of the groups that has had a growing influence in recent years, especially through the media. Its official name is the Unification Church of World Christianity.

"Moonie" religion has ceased being exclusively Christian, as it was delineated initially, and has become a kind of syncretism with elements of Buddhism, Confucianism, Taoism, spiritualism, and a supposedly scientific attitude. Overriding its religious nature are its ideological interests. Rather than a faith, it is a political line disguised as religion or Christianity.

The Moon Sect and the Unification Movement

41.   As we indicated in our *Statement on the Unification Movement* last August, this sect is dangerous because of the anti-Christian doctrine it presents, the questionable methods it uses to proselytize, and the new ideology it presents—"unificationism"—which cannot be separated from the theological principles of the "Moonie" religion.

In our region, the sect is connected to the "Confederation of the Associations for the Unification of the Societies of the Americas" (CAUSA), whose objectives are to defend the values of Western democracy and struggle against communism. This sect has made its presence felt in Panama by organizing seminars to which men and women from professional circles are invited (e.g., teachers, journalists, intellectuals).

The anticommunism of the Moon Sect and the "Unification Movement" is based on the messianism favored by its founder, which has no connection with the gospel, and is closely connected to an ideology that also entails geopolitics.

Attitude toward Pseudo-Christian Sects

42.   With regard to Mormons, Jehovah's Witnesses, the Moon Sect, and other groups that are really not Christian, we are obliged to warn our faithful of the deception practiced by these groups who claim to follow the Bible, when their teachings have very little to do with Christianity. Many Christians are brought into these groups under the pretext of studying the Bible, when the real purpose is to lead them to theories that are foreign to what is most essential to the gospel and Christianity.

Without intending to judge the personal intentions of these groups, we declare to our faithful that such groups do not take their inspiration from Jesus Christ and are not Christian. For us Christians, Jesus Christ is the Son of God who has fully revealed the Father to us and who teaches us with his word and his life the way to him. Only by clearly pointing out the non-Christian nature of these groups can we overcome the doubts that have caused so much harm among our people.

Pointing Out Their Cultural and Ideological Penetration

43. It is also important to unmask the cultural and ideological propaganda underneath the messages of these sects. In many cases, one finds a propaganda that uses a strange anticommunism for its own ideological ends, and it is more prominent than religious truth. The Moon Sect leaves no room for doubt in this respect.

"The Catholic Church cannot agree with Marxism either as a doctrine or as an ideology, since it is based on an atheistic philosophy, it absolutizes its ideological positions, and it promotes methods that are contrary to Christian morality . . ." (Panamanian Episcopal Conference, *Statement on the Unification Movement*). This is the true Christian position on communism, not what Moon preaches.

The Church does not close her eyes to the grave problems of dire poverty, hunger, and unemployment. She points out that the root of unjust structures is the sin that permeates with materialistic values the society in which we live. It calls for a conversion of structures that has to proceed through a conversion of human beings (cf. ibid.). We Catholics have to be clear about what has been pointed out above so as not to let ourselves be taken in by doctrines that, by promoting so-called anticommunism, depart from our very faith.

Conclusion

Reaffirming Our Vocation as Catholics

58. Pope John Paul II has invited the Catholic Church in Latin America to prepare to celebrate the five-century anniversary of the evangelization of our region:

As Christians and Catholics, it is fitting that we recall this date [1492] by looking back over these 500 years of work of proclaiming the Gospel and building the Church in our lands: looking toward God in gratitude for the Christian and Catholic vocation of Latin America and toward all those who were living and active instruments of evangelization; looking back in fidelity to your past in the faith; looking at the challenges of the present and the efforts presently being made; looking toward the future in order to see how the work begun will be consolidated (Opening Address to XIX Assembly of CELAM, March 9, 1983).

With regard to this anniversary, the pope calls us all to a new evangelization. "New in its fervor, in its methods, in its expression . . ." (*Informativo, Quinto Centenario,* CELAM, 1984).

Facing the challenge that the spread of new groups and sects represents for us, we reaffirm our Catholic vocation and we recognize the urgency of a renewed evangelization that may aid us to live as people of God, sign and instrument of the kingdom, which will reach its fullness at the end of time, when Christ will be all in all.

Working for Unity, with the Patience of God

59.   Our Christian and Catholic vocation impels us to seek the ways to respond to God's plan that we be sign and instrument of intimate union with God and of the unity of humankind (cf. LG, 1). However, we must act in conformity with the patience of God.

> Only God knows the times; nothing is impossible for him. His mysterious and silent Spirit opens persons and peoples to the ways of dialogue in order that racial, social, and religious differences may be overcome so as to mutually enrich one another. Behold the time of God's patience. The Church and every Christian community acts in him, since no one can force God to act at a faster pace than the one he himself has disposed. May the Church be capable of radiating an open Christianity toward the new humanity of the third millennium so as to await patiently with both tears and confidence the sprouting of the seed that has been planted (cf. Jas 5:7–8; Mk 4:26–30). (Secretariat for Non-Christians, *On Dialogue and Mission,* III B, 44)

Along with all Christians, we want to enter into this difficult task of praying and working for the unity that Christ so yearned for: "that they may all be one, as you, Father, are in me and I in you, that they also may be [one] in us, that the world may believe that you sent me" (Jn 17:21).

Panama   José María Carrizo V.
October 18, 1984   Bishop of Chitre
Feast of St. Luke, Evangelist   President of the Bishops'
                                               Conference of Panama

Carlos A. Lewis, SVD
Auxiliary Bishop of Panama
General Secretary of the Bishops'
Conference of Panama

José Dimas Cedeño D.
Bishop of Santiago

José Agustín Ganuza, OAR
Bishop of the Prelature of
Bocas del Toro

Jesús Serrano P., CMF
Bishop Emeritus of the Apostolic
Vicariate of Darién

Marcos G. McGrath, CSC
Metropolitan Archbishop
of Panama
Vice-President of the Bishops'
Conference of Panama

Daniel E. Núñez N.
Bishop of David

Carlos María Áriz, CMF
Vicar Apostolic of Darien
and Colón

Martín Legarra, OAR
Bishop Emeritus of Santiago

Marcos Zuluaga, CMF
Bishop Emeritus of the Apostolic
Vicariate of Darién and Colón

Argentina
Church and National Community
(1981)

Six years (1975–1980) of killing and bombing by guerrillas and of disappearances, tortures, and killing, often indiscriminately, by the armed forces left Argentinians disoriented and contentious. The bishops' conference issued a long document, excerpts of which are presented here, to express urgency for national reconciliation.

To those suffering the turmoil of the period, the bishops remind listeners that "the goal of opposition is not the elimination of those who think differently." To the military, whose rule has become highly repressive and imperious, the bishops cite the unifying mission of state authority, a "task that is not to be done mechanically or despotically."

Specifically, with regard to repression, the bishops take a position that "not all means are justifiable. Human rights cannot be abused in the name of a state of exception, internal war, or reasons of military efficacy. The theory of the so-called dirty war cannot suspend fundamental ethical norms that require of us minumum respect for persons, including enemies."

The bishops also address the question of violence from guerrillas and the possibility (in 1981) of external wars (such as with Britain or Chile).

Argentina suffers from a crisis of authority, a legal crisis, because the willingness to submit to the dictates of just law and legitimately constituted authority is absent, perhaps because authority has been uprooted from its ultimate origin, which is God. It has been forgotten that everyone should obey the law, those who have political, economic, military, and social power, as well as those who have none.

Argentines, individually and in groups, . . . should do a self-examination . . . in terms of moral behavior and be conscious of projecting their action in the community. The most significant groups in Argentine public life—professional associations, political parties, the armed forces, even Christian communities and their ministers—should not shy away from this self-study.

Opposition and dissent must be constructive. In a democratic political regime, there are adversaries but not enemies. The goal of opposition is not the elimination of those who think differently, but calm and just control over the conduct of the governing majority and the proposal of legitimate alternatives in the judgment of the people.

All citizens should feel their responsibility to be protagonists and designers of their destiny as a people, each according to his ability. They are the ones who, as depositories of the authority that comes from God and by their consent, give a democratic government its legitimacy. This implies the need to avoid unjust individual disqualifications, the arbitrary proscription of groups or parties, and diverse kinds of political conditioning that distort the citizens' free expression, unless it has to do with movements whose ideology and practices go against the very nature of democracy, which must justly watch out for and defend its existence.

State authority has the unifying mission of bringing together the interests and efforts of all for the common good. This task is not to be done mechanically or despotically, but by working as a moral force persuading free men and confronting them with their responsibility.

Although there can be just revolutions, nevertheless, it must be emphasized that a society should normally grow without them. Because they are means of force that are not subject to the normal control of authority, they may give way to injustices as great as those which they wanted to combat.

The Church opposes all intentions of cultural, political, economic, or military domination or hegemony of one nation over another. No matter how this domination is effected it always results in hindering . . . the subjected nation's development, growth, and maturity according to its own decision and timing. But the Church has also warned against an excessively narrow concept of national sovereignty, in the name of a false nationalism, that denies loyal collaboration of peoples and national States, even when as in Latin America, the common history, culture, interests, and destiny clearly point to the need for cooperation and integration.

The separation and balance of executive, legislative, and judicial power, which the Constitution guarantees, must be permanently and effectively observed, avoiding undue intervention of one power in the sphere of another and favoring free play and mutual control among them.

Political parties should be real schools of civic education and political clarification and practice an internal democracy that permits confrontation of ideas and a change of leadership.

Republican democracy demands the periodic rotation of public positions, ample publicity, and guaranteed respect for freedom of expression.

On Repression

The common good can never permit the suppression, but only the restriction, of some human rights.

Not all means are justifiable. Human rights cannot be abused in the name of a state of exception, internal war, or reasons of external military efficacy or of internal or external security. The theory of the so-called *dirty war* cannot suspend fundamental ethical norms that require of us minimum respect for people, including enemies.

Economic Policy

(Three Effects Linked to Social Inequities)

a) *Social isolation, individual segregation, personal aggrandizement.* This is the error of those who do not know what to do with their lives, their culture, or their possessions.

b) *Regimentation,* so that persons lose their individual characteristics and creative personal contributions are of no interest or are feared and destroyed.

c) *Grouping persons in classes as closed, competitive, and aggressive circles.* When men and women are put into groups by reason of maintaining inequalities, then social classes are divisive, foment hatred, and subjugate human rights.

Argentina
Way of Reconciliation
(1982)

The bishops' conference addressed a situation, grown worse since their appeal in 1981 to control repression on the part of the military government or to control violence that had given way to injustices on the part of guerrillas. In the interval between that letter and the present pastoral letter, Argentina had gone to war with Britain over the Malvinas/Falkland Islands. Argentina lost disasterously, and the bishops found the Argentinian people prostrate, not only from the war but from "old, longstanding injuries."

The bishops here make a plea for reconciliation, in part to heal "the animosity that is taking posssession of many Argentinians." The bishops recommend a number of measures to bring about reconciliation. One such measure was aimed at resolving a particularly acute problem: "It will be a great contribution to the recuperation of democratic life if effective steps are taken to resolve the serious problems of the disappeared, the prisoners who have not been charged [and] those who have completed their sentences and still remain imprisoned."

Our purpose is to serve reconciliation and peace. We are convinced that their Christian faith, in consonance with love for their country, will guarantee that the Argentine people will remain strong in order to overcome a kind of prostration that doubtlessly has not been produced only by the recent military misfortunes but also by old, longstanding injuries in the political, social, and economic spheres.

We have to construct upon the truth and, above all, upon the acknowledgment of the fact of people being God's image. "In the moment when Argentines are seeking to rebuild themselves so that they can continue with maturity toward their future, it is imperative to begin with a renewed and, if necessary, redefined concept of the person." (Statement of the Argentinian Episcopal Conference, May 1981).

The truth of the person as image of God concretely leads to two

113

fundamental affirmations: that of the person's individual dignity and that of their calling to live in community. The dignity of persons does not have its foundation in the State but rather in the Creator. Nor does it find its origin in power, in money, in science, or in some human authority, but only in God.

Upon calling for national reconciliation, the hierarchy of the Argentine Church is convinced that it is not simply a question of achieving conciliation between divergent points of view regarding the political organization of the country, but also a question of healing the animosity that is taking possession of the spirit of many Argentines. This animosity is being increasingly manifested: the wide divergence between social sectors and political groups; the inclination to exclude opposition; the actual banishment of opposition to the point of violently eliminating it. Since the nation is the fruit of social amity, all these signs of enmity are alarming because they are against the very stability of the country.

Reconciliation, understood as recovery of national unity, is the task of all citizens working together and of each group according to its specific function in society. Therefore, we ought to make every effort to include each sector of society—farmers, workers, industrialists, the military, professionals, and people involved in the arts—within the legal structure of the nation in the exercise of their rights, in the fulfillment of their duties, as well as with their corresponding political projection, "this being understood as a wise solicitousness for the common good" (*Laborem Exercens* [= LE], 20).

Each one of the sectors of society, for its part, should remain within the confines of its respective limits. "The essential sense of the State, as a political community, consists in that the society and people composing it are master and sovereign of their own destiny. This sense remains unrealized if, instead of the exercise of power with the moral participation of the society or people, what we see is the imposition of power by a certain group upon all the other members of society" (*Redemptor Hominis* [= RH], 17). Just as the social teachings of the Church reject the totalitarianism of the proletariat (OA, 26, 32–34), it also rejects the monopoly of political power by any other sector of the nation, regardless of how large, how powerful, or how enlightened it may be.

In the issue of national reconstruction, the political parties have a decisive role. In our system, they are the ones responsible for channeling the various possible options. In order to fulfill with honor their historical obligations, as well as admitting and renouncing their past mistakes, they ought to make perfectly clear, in advance, their understanding of the nature of persons, in their economic, social, political, educational, and religious aspects. Everyone has the right to be informed. Citizens cannot be asked to give them a "blank check."

The political parties will only have the right to the confidence of the people if the men who are proposed are actually people with political capabilities and moral integrity, which includes altruism and self-denial. The parties then, must be trustworthy not only because of their programs but also for the ethical qualities of their leaders.

The decision of the national authorities to restore institutional order is a measure that has earned the consensus of the majority of the people who see it in a recognition of their personal rights. All we citizens ought to commit ourselves clearly and firmly to support this move toward government by mandate, which is according to the fundamental law of the nation. In spite of its limitations, this law contributed to the organization of our political society in the midst of situations as critical, or more so, than our present one. To hinder or destroy this process of institutionalization would be tragic for the future of Argentina.

In preparation for the next elections, it is advisable to back the most complete exercise of democracy that is possible, the public and free discussion of national problems, the organization of the political forces. The honest, necessary interest in the well-being of the people cannot be discounted in the name of demagogy or populism. We think it is advantageous and opportune to lift the stage of siege. Democracy, as a style of life, has freedom as a minimum constituent. In leaving this state of emergency in which the exercise of rights was limited, it will not be surprising if there are excesses. Democracy cannot slacken in its defense of freedom, even though we see dangers involved in it. It is part of the risk that a nation assumes when it knows that the reality of its sovereignty is related directly to the measure of liberty of its citizens. It is necessary to defend effectively freedom.

Once again, the Argentine bishops impassionately discourage and condemn all guerrilla activity that would try to impede the Argentine people in recovering the complete exercise of their rights. The results of the elections will have to be respected by all people without exception, approving, supporting, and criticizing, if appropriate, the authorities that the majority has honestly elected. The soul of the people has to be nurtured by the deep conviction of the goodness and advantage of the democratic system that we have chosen. It, at least, has to have the ability to defend itself from the dangers that lie in wait for it, to survive and develop itself within the legal means of procedure. The need for continuity in institutional life should be a fundamental and unchangeable principle of the national political conscience, so that the "coup" spirit will disappear in our particular politics.

It will be a great contribution to the recuperation of democratic life if effective steps are taken to resolve the serious problems of the *disappeared*, the prisoners who have not been charged, those who have completed their sentences and still remain imprisoned. This could be done by providing information or freeing them, thereby alleviating forever the anguish of their families and the society.

The present economic situation urgently demands the exercise of justice and of charity. The high prices and the low salaries, the extensive unemployment and inflation, usury and indexing policies, and now the extensive flooding, have caused anxiety and anguish and have affected the peace and the lives of many individuals, families, and even entire towns.

The Church, in order to be the teacher of justice, has to show the most exemplary kind of charity. It is not enough that its members show mercy individually. It is necessary that we all act as a socially organized body. It is absolutely necessary that there be acts of mercy that are at the level of today's needs.

Because we know that everything comes from the merciful heart of our Father, we beseech everyone to pray without ceasing that in truth Argentina be a reconciled nation and that austerity and generosity on the part of those who have more, together with privation of those who have nothing, be one single sacrifice that is pleasing to the Lord.

August 16, 1982

Uruguay
Solidarity and Hope
(1983)

Observers of the Uruguayan Church received this pastoral letter with special interest. They had seen a Church attempting renewal even before the Medellín Conference (1968). This was especially true in the Archdiocese of Montevideo, where Archbishop Carlos Parteli and other priests such as noted theologian Juan Luis Segundo offered leadership, and lay involvement was promoted.

The ferment for change led some lay persons into antigovernment activities, sometimes violent ones. Military rulers responded both to Tupumaro guerrillas and persons dedicated to nonviolence with a repression more intense and more indisciminate than most Latin American countries suffered.

In a largely secularized society that offered little support to the Church, the episcopal conference went into long periods of silence. Solidarity and Hope *(1983) marks a new phase in which a wounded Church expresses hope for social peace and establishment of political democracy and calls for reconciliation. The bishops do not overlook the plight of many persons whose economic and human situation has worsened.*

Introduction

1.   The Holy Year of Redemption that we are living; the Visit that the Virgin of los Treinta y Tres,[1] Patroness of Uruguay, Mother of Jesus, and Mother of all human beings will make throughout all our dioceses; our option for the poor and most needy, which are the priorities of our *Pastoral Plan* and of our *1983 Pastoral Guidelines*; the coming Synod of Bishops on Reconciliation in the Church's Mission;

---

[1] *Los Treinta y Tres* ("the thirty-three") refers to thirty-three men who crossed the River Plate in an action that led to the independence of Uruguay as a separate nation in 1825.

the situation of the world and especially the situation of our own country—all of these strike us as propitious occasions for a personal and collective meditation on the need for a reconciliation that is personal and communitarian, political and social. As we conclude our assembly, these developments impel us as bishops to propose a word of enlightenment.

Meaning and Purpose of This Document

2.   Our intention is that this word be an invitation to prayer and to reflection, and a call to share the responsibility for this moment. It is directed first to all the faithful whom God has entrusted to our pastoral care as well as to the Uruguayan people in general.

We are speaking this word as bishops, pastors of the people of God, who make no claim to be experts in the disciplines of the temporal sphere but who are the keepers and transmitters of the Word of truth that Jesus Christ entrusted to his Church. It is proper to the Christian message to illuminate earthly realities with the light of faith, as a contribution and service to the community of the nation.

Social Solidarity and Common Good

3.   The evils within the community must be the concern of each one of its members, and no one has the right to pass over or ignore the dramatic situations people are experiencing collectively. Ultimately, these situations are simply the fruit of sin, the violation of God's Law, whose effects have negative impact on our personal fate as well as on the common destiny of communities. A discernment in faith also sees the presence of good in the midst of all these evils. The Christian response is to fulfill the command to love our brothers and sisters, with all its consequences. The result of this gospel love is the commitment to work for the common good, which, as Vatican Council II reminds us, "embraces the sum of those conditions of social life by which individuals, families, and groups can achieve their own fulfillment in a relatively thorough and ready way" (GS, 74).

4.   It is, in fact, morally obliging for political institutions that they have no other aim than the common good. Such institutions will be weak unless they are rooted in a strong sense of justice and of love for neighbor. This root of justice and love is the point from which to derive an institutional framework that can safeguard the stability of

institutions themselves and that can lead these institutions to serve the spiritual and material needs of all citizens.

Word and Witness in Relation to Concrete Problems

5.   What can be done to make this program of justice and love really take shape? For that to happen, Christians must make the spirit of the Beatitudes and the words of Jesus their starting point. The practice of the spiritual and corporal works of mercy is an authentic expression of gospel love. At this moment in history, it is utterly imperative that we show concern for our neighbors and aid their development in all their spiritual and material aspirations.

6.   Toward that aim, the preaching of the Word must be persistent, but witness must be even more convincing. If we want to translate these reflections into concrete acts of witness, we must all share the problems of our neighbor so as to understand those problems and find a way to resolve them. This is especially true when there is a social reality that reveals to us so many brothers and sisters who do not have the means necessary for a life in dignity, even to the extremes of indigency and hunger; brothers and sisters without a decent place to live; brothers and sisters who are unemployed and have no prospects for work; children left on their own; old people without care, even in their most basic needs; whole families who have no prospects for resolving their crises and problems.

Materialist Economic System

7.   We know that all this is largely the result of the attempt to organize personal and social life while ignoring God, who is the root and foundation of all social order. The result is a way of life and an economic system that places the financial realm above every other value and, consequently, ignores the specifically human dimension, plunging many into anxiety and despair.

8.   In this connection, we remind readers of our pastoral letter issued in April of last year. Among other issues, we there pointed to unemployment, low pay, and low payments for retirement and other pensions. We must now refer back to that letter, at this moment when those problematic aspects of life in our society have become worse, and all present indications are that the whole community will suffer painful consequences.

Personal and Social Dimensions of Problems and Solutions

9. It is utterly essential that we keep in mind that there are two aspects to the problematic situation we have today: the personal and the social. Those aspects that are personal, concrete, and immediate must be dealt with urgently by means of a kind of action in solidarity that is also personal, concrete, and immediate. This solidarity must be marked by a practice of justice and of social charity with regard to all the problems affecting our brothers and sisters these days. Such problems are aggravated by an economic and social system, which is also international, that assaults concrete human beings with its egoism, indifference, and coldness. Dealing with the social aspect will require organizing institutions that will move toward the protection and the social development of all, but especially of those who are weakest and most abandoned. Only joint efforts will permit the emergence of a just order, which is the indispensable condition for social peace.

Necessary Dialogue

10. This joint effort requires an adequate climate and channel: sincere dialogue at all levels is an urgent requirement of our time. By this, we mean a dialogue of the type proposed by Pope John Paul II for the 1983 Day of Peace: "Dialogue for peace must be established, especially on the national level, in order to resolve social conflicts and to seek the common good. Therefore, by keeping in mind the interests of different groups, it is possible to engage in a continual effort to come to agreement, through dialogue, in the exercise of democratic freedoms and responsibilities for all, thanks to structures of participation and the many instances of conciliation between employees and workers, in the way the cultural, ethnic, and religious groups that make up a nation are respected and brought together." The pope continues, "Unfortunately, when there is no dialogue between rulers and people, social peace is threatened or absent; it is like living in a state of war. But history and observation of the present show that many countries have been able to establish a true ongoing process of coming to agreement in order to resolve the conflicts that have arisen within them, as well as to prevent such conflicts, making use of truly effective instruments of dialogue. Such countries provide themselves with a continually evolving legislation that assures respect for appropriate jurisdictions so as to serve the common good."

Social Peace

11.   Social peace is the product of an explicit application of the elements that constitute the definition and practice of the common good. When the common good is in effect, the result is peace. That is the source of "agreement between citizens in order," as St. Thomas Aquinas defined social peace. Moreover, as the prophet Isaiah says, "peace is the work of justice." It exists where all are guaranteed justice. Peace is not the mere absence of conflict. It is a dynamic state in which justice is enshrined and respected and protected. It is not the result of weakness or of silence. It is the result of an "agreement between citizens in order." Order exists only to the extent that justice is the dynamic and driving objective of the community and its institutions. In a period in which the country is on the way to having democracy fully institutionalized, as obviously seems to be the case, it is essential that there be serious reflection on the content of the institutions being organized.

12.   Consequently, there should be set up political structures capable of offering to all citizens of good will the real possibility to take part, freely and actively in the establishment of the legal order of the community and in the governing of public affairs. Participation in public responsibilities and in the decisions that go along with those responsibilities is a right of all in the process of the community's historic development.

Freedom and National Security

13.   This aspect of political participation is intimately connected to the exercise of freedom and to the security of the nation. In this sense, Jose Artigas should be, once again, the one whom we hold in common as the inspiration for our direction as a nation. The leader of the *orientales*[2] left a very clear imprint on our history: the high price of the freedom of the people of Uruguay. The considerable obstacles that Uruguay has had to overcome in order to maintain its historic identity have shown simply how deeply it cherishes its love for freedom.

14.   It is also worthwhile to reflect on the relationships between se-

---

[2] José Artigas was the major figure in Uruguayan independence. Uruguayans became known as *orientales* ("easterners") in comparison to Argentina, to the west across the River Plate. The official name of Uruguay is still the Eastern Republic of Uruguay, and several times the bishops evoke nationalistic symbolism by refering to Uruguayans as *orientales*.

curity and freedom in the history of different peoples. Freedom that values itself seeks to be secure. Security that understands itself knows that it does not produce freedom, but is at its service. The freedom of a people that is territorially small and has no mechanism for self-protection in a world of growing violence is a freedom threatened with extinction in short order. On the other hand, a national security that does not show clearly that it is at the service of national freedom, but rather seeks to steady itself by manacling social freedom, is no longer national security, but slavery. If the way national security is organized should seek as its foundation the arbitrary restriction of freedom, it gravely compromises itself through a process of deterioration and a growing loss of legitimacy and credibility within the community of the nation.

National Reconciliation and Participation

15.   The spirit of the Holy Year prompts us to call for a sincere effort at reconciliation among all groups of Uruguayans who have found themselves on opposing sides or in conflict because of historic circumstances or for ideological reasons. The attitude of reconciliation demands repentance for errors committed and requires that all people, from both sides, make an effort to come together and to dialogue with those who were seen as adversaries. No one can remain passive, waiting for the other side to take the initiative on the way toward meeting up with one another. This spirit also requires that there be a readiness to reincorporate into the life of the social community all those who can make a positive contribution to the task of rebuilding the nation.

16.   A spirit of dialogue, reconciliation, and participation will give rise to a system of genuine democracy in which the social, juridical, political, and economic forces, developing fully, will cooperate and participate to attain the common good, without ever forgetting, we repeat, that the dynamic of such institutions must be especially oriented toward the good of those sectors that are most vulnerable and which therefore, in justice, have need of greater protection. Hence, it is essential not only that political institutions be functioning normally, but also that all the intermediate bodies such as families, labor unions, and professional groups also be functioning, so that all may fully carry out their mission responsibly and with respect for the freedom of all. In particular, the silence of the labor unions is one of the factors that weighs most heavily on our society, and that increases the sensation of vulnerability of those who can scarcely find any other way of making themselves heard.

A Word of Encouragement and Hope

17. Hence, at this point, we want to say a word of praise, of encouragement, and of stimulus with regard to the many initiatives taken in our Christian communities or in church bodies in connection with promoting, organizing, and seeking specific solutions for the new needs, by creating projects, institutions, or structures or by carrying out concrete acts of solidarity in response to these needs. We encourage all of these efforts to go forward in their work of creativity so as to find new solutions to the new problems arising every day.

18. Finally, it is our intention that our word be a heartfelt invitation to hope. With individualism and the selfishness of persons and groups overcome, and with all incorporated into the common task of building a society that will be more human, more just, and more family-spirited, a different spiritual climate will have to spring forth in our midst. With greater optimism and purpose, we will jointly face the future, and we will all be working together in harmony, without partisan interests, toward a better future for all Uruguayans. The present moment is difficult, and solutions are also difficult. However, if we are all committed in solidarity in this common action, there is no doubt that the power that comes from God, which is backed up by brotherhood and sisterhood among human beings, will aid us to overcome the difficulties of this moment, to seek concrete solutions, and to begin to live now a more hope-filled and hope-giving future.

Montevideo
April 1983

Carlos Parteli
President of the Bishops'
Conference
Archbishop of Montevideo

Orestes S. Nuti
Interim Secretary
Bishop of Canelones

José Gottardi
Vice President of the Bishops'
Conference
Auxiliary Bishop of Montevideo

Humberto Tonna
Bishop of Florida

Andrés Rubio
Bishop of Mercedes

Antonio Corso
Bishop of Maldonado

Roberto Cáceres
Bishop of Melo

Carlos Nicolini
Apostolic Administrador
Diocese of Salto

Carlos Mullin
Bishop of Minas

Daniel Gil
Bishop of Tacuarembó

Raúl Scarrone
Auxiliary Bishop of Montevideo

Uruguay
Pastoral Reflections
on the Present Situation
(1986)

The return to living in a "state of law with public guarantees" heartened the Uruguayan bishops, as most other citizens of Uruguay. After years of living with a highly repressive military government, Uruguayans found themselves searching for steps that would restore democracy.

Electoral freedom by itself would not suffice. Grave social problems continued: large numbers of Uruguayans were living in poverty, teenagers were dropping out of school in greater numbers, and confrontations between workers and their employers increased.

But in the minds of many Uruguayans was the question that needed to be resolved before anything else: Should there be closure on the possibility of prosecution of military officers for torture, disappearances, and killing? This has been one of the major issues in Latin America during the 1980s. Nicaraguans and Haitians faced the problem after deposing dictators. Brazilians, Argentinians, and Guatemalans, as well as Uruguayans, had to continue to negotiate with a strong military. The Uruguayan bishops addressed the issue without taking sides. Six weeks after publication of the letter, a law of closure was passed.

This letter is directed to all our brothers and sisters in the faith and to all men of good will. We wish them the blessing and peace of God, our Father, and of our Lord Jesus Christ.

1. Introduction

As pastors and servants of mankind concerned with serving faithfully the entire Uruguayan people to whom we have been sent, we have studied closely the present situation of our country with the eyes of men of faith.

We want to share our vision of the present situation and help you to discover the mysterious action of God that discreetly, but efficaciously, acts through our history to bring about salvation. This initiative of our Lord invites us to conversion, to renew our minds and hearts and allow ourselves to be led by the Holy Spirit. We believe this is the only way to inaugurate a new circumstance open to the hope of a better future.

The Church is preparing to celebrate Advent, a time of hope, of opening of new paths, of removing obstacles, of making present God's salvation.

During Advent, we commemorate the first coming of the Lord when, in total poverty and humility, the Word of God, the Eternal Truth that is Light and Salvation, became man among us.

Advent will also be for us Christians a time to raise our hearts to the second coming of the Lord in his glory to complete mankind's and the world's definitive, eternal liberation.

The Saviour who has already come and brought our salvation is the immovable foundation of our trust and hope. Surely, the Lord has brought us salvation.

But Advent does not only invite us to look with thanksgiving to the past and hope to the future. It is also a commitment to the present. Where the Lord and his Word are still absent, we must make the Nativity present and celebrate it. That is the commitment we assume, to prepare the way, to straighten out our paths and those of society.

From this faith perspective, we wish to contemplate the different situations our people are undergoing. We can certainly find many situations that offend human dignity, but we believe that the Lord has conquered the root of those evils, which is sin. And though the consequences of sin still oppress and tyrannize us, causing anguishing situations, the hope of Jesus, "God with us," and of his second coming introduce a new reality for present times. That is our faith conviction.

2. Our Situation

Guided by God's way of acting in history and finding that to save us he became incarnate among us and took on all human situations except sin, we also wish to be aware of our situation and take it up both in its positive and negative aspects and bring to it the proclamation of the gospel message.

In an effort to discern the different circumstances that afflict our people and challenge our pastoral action, we will enumerate some of them.

2.1 Though it is true that we Uruguayans are happy at recovering institutional normality, the reality we are living shows us that other steps are still missing if we are to reach the fullness of an authentic democracy.

Without a renovation of the attitudes and criteria that govern political and social action, and without the transformation of certain structures incompatible with distributive justice, electoral freedom alone is not enough to sustain a way of life that, through the just interplay of rights and duties, can avoid frustrations and permanent conflicts.

There are clear indicators that permit us to recognize the presence or absence of those basic values that make up a real democratic way of life, for example: equal possibilities for everyone to satisfy the basic necessities of a life in dignity or, on the contrary, the notorious situation of material and spiritual misery of great sectors of the people; the free and effective participation of all in intermediary organisms or, on the contrary, the silence of and the contempt for those voices that express the desires of the people; the privileged situation of the rich or, on the other hand, the complete abandon in which the poorest find themselves—all are signs that demonstrate the degree to which there exists a true democratic consensus within a human community.

There is real confusion at the sight of the discord that has followed other moments of consensus. School desertion is increasing, a clear sign of the material misery that makes child labor essential, forces children to beg, or, what is worse, moves them into delinquency. All this darkens the future of each generation.

At times, the political crises take on a threatening tone. The confrontations between unionized workers and employers constitute serious obstacles to the workplace, becoming the hub of our complex social problem (cf. LE, 3). Internal and external emigration continues, with all the problems this uprooting involves. The use of drugs by adolescents and youth increases. Pauperization grows, to the extreme that some of our brothers and sisters live on the garbage of others.

Abortion, an abhorrent crime, continues to be a tolerated practice. An excessive politicizing of problems prevents seeing them within a realistic perspective and thus prevents adequate solutions. The payment of the enormous foreign debt oppresses and diminishes any hope of restructuring the national economy with a real social sense. The growth of delinquency causes anguish and insecurity for everyone.

Our national culture is weakened by the cultural aggressions of the world power centers and moral decadence generates insecurity in our behavior among ourselves. We see every day how the misery and pain of others are used to advantage by certain groups. The family, especially, suffers the impact of all these evils.

It also hurts us to see how many are losing their faith, falling into a despair expressed by the painful experience of the absence of meaning of life.

2.2   Fortunately, however, these sad aspects of our present situation are partly counterbalanced by many other positive signs.

We are living in a state of law with public guarantees. We see in the people a deep desire for social peace and historical reconciliation. The degree of participation of many organisms in social life is satisfactorily augmented, and social conflict is ordered through civilized channels and mechanisms for just agreements. The people want a governable country.

It pleases us to see that human rights are an aspiration of all social groups and that all determinedly seek ways of making them respected in our country. We see with satisfaction how many Christians are assuming their faith commitments in their professional, political, and social activities.

It fills us with hope and joy to see so many honest and sincere men and women who perhaps have not explicitly discovered the Lord of our faith, but who struggle loyally for an Uruguay with justice and with more solidarity in accord with perennial ethical values, which they encourage in people of good will.

It is now fitting that we let these events speak to us and question us and that those with faith be disposed in a spirit of prayer to listen to the voice of the Lord, who speaks through these events. Concerning all this, we formulate the following questions:

- What kind of world, values, ideals are we preparing for the coming generation? What kind of Uruguay do we wish to build?

- What degree of conversion does the Lord ask of us if we are to be his faithful disciples?

- Are we collaborating in the exploitation of the weak, or are we resigning ourselves to a materialistic system, inspired in the desire for gain, which marginates and destroys large sectors of our people?

- Has the religion of the God of Money, the God of Pleasure, the God of Power taken root in our lives? Do we place our faith in illusory materialistic messianisms, which do not recognize Jesus of Nazareth as the Lord of History?

3. The Validity of Human Rights

We share with so many of our fellow citizens the demand for respect and the promotion of human rights.

3.1   These rights, as recognized by all, are those values that everyone can accept without violating their responsibly formed consciences. Even though we Uruguayans make up a nation that gave the example of an advanced social legislation, especially in the area of labor relations, one of whose great backers was Bishop Mariano Soler, first archbishop of Montevideo, still the violation of human rights is also part of our history. We recall the low birthrate, the discrimination between students who received a free education and those who, coherent with their religious principles, had to pay for the school of their preference. These are some of the examples of lack of recognition of human rights, preceding the recent period of our history, so agitated by the violence of subversion and repression.

3.2 During this present moment to which we are all committed, a Christian must be guided by the demands of the common good, which take precedence over interests of parties or sectors of society. The respect for human rights is not optional. It is required of us all. It is the "common patrimony" of all Uruguayans and, as such, no one has a monopoly.

With regard to the Projects for National Pacification, which have been the occasion of confrontations in our political and social life, the following should be said: A people elaborates for itself a juridical body for ordering society as an expression of its social conscience and, as such, demands exact fulfillment. Only in extraordinary cases is it permissible to recur to an amnesty that suspends the application of those norms considered obligatory for all. An excess of such exceptions would weaken efforts at moral improvement and lead to impunity, to a social permissiveness leading to dissolution. On the other hand, not to recur to it, when it is reasonable, would lead to more evils than those one is attempting to avoid and would harm the common good out of consideration for particular situations.

We believe that the people's representatives should decide in each situation if the conditions that legitimize an amnesty are present.

3.3 Given the importance of the subject of human rights, we hope that national legislation will provide new norms that will cover the defense of the citizens in cases of torture and mistreatment and other human rights, as we are convinced that the defense of these rights takes precedence over any political option. It is the person and his or her dignity that are in question. The importance of the subject of human rights obliges us to leave it for a more ample and profound treatment on another occasion.

4. Our Goals

On December 12, 1985, we bishops invited the whole church community, in our pastoral orientations, to "accompany evangelically each man and woman and the Uruguayan people, as such, so as to help transform our culture from within; to accompany them in salvific acts, in the new events of their history, their life, and in their concrete circumstances."

Today, one year after that invitation, we reaffirm our commitment to serve our people in the same terms we proposed then: "to defend and promote the rights of all the oppressed and denounce anything that places them in danger"; "to favor dialogue, tolerance, and legitimate pluralism at every level."

However, we are aware that we cannot limit ourselves to offering these reflections. We also commit ourselves to continue promoting an effective social projection that will educate in justice, according to the social doctrine of the Church. Above all, is the magisterium of Pope John Paul II, whom we will soon have the joy of receiving among us.

We firmly support Christians committed to political, trade union, business, and student activity; teaching; cooperative and rural organization; and to scientific tasks. We are sure that the next Synod of Bishops, the theme of which is "The Vocation and Mission of the Laity in the Church and the World," will amply illuminate the meaning of your Christian commitment.

Through this message, we wish to encourage both those who confront the inescapable urgency of the present, and those who are attempting to seek in a reflective manner the root cause of the problems we are suffering from.

We understand this whole effort at recuperating an authentic social peace and at respecting human rights that no one can responsibly escape as an experience proper to the liturgical season of Advent. It is a question of taking up once again and liberating in Jesus everything—both people and material things—that the Father summed up in his Son in the transcendental event of the Incarnation. For that reason, our hope, though passing through the human, transcends it. We seek and struggle for a total liberation, for the salvation revealed and made reality in history by the Lord, we await again.

5. Conclusion

Today, contemplating our nation, Christian by the baptism of the majority of its children but wounded by the scandalous breach of poor ever more numerous and rich ever richer, we opt for a social justice that will satisfy the hunger for bread and the hunger for progress and peace. And as administrators of the gifts of God, we commit ourselves to satisfying the hunger for God that so many of our brothers and sisters are suffering. We hope that the day will come when every man and woman will recognize him or herself as a child of God in the world, created in his image and likeness, and called to be Lord of creation and not its slave, and brother or sister of every other man or woman. This is the hope that encourages us to make every effort to make the dignity of every Uruguayan a reality.

We place our hope in the hands of the Virgin of the Thirty-Three, who, from the dawn of our nation, has been leading us toward liberty as the guiding star of our evangelization.

With the sense of responsibility that is ours as pastors, but, above all, with the joy and the happiness of being Christians, we take our leave and bless you in Christ, the Redeemer of the world.

Bolivia
National Convergence
(1984)

Many Bolivian leaders, including President Victor Paz Estenssoro, have praised the efforts of Bolivian bishops in recent years to conciliate effectively major political crises. In 1984, and at other times since then, crises became so acute that civil strife was threatened. Time after time, the bishops were able to work out an agreement among the government and labor unions and other opposing political actors.

One of the bishops' key statements, that of October 1984, is presented here. The bishops address the crisis as perhaps the greatest in Bolivian history. They see more than internal conflict: the larger world situation, including the problem of external debt repayments, strongly influenced the deteriorated economic situation.

Introduction

We bishops of Bolivia are addressing our people on the occasion of our Plenary Assembly in order to offer help to them in their search for solutions to the grave problems facing our country at present.

Our message comes from the gospel. Out of the gospel, we want to enlighten the minds and move the hearts of our fellow citizens, in order to arouse the hope we all need.

In one of our previous messages, we stated that the present crisis is perhaps the most serious in our history and that to overcome this crisis there must be an effort to rescue the nation.

Today, we urgently address all vital forces in our country: the Executive, Parliament, Central Labor Federation, National Association of Private Business Managers, Unified Central Peasant Federation, Armed Forces, and the population as a whole, in order that, putting aside divisive attitudes for the sake of the unity that is indispensable, they may all harmonize their viewpoints and their strengths.

As pastors, our mission is to appeal once more for convergence, inspired not by human ideas but by the transforming power of reconciliation, the only power capable of achieving understanding among those whose thinking and feeling differ.

We are aware that there cannot be true reconciliation unless there is a search and struggle for justice. We observe that the people have been admirable in the way they have been bearing up under the present situation, but, as Pope Paul VI noted, "the patience of a people must not be abused."

Economic Aspects

In the economic realm, the crisis has reached incredible levels. We are experiencing it every day. But this crisis is much more serious for those who are poorest, for those who are living on their wages, and even worse for those who are out of work.

The Bolivian people are used to austerity and poverty. Our people are taciturn and long suffering, but the present low economic levels are unsustainable. Adding to the pressure of a foreign debt that is quite beyond Bolivia's present economic ability to pay, and with production down to very low levels, inflation is destroying day by day the buying power of our money, destroying internal savings, and unleashing public and private immorality.

The people expect the government to put into effect coherent measures to make economic recovery possible and enable them to believe once more in their own capabilities. Mere economic patchwork or emergency measures make the situation of the majority much more dramatic over the long run.

It is in this extremely sensitive area of the economy, much more than anywhere else, that there must be a social pact, a process of harmonization, and a convergence of common interests.

The government has an obligation to consult with the most capable and most honest people and with the productive forces of the country. But the political and social forces are also obliged to offer their country an efficient and honest collaboration, without getting locked into fixed positions.

We cannot ignore the fact that there are very strong and unjust pressures on our raw materials, and that they make us a dependent country, like most Third World nations.

From this corner of Latin America, we can only believe that in the light of the poor, whose rights God assumes as his own, Bolivia expects specific kinds of international cooperation that may enable it to start a recovery process.

We regard the position of international banks as unjust, for it does not offer viable alternatives for overcoming our crisis, which was largely caused by those very banks, with their loans and excessive interest rates. The ordinary simple people have not had anything to do with these international credits, but they are paying the bills and interest payments with their hunger, illness, unemployment, and unbearable privation. In this connection, we make our own the words of Pope John Paul II, spoken during his recent visit to Santo Domingo: "I want to emphasize the grave problem of the foreign debt of Third World countries, and particularly of Latin America. It can condemn whole countries to permanent indebtedness, with serious consequences that would lead to ongoing underdevelopment and unending social immobilization."

Political Aspects

The Bolivian people have a sincere political will to consolidate the democratic process. This will is the focal point for their fierce determination to put up with the economic and social situation that is subjecting them to all kinds of privations. Without this manifest will, which is a source of energy and hope, the democratic process, which has been achieved at the cost of so much effort, would already have fallen apart, as it fell apart so many times in the past. The people are expressing their faith in the political future of our country. The Bolivian people want to live, they want to work, they want an authority founded on rights and law. The people want peace and freedom.

But there are power groups who claim exclusive rights over the democratic process and want to impose their own party banners and their group interests over the common good.

Such attitudes mask totalitarian maneuvers, contrary to the thought and feeling of the people who want to bring about a genuine democracy.

The struggle for political and economic power in our society makes us think that there may be international interests from one side or another involved. The ideologies of Marxism and capitalism may be engaged in irreconcilable struggle to keep the journey toward democracy in Bolivia from reaching its destination.

We want to reaffirm with utter clarity that selfish capitalism, which is firmly in place in our society is just as evil as totalitarian communism, which has made its way into government circles and in various sectors of our population. It would be a dramatic tragedy if alien and restricting ideologies were to succeed in turning Bolivia into a battlefield of fratricidal struggle, as is the case in other Latin American nations.

Whether we can avoid such a catastrophe depends on us, on whether we can be open to others and subordinate our interests of party and ideology to the common good, to our common life together, and to sincere collaboration.

Social Aspects

Economic problems have plunged the country into a social up-heaval, tending toward anarchy, such as has never been witnessed throughout our conflictive history. We regret to see that every day the number of the impoverished is growing, and yet their cries of pain are not heeded by a minority that is getting rich in a scandalous manner.

The channels for participating in the affairs of the nation are being closed due to the almost dictatorial blindness of leaders who speak, act, and decide in the name of a people that is usually not consulted.

We live in a situation of constant conflict: regionalism is on the rise; an excessive use of strikes has made the decision to go on strike meaningless; the use of pressure tactics has become common, in a kind of race against the clock in order to have demands satisfied, without any effort to contribute with patriotic realism toward seeking genuine solutions. We are enveloped in an atmosphere of anarchy, which integralist and ideological groups foreign to our culture desire and seek. What is worse, such an atmosphere is tolerated by those who bear the responsibility for leading the country within the frame-work of our laws. Contradictions within political parties are being accentuated, and group appetites are coming to the surface. Sectar-ianism is the most significant thing offered to a people that is frustrated at having no guides.

Moral Aspects

The measure of a people's strength is its ability to transmit life and safeguard life for all. When the ethical and moral dynamism is no longer what animates a society, there sets in a process of decay or death.

On various occasions, we have pointed to immoral situations with the hope of helping our country summon the dignity to rise from the crisis affecting it. Unfortunately, the lack of moral principles has gone so far that it seems impossible to find any sector uncontaminated:

- Private and government groups devote themselves scandalously to hoarding basic consumer goods, to encouraging a contraband that is both organized and immune, and to trafficking even in the public services the people most need.

- We are trapped in a dependence that is not only economic and political, but cultural as well: the soul of the Bolivian people is being destroyed as the state and private media devote themselves exclusively to mimicking the life patterns of consumer societies, which are making their way into our country, leading to contempt for our values.

- Drug traffic is spreading through all circles and to every corner of the country: consciences are corrupted, young lives are destroyed, and campaigns to eradicate it seem to be condemned to failure.

The fate of our country as a nation is at stake. Its destruction or survival is in our hands. Only if there is a change of attitude will we really be able to build up our country.

Final Exhortation

Once more we want to be the voice of the voiceless. We turn to them to offer a word of hope. At critical moments in our history, the suffering people have always found their support in Jesus Christ, the one who liberates from everything oppressing human beings, and in Our Virgin Mother, who has always journeyed with her people.

We urge all to seek in Jesus Christ the way that will lead us to a true reconciliation in justice, freedom, and love.

We invoke the blessing of God our Father upon each and every one of our Bolivian brothers and sisters.

Cochabamba
October 20, 1984

Guatemala
To Construct Peace
(1984)

Two years after their letter about the massacre of peasants in Guatemala, the bishops return to the theme of violence and unrest. They do so in a measured and constructive way, looking to find in the new Constitution guarantees for greater justice and a measure of peace.

By 1984, the time of the pastoral letter, violence continued but at a diminished rate. The bishops found ominous changes in the restriction of the right of movement within the country. Guatemalan army troops caused the relocation, or flight, of hundreds of thousands of Indians and blocked their return to places of origin. Government forces even restricted the freedom of Caritas, the Church's official social welfare agency, while favoring more compliant, usually evangelical, agencies. The bishops, moreover, question the policy of forcing peasants to join civil defense patrols without pay.

To construct peace, which is a task of national urgency, the contribution of all of us who love Guatemala is essential. We Catholics, who represent the great majority of the Guatemalan people, cannot be nor do we want to be absent from the daily, wearingly persistent process and work of building peace. In truth, it is a demand of the gospel if we desire to "be recognized as sons and daughters of God" (Mt 5:9). A year ago, Pope John Paul II, in his historic visit to Central America, demanded "that no one be excluded from the efforts toward peace" (Sermon in San Salvador).

We bishops, as spokesmen for the Catholic people whom we guide in Christ's name, express our overwhelming longing for peace that springs from the hearts of all our faithful. As teachers appointed by Christ to illuminate the way of our people, we want to point out paths that will bring us to the desired national peace. We passionately beg all our faithful and all people of good will to read these pages and to study them with a quiet mind. Urged on by charity, we explain our arguments in careful detail, with the hope that they be an effective contribution to the goal that all Guatemalans long for: to build peace.

Vision of the Reality

1.1.   The eyes of Guatemalans are directed with expectation toward the new Constitution of the country, which ought to be made public soon. They know that the legal foundation of the country depends on it and that it will indicate the course that the nation will undertake to solve the acute problems that exist. The approaching election has far-reaching significance for the institutional life of the nation because it is hoped that it will make a positive contribution to the opening of a new way to a better future. We must remember that during 163 years of independence, various constitutions have been promulgated that have not fostered adequately lasting foundations for real democracy nor the establishment of economic, social, and political structures capable of assuring opportunities for the participation of the entire society.

The return to (democratic) institutions and the formulation of fundamental norms of our society are not gifts from those who hold power; they are their responsibility. They are social necessities demanded by the people and must be constructed on concrete facts in order that the Constitution be binding and lasting. Therefore, we bishops cannot be less than profoundly happy and greet with optimism this opportunity that is being given to Guatemalans at this present time.

1.2.   The deputies to be elected to form the constituent assembly are not going to legislate for a country in abstract but, rather, for a nation with a particular social background, with its own history and culture, one that is immersed in a particular reality. If they do not take into account this reality and assume a position that is removed from that which Guatemala has lived, suffered, and borne, if they do not consolidate the constituent bases to solve the huge, serious national problems, we will be even more overwhelmed in the abyss of social and human evils that are being endured. It is, therefore, extremely important that all Guatemalans have a clear understanding of our reality, the profound values that sustain our nationality, and the grave dangers that are lying in wait for us.

1.3.   Therefore, we bishops of Guatemala wish to dedicate the first part of this pastoral letter to an objective, calm, and impartial analysis of the social situation of our people. To do so, we are not entering areas that are outside of our pastoral work, since our service to God ought to show itself in an attitude of concern for the concrete needs of men and women, to those whom we ought to help to be saved. We are not indifferent to the sociopolitical economic structures in which these people live. It is not possible to look at our flock with the eyes of shepherds without discovering the tragic situation that actually exists in the country, inherited from multifaceted institution-alized injustice.

1.4.   In pointing out the problems, we must not forget the great moral and spiritual resources of our people which, together with the material resources that God has given Guatemala, assure us of the complete possibility of overcoming the present crisis and of acting in more human, more Christian, more just ways.

1.5.   Shortly after the earthquake that devastated our national ter-ritory in 1976, the Guatemalan bishops published the pastoral letter *United in Hope,* which we began precisely with a presentation of the reality in which the country was living. We pointed out that there existed a situation of "constant exploitation" to the extent that people "are being dragged down to an unjust and inhuman life." We showed how "in the economic field, a minority receives the major part of the gross national product, while the huge majority has to share the smallest portion to the point that there are areas where the real income does not satisfy the basic needs of human beings." We saw that the situation was not any less serious in regard to housing, food, sani-tation, education, and work. We believed that the root of the socio-economic situation in Guatemala lay in the serious problem of landholding. We said, "It is here that the injustice that exists in our country appears the most clearly and the most dramatically." We expressed our sorrow at seeing that "while millions are invested in armaments, in excessive salaries, in luxuries and superfluous ex-penses, serious problems and fundamental needs remain without solution."

1.6.   This tragic picture that the bishops described in 1976 not only persists but has deteriorated even more because of internal and ex-ternal factors that have arisen to the detriment of our social peace.

1.7.   Violence in its various forms has taken possession of Guatemala. We are all witnesses of this violence, and we have all suffered from it. We all know that for a number of years now, mourning, terror, anxiety, and pain have taken over numerous Guatemalan households. They have been whipped by the growing wave of violence that has broken over all social levels and classes, striking especially *campesinos* and indigenous people.

A synthesis of the violent acts that daily accost and punish the people includes:

- kidnappings, disappearances, detentions, without authorized le-gal orders;

- senseless use of torture;

- massacre of entire families and groups, especially indigenous and *campesinos,* including children, pregnant women, and old people;

- massive displacements of families and communities in search of security, with the accompanying loss of homes and property that results in the appearance of refugees faced with prospects of the most inhuman levels of misery and uncertainty in foreign countries; and

- increase in accusations and violations of homes, correspondence and private communication, and all norms that are the context of human rights in all civilized countries.

1.8.   We all ask ourselves—frequently in a whisper because of fear—from where does such violence stem? It is not easy to arrive at a simple answer to such an extremely complex problem. By describing in detail the various forms that violence in Guatemala takes, possibly we can begin to grasp its causes and discover its roots.

1.8.1.   In the first place, we point out what we refer to as institutionalized or structural violence that manifests itself in unjust economic and social differences between the various sectors of the population, in the prostration of our people, in the systematic margination of participation and decision making, and in the loss of effective citizens' rights. We have to recognize that the majority of Guatemalans have found themselves deprived, throughout the centuries, of the possibility of a decent level of personal development.

1.8.2.   Aware of their dignity and their rights, marginal people have begun, in various ways, a process of liberation. Everywhere, initiatives are being made that favor the formation of base organizations that, in an authentically community atmosphere, conciliate the integral development of the human person. They are completely just initiatives, in line with existing laws in the country, advocated by humanism, and carried out in the full light of day. At the margin of this orderly, peaceful movement of the people, appear the guerrillas. Easily organized and directed by extremist sectors and motivated by messianic ideas, they fall into the paths of subversive violence.

1.8.3.   Those, then, who retain power and wealth—with fortunately some, though very few, exceptions—rather than accept, incorporate, foster, and channel the efforts of those who are seeking orderly and peaceful change, include them with those groups that have taken up arms and let loose an indiscriminate, bloody repression that, apart from other most painful consequences, has caused not a few Guatemalans to lose hope. In their despair, with no other alternative, they are incited to become collaborators with subversion. This repressive violence in which "death squads," paramilitary groups, and even police forces have participated, has increased the discontent of the people and has succeeded in becoming a spiral of violence, the consequences of which we have all felt in our own flesh. Only God knows the unbounded suffering that our people have had to bear, especially the most humble and defenseless ones.

1.9. This growth of violence has produced an ideological and political radicalization that has brought us to a point of polarization that is very difficult to overcome.

1.9.1. On the one hand, the traditional positions of power have been strengthened on the pretense of the return, at all costs, to liberalism. Deaf to the urgent demands of social justice and firmly determined to maintain, at whatever price, the secular structures that define the status quo, they try to keep the majority of the population subjected to a situation that is increasingly unbearable.

1.9.2. On the other hand, materialistic Marxism has appeared. It advocates the struggle of the classes as a social principle and has begun to acquire power, justifying whatever method, even the most violent, to obtain it.

1.9.3. As a third element of dissociation, in recent times there has appeared the doctrine or ideology of national security which, in exaltation of the nation personalized in the state as the absolute value, encourages totalitarian regimes in which the security forces are not at the service of the people but rather of the state. Frequently, by damaging and violating human rights, it collaborates with, as a means of repression, the creation of an atmosphere of terror and violence.

1.9.4. Complicating our sad situation even more is the fact that Central America, and therefore Guatemala, has become a battlefield where the great hegemonic powers of the world are waging a bloody war, thereby augmenting an uncontrollable movement of arms and ideologies.

1.9.5. Finally, as a result of a situation of total economic and political calamity, there has been unloosed an uncontrollable wave of common violence manifested in numerous and continuous armed assaults and murders.

1.10. Governments that have arisen as a result of electoral frauds and are corroded internally by insatiable corruption and deprived of authentic popular support are in need of moral solvency and the technical ability to order life in Guatemala and to distribute adequate justice.

1.11. To the immeasurable suffering that our people have endured in such dramatic ways, there has been added in the last two years the presence of civil self-defense patrols. It is not our desire to treat this matter from a strategic or tactical point of view. We look at it strictly from the ethical and human viewpoint. This obligatory service means a new responsibility on the shoulders of the most weak and most needy of our country. In effect, to have to submit themselves to gratuitous service that is incompatible with the needs of their work represents, for men in rural areas and in indigenous communities, a new sacrifice that aggravates their hardships.

1.11.1. What concerns us even more is the moral damage that is done to the consciences of some of our brothers when they are obliged to act against innocent people and when a bellicose spirit is encouraged to be instilled within them. We believe that the benefits that have been obtained in ordering the pacification of the country must not be maintained at the cost of permanent deterioration of values nor of new negative visions, the consequences of which are not yet known.

1.11.2. We bishops, who feel in the depths of our hearts the suffering of our people, take advantage of this opportunity to present respectfully our anxiety to the high military authorities of this country and beg them, with vehemence, in God's name, to lift or modify substantially this enormous weight, which our humble brothers in the rural areas should not have to bear. In this sense, the high authority of the government ought to fulfill its promise to assume this obligation.

1.12. Finally, we cannot end this first part of our pastoral letter without addressing ourselves to the state of the Catholic Church in Guatemala since it forms a very important part of the whole social conglomerate. For the Church, this time of such suffering has been, without any doubt whatsoever, a time of faithfulness to Christ, with the unceasing proclamation of the gospel and the presentation of its demands for reconciliation, unity, love, and respect for the dignity of the people. For that very reason, it has been a time of fidelity to the people who have been scourged by the violence. In fact, the Church has been constituted for the defense of people. By denouncing the abuses and violations of human rights, it has been and is like the Good Samaritan, who draws near to help the numerous victims of violence. The Catholic Church has also wanted to be faithful to Guatemala, announcing the only way that can lead to peace, which is the way of justice and brotherly love.

1.12.1. But exactly that faithfulness to Christ, to people, and to Guatemala has cost the Church the price of living in a time of intense persecution: there have been numerous priests and religious who have been murdered, have disappeared, or have had to leave the country; there have been even more catechists who have died for proclaiming the gospel; and our institutions have been the object of continuous suspicion, many times having had serious difficulties in doing their pastoral mission.

1.12.2. We have, nevertheless, the certainty that the blood of our martyrs is and will be the seed of redemption for our people, who have not lost their faith in their Church, who put their faith in it, and who have confidence in its guiding voice in spite of campaigns made to slander it and in spite of attacks by numerous fundamentalist Protestant sects.

The reply that was given, and continues to be given, to the people by the presence and message of the Holy Father, the pope, in his unforgettable visit to our country, is convincing proof of the feelings and thoughts of our people, who are fundamentally Catholic. Whoever tries not to recognize or to ignore this fact will neither be able to understand the Guatemalan people nor lead them by means of adequate legislation to ways of peace. The very soul of our people is radically religious, and it is their faith that gives them motivation to overcome most effectively their anxiety and to maintain their hope.

Practical Applications

Having indicated some basic principles that ought to guide the development of a duly organized national community, we want to dedicate the last part of our pastoral letter to an emphasis of some cases that, due to the specific situation in Guatemala, deserve special attention.

1. Life

To defend and protect human life, the first and basic gift of God, is the duty of the state, and it is incumbent upon the state to fulfill this duty for all social institutions.

1.1.   Life should be respected and protected from the first moment of gestation in the maternal womb and, for this reason, the practice of induced or provoked abortion must be penalized; birth control campaigns, sometimes subtle, should be disallowed; and all criminal practices of mass sterilization should be outlawed. It should be made perfectly clear that the law protects and respects the inalienable right of married couples to be open to life by means of responsible parenthood.

1.2.   Human life is a gift of God and belongs only to him. Only he has the right to give life and to take life. The constitutive laws of the nation must recognize and respect this principle. Therefore, legislation should be passed in such a manner that the horrendous massacres, which have caused so much dismay throughout the world, can never be repeated.

1.3.   To provide for the conservation of life, God has put the things of this earth at the disposal of all his children. Therefore, it is a sin and an injustice when the earth and its goods are monopolized for the benefit of a few. It is a responsibility of the state to assure, by means of adequate reforms, that all its citizens have access particularly to the land. Appropriate legislation, therefore, ought to grant just distribution of the land and its riches so that no one dies of hunger in a land as generous as the one that God has given us.

1.4.   Respect for life ought to lead to respect for the physical integrity of all people. Legislation ought to condemn, as abominable crimes of a warped humanity, the abduction, torture, and disappearance of persons. The practice of these crimes which, to Guatemala's disgrace, have become so frequent, is an affront to Guatemala and has placed us in a sad position in our relationships with other civilized nations.

1.5.   To watch over the health of its people is also a solemn obligation of the state and ought to remain linked to the constitutional charter. In this respect, we believe that steps ought to be drawn up clearly to assure that all Guatemalans, especially those with the least resources, have access to health centers and receive adequate health care. This has to be a privileged area and sufficient funds from the public budget must be set aside so that medicine and adequate services in hospitals are assured. Resolute legislation ought also to be drawn up to stop the irrepressible greediness of the producers and distributors of medicines who put them out of the reach of the majority of Guatemalans.

1.6.   The levels of social security are not sufficient; in the majority of cases, social security is inoperative or manages only to cover very few Guatemalans. It is necessary to establish legislation that obliges social security to be extended to all inhabitants of this country and against everything that implies uncertainty for the working person, to give him or her security against both accidents and common illness, for workers both in the cities and in the rural areas. Furthermore, it is necessary that more social provision be made to protect adequately the aged and invalids, who ought to occupy a predominant place in society.

1.7.   It is not any less important to protect the psychological or mental health of all Guatemalans, especially of the youth; it is being put in serious jeopardy by some movie and television programs that are geared to excite the lowest sexual and violent instincts. Responsible authorities do not make even a minimum effort to brake this wave of filth. To this is added, especially in the cities, the appearance of electronic games that awaken in children and adolescents destructive instincts of violence and death. There should be legislation to stop those who thrive on helping to make people unstable.

1.8.   The Church and other charitable and service institutions ought to have unrestricted legal aid to collaborate in such an important area as the physical and psychological health of Guatemalans.

It is inconceivable that attempts should be made to control, limit, or hamper the charitable work of the Church, especially CARITAS, the organ of our social ministry that works on behalf of the people.

2. The Family

2.1.   The essential cell of the society, the family, has been instituted by God to be open to life, to transmit values, and to assure the orderly growth of the social fabric. Many of the evils that exist in our national community have their roots precisely in the weak and, at times, non-existent family cell. The high index of single mothers, broken homes, and disintegrated families has doubtlessly something to do with the whole national problem. The Constitution ought to make very clear principles that assure respect and esteem for the institution of the family and that protect steadfastly the inalienable rights of the family to procreate, educate, and orient the children.

2.2. It cannot be forgotten that the family is an institution preceding the state and, for that reason, the laws ought to recognize its priority and avoid all abusive interference that could limit its rights and re-sponsibilities.

3. Religion

3.1. Another inalienable right of all people is to worship God and to manifest their religious faith with complete freedom, without any more limitations than those that just social order and the rights of others prescribe.

3.2. The Catholic Church, which for almost 500 years has been pres-ent and working in the life of Guatemalans, does not ask for itself any privileges whatsoever, but does demand, with all the force of its divine-human nature, its right to act for the benefit of the Guatemalan people. The separation of church and state should be stated very clearly in the new Constitution. Since the same people are the object of the attention of both the church and the state, there ought to exist among them a climate of collaboration and mutual respect that rec-ognizes the parameters of each other's task.

3.3. Accordingly, the Constitution must clearly state the right to freedom of religion and recognize the legal status of churches that have been duly constituted. Because they belong to the people, they ought to be exonerated from all types of taxes in relation to their worship services and their work of education and human develop-ment. They should enjoy full liberty to develop all the activities that pertain to their mission.

4. Native Cultures

4.1. One of the greatest riches of Guatemala, which gives it its own character in harmony with other nations, is the plurality of native cultures, manifested in the different ethnic groups in the country.

As descendants of the immortal Mayas, our indigenous population deserves complete respect and admiration. Unfortunately, throughout the centuries since the conquest, this has not been the case. Rather, the entire socioeconomic structure of Guatemala has rested on a structure of subjugated and impoverished indigenous people. We must not forget that the indigenous are the majority of the Guatemalan population and have inalienable rights.

Recognizing the great values of our native cultures, the new Constitution should establish firmly the bases of a legislation that respects and fosters those very cultures and responds to the cultural patterns of our ethnic groups. All forms of racial discrimination, which even now still exists, must be absolutely avoided. Our native peoples' rights to their own languages, their traditions, and their ways of life should be taken seriously into account in an attempt to bring about a gradual and respectful integration into the Guatemalan nationality.

5. Freedom

5.1. God, the Supreme Creator, gave people intelligence and freedom. He wanted sons and daughters, not slaves. For this reason, we are responsible before him for our acts, and by our work, we will make ourselves worthy of reward or punishment. The state, an institution at the service of humanity, has the serious obligation to watch over and protect the freedom of all citizens. Any legislation that eliminates, impedes, or diminishes freedom must be considered as an unacceptable abuse. Nonetheless, the just and peaceful coexistence of all citizens requires that, within a state of law, appropriate legislation organizes and guides the forms of life.

5.2. There are some cases of individual and collective freedom that must be especially protected and clearly expressed because, in practice, they have repeatedly been trampled upon in our civic life.

5.2.1. *Freedom of expression and the right to objective information.* All citizens should benefit from this unrestricted right, and the government should guarantee it. We must abolish all practices of coercion, intimidation, and other actions that are used frequently to impede people from expressing their ideas and demands or from receiving, by way of the mass media, objective and truthful information.

5.2.2. *Freedom of movement.* This must be established clearly because every citizen has the right to move about freely within the national territory. The fact that some residents must seek permission from the military in charge or from other military or paramilitary authorities to move from one area to another is not admissible; this is what is currently happening in some parts of the interior of the country. This practice is a flagrant violation of a universally recognized right and makes people feel frustrated and asphyxiated.

5.2.3. *Freedom of association.* For a just development of individuals and communities, the social fabric requires the existence of intermediate bodies such as neighborhood committees, cooperatives, and other institutions. Therefore, it is indispensable that legislation guarantees the freedom of association, duly regulated, but never diminished nor manipulated as unfortunately happens frequently.

5.2.4.   On this subject of freedom, we cannot help but point out the moral problems that are created by the existence of civil self-defense patrols to which we have referred in another part of this pastoral letter.

5.2.5.   In the constituent law of the country, it ought to be made very clear that no one can be obligated to give service imposed by the authorities without pay or by force. The defense of the integrity of the national territory is the responsibility of the army, and it cannot oblige anyone to join its patrols against his will, except in extreme cases already established by law. Likewise, vigilance is the responsibility of the police, and civilians cannot be obliged to organize vigilance to the detriment of their work, family, religious, or scholastic obligations.

6. Education

6.1.   All citizens have a right to education, appropriate to their age and abilities. Therefore, the state has the obligation to provide mandatory education that is free to everyone. This way, freedom of instruction, without a determined ideology being set, will be guaranteed. All citizens should receive at least the primary level of education; it must be financed by contributions taken by the state from funds received through taxes. Nonetheless, we know the tragic reality of education in Guatemala. We are not going to repeat here the shameful facts about the deficiencies of our national system of education. However, we do believe it is necessary to remember that it is one of the most urgent tasks and one that must be taken more seriously.

6.2.   The state is responsible for assuring that all people receive education, but it should respect the beliefs of parents and educators. Therefore, within the constituent law, it should be set down clearly that it is the right of parents to choose the kind of education that they want for their children. It should also be set down that private institutions, such as the Church, have the right to establish schools and the freedom to choose the teaching staff.

The Catholic Church is willing to make available all of its schools and to put them at the service of everyone, without charge, provided that the state commits itself to paying the teachers' wages and the operating costs of the primary and secondary schools.

7. Work

7.1.   The right to work, which is properly remunerated with a salary that covers the needs of a worker and his or her family, is a universally recognized right. Therefore, we must not forget that it is the responsibility of the state, as well as those who possess goods and wealth, to create new sources of employment.

7.2.   The owners, as well as the workers, should defend their rights and interests. To do so, they may organize in various ways, the former creating chambers (of commerce) and business associations, and the latter forming unions. Unions are the institutions fundamental to obtaining just living and working conditions. They are necessary so that workers are recognized as persons, because when they are isolated, they are totally subject to the law of capital. The function of a union is to develop in salaried workers an awareness of their dignity and a will to advance. In addition, it should undertake activities and create organizations that bring about the workers' advancement.

7.3.   The Church, within which the guilds of the Middle Ages were born, has reaffirmed solemnly the right to organize, first recognized by Pope Leo XIII in 1891, and confirmed by his successors, as a fundamental right that no legislation or practice can abolish.

Pope John Paul II, speaking in the Sao Paulo (Brazil) stadium before 120,000 workers, remembered the still valid right of wage earners to establish free association in whatever system. In his encyclical *Laborem Exercens* (20), he demonstrated the "importance of unions."

7.4.   This universal right of workers, in the private sector as well as in the public, should be established clearly in our legislation and all means anticipated to defend it firmly.

We all know the history of the unions in our country and that, at present, their ranks are diminished. Some of the main leaders have been murdered, others have disappeared or have had to seek refuge in a neighboring country. This situation must end; the Constitution must guarantee fully the freedom to form unions.

7.5.   Workers have to understand that the strength of the unions lies in unity and in remaining within the confines of their union organization: to enter into areas of party politics or to allow their unions to be infiltrated by one ideology or another will always weaken the unions' struggle.

7.6.   Investors and employers should also find within the legislation ample protection of their rights and interests, without forgetting that wealth has a "social mortgage." That is to say that wealth was not created only for the enjoyment and pleasure of a minority but rather that it should serve for the balanced development of the entire community.

7.7.   Finally, our legislation should establish the foundations to assure that special care be taken in regulating the work of women, the handicapped, and minors.

8. Political Participants

8.1.   The political task, that is, the conduct of *res pública* (public matters) is the obligation and responsibility of all citizens. No citizen can be prohibited legitimately or marginated from this activity for ideological, religious, racial, or any other reason. Each citizen has the full right to manifest his or her political preference, and it is the duty of the state to facilitate legitimate channels for this free and responsible expression. The very apathy that we see in our people in regard to political matters clearly demonstrates that the huge majority of citizens rejects leadership that is manipulated by politics and plagued with fraud, cheating, and lies.

8.2.   Catholic citizens, as we have said on other occasions, have still another reason for participating in the political life of a nation. It is their faith that shows them that the kingdom of Christ is to be brought about in the "here and now" of public events and that, through the mediation of institutions, legislation, and the organization of the republic, day by day, a civilization of love must be forged.

8.3.   But the Catholic Church has no political party nor does it endorse any faction that fights to take power. It respects and values all of them because it defends fully political pluralism.

In a civilized nation, citizens have the right to choose a government that, in their judgment, responds best to the interests of the country. The state has the duty to regulate and legislate political activity, being careful, nevertheless, not to limit arbitrarily the freedom of its citizens. It is not legitimate to overturn all economic, political, and military power in favor of one particular political faction. That this has happened in the past is one of the reasons for the tragic situation that our country is presently experiencing.

8.4.   In this respect, we also share the concern expressed by different sectors in the country about the existence of the civil self-defense patrols during the current electoral process. The vague situation of the patrol members, submitted to military or paramilitary discipline, makes them susceptible to manipulation or limitations in the exercise of their civil rights. We trust that the government will find a proper solution to this problem.

9. Authority

9.1.   Legitimately constituted authority should merit all the esteem and respect of the citizens since it exists to render enormous service to the nation. We understand authority to mean not only the supreme government representing the power of the state, but also public officials and security forces.

Since the beginning, we Catholics have learned to honor and respect legitimately constituted authority (cf. 1 Pt 2:13–17). We also have a clear awareness of our right to demand that these same authorities faithfully fulfill the law because no authority is above the law, and none can reach unlimited power since no authority is owner of the country but rather is its servant.

9.2.   In order to be effective, the strength of any authority should be rooted in its attachment to the law, its honesty, and in the respect it shows its citizens. When public authority falls into a practice of crime, which unfortunately has happened and continues to happen in our country, it loses all strength and, in order to gain control again, has no other recourse but to call upon the brute strength of arms. Illegal arrests marked by abductions, disappearances, and the abominable practice of torture, among other repugnant actions, have put the nation's forces of order in a serious predicament. We hope that these practices will disappear from the national scene. The constitutive law of the nation must be very definite and clear in order to prevent such abominations from being repeated.

10. International Relations

10.1.   As a developing country, we are subjected to the influences of more developed countries and, in particular, to those of the great powers. Therefore, those with public power should be conditioned and limited in order to guarantee that a permanent neutrality be maintained and to avoid our being converted into an instrument of war by international hegemonic forces and into participants in the arms race. "The arms race is the most serious plague of humanity and endangers the poor in an intolerable manner" (Pope John XXIII, *Pacem in Terris*).

10.2.   International cooperation for security, in both the social and the economic spheres, cannot be accepted nor promoted under negative norms. The dignity of the human person extends to the social realm. Relations with neighboring countries, as well as the entire international community, should be maintained under this same principle of dignity. Our vision is guided by the papal encyclical *Populorum Progressio* which, when speaking of the brotherhood of peoples, defined these relations as a duty that concerns, in the first place, the more developed countries: "Their obligations stem from a brotherhood that is at once human and supernatural, and take on a threefold aspect: the duty of human solidarity—the aid that the rich nations must give to developing countries; the duty of social justice—the rectification of inequitable trade relations between powerful nations and weak nations; the duty of universal charity—the effort to bring about a world that is more human towards all people, where all will be able to give and receive, without one group making progress at the expense of the other. The question is urgent, for on it depends the future of the civilization of the world" (PP, 44).

Conclusion

Through these pages, we bishops of Guatemala want to make, with clarity and simplicity, our contribution to peace in our country. We ask God, the Lord of History, to move the hearts of all our faithful and of all people of good will so that, in light of the teachings we have offered, they might work actively and decisively in the long and hopeful process that has begun in our country.

We all can and should collaborate, with our serious, responsible, and informed vote, to elect the men and women who will write the new Constitution of our country. And those who are elected for such a noble and determinant task have the enormous responsibility, before God and history, to carry out this work with honesty, efficiency, and wisdom.

May Mary, Mother of God and our Mother, who has been so close to the hearts of Guatemalans throughout history, who protects us with maternal care and reminds us continually that we are all brothers and sisters, bring us the strength through her divine Son to "build upon rock" and to construct with enthusiasm and optimism the roads that lead to peace.

Guatemalan Episcopal Conference
Guatemala de la Asunción
June 10, 1984
Pentecost

El Salvador
Called to Be Artisans of Peace
(1984)

A year after the visit of John Paul II to El Salvador, the bishops reinforce the task the pope left for Salvadoreans: to be artisans of peace. That the papal visit caused an intense emotional reaction, the bishops do not question. Everyone seems to remember the ten hours John Paul II was in the country March 6, 1983.

Rather, they ask if the papal visit had a lasting effect. Testimonies from priests in contact with diverse communities unanimously reported evidence of a spiritual revival that took many forms. However, the renewal has not done away with the forced exodus of thousands of Salvadoreans, the lack of priests for villages, nor especially with uncontrolled violence. It is this latter issue that the bishops address in this letter.

The bishops also speak about the role of the United States and the Soviet Union, when they decry "the spiral of violence being increased by the undue interference of foreign powers who 'are waging a war in some one else's house,' with grave danger of internationalization of the conflict."

The bishops devote the rest of the letter to the steps necessary for bringing about interior and exterior peace.

To our diocesan and religious clergy and seminarians; to brothers, sisters, and members of secular institutes; to our lay co-workers in the apostolate; to all our children in the faith of Jesus Christ and to all people of good will, greetings and blessings.

Dear Brothers and Sisters:

As the end of the "Year of the Jubilee of the Redemption," which will culminate with the celebration of Easter this coming April 22, draws near, and just a few weeks away from the first anniversary of the unforgettable and providential visit of His Holiness, John Paul II, to our country, we bishops of El Salvador want to share with you some thoughts, concerns, and hopes. Our message also takes its inspiration from the recent Synod of Bishops on "Penance and Reconciliation in the Mission of the Church," as well as the illuminating guidelines of the Holy Father for the XVII World Day of Peace. Its theme, "peace arises out of a new heart" is a whole program for us, whom the Supreme Pastor so emphatically invited to be "artisans of peace."

It has been almost a year since we wrote our collective pastoral letter *Awaiting the Vicar of Christ*, as part of our feverish and enthusiastic spiritual preparation for welcoming the man of God who was to come to visit us in the name of the Lord. The purpose of the letter we offer you today is to make an initial assessment of the fruits that visit has produced among us and to give further impetus to the spiritual renewal and the commitments that his presence and his message awoke in many hearts.

I. Evoking the Holy Father's Visit

An Extraordinary Grace

In our pastoral letter *Awaiting the Vicar of Christ*, we pointed to the pastoral style of John Paul II, the expectation his visit had aroused in El Salvador, and the deep pastoral concern he had shown toward our country. Now as we evoke the ten hours that he spent under Salvadoran skies, we feel an overwhelming joy over such an extraordinary grace. We also once more thank those who, with exemplary devotion and abnegation, made possible the welcome that so moved the pope during his brief and very intense stay with us. We have in mind both those who served on the commissions that were formed to prepare the different aspects of the papal visit and those who welcomed the pope in an anonymous and spontaneous manner.

Almost twelve months have gone by since then, and our pastors' hearts bless the Lord as we recall what the presence of John Paul II in El Salvador meant to thousands upon thousands of Salvadorans. That is why March 6, 1983, has remained indelibly imprinted on the soul of our country, which trembled with emotion and was filled with light and hope. And the seed that His Holiness sowed liberally in the furrows of our ancestral land is now giving fruits in conversion, in reconciliation, and in peace.

However, the point is not simply to relive emotions, but especially to ask ourselves how we are carrying out the task that John Paul II left us: to be artisans of peace and reconciliation in El Salvador. That is the task that he exhorted us to carry out, stimulated by the Holy Year that he inaugurated a few days after visiting us, and by the

Synod of Bishops that took place in Rome in October of last year. Thus, the celebration of the first anniversary of the papal visit will signify a step forward in our following of the Lord and in our commitment to the peace for which there is so much yearning.

An Intense Spiritual Renewal

The Holy Father's visit has stimulated a true spiritual renewal throughout our country and in all circles. Priests who are in direct contact with the various Christian communities are unanimous in witnessing to the thirst for God that the papal journey aroused in many souls and to the rediscovery of the sacrament of penance and of the Eucharist made by many Christians, as well as of the interest in absorbing the Word of God and of having a deeper knowledge of their faith. Moreover, the suffering caused by the war has brought many of our brothers and sisters closer to the Lord, especially when they have felt disillusioned by the various groups that say they are seeking the good of the country. It is impressive for us to discover this hunger for God also in young people who are ever more numerous and active in our parishes and in the various groups for formation and apostolate. In this atmosphere, more priestly, religious, missionary, and lay vocations are arising. The movements of the secular apostolate and pious associations are reflecting also this renewed joy and enthusiasm for the things of God and this holy pride at being part of the Church.

The very consoling picture we have just described does not lead us to forget the shadows and the problems that occur in the realm of living out the faith. For example, we cannot ignore the enormous problems produced by the forced exodus of thousands and thousands of Salvadorans, thrown out from where they lived, often with nothing in their hands, and pushed out into uncertainty, unemployment, and all kinds of suffering. All of this has made it difficult for them to live their faith.

The situation becomes all the more painful for us when all around us we hear the heartrending cry of communities pleading for a priest and, in many cases, we are unable to satisfy these requests, which are so justifiable.

The Exhausting Journey toward Peace

However, the most anguishing problem disturbing Salvadorans is undoubtedly that of unrestrained violence, terrorism in all its forms, and the unprecedented suffering to which our noble people are subjected. Peace seems a long distance away, and according to some, it is impossible. Although the Holy Father pointed so clearly toward the ways of peace, those who have opted for the ways of violence seem deaf to every voice raised calling for conversion, reconciliation, justice, and mutual understanding in order to attain it. A small consolation in this way of the cross, which has been going on for more than four years now, is that beyond our borders there is a growing recognition that the vast majority of Salvadorans are not offering their support to those who want to change or to maintain the present state of things by violent means. Unfortunately, on top of the undeniable situation of injustice that partly caused this spiral of violence, there comes the unlawful involvement of foreign powers, which—as a high Roman prelate said—"are fighting a war in someone else's house," with the grave danger of internationalizing the conflict.

Hence, it is not surprising that a sensation of impotence invades many hearts, and many feel tempted to evade their own responsibilities for building peace. It is also understandable that sometimes people think the only solution is one of forceful action to get rid of violence once and for all and enable us all to live and to work in peace.

As pastors of our people, we have examined this situation with a great deal of concern in order to discover the ways that the Lord wants us to proceed, or the ways he wants us to continue traveling, in order to offer our contribution as Church to the cause of peace. This contribution must be built on the illuminating and solid foundation laid by John Paul II during his Central American journey and should take inspiration from the spirit of the Holy Year for Redemption, so masterfully translated in terms of peace when the pope tells us, "peace springs from a new heart."

II. The Way of Artisans of Peace

It is our lot to be bishops of this local Church during an especially difficult period. Sometimes, we feel that the task is immeasurably above our weak capabilities. How much we need the support of prayer and intense Christian life from you, beloved children entrusted to our care! The paternal exhortation that the pope addressed to us when he arrived in Costa Rica, comforts and stimulates us in this mission: "May you strive to be guides and examples for your flock, and like Jesus, may you know how to be good Shepherds, always going before your faithful, to show them the sure way, heal their wounds and miseries, their divisions and falls, and reconcile them in a new unity in the Lord, who does not cease to call out to unity in him."

Our pastoral mission includes aspects that are diverse and inseparable: We are called to be teachers of truth, signs and builders of unity both within the Church and in society, as well as promoters and defenders of human dignity. This latter aspect becomes especially important when it is our lot to serve a people that has been so battered by suffering. It is within this harsh reality that our work for the peace that is so desired, must take place, a peace that, if it is to be genuine, must be built upon truth, justice, love, and freedom.

In this pastoral letter, we want to reiterate some of the Holy Father's thoughts and propose some reflections of our own to illuminate and maintain our Christian commitment in the situation, painful but full of hope, in which we must respond to the Lord.

Why the Pope Came

On the eve of his journey through the Central American countries, Belize, and Haiti, John Paul II addressed us with these words from Rome: "It is precisely this situation in which you live that has impelled me to undertake this journey. To be closer to you, children of the Church and of countries whose root is Christian, you who are suffering intensely and experiencing the scourge of division, of war, of hatred, of age-old injustice, of ideological conflicts that make the world tremble and that turn innocent populations yearning for peace into the scene of conflict."

In this same message, he expressed what he wanted to obtain as the fruit of his visit: "It is my ardent desire that my visit, through which I want to share the Gethsemani and Calvary of your peoples, with its message of faith, brotherhood and sisterhood, and justice, should encourage an effective change, especially in inner attitudes, one that might open so many weary hearts to the hope of a better future."

And thus he began his pilgrimage, "moved by this desire, impelled by love for human beings and for the image—so often violated!—of the love of God that they bear on their forehead, convinced that every heart can and must feel the touch of grace, urging it to seek better moral paths."

The intense and emotional days that John Paul II lived in each of our nations constituted the best commentary on his words, for the pope not only spoke with his limpid messages, but also with his gestures, which were so moving and filled with love. His first greeting as he landed on Central American soil set the tone of intense solidarity with the sufferings of our peoples, which was to characterize his whole journey. "The battered cry that arises from these lands has resounded urgently in my spirit, the cry that calls for peace, an end to war and to violent deaths; that pleads for reconciliation, uprooting divisions and hatred; that yearns for a justice that has been awaited for so long and thus far in vain; that wants to be called to a greater dignity, without giving up its religious core."

And in order to clarify any doubt over the strictly pastoral thrust of his mission, he added, "My word is one of peace, of harmony, and of hope. I come to speak to you with love for all and to exhort you to family spirit and understanding as children of the same Father. It is precisely this reality that moves me to exert pressure on consciences so that an adequate response may bring forth hope in these lands that need it so much."

Sharing the Pain and Opening the Ways to Peace

We guard the words of the Holy Father in El Salvador as a precious legacy in our minds and hearts. Let us recall some of those words so as to once more make present in our spirit all their power and inspiration so that they may sustain our efforts toward conversion, reconciliation, and peace.

Who could forget the moving confidence he shared with us as he arrived at Ilopango Airport? "For a long time I have been yearning for this day to come, in order to give witness with my presence to something that you know to be true: that the pope is close to you and shares in your sufferings. How could a father and brother in the faith remain insensitive to the travail of his children? El Salvador has been in my prayers constantly, in my persistent appeals for peace, both stated and written, as I sought to keep your faith from failing and the hope in your spirits from waning, due to a situation that is still not beyond repair. That situation has been a seedbed of harmful divisions and, worse yet, of the spilling of so much innocent blood throughout your nation's soil."

And then, with fine human and Christian sensitivity, His Holiness declared what he hoped would be the fruit of his presence among us: "May this visit among you, which I make under the emblem of peace, help restrain the conflict and once more reunite this beloved Salvadoran family in a peaceful home, where all may truly feel that they are brothers and sisters. With every feeling of selfishness and hatred set aside, from now on, may the good will of all, and especially of the children of the Church, be devoted to promoting justice, the basis for hope, in order to achieve a new earth, abounding in the fruits of truth and of Christian reconciliation."

Conversion, Reconciliation, and Peace

From the moment he set foot on our land, the pope's expressive gestures shed light on the meaning of his words, which in turn explained the meaning of his gestures. For example, his visit to the tomb of the murdered Archbishop Oscar Arnulfo Romero must be placed in this perspective.

However, the most glorious moment of his stay was the massive eucharistic celebration in Metrocenter where, under the burning March sun, John Paul II made a compressed summary of our tragedy: "How many homes destroyed! How many refugees, exiles, and displaced people! How many noble and innocent lives, cut short in a cruel and brutal manner!"

Faced with such an inhuman and frightful situation, the pope added his authoritative voice to "the anguish, the pain, the weariness, the fatigue of so many people who want to live, to arise from the ashes, to see the warmth of children's smiles, far from terror and in a climate of democratic life in common."

For the Vicar of Christ, this situation is not beyond repair, but the solution goes by way of conversion of hearts, which is difficult but not impossible: "Hence, the Christian knows that all sinners can be saved; that the rich—if they are unconcerned, unjust, satisfied with the selfish possession of their goods—can and must change their attitude; that those who make use of terrorism can and must change; that those who seethe with spite and hatred can and must free themselves from such slavery; that there are ways to overcome conflicts; that where the prevailing language is that of weapons in battle, there can and must reign love, the irreplaceable element of peace."

With pained conviction, with a voice of appeal and almost of command, he exclaimed: "There is an urgent need to bury violence— enough of violence!—which has cost so many victims in this and other nations. How? Through a true conversion to Jesus Christ. Through a reconciliation that can make a family out of all those who today are separated by political, social, economic, and ideological walls. Through mechanisms and instruments of genuine participation in the economic and social realms, through access to the goods on the earth for all, through the possibility of self-realization in work; in short, through applying the social teaching of the Church. It is in this context that there must be a courageous and generous effort for justice, which can never be disregarded. All this must take place in a climate in which violence is renounced."

We Must Be Artisans of Peace, Each and Every One of Us

In his ringing homily in Metrocenter, the Holy Father comes down to the practical details when he indicates our task. But he first expresses his confidence in us: "In this multitude of believers and those united to us throughout Central America, I contemplate a vast reservoir of energy for reconciliation and peace. You thirst for peace, and rightly so. Out of your breasts and throats there arises a cry of hope: we want peace!"

Peace! this word has a great impact on each one of us. But the pope specifies the exact meaning he gives this idea: "When I speak of conversion as the way to peace, I am not advocating a slick peace that hides problems and passes over the worn-out mechanisms that must be repaired. What is needed is a peace in truth, in justice, in complete recognition of the rights of the human person."

The source of this peace must be sought beyond ourselves: "Christ, who offers himself for the world, and toward whose mystery of reconciliation on the cross we must move during the present period of Lent, is the Lamb of God who gives peace. . . . Peace comes from Christ and is the genuine embrace of brothers and sisters in reconciliation."

Indeed, peace is God's gift, but it is also the task of each one of us: "Each and every one. . . in this noble nation that is proud to bear the name of El Salvador [The Savior] . . .; each and every one, governors and governed, people who live in the city, towns, or villages; each and every one, business people and workers, teachers and students, all have the duty to be artisans of peace."

In this fashion, the pope leads us to the core of the gospel: "The Sermon on the Mount is the Christian's charter: 'Blessed are the artisans of peace, for they will be called children of God' (Mt 5:9). That is what all of you should be: artisans of peace and reconciliation, praying to God for it and working for it. May it be stimulated by the extraordinary Holy Year of Redemption, which we are about to begin, and the coming Synod of Bishops."

III. Our Task: Praying and Working for Peace

John Paul II left us on the eve of the Holy Year, and he aroused our interest in the work of the Synod of Bishops that was to take place some months later; shortly afterwards, we artisans of peace found new light shed by the papal message for the XVII World Day of Peace, celebrated this past January. In this fashion, we have been discovering the roads we must travel in order to build peace.

Opening the Doors to the Redeemer and Being Reconciled to One Another

Last year, on March 25, the pope inaugurated the "Year of the Jubilee of the Redemption," which is an extraordinary Holy Year convoked to commemorate the 1950th anniversary of the salvation achieved by Christ through his death and resurrection.

The aim of this jubilee celebration fits remarkably well with our yearnings for peace, since it reminds us that "all Christians are called upon to realize more profoundly their vocation of reconciliation with the Father in the Son . . . [which] leads to a fresh commitment by each and every person to the service of reconciliation . . . among all men and women. It must also lead to the service of peace among all peoples" (Papal Bull *Aperite portas Redemptori*, 3).

The fact that this time of grace has been received so favorably in our Christian people, and that our priests have been exemplary in their availability for the ministry of reconciliation, fills us with consolation and hope. We earnestly desire that in the few weeks remaining before the close of this Year of the Jubilee, this effort of deep interior renewal, which leads us to a reconciliation with God and with our brothers and sisters, will continue. Thus, we will be able to receive the gift of Christ, who, as he was carrying out the supreme act of love exclaimed, "My peace I give you" (cf. Jn 14:27). This peace is the one we are called to share with our brothers and sisters, communicating to them the power of our Christian hope.

Very closely connected with the Holy Year is the Synod of Bishops that was held in Rome last October in order to reflect on "Reconciliation and Penance in the Mission of the Church." There, it was emphasized that the Church is a community called to be in a permanent state of conversion and reconciliation. The road to peace passes along this way, and that peace is authentic only if there is a previous conversion of mind and heart leading to reconciliation. As they finished their work, the bishops, united in the Synod, sent a message to the world, from which John Paul II took these expressions: "The Word of God urges us to repentance: 'Change in your heart and allow yourself to be reconciled with the Father.' The Father's design for our society is that we live like a family in justice and truth, in freedom and love."

Along this way, together with the whole Church, "we share in the mission given by Christ to create the civilization of love, healing, reconciling, and repairing this divided and broken world." This is an urgent and all-consuming task for artisans of peace.

Peace Arises from a New Heart

The theme of the Holy Year also provides the inspiration for the message of the XVII World Day of Peace, which we have just celebrated. It is our lot to be artisans of peace in a situation that is extremely serious and agonizing, and that seems to be beyond our control. We feel the temptation to flee, but John Paul II reminds us of our task of bringing hope and of working for brotherhood and sisterhood, each of us offering his or her collaboration for peace, without shifting the responsibility to others.

Indeed, our situation is grave. It could be described by taking elements from the analysis that the pope makes of the situation around the world in his *XVII World Day of Peace Message:* Clearly, in El Salvador, peace is precarious and injustice abounds. Armed conflict is cutting down more lives every day, apparently without any progress toward a solution. Violence and terrorism of all kinds are mercilessly increasing destruction and the suffering of many innocent people; assaults on human rights continue; weapons of death continue to arrive to the army and to the guerrillas, placing more lives in danger. We are the bloodstained scene for the clash between East and West, as we ourselves pay a high price in human lives. But our conflict also has internal causes that are not ideological, which sink their roots in the manifold forms that injustice has taken in our midst.

How can we deal with such terrible problems? The Holy Father replies by calling to the renewal of the heart: "peace springs from a new heart." In the heart are found the roots of these problems and that is where the key to the solution is to be found as well.

This conviction is expressed compactly and emphatically by the pope: "War is born in the human heart. It is the human being who kills and not that person's sword." In biblical language, the *heart* is what is deepest in the human person, in relation with good and evil, with other people, and with God.

A new heart cannot accept violence as the way to peace: "The recourse to violence and war clearly is born of the sin of human beings, of blindness of spirit, of a disordered heart, which invokes injustice as a reason for developing or aggravating tension or conflict" (*Message,* 2).

A new heart is ultimately one that "allows itself to be inspired by love. There cannot be true external peace," John Paul II tells us, citing Pius XI, "among human beings and among peoples where internal peace does not exist, that is, where the spirit of peace has not taken hold of minds and hearts . . ." (ibid.).

Peace Must Be Won

If violence is not the way, the conclusion is clear: peace must be won. Every Christian must make efforts at this task in the environment where he or she lives: family, school, work, and so forth. Naturally, the greatest responsibility falls on heads of state and on political leaders. To them the pope says, "More than others, they must be convinced that war is inherently irrational and that the ethical principle of a peaceful solution of conflicts is the only way worthy of human beings. Peace must be won. Even more, the consciences of those in positions of political responsibility must prevent them from being swept into dangerous ventures in which passion prevails over justice, sacrificing in vain the lives of their citizens, provoking conflicts in other people's homes, and using the precariousness of peace in a region as a pretext for extending their own hegemony over new territories" (*Message*, 4).

But peace, insists the Vicar of Christ once more, is the duty of all; and he immediately issues a call to those who exercise an influence on public opinion through the media; to those who devote themselves to educating young people and adults; to young people who, certainly more than anyone else, yearn for peace; to women, who are so connected to the mystery of life; and to all, both men and women, who are called to contribute to the cause of peace.

This call is directed especially to us Christians. To respond to it is to cooperate with God's plan, to allow the Lord to convert us, to allow our lives to be transformed for "everything comes from God, who has reconciled us to himself through Christ and has given us the ministry of reconciliation" (2 Cor 5:18).

For that purpose, we especially need to seek the power of prayer: "To pray is to conform ourselves to the one we invoke, the one we encounter, the one who gives us life. To experience prayer is to receive grace, which changes us. The Spirit, joined to our spirit, commits us to shape our lives according to the Word of God. To pray is to enter into God's action in history; he is its sovereign protagonist and he has chosen to make human beings his collaborators" (*Message*, 5).

Pursuing Specific Paths

Our prayer leads us to encounter Christ, "our peace, he who has made both peoples one, knocking down the wall of separation, enmity" (Eph 2:14).

However, John Paul II tells us, if we believe in forgiveness, "Can we continue to battle each other endlessly? Can we be adversaries, invoking the same living God? If the law of love is our law, can we continue not to speak and not to act when a wounded world is waiting for us to march at the head of those who are building peace?" (*Message*, 5).

We bishops of El Salvador have accepted this exhortation and have repeatedly called for a peaceful solution to the conflict that is costing our blood. Together with the pope, we have repeated our conviction that true dialogue is not only the only possible solution, but indeed the only solution that is human and Christian. We cannot accept an illusory peace built over the bodies of more Salvadorans.

On this solemn occasion, as the first anniversary of the papal visit draws near, we once more exhort those who are combating with weapons in hand to open themselves to dialogue and to halt the senseless spilling of Salvadoran blood. With the same vigor, we also emphasize that true dialogue must respond to the conditions so masterfully laid out by the same Holy Father, especially in his message of "dialogue for peace, an urgent need of our age," and in the homily he gave on March 6, under our skies.

Because we believe in the human being and in a peaceful solution, we have been willing to be present in the Peace Commission, through a member of this episcopal conference. We do so without commitments to any political group or ideology, since our commitment is only to the Lord and to Salvadorans, whose dignity we are obliged to defend.

We bless you with all our heart, and we support all initiatives undertaken to celebrate the first anniversary of the Holy Father's visit. May the Queen of Peace sustain the efforts of each and every one of us, who are called to be artisans of the peace that springs from a new heart.

San Salvador
February 1984
Feast of the Presentation
of the Lord

Marco René Revelo
Bishop of Santa Ana
President of CEDES (Episcopal
Conference of El Salvador)

Arturo Rivera Damas, SDB
Archbishop of San Salvador

José Eduardo Alvarez, CM
Bishop of San Miguel
Military Vicar

José Oscar Barahona Castillo
Bishop of San Vicente

Gregorio Rosa Chávez
Auxiliary Bishop of San Salvador

Rev. Leopoldo Barreiro Gómez
General Secretary of CEDES

Nicaragua
Christian Commitment for
a New Nicaragua
(1979)

Many groups and individuals, committed Catholics,
took part in the overthrow of the Somoza dictatorship.
In the last months of fighting, the bishops declared that
all peaceful means of political resolution had been at-
tempted and stated that insurrectionary violence could
then be justified.

Somoza left Nicaragua in July 1979, and Nicaraguans
began to rebuild. They faced a formidable task. Some
50,000 persons had been killed, more than 100,000
wounded, and up to a half million at least temporarily
homeless. All this occurred after a terrible earthquake
that left the center of Managua still in rubbles.

At this early stage of the revolution, the Church urged
all to work energetically to rebuild Nicaraguan society.
Many Catholics (Protestants, as well) responded to the
challenges on the basis of their Christian faith.

To the clergy, men and women religious, basic Christian communities, delegates of the Word, and all people of good will, peace and
blessings in the Lord.

Introduction

We address the Nicaraguan community, of which we form a part,
which is searching for the path of truth and for justice during the
current stage of the revolutionary process in our country, a process
that is being watched by many people in the world today. We wish
to speak with the clarity demanded in the gospel (see Mt 5:37) and
by the Catholic community and all the people of Nicaragua to whom
we have an obligation. We speak as pastors of the Church, aware that
many Christians participated actively in the insurrection and work
today for the consolidation of its triumph. We believe that this message
can be of service to the people of God by encouraging them in their

commitment and helping them to discern that which is the role of the Holy Spirit in the revolutionary process. As a Church, we are convinced that there is much to be done and that we have not always been fully aware of the needs of our people.

We cannot make this discernment alone. We recall and make our own the wise words of Pope Paul VI: "In Christian communities, it is necessary to determine, with the help of the Holy Spirit, in communion with the bishops involved, and in dialogue with our fellow Christians and all people of good will, the options and commitments that must be made in order to carry out the social, political, and economic changes that are felt to be urgently needed in each case" (OA, 4). For this reason, this pastoral letter is also an appeal to continue the dialogue with the Christian communities and a request that these communities, which are in closest touch with our realities, will be able to find the true spirit "to join Christ in effectively moving the history of our people toward the Kingdom" (*Puebla*, 274). We know that what we have to offer is not "silver and gold" (cf. Acts 3:6) nor is it to provide political and economic solutions, but to proclaim the Good News.

We wish to speak humbly and simply because we are pastors and members of a Church that is "holy and at the same time in need of purification" (LG, 8; EN, 15).

We will discuss the following points in this letter: (1) Christian commitment for a new Nicaragua; (2) evangelical motivation; and (3) the responsibility and challenge of today.

I. Christian Commitment for a New Nicaragua

A. Accomplishments

We would like to begin with a few remarks about the achievements of the revolutionary process that help us to:

1.   Recognize that, through years of suffering and social marginalization, our people have been accumulating the experience necessary to transform this situation into a broad and profoundly liberating action. Our people fought bravely to defend their right to live with dignity in a peaceful and just society. This struggle has given profound significance to the activities conducted against a regime that violated and repressed human, personal, and social rights. As in the past, we denounced this situation as one that was contrary to the demands of the gospel, so now we wish to reaffirm that we accept the profound motivation of this struggle for justice and for life.

2.   Recognize that the blood of those who gave lives in this lengthy struggle, the devotion of youth who want to build a just society, and

the outstanding role of women in this whole process—elsewhere in the world postponed—signal the development of new forces for constructing a new Nicaragua. All of this underscores the originality of the historic process we are now living through. At the same time, our people's struggle to control their own future has been affected strongly by the thought and work of Augusto Cesar Sandino, which emphasize the uniqueness of the Nicaraguan revolution, giving it its own style and its clearly defined banner of social justice, of affirmation of national values, and of international solidarity.

3.   Observe in the joy of an impoverished people who, for the first time in many years feel that they are masters in their own country, an expression of revolutionary creativity that opens up broad and fruitful opportunities for a commitment by all who seek to fight against an unjust, oppressive system and build a new humanity.

4.   Appraise the determination to start on the first day of victory to institutionalize the revolutionary process by providing a legal basis. This was evident in the decision to keep the programs announced prior to victory. Some examples are the promulgation of the Statute on the Rights and Guarantees of Nicaraguans; the consequent practice of freedom of information, of partisan political organization, of worship, and of movement; naturalization to recover the country's wealth; the first steps in land reform; and so forth. Other examples include the ability to start, on the first days of the process, to plan and organize a national literacy campaign to ennoble the spirit of our people and make them more capable of guiding their own destinies and participating more responsibly and with greater vision in the revolutionary process.

5.   Recognize the existence in Nicaragua of conflicts between opposing interests brought about by land reform, expropriations of large estates, etc., conflicts that can be aggravated by changes in the economic, social, political, and cultural structures.

6.   Recognize also the risks, dangers, and errors in this revolutionary process, aware that there is no absolutely pure human undertaking in history and, with this in mind, to consider freedom of expression and criticism as an invaluable means of pointing out and correcting mistakes and improving the accomplishments of the revolutionary process.

B. Tasks

We believe that the present revolutionary moment is an opportune time to truly implement the Church's option for the poor. We must remember that no historical revolutionary event can exhaust the infinite possibilities for justice and absolute solidarity of the kingdom of God. We must state that our commitment to the revolutionary process does not imply naivete, blind enthusiasm, or the creation of a new idol before which everyone must bow down unquestionably. Dignity, responsibility, and Christian freedom are essential attributes for active participation in the revolutionary process.

During this process, as in all other human undertakings, mistakes may be made and abuse may occur. Many Nicaraguans have certain concerns and fears. It is our pastoral duty to listen to the anxieties of the people whom we have served and discern the reasons behind these concerns. We must report those that are caused by abuse or negligence, and we must make certain that concerns arising from a lack of material resources and current conditions are not used demagogically.

The government has created channels that we believe will become increasingly more useful for collecting complaints about the revolutionary process. This creates the need for a dialogue, although it may be brief, and we know that not everyone shares our point of view on some concerns that we have heard and that we think are important.

1. Although the policy followed by the authorities has been that of avoiding executions or mistreatment of prisoners and appealing to the people not to take justice into their own hands, abuses have still occurred. These distressing situations have been caused by some local leaders. Our task will be to give national authorities the evidence that we have received of such abuse, confident that they will know how to correct it as the possibilities for effective control and national integration increase.

2. There is much talk about the disorder and even administrative chaos of the country, but we must remember that we are living in a time of creativity and of transition and that reconstruction is everyone's work not that of just certain sectors.

3. Insofar as the freedom of political parties is concerned, it seems to us that responsible, active participation by a majority of Nicaraguans in our current revolutionary process is most important and should occur both through the existing organizations for direct popular democracy as well as through organizations that will be created out of national dialogue. Various forces have contributed generously to the historic process, and no one should prevent their continued contribution. Leading all these forces, the *Frente Sandinista de Liberación Nacional* has clearly earned a place in history. In order to strengthen that position, the Frente's principal task is to continue calling on the whole people to make their own history through strong participation by the many in the life of the nation. This requires absolute faithfulness to the community of poor people on the part of the present leaders so as to maintain unsullied the principles of justice and the name *Sandinista*, earned in the struggle for freedom.

C. Socialism

The fear is expressed, at times with anguish, that the current process in Nicaragua is heading toward socialism. We bishops have been asked for our opinion on the matter.

If socialism, as some people imagine, becomes distorted, denying people and communities the right to decide their own destinies, and if it attempts to force people to submit blindly to the manipulation and dictates of individuals who have arbitrarily and unlawfully seized power, then we cannot accept such false socialism. We cannot accept a socialism that oversteps its limits and attempts to take away the individual's right to a religious motivation in his life or his right to express this motivation and his religious beliefs publicly, regardless of his faith. Equally unacceptable would be a denial of parents' right to educate their children according to their convictions or a denial of any other right of the human person.

If, on the other hand, socialism means, as it should, that the interests of the majority of Nicaraguans are paramount, and if it includes a model of an economic system planned with national interests in mind, that is, in solidarity with and provides for increased participation by the people, we have no objections. Any social program that guarantees that the country's wealth and resources will be used for the common good and that improves the quality of human life by satisfying the basic needs of all the people seems to us to be a just program. If socialism means the injustice and traditional inequalities between the cities and the country and between remuneration for intellectual labor and manual labor will be progressively reduced, and if it means the participation of the worker in the fruit of his labor overcoming economic alienation, then there is nothing in Christianity that is at odds with this process. Indeed, Pope John Paul II, while recently addressing the United Nations, has drawn attention to the concern arising from the radical separation of labor and ownership.

If socialism implies that power is to be exercised by the majority and increasingly shared by the organized community so that power is actually transferred to the popular classes, then it should meet nothing in our faith but encouragement and support.

If socialism leads to cultural processes that awaken the dignity of the masses and give them the courage to assume responsibility and demand their rights, then it promotes the same type of human dignity proclaimed by our faith.

Insofar as the struggle among social classes is concerned, we think that a dynamic class struggle that produces a just transformation of the social structure is one thing; however, class hatred directed against individuals is quite another matter and goes completely against the Christian duty to be guided by love.

Our faith tells us of the urgent Christian responsibility to subdue the earth and transform the land and all other means of production in order to allow people to live fully and make Nicaragua a land of justice, solidarity, peace, and freedom in which the Christian message of the kingdom of God can take on its full meaning.

We are further confident that our revolutionary process will be something original, creative, truly Nicaraguan, and in no sense imitative. For what we, together with most Nicaraguans, seek is a process that will result in a society completely and truly Nicaraguan, one that is neither capitalistic nor dependent nor totalitarian.

II. Evangelical Motivation

On various occasions in the past, we have sought to address the situation of our country in the light of the gospel (cf. our messages of January 8, 1977 and January 8, 1978). More recently, on June 2, 1979, we proclaimed the right of the Nicaraguan people to engage in revolutionary insurrection. Each time, we have relied on fidelity to the gospel and the traditional teaching of the Church.

It now falls to us again, in this new situation, to offer a word of faith and of hope concerning the present revolutionary process and how, through it, we can accomplish what the gospel requires of us.

We would like, therefore, to recall a fundamental truth of our Christian faith, one which we are rediscovering and seeing again as central in the present situation of our country and in the orientation of the process of revolutionary change.

A. Announcement of the Kingdom of God

1.   The heart of Jesus' message is the announcement of the kingdom of God, a kingdom founded on the Father's love for all mankind and in which the poor hold a special place. "Kingdom" signifies universality; nothing is outside it. Proclaiming the kingdom of God means proclaiming the God of the kingdom and his fatherly love, the foundation of solidarity among all people.

Jesus tells us that the kingdom means liberation and justice (cf. Lk 4:16–20), because it is a kingdom of life. Our need to build this kingdom is the basis for our accepting and participating in the current process, whose purpose is to ensure that all Nicaraguans truly live. Our faith in this God moves us to emphasize what we have always preached but which has now moved urgently to the fore. To believe in this God is to give life to others, to love them in truth and to do justice. The particular life that God wants for Nicaraguans can only be achieved by radically overcoming the selfishness and casting aside the self-interest that have festered in our country for so many years and have, we must tragically recall, caused the deaths of our brothers and sisters. Each of us must be made to live a life of love and justice, to forget about ourselves, and to consider what we can contribute.

B. Evangelical Commitment

2.   To announce the kingdom means that we have to bring it into our lives. On that effort, the authenticity of our faith in God is staked, establishing what the holy Scriptures call "justice and right" for the poor. It is commitment that tests our faith in Christ, who gave his life to proclaim the kingdom of God. There is no life of faith unless there is witness to it, which is given in our acts. Only then can the announcement through the word be understood and be confirmed. In our commitment to help the poor and to fight against social injustice, our faith becomes truly productive, for others as well as for ourselves. By acting as Christians, we become Christians. Without such solidarity, our announcement of the Good News is but an empty phrase. An evangelical movement of liberation implies a commitment to the liberation of our people. In the words of the bishops at Puebla, "Confronted with the realities that are part of our lives today, we must learn from the gospel that in Latin America we cannot truly love our fellow human beings, and hence God, unless we commit ourselves on the personal level, and in many cases on the structural level as well . . ." (*Puebla*, 327). After a long and patient wait, our people have committed themselves to the struggle for their full and total liberation.

C. Liberation in Jesus Christ

3.   Liberation in Jesus Christ encompasses the various aspects of human existence because God wants people to live and to live fully. He thus created humanity according to a plan in which our relationships with nature, with our fellows, and with God are linked closely together. First is the relationship with nature, whereby human beings can satisfy their most elemental needs. Harnessing it through a planned economy to the benefit of humankind forms the basis for a just society. There is also the relationship between individuals in society, which must be marked by fellowship implying genuine brotherhood and effective participation by all in the society to which they belong. For us today, this must be primarily the work of justice for the oppressed and an effort to liberate those who need it most (cf. *Puebla*, 327). Yet, liberation also signifies a relationship with God. As children who accept and live in the light of his freely given love, we are inextricably linked to nature and to society. When we reject our fellow man, we

reject God himself. The act of love for the poor and oppressed is an act of love for the Lord himself (cf. Mt 25:31–46). Complete liberation encompasses these three, mutually inclusive, aspects. In neglecting one of them, we diminish the rights and the potential of the human person. In accepting the free gift of the Father, we are committing ourselves to the struggle for justice and the establishment of brotherhood. This, in turn, acquires its full significance in the acknowledgment of the presence in history of God's liberating love.

D. Social Commitment

4.   The kingdom of God, the heart of Christ's message, is at the same time a requirement for social commitment, which incorporates a critical judgment of history and refuses to deny change. It is open to human creativity and to the outpouring of the Lord's grace.

The situation in our country today offers an exceptional opportunity for announcing and for bearing witness to God's kingdom. If, through fear and mistrust, or through the insecurity of some in the face of any radical social change, or through the desire to defend personal interests, we neglect this crucial opportunity to commit ourselves to the poor, urged by both Pope John Paul II and the bishops at Puebla, we would be in serious violation of the gospel's teachings.

This commitment implies the renunciation of old ways of thinking and behaving and the dramatic conversion of our Church. Indeed, the day when the Church fails to present the appearance of poverty and to act as the natural ally of the poor will be the day she has betrayed her divine creator and the coming of God's kingdom. Never before has Nicaragua been faced with such an urgent need to confirm persuasively this commitment to the poor.

The poor of whom Jesus speaks and who surround him are the truly poor, the hungry, the afflicted, the oppressed, and all those for whom society has failed to provide a place. Through this solidarity with the poor, Jesus proclaimed his Father's love for all humankind, was persecuted, and died.

E. Preferential Option for the Poor

5.   Brothers and sisters of Nicaragua, our faith in Jesus and in the God of Life must enlighten our Christian commitment in the current revolutionary process. The first contribution of the Church and of each Nicaraguan is the preference for the poor; thus, each should support the measures and laws that bring the poor out of their oppression, restoring their rights and strengthening the institutions that assure their freedom. We cannot and must not close our eyes to the dangers and possible errors inherent in any historical process of change;

indeed, we believe that we must clearly and boldly lay them bare, working from the gospel, whose word it is our task and responsibility to spread. But we are convinced that this commitment will be authentic only if we listen humbly and perceptively to what the Lord is telling us through the signs of our times. We wish to share this discernment and this commitment with the entire Nicaraguan ecclesial community, where we hope to encounter a spirit and a vocation in unity with the poor, whose "evangelizing potential" we have discovered and who call the whole Church to conversion. (cf. *Puebla*, 1147)

III. The Responsibility and Challenge of Today

The eyes of Latin America and of the Latin American Church are on Nicaragua. Our revolution is occurring at a time when the Catholic Church, through the experiences of Vatican II, Medellín, and Puebla, is becoming increasingly aware of the fact that the cause of the poor is her own.

Many are the church people of this continent who have lately given clear witness to this solidarity. Aware that the revolutionary process demands generosity and sacrifice, we urge all of you, our brothers and sisters, to join with us in finding the motivation and strength in our faith so that we will be the first to accept the sacrifice and to devote ourselves to the task of building a new Nicaragua.

In the first place, the revolution requires us to undergo a profound change of heart. It also demands austerity in our lives. The war and, above all, the previous social order have left us a legacy of economic poverty, despite the richness of our country. The exodus of competent administrative personnel and the inevitable confusion when any such radical change in systems occurs, only worsen the problem.

We must be prepared to support the lean years with austerity and prevent those who must bear the consequences from being in the majority. As Christians aware of the Lord's exhortation to poverty, we must be the first to accept, joyfully and generously, this period of austerity. We are certain that it will lead to a more fully human and fraternal way of life. In this way, we will learn, as John Paul II has maintained repeatedly, that peoples' fulfillment and the satisfaction of needs are not predicated upon abundance and still less on consumerism. The human person, rather, finds fulfillment as an individual from the solidarity, which enables each person to satisfy basic material needs and to create a higher level of culture, to labor more productively and humanistically, and to achieve a peace more receptive each day to spiritual progress. At the same time, we appeal for a halt to capital flight and for increased repatriation and reinvestment. We call for more equitable international trade practices and fairer conditions for renegotiating Nicaragua's foreign debt, in the certainty that this will help alleviate the shortages and prevent much human suffering.

A. Generosity of Our Young People

The hope of this revolution lies, above all, in the youth of Nicaragua. They have shown an outpouring of generosity and valor that has astonished the world, and henceforth, they will be the principal architects of this new "civilization of love" (cf. *Puebla*, 1188), which we hope to build. It is up to them to incarnate in the revolutionary process the authentic values of the gospel. The evangelical effort of the whole Church must be channeled to them with special care.

B. Freedom in Our Apostolic Mission

We Nicaraguan bishops want no special privileges for the Church other than the ability to accomplish her evangelical mission of humble but valued service to the people. To do so, the Church desires only that "broad area of freedom that will enable it to carry out its apostolic work without interference. That work includes the practice of cultic worship, education in the faith, and the fostering of those many and varied activities that lead the faithful to implement the moral imperatives deriving from the faith in their private, family, and social life" (*Puebla*, 144). The people of God must become revitalized through the basic Christian communities, which create a growing sense of fellowship. The Church must learn and teach others to see things from the perspective of the poor, whose cause is that of Christ. By adopting the cause of all Nicaraguans as her own, the Church believes that she will be able to make an important contribution to the process that the country is now experiencing.

May the Virgin of the Magnificat, who sings of the fall of the powerful and the exaltation of the humble (cf. Lk 2:52), guide us and help us in fulfilling our role in the arduous and exciting task of building a new Nicaragua in this hour when the commitment to the poor makes it possible to "create new horizons of hope" (*Puebla*, 1165).

Managua
November 17, 1979

Archbishop Miguel Obando Bravo
Managua

Bishop-Prelate Pablo A. Vega M.
Juigalpa

Bishop Rubén López Ardón
Esteli

Bishop Manuel Salazar Espinoza
Leon

Bishop Leovigildo López Fitoria
Granada

Bishop Julián Barni
Matagalpa

Bishop Salvador Schlaefer
Bluefields Viacriate

Nicaragua
Eucharist: Fount of Unity
(1986)

Between the time of the bishops' pastoral letter of 1979, urging cooperation in the rebuilding process, and the present pastoral letter, great debates raged in Nicaragua over the role of the Church. In Managua alone, some 2,300 articles, editorials, and commentaries about religion in Nicaragua appeared in eighteen months in the three daily newspapers of Managua.

The bishops utter a cry: "Enough of blood and death. The blood shed by so many Nicaraguans cries to Heaven." They argue: "It is essential for Nicaraguans, free from foreign interference or ideologies, to find a way out of the situation our country is experiencing."

The bishops continue: "We hold that every form of aid, no matter where it comes from, that leads to destruction, sorrow, and death in our families, to hate and division among Nicaraguans, is to be condemned."

Ultimately, the bishops plead for unity and reconciliation "through opportune dialogue and sincere rectification of past mistakes."

To the priests and deacons of our diocese; to the men and women religious; to all our beloved faithful; and to men and women of good will. The grace and peace of God, our Father, and of our Lord Jesus Christ be with you (cf. Eph 1:2).

Dear Brothers and Sisters:

We call on the grace and power of the resurrected Lord, that our word may be a reflection of his Spirit, which we call on to enlighten the hearts of all Nicaraguans during this year that, today, we officially proclaim the "Eucharistic Year."

We want this Eucharistic Year to serve as a preparation for the National Eucharistic Congress that will be celebrated the last week of the liturgical year.

No mystery of our faith seems more fitting than the Eucharist, whether to renew the spiritual vigor of the community and the strength of every Christian, or to confirm the unity of the diverse groups within that community.

May the people of God express and joyfully celebrate the mystery of the mystical Body of Christ during this time. May they discover in the Eucharist the resources and the fortitude to bring unity and concord to all Nicaraguans.

Jesus is our Peace, he who has battered down the walls of enmity and reconciled all with God in one Body on the cross (cf. Eph 2:14–15).

It is he who, really present in the Eucharist with his Body, Blood, Soul, and Divinity, offers himself in sacrifice for the salvation of the human race and gives himself to us as food and strength to fulfill his own mission in the world.

I. The Eucharist: Unity and Reconciliation

A. *The Eucharist, Sacrament of Unity and Reconciliation*

The Eucharist is the living reality of God among us. Thus, it is also the living fountain of love that can and should unite us. The reconciliation of Nicaraguans, something to be hoped for we think, should spring from the only source that is capable of producing it, the Heart of Christ—fount of mercy and pardon, of unity and charity—which in the Eucharist opens to us in all its redemptive power and all its liberating force.

Let us receive the fount of peace, and we will create peace. Let us receive the fount of pardon, and we will bring about reconciliation. Let us be united to God in Jesus Christ, and God, who is the Father, will teach us to be brothers and sisters. Let us keep our hearts open, praying and participating in that mystery of love that makes up the Church, which is united with Christ so that with everyone participating of the same bread, we make up one Body.

B. *The Church, Sign and Instrument of Unity and Reconciliation*

The Nicaraguan Church wants to be a sign and witness that unity among Nicaraguans is possible and wishes to be an efficacious instrument in bringing it about.

This service summarizes the mission proper to the Church, called to point out and offer the means, the way, to reconciliation, which are "the conversion of the heart and victory over sin, whether that be selfishness or injustice, prepotency or exploitation of others, the attachment to material goods or the frenzied search for pleasure (*Reconciliation and Penance*, 8).

We know that in the course of history, the Church has met with obstacles in carrying out this unavoidable mission. His Holiness, John Paul II, on the occasion of the celebration of the feast of the Immaculate Conception, said: "You know very well, dearly beloved bishops, that you have been specifically given the ministry and the word of reconciliation (cf. 2 Cor 5:18–19). "Beloved brethren, you are especially aware of this obligation as you have shown by addressing a *Pastoral Letter on Reconciliation* to the Catholics of Nicaragua on April 22, 1984, on the occasion of the Feast of the Resurrection. I am sure that you will continue faithfully to fulfill the mission Christ has given you."

We are aware that national reconciliation will not come about by simple readjustments, but that there must be an authentic transformation that includes all the people in the determination of their destiny [and that] it is not the rights or aspirations of any political group that we wish to defend or praise, but those of all, and concretely, our brothers and sisters of Nicaragua. It is this person, concretely, our Nicaraguan brother or sister, who is the object of our preoccupation (cf. pastoral letter of the Nicaraguan bishops, *On the Principles Governing Political Activity of the Whole Church, as Such*, March 19, 1972).

We are convinced that reconciliation will be possible only through dialogue. The dialogue of which we speak is not a tactical truce giving time to reenforce positions so as to carry on the struggle better, but rather a sincere effort to seek opportune solutions for the misery, the sorrow, the weariness, and the fatigue of so many people who aspire to peace. So many who wish to live, to be reborn from the ashes, to live again the warmth of a child's smile, far from terror and in an atmosphere of democratic sharing. The violence must be buried. Enough of violence! It has caused so many victims in this and other nations (cf. John Paul II, *Visit to San Salvador*, March 6, 1983).

Today, we wish to encourage Nicaraguans to assume the responsibility that pertains to each of you in making reconciliation, unity, and peace possible in Nicaragua.

II. Ecclesial Unity and Reconciliation

A. A Living Church

We have seen with joy the solidity and the depth of faith of our people in general. They are faithful to their religious beliefs and traditions. They cultivate the love of the Eucharist and of the Blessed Virgin. They recognize and accept their legitimate shepherds, with a proven loyalty to them and to the person of the Holy Father, in spite of the institutionalized ideological pressure and the scandalous disobedience of some clergy.

We live in a privileged time when the Holy Spirit is renovating the Church, renewing its strength, making it capable of carrying out its universal mission. We note with hope the growth in priestly and religious vocations and the existence of a lay people that seeks to live its Christianity with greater fullness and responsibility. We know of the intense life of prayer and the courage of many Catholics who give witness of their faith and are disposed to give their life for Christ and for their Church.

We thank God for the love and mercy that the Lord has shown to Nicaragua, and we beg the faithful to remain strong in their faith.

Along with this reality, there exists, however, a sector of the Church that is the object of our pastoral preoccupation, and we call on them to return to reconciliation and unity.

B. A Church Put to the Test

A belligerent group of priests, religious, and lay people of different nationalities, insisting on their pertinence to the Catholic Church, in reality and in fact, actively work to undermine the unity of the Church itself, collaborating in the destruction of the principles on which the unity of the faith in the Body of Christ are founded.

There is a nucleus of people, frequently sincere and well intentioned, but not any less at fault, who follow this group. Together, they are known as the "popular church." The Holy Father gave his opinion several times concerning their nature and their behavior, pointing out their errors and condemning their attitudes.

Those who make up the so-called popular church share the following characteristics:

1.   They manipulate the basic truth of our faith, giving themselves the right to reinterpret, and even rewrite, the Word of God, to shape it to their ideology and use it for their own purposes. As the Puebla document warns us: "every ideology is partial because no one group can claim to identify its aspirations with those of society as a whole" (*Puebla*, 535). "Ideologies have a tendency to absolutize the interests they uphold, the vision they propose, and the strategy they promote. In such a case, they really become 'lay religions.' People take refuge in ideology as an ultimate explanation of everything: 'In this way, they fashion a new idol, as it were, whose absolute and coercive character is maintained, sometimes unwittingly' (OA, 28)" (*Puebla*, 536).

2.   They try to undermine the unity of the Body of Christ, defying

the constituted authority of the Church with acts and attitudes of clear rebellion and protesting the most elementary measures of ecclesiastical discipline.

3. They try to lessen or undermine the faith and the loyalty of the people in their priests and bishops, in the Church as an institution, and in the very person of the Holy Father, inventing or spreading accusations and calumnies of all kinds or divulging them in communications media largely financed by groups contrary to the Church or that the state itself places at their disposition.

They try especially to present the bishops as persecutors of the clergy and as allies, pawns, and proponents of the imperialistic plans of the United States, and the Holy Father as the executor of such plans.

4. They try to divide the Church by internally fomenting the "class struggle" of Marxist ideology. They attempt to identify the Church with the interests of the powerful, reserving to themselves that they applaud the expulsions of priests who have given a great part of their lives serving and living among the poorest and most marginated of the people.

C. Ecclesial Reconciliation

Without excluding anyone, we invite these brothers and sisters to reconsider their errors and attitudes, to renew their loyalty and correct their ways, to avoid what today is a splintering and a distancing within the community, but may one day become complete division and schism.

In the same way, we warmly invite all the people of God—priests, religious, and lay people—to strengthen their unity with their shepherds by celebrating the Eucharist and expressing their communion, abhorring negative or indifferent attitudes, which lessen the unity of Christ's Church.

"I appeal to you, brothers, for the sake of our Lord Jesus Christ, to make up the differences between you and, instead of disagreeing among yourselves, to be united again in your belief and practice" (1 Cor 1:10).

"So be very careful about the sort of lives you lead. Do not act like senseless people, but be intelligent. This may be a wicked age, but your lives should redeem it" (Eph 5:15–16).

"Thus, all the sons and daughters of the Church should try, in this historic moment for Nicaragua and the Church in this country, to help keep the communion with your shepherds strong, avoiding every trace of breach or division" (John Paul II, *Letter to the Nicaraguan Bishops,* June 29, 1982).

III. Unity and National Reconciliation

A. The Church Opts for Humanity

The Church, tested from within, is also being tested from without. There is an attempt to take away its legitimacy and subjugate it in the midst of applause, while the unwary are bombarded by institutionalized lies and half truths.

It is accused of keeping silence, while it is silenced by taking away its radio station, and in the communications media, the news of attacks and its words of defense are censored.

The only thing left to the Church is to raise its voice in favor of peace, but when it tries by way of reconciliation and dialogue, it is calumniated and battled because this is not seen as a moral orientation but as the manipulation of a declaration.

When it risks making itself heard, those who admit hearing its word criticize it, not for what it has said, but for what it *should* have said and did not.

The Church is accused of practicing politics, while at the same time the demand is made that it pronounce on the most delicate questions of national and international politics.

In this situation, we insist that our Church choose only to be for humanity: for all Nicaraguans.

B. The Church, Worker for Peace

In favor of this humanity, because "we cannot silence what we have seen or heard" (Acts 3:20), we raise our voice to say: enough of blood and death! The blood shed by so many Nicaraguans cries to Heaven!

It is urgent and essential for Nicaraguans, free from foreign interference or ideologies, to find a way out of the situation our country is experiencing.

Today, we reaffirm with renewed emphasis what we already said in our April 22, 1984, *Pastoral Letter on Reconciliation:* "Foreign powers are profiting from our situation for their own economic and ideological benefit. They maintain us as an object of support for their power, without respecting our person, our history, our culture, or our right to decide our own destiny. The result is that the majority of the Nicaraguan people live in fear of the present and insecurity concerning the future. They experience profound frustration, and demand peace and freedom. But their voice is not heard, smothered as it is by the war propaganda of one side or the other."

We hold that every form of aid—no matter where it comes from—that leads to destruction, sorrow, and death in our families, to hate and division among Nicaraguans, is to be condemned. To choose the annihilation of the enemy as the only way to peace is, inevitably, to choose war.

The Church is the first source of peace and tries to build it through conversion and penance.

C. The Judgment of History

With the passage of time, passions cool and people see more clearly how imprudent and irresponsible were the arguments or reasons on which they founded their intransigence and political precedents for avoiding dialogue and thrusting our people into war.

Before the judgment of history, all the fraticidal wars of the past could have been avoided, and none brought a solution that could not have been reached through opportune dialogue and a sincere rectification of respective mistakes.

Today, the reasons given to justify wars suffered by Nicaragua throughout its history seem unjustifiable.

If, in all these situations of conflict, the spirit of concord and reconciliation had prevailed, if the political interests and the brutal realities of war were weighed with a Christian criterion, how much destruction, how many deaths, how many exiles, how much hate would have been avoided.

Thus, this vision that time gives, this serenity that history could teach us, this recognition of the damage and the capacity for correction offered by the Christian conscience are very necessary today so as not to repeat the mistakes of the past.

To build a new history means to bring about peace, where our fathers blundered into wars. It means stressing the love of brothers and sisters, where formerly we were plagued with hate.

Today, we are again in a situation of war, but it is possible to avoid it if those defending positions in the struggle thought about their historic responsibility not to increase the portion of sorrow and death brought to the Nicaraguan family.

D. Conquer Evil with Good

The root of all evil is definitely rooted in the heart of man, and evil produces in the mind and heart of the people an irreversible damage.

Confronted with the dehumanizing effect of a fraticidal war, which not only kills our youth on the battlefield but is already killing and destroying all our better human and moral values, rooted in our profound Christian tradition, we raise our voice to say that the love of Christ, the supreme manifestation of which is his cross and his Eucharist, begs us to conquer hatred with an effective love, to change the desires for vengeance into concrete gestures of repentance and pardon, to defend human life from its beginning in the mother's womb, to make language a vehicle of unity, and to respect everyone's dignity and inalienable rights.

"The option of the Christian, and even more of the priest, is at times dramatic. Though reacting strongly against error, he can not be against anyone because we are all brothers and sisters or, at least, enemies that we must love according to the gospel. He should embrace everyone, because all are sons and daughters of God, and should give his life, if necessary, for all his brothers and sisters" (John Paul II, *Speech on Reconciliation* [El Salvador] March 6, 1983).

E. Closing Exhortation

We hope that the Eucharistic Year, during which we are preparing to celebrate in a worthy manner the National Eucharistic Congress, may be an occasion of special grace, so that we Nicaraguans may be able to build peace through love, pardon, and reconciliation.

We lovingly recommended the conscious and full participation of the faithful in the Sunday Mass, in Vespers, especially on Thursday, the day our Catholic people traditionally honor Jesus in the Blessed Sacrament, as well as in vigils of prayer and penance, reciting of the Rosary, and so forth.

May this year represent a serious effort for Catholics to honor Jesus in a very special way in the Blessed Sacrament if they are interested in knowing profoundly their Catholic faith and working apostolically. These are the main objectives to accomplish in this Eucharistic Year and the best fruits of the Eucharistic Congress.

May the Blessed Virgin Mary, to whose Immaculate Heart we are consecrated, help Nicaraguans prepare the triumph of the Eucharistic Heart of this divine Son, and in this way make us worthy of receiving his merciful love, which is the only thing that can enable us to find tranquility and the fullness of order, which is authentic peace.

We trust in the fidelity and power of him who said, "Do not fear, I have conquered the world" (Jn 16:33) and just as he promised, sacramentally in the Eucharist, he is with us all days, till the end of time. Alleluia!

Haiti
Priorities and Changes
(1986)

A number of bishops, priests, and committed lay persons actively called for democracy and economic justice in Haiti—actions that contributed to the flight of the ruling Duvalier family on February 7, 1986. Since that time, the Haitian Bishops' Conference has tried to contribute to the rebuilding process. In a relatively brief time, they issued seven pastoral letters, trying to foster a national dialogue.

One of the functions the bishops sought to play is that of helping to clarify issues in a very chaotic situation. Invoking the principles of equality and justice, the bishops urge a national campaign to reduce illiteracy and other measures, such as agrarian reform and greater employment opportunities, aimed at improving the living conditions for the great majority—the poorest in the hemisphere.

Beloved Brothers and Sisters:

1. Once again assembled in the episcopal conference, the bishops of Haiti feel the necessity to address you in a pastoral message about certain urgent issues that we feel should be priorities, and certain changes that we consider essential for involving all Haitians in the work of reconstructing the country.

2. As we underlined in our last Message of March 7, 1986: "The principal personage in Haiti is the Haitian people. It is they who must be at the center of all concerns. It is toward serving them that all social and economic development must be structured."

3. Who are the Haitian people? The Haitian people are not an inert "mass" susceptible to being manipulated from the outside, nor an easy toy in the hands of whoever wishes to exploit them. The people are even less a vulgar mass others can bribe and push to all sorts of dishonest acts. "The life of the people depends on the fullness of life in which each person—in the place and manner that he or she deems fitting—is a conscious person, with his or her own responsibilities and convictions" (Pius XII, *Christmas Radio Message*, 1944).

4.   The Haitian people are peasants, workers, artisans, low-wage earners, unemployed, homeless, socioprofessionals, all those—literate or not, youth or adult, men or women—who have a mentality of the poor and who aspire to the construction of a Haitian community based on justice, truth, liberty, and fraternity.

5.   What are the priorities of these people? The first priority of these people is literacy. We insisted on the urgency of this at the official inauguration of the Literacy Mission on March 7, 1986. But we feel the need to restate it today.

6.   The new society to which the Haitian people aspire requires their participation in the major decisions concerning the life of the nation. The drafting of a constitution, of an electoral law, of a law on political parties, requires the participation of the people. The constitution and laws must be submitted to the nation for ratification before their official adoption. This presumes that a charter and the laws be drafted in simple terms and a language the people understand.

7.   The population must take an active part in the designation of its leaders at the rural, country, district, department, and national levels. Also the people must choose freely their chief of rural police, mayor, deputy, senator, and president.

8.   The Haitian people must be able to participate validly in the organization of the life of political parties. They must equally exercise freely their right of association: the right to organize unions, cooperatives, community groups, and so forth.

9.   Literacy, an indispensable condition for this participation, must mobilize the whole population. The government of the republic is called to contribute effectively to this project. The private sector is invited to cooperate actively.

10.   Haitians living abroad are requested especially to furnish financial aid for this project, as the Church counts on their help and asks them to offer it through the priests who serve the Christian community. As for the youth who have on several occasions expressed their enthusiasm for this mission, they are invited to participate in a special manner. We ask the competent authorities to structure the scholastic calendar so that a program for youth training allows them to dedicate the necessary time to this important work, the literacy of the people.

11.   This work is vital for the present and future of the country because it is inextricably tied to the socioeconomic development of the Haitian people. It is for this reason that we insist on underlining another extremely important priority: the urgency of agrarian reform. Four million men and women of the country draw their revenues almost exclusively from agriculture. But the socioeconomic condition of the peasants is dramatic. On the one hand, they usually do not have land; on the other hand, they are only sharecroppers who are at the mercy of all forms of exploitation and dispossession.

12.   There is a vast amount of land owned by the state, and other land improperly ceded to individuals and groups, which must be reclaimed.

13.   The primary objective of agrarian reform ought to be equitable distribution of land to peasants who can manage it responsibly and who will make it bear fruit. The agrarian reform must assure the protection of the peasant, for as we wrote in *The Charter of the Church for Human Promotion,* public powers have as their mission to "protect the peasant from expropriation, assure them of their land titles, regulate the condition of farming and sharecropping, and make fallow land productive by distributing it to the poorest" (cf. art. 37, par. a, b, d).

14.   A third priority concerns the problems of employment. For many years, the standard of living in Haiti has been dropping in a disturbing fashion, and this deterioration has struck the poorest sector very hard. Less than 22 percent of the urban population earns a salary. The unemployment percentage is enormous. Added to this is the fact that recent reduction of prices is still far from corresponding to the real level of salaries.

In brief, unemployment and the disproportion between salaries and prices contribute to the diminishing buying power of households. It is of the greatest urgency to lower the price of essential consumer products. To fight unemployment, industrial and agricultural production must be encouraged for the local market, and a program of public works must be initiated with great urgency: road construction and repair, reforestation, construction of schools, sanitation works, and so forth.

15.   In this perspective, a problem exists in the glaring disparity of incomes of the large majority of the population who live below absolute poverty level, while a small minority absorbs a considerable part of the national wealth.

16.   A political will is required for the development of the country. This should respond to the will of the people in line with the priorities that we just enumerated:

- priority of literacy to permit the people to participate truly in the life of the nation;
- priority of agrarian reform to give peasants access to land ownership and stability in working and managing the land;
- priority of employment to help the buying power of both urban and rural populations, and to encourage local production.

But this political will can only become an effective reality to the extent there is a profound change in the system of government and in the mentality of the people.

17. It is true that since February 7, there has been a change of a few individuals, but there has not been any change in the political system. It is equally certain that some efforts have been made to abolish some taxes, to lower the prices of certain products, but it does not appear that, beyond these measures, there has been any policy change in socioeconomic areas.

18. How do we, in these conditions and realizing these priorities, respond to the needs of the population? There must be a change of mentality, a new vision that calls for a new way of acting.

19. Under the former regime, the life of the country was organized in the realm of one individual, one family, one group. The people were forced to submit to the authority of one chief. Everything revolved around the individual good.

20. In the new regime, the life of the country must be organized to serve the whole population. Authority must be at the service of the people. Everything must be structured toward the realization of the common good.

21. This is the only way to respond to the expectations of the people. To succeed, certain immediate measures should be implemented:

- The public administration must be purified from corrupt elements of the regime, because corruption engenders favoritism, despotism, waste, bribes, and theft—all vices that corrode the foundation of any will toward progress.

- There must be a decentralization of political, economic, and social power to promote the development of the provinces. Toward this end, regionalization must be favored, with a relative autonomy of counties, provinces, and departments and a financial equalizing of the different administrative divisions.

- We must have a deep sense of humankind, of its dignity, of its rights, of its responsibilities; of respect for its person; of its legitimate aspirations, favoring honesty, righteousness, and loyalty and eradicating mistrust, back-stabbing, lies, scams, or the dubious combinations of these.

22. The event of February 7 summons us all. It presents us with a decisive turning point in our history. There can be no question of our failing to make this turn. The youth have given us proof that they were bearers of ideals—ideals of beauty, courage, and solidarity. The people as a whole give witness to an unshakable faith and an invincible hope for the future. They surmounted obstacles and overturned barriers.

Beloved Brothers and Sisters: From here on we must construct a strong and prosperous nation, toward which the first steps have been taken by the youth and the people. To succeed, we must arm ourselves with courage and confidence to bring about in us the necessary changes and to make the priorities of our people a reality in our society.

With the help of the Virgin Mary, Mother of Perpetual Help, following Christ the liberator, let us be firm in faith, diligent in prayer, and united in love.

Episcopal Conference of Haiti
Port-au-Prince
April 11, 1986

Francois Gayot
Bishop of Cap-Haitien
President of C.E.H.

Willy Romelus
Bishop of Jeremie
President of C.E.H.

Frantz Colimon
Bishop of Port-de-Paix

Petion Laroche
Bishop of Hinche

Francois Wolff Ligonde
Archbishop of Port-au-Prince

Emmanuel Constant
Bishop of Gonaives

Alix Verrier
Coadjutor Bishop of Cayes

Haiti
Christmas Message
(1987)

Jean Claude Duvalier, president-for-life, fled Haiti in February 1986, but the underlying system under which he ruled did not depart the country. This did not become immediately evident, as political prisoners were freed, the secret police disbanded, and the press allowed freedom. And in March 1987, the Haitian people turned out to vote solidly in favor of the new constitution.

So, with shock, the bishops and the people witnessed the long-awaited elections of November 1987. They watched in horror as the Tonton Macoute (former secret police) killed scores of voters. The violence and the unstable politics added further misery to a very difficult economic situation.

In a letter issued the next day, the bishops ask that the Haitian people be allowed to choose their leaders freely and not be treated as children or slaves. The bishops call for trust and safety as necessary conditions for voting. They petition for the end to the smear campaign conducted against the Church. They appeal for unity of the Haitian people, as a basic value.

1.   In almost all parts of the world, people are preparing to celebrate Christmas.

2.   In Haiti, on the other hand, at the end of 1987, we are living a sorrowful situation of confusion that creates anxiety and anguish:

- How can Haitian families, dislocated by an exodus; overwhelmed by the disappearance of a child, a father, a mother; afflicted by deaths; celebrate Christmas?

- How can the poor, without food, without clothing, without shelter, without means of subsistence, celebrate Christmas?

- How can the children and the young, left to their own resources, living from day to day, deprived of everything, without future, without hope, celebrate Christmas?

3.   How to celebrate Christmas in Haiti in this year 1987? How to celebrate Christmas in this climate of fear and insecurity? How to

celebrate Christmas in this atmosphere of lying, discord, division, and hate?

4.   Still, Christian hope lives in our hearts, and "this hope will not leave us disappointed" (Rom 5:5). It must sustain us and comfort us to the end. We must celebrate Christmas this year as a special appeal to God to revivify our hope.

5.   When the Christians of the first centuries suffered persecution, Saint Peter, in his First Letter, invited them to be ever ready to give a reason for the hope that is within (cf. 1 Pt 3:15). Following his example, we urge you to reflect with us now on the reasons for the hope that is within us and the manner by which we can revivify this hope.

Reasons for Our Hope

6.   The first reason for our hope is the presence of God among us. Indeed, Christmas is the birth of a very small child who is God and who submits to a treatment unworthy of the human condition (cf. Phil 2:7). He is rejected, persecuted, and obliged to go into exile to escape a massacre. "Though he was in the form of God, he did not deem equality with God something to be grasped at. Rather, he emptied himself and took the form of a slave. . . ." (Phil 2:6–7). In this state of abasement, God directed his Son through ways incomprehensible to us, but which led to the realization of his plan of salvation for all persons. God did not abandon his Son in this state of abjection in which he found himself. Neither can God abandon us in this distressing situation in which we find ourselves.

7.   God's fidelity to his plan of salvation is the second reason for our hope. Everything possible was done to make this child disappear. The great and the powerful of that time tried to thwart God's plan, but "God who is mighty has done great things . . . holy is his name; his mercy is from age to age on those who fear him. He has shown might with his arm; he has confused the proud in their inmost thoughts. He has deposed the mighty from their thrones and raised the lowly to high places" (Lk 1:49–52).

8.   God reversed the Devil's project. God accomplished his plan of salvation in Christ, who was born in a stable in Bethlehem, and through Christ, who lives with us all the events that we undergo today in his Body, which is the Church. For he is Emmanuel: God-with-us.

9.   In the situation in our country today, the Haitian people, threatened in their existence and in their legitimate aspirations, live the mystery of this Emmanuel, poor child, rejected and persecuted. This is the third reason for our hope.

10.   Strong with this hope brought by Christ, we have the certainty that God has not abandoned us, that he is present among us, and that he lives with us.

To Revivify Our Hope

11.   We invite you, then, to interiorize more deeply the mystery of Christmas. We continue to ask that you stress the spiritual dimension of the mystery. Often, one is tempted to reduce the celebration of Christmas to its profane and commercial aspects, which reveal themselves in noisy external manifestations: festivities, decorations, illuminations, midnight parties, singing of carols, and so forth. In this way, one drains away the spiritual content of the feast of peace, of reconciliation, of life, and of love.

12.   Everyone—Christians and persons of good will—we are all compelled to enter into ourselves and to make a true examination of conscience. Faced with so many crimes, the disquieting depreciation of the sacred character of life and of the human person, we ask ourselves:

- How can one kill, in cold blood, human beings, simply because they belong to another group?

- How can one destroy the life of a child, of an old man, of an old woman, who are defenseless?

- How can one trifle with human life to the point of assassinating weak human beings and leaving them on the roadsides?

13.   How far away we are from the message of life brought at Christmas by him who "has come that we might have life and life in abundance." How far we are away from the message of love brought by the Messiah-Savior, who came to tell us that we are all brothers and sisters, that the Father wants the happiness of all in his kingdom of truth, of justice, of love, and of peace. A kingdom that must begin here below.

14.   Faced with the deterioration of the situation in Haiti, some are discouraged: "there is nothing that can be done in this country," they say. They think that all hope is irretrievably lost. Others, confronted with ineffectual efforts and the failures of their efforts, try to drown their sorrow in drugs or alcohol or plan their escape in the form of voluntary exile, telling themselves: "we can foresee no future in this country." Still others, see themselves giving rise to sentiments of revolt and consider violence as the only means of changing the situation. None of these sentiments can solve the problems of this country. . . .

20.   On this feast of Christmas 1987, we beg you our beloved brothers and sisters: "Do not be surprised, beloved, that a trial by fire is occurring in your midst. It is a test for you, but it should not catch you off guard. Rejoice instead in the measure that you share Christ's sufferings. When his glory is revealed, you will rejoice exultantly. Happy are you when you are insulted for the sake of Christ, for then God's Spirit in its glory has come to rest on you. See to it that none of you suffers for being a murderer, a thief, a malefactor, or a destroyer of another's rights. But, if anyone suffers for being a Christian, however, he ought not to be ashamed" (1 Pt 4:12–16).

21.   We ask you, then, brothers and sisters, not to let yourselves fall into despair. On the contrary, we wish that you will live as men and women of hope: that is, to renounce lies to live in truth; to renounce hate to live in love; to renounce violence to live in peace and fraternity. This is our most sincere wish, and, for its realization, we remain with you in union of thought and of prayer.

May Mary, sign of sure hope and sign of consolation for God's people on pilgrimage, walk with you toward him who is our way, our light, and our life—Jesus Christ, our Lord.

Episcopal Conference of Haiti
December 20, 1987
Fourth Sunday of Advent

Chile
The Rebirth of Chile
(1982)

This brief statement reflects the starkness of the period. By 1982, Chile had reached probably the lowest point in its contemporary history. The economic situation worsened to the extent that leading financial institutions found themselves on the brink of bankruptcy. Unemployment increased, production diminished, sectors of the work force were eliminated, wages dropped, and foreign debt grew. In the streets, the poor were to be seen everywhere.

Chileans faced other crises, including the elimination of such intermediate structures as political parties and labor unions and the loss of democratic institutions. Many Chileans felt a sense of insecurity and disquiet. The bishops decried the crises and searched for constructive responses.

1. A Word of Warning and of Hope

As many Chileans, we, the bishops of Chile, are concerned about the difficult moment our country is passing through. Having exhausted private efforts and fearing events may rush headlong down the road to violence, we feel impelled to speak a word of warning and of hope. From our perspective as Christians and as pastors, we wish to help Chile find a constructive solution to the present crisis.

2. Economic Crisis

This is the most visible and indisputable crisis: high unemployment, the collapse of production, the elimination of important sectors of the work force, a drop in real wages, high interest rates, an excessive foreign debt, and a low rate of investment all add up to a very serious problem.

In addition to the national economic crisis, we are also affected by the world recession, which has brought about a loss of credibility and confidence in economic policy, making it even more difficult to overcome the problem.

3. Social Crisis

The economic crisis is accompanied by a profound social crisis that is manifest in growing misery, signs of violence, insecurity, and fear. Independent, intermediate organizations have been destroyed or dissolved, and the communications media are limited by censorship.

4. Institutional Crisis

The participation of all in the search for the common good is a basic principle of the Church's social doctrine. And government authorities should promote participation. Unfortunately, the disappearance of democratic structures has left the majority of Chileans without any real possibility of participation.

In the area referred to as integral respect for human rights, the 1980 Constitution is not observed. This is, in part, due to the implementation of the "transitory articles." Legislation establishing the full exercise of democracy has yet to be implemented. "The rights of authority," says John Paul II, "cannot be understood in any way that is not based on respect for the objective, inviolable rights of the human person" (RH, 17).

5. Moral Crisis

This is the most important and the cause of all the others. The loss of fundamental Christian values has done violence to Chilean tradition and has led to current tensions. Outrages against human dignity, the unjust constraints to which some prisoners are submitted, the exile of others, unrestrained economic liberalism, speculation instead of honest work, and the coexistence of extravagance and misery all confirm this loss of values.

There are some who seek a solution in Marxism, even in its atheistic and totalitarian expression. Others silently nurture rancor and await the moment of revenge. Still others, having lost hope in the democratic way, opt for violence. All these postures make the peaceful resolution of the crisis difficult.

6. A Christian Solution

Faced with the situation described, we want to participate in the search for a constructive solution while there is still time. As Christians, we know that suffering, when it is honestly taken upon oneself, is the seed of resurrection. We hope that the suffering of the unemployed, of so many families, so many youths—the suffering of Chile—will open a new way to us.

This is possible. Failures and frustrations teach us to be humble, to listen to our former adversaries, to mistrust easy success, and to value spiritual wealth.

7. Three Conditions

The rebirth of Chile requires three basic conditions:

a) *Respect for human dignity.* Each Chilean is a child of God, unique and irreplaceable. The life, freedom, and opinion of the other merit respect, even when he or she does not think as we do. The country belongs to everyone, and we must learn to share it as brothers and sisters.

b) *Recognition of the value of work.* Work is the human element in the economy and should guide all economic policy. Let there be work for all, as well as just wages for that work. Let no one live extravagantly while there are brothers and sisters in such need. Let us give the example of a modest life style. Let the state actively seek the common good and hear the just desires and needs of all.

c) *The return to full democracy.* Democracy has been the Chilean tradition. Thanks to that tradition, we lived in peace for many years and were respected throughout the world. The abuses that may have been present do not justify so long an interruption of the normal life of the nation. This is not healthy and has led to consequences that we now lament. To open the way to political participation is an urgent task. It should be undertaken before the level of tension provokes a possible tragedy.

8. There Is Always Hope

In spite of the negative signs, we invite all to hope. Hope is an essentially Christian virtue. It is based on the certainty we have that, in the death of Jesus Christ, God has assumed all our sufferings and failures, and in his resurrection, he has conquered every evil. His life is more powerful than death.

We Chileans have suffered long enough, and we will not forget the lessons learned during this time. We are capable of forgiving each other and of building a nation of brothers and sisters based on Christian principles.

We want to work and to produce, in order to overcome our economic problems. We need more free space to participate and take responsibility for the future of the country. We believe that generosity conquers hate and that wisdom solves more than violence.

The Holy Father has invited us to celebrate a "holy year of redemption" in 1983. We Chileans can give a fine response to that invitation. We have been Christians for 400 years and want to be faithful to our commitment.

The Virgin of Carmen, mother of the Chilean people and patroness of the armed forces, has shown throughout our history that she can unite us. To her, we send our invocations, at this crossroads in the history of our country.

The Bishops of Chile
Punto de Tralca
December 17, 1982

Chile
Lent and National Life
(1987)

Many Chileans looked forward to the visit of John Paul II to their country just before Holy Week 1987. A series of incidents preceded the pope's visit, including statements by Bishop Carlos Camus condemning the repressive nature of the political and social environment.

The bishops' conference through its Administrative Board, emboldened by the impending visit, issued statements, one of which is included here. Statements made in Chile by Pope John Paul II reinforced the bishops' pastoral communications.

The bishops comment on events affecting Chilean Catholics. They spoke more strongly than they had for some time, emphasizing the government's need for "morally valid" consultation with the Chilean people about the structuring of national political life.

Dear Brothers and Sisters:

At the moment when Lent, a time of conversion, is just beginning; when the activities proper to summer come to an end and the pastoral year begins again; as the hour draws closer when the Holy Father will tread the ground of our homeland for the first time; we wish to express our opinion, as pastors, concerning some recent events that affect our national life.

The Firing of Teachers

Throughout the country, there have been several thousand teachers fired recently. We understand that there might be just motives why some teachers must be fired. But we consider that, when it is a question of professionals whose vocation is to teach, and they have no other, and they have families who must live, one cannot have massive dismissals for purely budgetary reasons.

We are not going to discuss whether there are too many teachers or whether there are too many students per teacher; whether the decrease in the birth rate should necessarily lead to a reduction in teaching positions or whether, on the contrary, the improvement of education should require added teaching personnel; nor what is the percentage of the national budget that ought to be dedicated to education, taking into account the common interest of all Chileans. Whatever the case, measures that mean cutting off a professional career dedicated by vocation to a noble and difficult task and leaving a family without resources for survival should be the subject of dialogue with those involved or with their union leaders, in a spirit of equity and respect, and not just an economic criterion.

A family whose resources have diminished for some reason does not just decide that from today on, some of the children will have to stop eating. The situation is talked over among all the members and the imposed deprivations are shared equitably among all. We believe that, in the case of the great Chilean family of teachers, it would have been fitting to act in the same manner. And we hope that at least some of the most dramatic cases can be reconsidered.

We have been deeply preoccupied at seeing the climate of insecurity and even fear that the measures taken have produced among teachers and believe that this is prejudicial for national education. We also think measures such as these lend themselves to arbitrariness when it is a question of deciding who should resign their functions.

The Declarations of Former Army Major Armando Fernandez Larios

One of our former army officers has made declarations that seriously compromise high officials within the armed forces. A crime was planned. This crime was committed. Then the crime itself was covered up.

The country's moral welfare and the Chilean Army's prestige demand that this subject be clarified totally, not only at the level of the Courts of Justice but, above all, by the institutions to which the accused belong or belonged. Given human weakness, we could understand that members of the armed forces, just like those of any other institution, might commit abuses, especially in politically difficult circumstances. But the country needs to know that the institution itself is trying seriously to clarify the criminal acts and sanction those who are proved guilty.

Public Services

It worries us that some public services are lessening or terminating their service to distant places because the service is not economically profitable. This situation will worsen on the day these same services are handed over to the private sector. This is happening, for example, in the mail service. Post offices in the small towns are being closed, so that the inhabitants are left isolated as far as written correspondence is concerned.

We believe that the services, insofar as possible, should be extended to all and that the most profitable sectors should underwrite the less profitable. A large portion of the inhabitants of our country do not earn enough even to pay indispensable costs. The public services—education, health, communication, transportation—help to redistribute resources to the benefit of the poorest and the most isolated. It does not seem suitable for a purely economic criterion to replace the social solidarity that has been traditional in our country.

The Handing Over of National Enterprises to the Private Sector

We are also preoccupied, like many other Chileans, by the handing over of important enterprises, which make up part of the national patrimony, to the private sector. At the very least, these bids should be made with maximum transparency, and the country should be kept informed as to the use to which the income from these sales is destined.

Political Laws

We neither are nor pretend to be technicians in electoral records or political parties. We do rejoice at any step taken toward full participation by the Chilean people in the realization of its historical destiny. Some judge that the recently promulgated laws are good. Others do not consider their hopes fulfilled. Whatever the case, the Chilean people want to be sure that, when the moment arrives for the country to be consulted about its future, it can express its opinion in possession of all necessary information and with complete freedom and be assured that the will of the majority will be respected.

We wish to reiterate what our plenary assembly stated on the eve of the 1980 Plebiscite on the required conditions for a consultation of the people to be morally valid.

Human Rights

We do not want the bishops' relatives to receive treatment any different than anyone else. But the fact that a young woman, 18 years old (the niece of Bishop Camus), whose only crime is to be the sister of and share the apartment of a young woman sought by the police, has been subjected to mistreatment that constitutes real psychic torture makes us think of those thousands of Chileans who have suffered or are liable to suffer similar or even worse violence. Once more we say that this must come to an end.

We are told that in other countries and under other regimes the same or worse things happen and the bishops of those countries cannot even protest. For that very reason, we have the obligation of protesting for the victims here and those abroad, for yesterday's victims and tomorrow's possible victims. Once more we say: human beings must be respected because they are sons and daughters of God.

Dear Brothers and Sisters: Lent, which begins today, will be the immediate preparation for the Holy Father's visit to Chile. Let us prepare our hearts, with prayer and penitence, to receive his message of truth and justice, love and peace. And let us be disposed to keep on working so that his word, his witness, and the grace that comes to us through him may help us to overcome all our problems and reach the longed for reconciliation.

Permanent Episcopal Committee
Episcopal Conference of Chile

Paraguay
A Call for National Dialogue
(1986)

The Catholic Church in Paraguay has gone through several phases in its existence of more than thirty years under General Alfredo Stroessner's military rule. In the early years, members of the Church spoke up vigorously in opposition. In response, the government expelled some foreign priests, and the Church's opposition lessened.

As Stroessner gained increased control of many aspects of life of the country, the Church fell into a long period of silence. But now, in the last fifteen years, the Church has developed a clearer voice. The episcopal conference and individual bishops have spoken forcefully on such issues as human rights, agrarian reform, and land titles. A Call for National Dialogue *exemplifies a later development in the evolution of the bishops' teaching.*

A Message of the Paraguayan Episcopal Conference

The following pastoral letter was approved in its general assembly, signed by all members of the Bishops' Conference of Paraguay, and published on April 20, 1986. It represents a break with silence after strong protests by the hierarchy some ten years ago failed to provoke change.

Frequently, we Paraguayan bishops, fulfilling our "principal duty as teachers of truth" (cf. John Paul II, *Puebla*), personally or collectively address the national community. Our word reaches many people, always with the aim of announcing the gospel message and keeping in mind the reality of the world and of the concrete persons we are addressing.

The mission is difficult and delicate. We must be faithful to Christ and his doctrine, which is the doctrine of the Church. We must be faithful to our people, a people to which we belong. We have been sent to them by God, and we wish to, and must, serve them. That people lives amidst problems and preoccupations; labors and has hopes; suffers and becomes happy; at times is disenchanted; and always trusts it will find in its Church the understanding and support it needs.

Aware of that responsibility and that hope, all of us, bishops of the Paraguayan Episcopal Conference, sign this message and invoke the person of our beloved bishop, Juan Sinforiano Bogarín, a great bishop who, for fifty-four years, served his people as their true shepherd. Not long ago, we celebrated the hundredth anniversary of his priestly ordination, recalling his example of constant preoccupation for the Paraguayan people and their unity. For that reason, his name can never be used to encourage rancor nor confront Paraguayans one with another. His letters and pastoral visits clearly testify to that concern. His intervention to avoid conflicts, to bring an end to armed struggles, or to support the defense of our native land in the Chaco were truly magnificent. He was a bishop unafraid of acting energetically when the circumstances demanded it.

With that spirit, we have undertaken the task of attempting to bring about a great National Dialogue. That is what we wish to refer to here. We know that, ever since the announcement of the Permanent Episcopal Council of the Paraguayan Episcopal Conference last January 22, this theme is uppermost in everyone's mind. Some have offered their enthusiastic support and solidarity with the task undertaken. Others have manifested their displeasure and rejection. The fellow citizens, from the most diverse sectors of society, who have spoken out are many. And many who are sincerely worried are asking themselves what the bishops are looking for or why the Church takes an interest in these affairs. Respecting everyone's opinions, we will try to answer these questions and clarify existing doubts. We do this out of love for the truth and out of a deep affection for our brothers and sisters who live in this land, with no limitations or exclusions.

1. What Is This National Dialogue?

In the first place, it is a gesture of service the Church offers to the whole country. As "Mother" and "Teacher," the Church perceives that the situation of the country is delicate and feels obligated to do something for it. In fact, the constant confrontations and the growing disunity that we see in all sectors of national society; the deterioration of public and private morality we have been denouncing for years (see *The Moral Healing of the Nation*, 1979); and the dangerous sensation of a fragile way of life not founded on love, justice, and truth—all of this constitutes a worrisome situation that motivates our intervention. The Church does not forget that all of us, to a greater or lesser degree, are co-responsible for this situation. No one has the right to avoid his or her own responsibility. For that reason, we all have the obligation of trying to overcome the evils that afflict our country. The Church offers its service with no other aim. It does not pretend to impose a program for government, nor does it aspire to gain anything. It wishes to facilitate dialogue, support dialogue, make space for dialogue. For that reason, it undertakes a responsibility that, though difficult and delicate, is eminently evangelizing.

Dialogue is a useful means or instrument for gaining the objective proposed. We dialogue when we know how to speak and how to listen. It does not mean renouncing one's own convictions or canceling or covering up existing differences without offending anyone, without always trying to win the day, without believing that only we are always right. When we dialogue, we find we have many things in common. Thus, the Church has great faith in fraternal, respectful, humble, sincere dialogue.

The National Dialogue is a call to all sectors of opinion to analyze and study the country's problems and our responsibilities in solving them. It is an invitation. It is not limited to political parties, because we think it ought to include all the different kinds of relationships and social enterprises in which people are involved. It is addressed to all sectors that make up the national community: political, union, farm, military, professional, business, student, cultural, church, as well as family and youth. For that reason, we say it is national, because it reaches the whole country and refers to all the problems affecting Paraguayan men and women, the Paraguayan families, the national community. The good sought is the common good, not one that might interest only a part of the nation.

Dialogue is a right and an obligation of all our country's inhabitants and all sectors of our society, because we are responsible for the construction of a just and a free society. Dialogue is a continuous and growing process. It is not just a momentary need arising from a difficult situation, but rather a climate in which the relationships of a people in process of continuous growth normally develop.

2. What Is the Church Seeking in This National Dialogue?

It is obvious that the Church does not pretend to enter the arena of partisan politics, to change governments, or to dictate laws. After all, that is not its role or its intention. Neither does it pretend to form a tribunal to judge anyone nor does it wish to begin a litany of accusations. No one has any right to attribute such intentions to the Church, and those who do, do so out of ignorance of its true mission or out of self-interest, with evil intent.

The National Dialogue has as a goal the participation of all in the construction of the common good. All Paraguayans, and all who inhabit this land, are called to do something for the good of this country, to work together in the construction of the good of all. We are called to begin a new way of living, without blaming our brother or sister for all past or present evils, but rather assuming seriously and patriotically the responsibility we all bear. The aim is that the coincidences that arise through dialogue become the basis of an effective community work. We must trust the ability we have as men and women, but we must be realistic and not deceive ourselves that everything will be easy and simple.

It is opportune to call to mind the words of Pope John Paul II, addressed to the diplomatic representatives of different countries to the Holy See on January 11 of this year: "The Church commits itself with pleasure to promoting all true dialogues for peace, all forms of sincere negotiations, of loyal cooperation." The pope went on to say: "Above all, [the Church] wishes to educate consciences for openness to others, respect for others, in tolerance, which always accompanies the search for the truth, for solidarity." These words of the Supreme Pontiff express the great goal of the Church, and we believe they will help people understand that the National Dialogue is a pastoral, not a political, undertaking.

Once more, we affirm that the mission proper to the Church is to evangelize. If we assume the responsibility of convoking the National Dialogue, it is because we are convinced of the need for seeking unity, concord, and the participation of the whole Paraguayan people. This is one of the fruits of evangelization. That is the only way we can make into a reality the ideal of a society more just, more fraternal, more open to God. A society in which there are no privileged or marginated or, as we sing in the National Anthem, without oppressors or servants, but with union and equality. Finally, a society looking to the future and capable of growing in acceptance of the differences there may be among us, but without lessening fraternity, peace, and love. This is what we call living together. And this is the vehement desire of the people.

Thus, it is understandable why the Church asks for everyone's collaboration and why a petition for this intention is included in the prayer of the faithful of all the Masses. We beg all believers, Catholics or not, to support this effort of the Church with their prayers. We make a special request in this sense to the priests, the religious communities, the secular institutes, and the contemplative monasteries. We hope for the collaboration of all Paraguayan men, women, and families. Let us promote a climate of understanding and peace. Let there be no offensive words or violent attitudes. Let us avoid grudges, prejudices, and distrust. The human and Christian values of our people have been capable of producing memorable exploits throughout the history of our homeland. Those values make up the starting point.

Let us begin to walk together and work in unity for the good of our beloved Paraguay.

Our Lord's resurrection, celebrated recently in an atmosphere of joy, invites us to assume this journey with courage and hope. Today we, the Paraguayan bishops, repeat our determination to accompany and share the life of our beloved people, in whose debt we are. We perceive the ardent desires and hopes of our country's young generations, whose noble spirit and generous purpose we recognize. We have often seen evidence of our people's capacity for sacrifice and their determination when it is a question of a common work, beneficial for all. All this animates us and makes us believe that undertaking will be of real benefit to the country. For us, the bishops, the National Dialogue is a call to all sectors of the country, a gesture of service, and a means of participation. But, above all, it is also a testimony of love and giving to our noble, long-suffering people.

In that spirit, we place this initiative in motion, invoking the intercession of the Immaculate Conception of Caacupe. May the Blessed Virgin of Miracles, mother and advocate of the Paraguayan people, obtain for us from God the graces necessary to reach the proposed objectives.

Chile

I Am Jesus, Whom You Persecute
(1980)

In the darkest days of military repression, the Chilean Church found not only that it was the sole institution free to speak on occasion in Chilean society but that it was vilified by newspapers and radio and television stations, largely controlled by the military government. In response, the Administrative Board of the bishops' committee repeated the cry Saul heard at the stoning of Stephen: "I am Jesus, whom you persecute."

The campaign to discredit priests, individual bishops, and the episcopal conference leadership resulted in confusion on the part of many Catholics, who were left wondering what to believe. So great was the fear of repression generated during this period that some Catholics would not attend catechism classes, lest they be mistaken for attending political meetings.

Dear Brothers and Sisters:

The recent events in Linares, Talca, Santiago, and other regions of the country, as well as the campaigns of the press, radio, and television against the Church and its leaders convince us that there are people who have decided to diminish the Church, some bishops, and priests— including the Permanent Committee—depriving us of our spiritual leadership. They use isolated facts, often invented or distorted. They intend to frighten us so that we will be afraid to talk about human dignity and social justice. We cannot refrain from talking about these two issues; they are an integral part of the gospel of Jesus Christ.

Our concern at this moment is the lack of information available to the Catholic community. They receive all the news through the mass media, and they do not have access to the same media for the purposes of clarification and self-defense. We are also concerned because the Christian communities are threatened in their activities. Some of them do not want to meet for worship or biblical study because they are afraid that they will be denounced as political meetings.

Through this letter, we want to alert all of you concerning the false information and sometimes insidious presentation of the news by some of the media. It would be easier for us to disregard the suffering of the poor and the cries of those who have been abused and tortured. It would be easier not to be concerned about justice in our country. But if we were not to speak out, we would be irresponsible.

Some people might think that the Church is being persecuted for good reasons. That is what Saul was thinking when he was witnessing the martyrdom of Stephen. Others will be happy because the Church needs to be purified of the infiltration and manipulation by others. To all of them, we repeat, "I am Jesus, whom you persecute."

There are not two churches, but only one: the community of Christian people united with its leaders. The bishops have the responsibility of teaching Catholics and anyone who wishes to hear. Our first commitment, as church leaders, is to teach about faith and Christian behavior. Some people pay attention to us when we talk about "spiritual" matters. But they are very disappointed when we show the practical implementation of our teaching.

We reaffirm that faith and Christian morality are preached to be lived and form the basis of the social teachings of the Church, which are obligatory for every Catholic. The example of Jesus and the history of the Church tell us that it will be difficult always to announce the gospel. We also know that the disciple cannot be greater than the Master. We are committed to continue talking so that no one can be deceived or separated from their bishops.

The bishops of Chile, as all Chileans, can have different interpretations of the reality. But we have united in one thing; we are leaders of the Church trying to incarnate the gospel in the life of Chile. If some people think that we are Marxists or pro-Marxists, they are wrong or could be of bad will.

When we see the restrictions of the press in our country, we realize how easy it is to depreciate the Church through the mass media. We will continue to be vigilant so that no sector of society manipulate the Church.

We remind all who suffer with us, and many times much more than we, of the theme of the Eucharistic Congress: "Do not fear. Let us open the doors of our heart to Christ."

The Permanent Committee
Santiago, Chile
May 29, 1980

Guatemala
Massacre of Peasants
(1982)

*No group in Latin America has suffered more in con-
temporary history than the Guatemalan peasants, most
of them Indians. Thousands have been killed since 1954,
when the military moved into the presidential palace for
the next three decades.*

*The killing intensified in 1981 and 1982. The Church
was touched directly by repression carried out, for the
most part, by right-wing and paramilitary units. Over
a dozen priests and religious were murdered and others
had to leave the country because of death threats, including the bishop of El Quiche and his entire pastoral
team. But the bishops' conference focused here not on the
Church but on the major happening in Guatemala: the
massacre of peasants leading to genocide.*

Faithful to the mission bestowed upon it by Christ, its Divine Founder, the Catholic Church cannot remain indifferent in the face of the
suffering of those it evangelizes and sanctifies. The bishops of Guatemala make their own the anguish of the people, especially those
most helpless and innocent. Faithful to the mission to proclaim and
defend the dignity of all human beings, we express our profound
concern over the latest incidents, specifically the massacre of numerous peasant and indigenous families.

The Events

1. With deep sorrow, we have learned about and have been able to
verify the suffering that our people have been forced to bear because
of these massacres, which the communications media has reported.
Many families have been vilely assassinated. Not even the lives of
the elderly, of pregnant women, and of innocent children have been
respected.

2. The consequences of this irrational violence may be easily seen

in the dismal situation of the survivors: orphans, women made widows before their time, insecurity, fear, and hunger because the lands are uncultivated and the villages abandoned and destroyed.
3.   We are of the opinion that citizens do not have a clear idea of the significance of the number of refugees within and also outside the country, nor of the continuing desertion of schools by both the teachers and the students in the interior of the country.

Christian Reflection

In the face of this harsh reality, the bishops of Guatemala feel compelled to reflect the following:
1.   Never in our nation's history have we been at such a grave point. These assassinations are now cataloged as genocide. We have to recognize that these actions are the worst violation possible to the divine commandment: "You shall not kill" (Ex 20:13).
2.   "God, who looks upon all with fatherly care, has willed that all people become one family, treating one another with brotherly spirit" (GS, 24). The most basic of human rights is the right to life and physical safety. If this fundamental right is not respected, cared for, and effectively protected, it will be impossible for Guatemalans to live under that just and amicable social order that God desires. We take for our own the words of Pope John Paul II: "You have to call homicide by its name: homicide is homicide. Political and ideological motivations far from justifying the act, only manage to destroy their own worth" (*World Day of Peace Message*, 1980).
3.   It grieves us that there are certain sectors of the extreme right and the extreme left who try to justify murder. We recall what we pointed out in our communique of May 15, 1980: "Neither the fear of communism nor the frustrated yearnings to change the present unjust social structures can be pretexts or justification for the killing of one's fellow man" (3.2).
4.   Being that Guatemala is a country for the most part Christian, it is inconceivable that these same Guatemalans are mutually destroying one another in an irrational and absurd conflict, perverting the marvelous order that God himself craves. True peace, as we have repeated consistently in all our communiques and pastoral letters during recent years, can only be the fruit of justice and love. It would be really tragic if the words of the prophet Isaiah, inspired by God, would be applied to our country: "This people honors me with their lips, but their hearts are far from me" (Is 29:13).

Conclusions

1. As Guatemalans and as bishops, we feel a profound obligation to once again condemn a violence that has come to such extremes as this massacre of the *campesinos*. We hope that all honest Guatemalans will condemn these acts of unspeakable barbarity.

2. Taking as our own the pain of the many families that have been so cruelly victimized by this violence, we ask and insist, in God's name, that the lives and physical integrity of our peasantry be respected. We ask the authorities who have been entrusted with the responsibility of effectively safeguarding the security of persons and the common good, to investigate these sorrowful events, preventing the guilty from going completely unpunished.

3. We ask all our Catholic faithful, as well as all people of good will, to contribute by their attitude to the creation of an atmosphere of true harmony and true justice. We believe that there is still time to retake the road that leads to just and amicable living-together and to attain the peace that all honest Guatemalans desire. In this historic moment, which has been our destiny to live in, one filled with light and shadow, with anxiety and hope, we are confident that Christian understanding of life will be able to replace the ideologies of hatred that have caused us so much damage. We hope that, despite all the painful events, we will never lose our hope of discovering how the value of suffering is the first step on the path to life together as a family of human beings. We beseech Mary, the Mother of Christ and of the Church, to protect us and inspire within all Guatemalans that feeling of faith and love which she reflected and which made her obedient to the Father's will.

Guatemala
May 28, 1982

Ecuador

Building a Society with Dignity
and Morality
(1986)

"When entire human groups in rural areas and urban slums, in childhood and advanced age, lack the living conditions necessary for human dignity, we feel the need to speak out," so begin the Ecuadorian bishops. They carefully delineate why the Church believes it has the right to make moral judgments, even on matters touching the political order. The Church's religious mission has consequences for society.

They go on to take up some crucial problems in their society, problems addressed after study and reflection. In speaking, first, of public morality, the bishops assert that the norm of morality leads to humanity and progress and to responsibility before God. They urge an uncreasing catechesis in essential values. They then examine various facets of violence that have become evident in Ecuador. Among other "most difficult" questions is foreign debt, which they treat following closely the lead of Pope John Paul II at the United Nations. Ecuador possesses rich hydrocarbon resources, and the bishops urge careful stewardship of this wealth and distribution that would give preferential attention to the neediest. Lastly, the bishops address the importance of landholding and cultivation "that goes far beyond a set of socioeconomic factors."

Many in Ecuador suffer from material poverty, as well as spiritual poverty, and find their happiness undermined. We know well that it is only in our future homeland that every tear will be wiped away (cf. Rv 7:17). But this, the root of our hope, far from sowing indifference in our hearts as pastors of the Ecuadorian churches, enlivens in us a greater sensitivity for the serious problems afflicting the Ecuadorian nation. When entire human groups in rural areas and in urban slums, in childhood and advanced age, lack the living conditions necessary for human dignity, we feel the need to speak out.

What we say about some of the more crucial problems that appear on the national scene is the fruit of study and reflection on the part of all members of the Bishops' Conference of Ecuador, as pastors of the churches that have been entrusted to us. Therefore, we want what we say to be understood within the framework of the Church's mission and to be an expression of its following of Jesus Christ, the Son of God made Man.

As the Second Vatican Council pointed out, "Christ, to be sure, gave his Church no proper mission in the political, economic, or social order. The purpose which he set before her is a religious one." But precisely as the Council explained, "Out of this religious mission itself come a function, a light, and an energy which can serve to structure and consolidate the human community according to the divine law" (GS, 42).

Therefore, we do not enter into the discussion of technical solutions that go beyond our competence. Nor do we wish to take a position in partisan politics. We are motivated by the commandment that "bishops should so preach the message of Christ that all the earthly activities of the faithful be bathed in the light of the gospel" (GS, 43). This brings with it "the right to pass moral judgments, even on matters touching the political order, whenever basic personal rights or the salvation of souls make such judgments necessary" (GS, 76).

Politics, understood as the whole of those actions aimed toward the common good, has as its basis the rights and duties of persons. These rights and duties constitute the purpose of our dialogue with civil authorities and with all groups or individuals who are interested in the good of the collectivity. This is so because, on the one hand, these rights and duties are inferred from the gospel message that the Church proposes to real men and women. And on the other hand, these rights and duties constitute the reason for the existence of our country's constitutional order and are present in solemn international treaties signed by Ecuador. In fulfillment of our inalienable duty, we turn our gaze to these rights and duties as well as to the dangers and distortions that lessen and threaten personal dignity.

We offer these considerations with a loyal desire to contribute to the good of the nation, supported by the Ecuadorian people's vocation to the faith, which has been a part of the national spirit for almost five centuries. We want to offer elements that can provide a foundation for justice and charity in order to generate peace, freedom, security, and development in all spheres and for all people while overcoming many difficulties. We are aware that the present moment's pressing needs cannot be satisfied through the isolated efforts of the national government. The extent and seriousness of these needs question the civic and Christian responsibilities of each citizen and of the various public and social powers. On our part, we want to be consistent with our pronouncements, and we commit ourselves to doubling our dedication, by appropriate ways and means, to the solution of the problems we will now indicate briefly.

Public Morality

Immoral actions of such depth and extension have been perpetuated and publicized that public opinion now tends to be confused as to the boundaries of honesty. This leads to a pernicious moral relativism in society. We believe that the root of such deterioration is to be found in a personal and societal orientation whose goals are power, possessions, and pleasure.

Thus, our society finds itself crisscrossed by drug traffic routes, which cause irreparable damage to youth and corruption that affects the guardians of justice. Assaults and robberies grow in number, either as a means to finance subversion or as a way of life. The anti-conceptive campaigns, which enjoy international financing and which attack family life and freedom, are radically immoral. A subtle mentality of negative values, such as the exaltation of money, sex, violence, and consumerism, is transmitted more and more clearly through the mass media.

In political life, party interests prevail above national interests, with a reprehensible narrowness on the part of opposition groups as well as those who make up the government. Services performed for the party are sometimes repaid by naming persons to positions for which they are unqualified, and by manipulation of public funds. A sufficiently operative awareness about disproportionate arms race expenditures has yet to be reached. Shadows are cast on respect for freedom of expression and the acceptance of a healthy pluralism. The rationale of state security threatens to override peoples' rights. The exaggerated tension among the different powers of the state causes continuous uneasiness, and while we appreciate the importance of strengthening the principal of authority, we also hear those who fear excesses of authoritarianism.

As to the relations of economic coexistence, we are sorry to see that old failings persist: business immorality through the traditional abuse of middlemen, tax evasion, and bribery in order to get favors from public authorities; even with respect to projects in the public interest.

Lastly, in this brief account, we must mention the collapse in the administration of justice, which often turns out to be so far from truth and equity. This constitutes a source of frustrations, which weigh particularly heavily on the backs of the weakest.

Now then, we must say very clearly that the expansion of immorality neither makes it dignified nor qualifies it as plausible behavior. Many extinguish the sources of life in their homes or profit from carrying out abortions; yet, their actions continue to be abominable crimes. Many people lie in different ways, but their conduct continues to evidence deceit, not talent. The public sector can be thought of as a playing field where employees and private citizens can abuse the public treasury, but this greed is inadmissible and has a name: theft.

We should all feel the invitation made by Pope John Paul II in his recent apostolic visit to Ecuador: "Let us build together a civilization of human dignity and an incorruptible worship of morality" (*Compānía*, 5). "Let us work," added the pope, "to strengthen the national character, starting from its roots of gospel morality, enlivened and nourished by the Church's doctrine" (ibid., 6). John Paul II's words point to the inseparable connection between the establishment of public morality and the attainment of a social coexistence worthy of Ecuadorian persons.

All of us, therefore, should exert ourselves to take as our own the objective norm of a morality that leads to humanity and progress, as well as being the key to our responsibility before the eternal God. Everyone—parents, educators, the mass media—has to respond and struggle to correct the direction of our individual and collective lives. Public authorities should take action to exercise self-control in accordance with justice and the law, as well as to promote the legislation and collateral measures necessary to subject excesses to the legal process. As for us, we repeat our word of encouragement to priests, religious, and lay people who collaborate in an unceasing labor of catechesis so that, dedicated to truth in charity (cf. Eph 4:15), their example and their word bring those they can to the practice and extension of essential values. Among these values are respect for life, integrity, personal honor, justice, honesty in the use of one's own goods and the goods of others—whether these be private or public—truthfulness, and industry.

Violence

The irruption of subversive violence in Ecuador is a specific consequence of the immorality mentioned above. Our country was included in the condemnation, made by the Latin American bishops in Medellín and in Puebla, of institutionalized violence, expressed in structures by which some groups oppress others. But we were not yet familiar with the violence of assaults, kidnapping, and guerrillas, with its sad retinue of ransoms, attacks, and other manifestations of contempt for life. It is deplorable that this violence almost inevitably generates violent reactions that multiply injustices instead of resolving them. We must recognize that this kind of violence is right at our doorstep. It is urgent that we get rid of it before it puts down roots in our environment and poisons the Ecuadorian family as it has other peoples, impeding work, production, and distribution—in a word, existence.

In order to combat subversive violence effectively, it is indispensable that the causes that nourish the sprouting of violence be known. We understand that, in the end, hate germinates in the selfishness of the human heart, from which also come bitterness, resentment, and greed. But social injustice is also a cause, as John Paul II explained in Ayacucho: "It is not by coincidence that the seeds of violence appear exactly in the most abandoned and crushed areas of the national community."

There exists a contrast between the greater awareness of human dignity, of fraternity in Christ, that promotes, on the one hand, undeniable aspirations to truth and justice, and on the other hand, unequal participation in social goods, such as education, housing, food, health, and so on. This creates an environment that favors actions oriented toward violently changing social living conditions. In addition to these contrasts, there is the certain ineffectiveness of the legal order: while laws exist to protect the rights and obligations of persons, and principles exist to channel the participation of citizens in government, these laws and principles are frequently applied to groups and individuals with censurable discrimination.

Another cause of subversive violence is the ideology that proclaims that hate and anger are the motors of history, together with those ideologies that reduce the human person to merely economic dimensions and, as a part of their message, promote passive resignation on the part of the least favored.

In the religious field, the presence and aggressive spreading of numerous sects cause division in the Ecuadorian family, especially in the marginal sectors and with special importance among native peoples, occasionally provoking deplorable confrontations.

In this review of the causes of violence, last to be considered are the international causes, which run from injustice in the terms of commercial trade to the activity of groups organized abroad to spread subversion. In the way that one evil brings another, these groups enter into close alliance with drug traffickers.

The darkest aspect of this picture is the widespread influence these factors have on our youth. Abusing their generous spirit, young people are manipulated, especially when they lack an integral formation in values. We cannot refrain from insisting that crime and robbery will never be a way to justice. The unjust attack on human life—which, to our disgrace, has already been demonstrated in our country in all its crudeness—cannot be justified in any way, whatever the subjective motivations might have been, even if they are theoretically linked to noble ends. The impunity of crime will render justice more vulnerable.

In the face of this panorama, we recognize the state's right and obligation to defend society by putting into action mechanisms that are part of the juridicial order and that can be perfected. But we are deeply concerned by the possibility that representatives of public authority slide—through hurried arrests that involve innocent people, excessive vigilance, and even tortures—toward a repression that despises the dignity of the human person, present in everyone, including the criminal and subversive. When the state exercises violence by decidedly employing force in a war without quarter against subversive violence, a growing spiral is traced which, according to the experience of other countries, leads to generalized terrorism, the collective devastation of values, and to conflicts that are almost impossible to resolve.

We propose, together with John Paul II, "to struggle against violence with the weapons of peace; to convince those who have fallen into the temptation to hate, that only love is effective." The first change, and the most profound, is that that must be achieved in each one of us, in order to treat each other mutually as brothers and sisters.

It is a difficult and long-suffering path that follows Jesus Christ. He suffered as a victim of destructive violence. With the strength of his Spirit, he was rich in mercy to pardon and open the doors of his kingdom even to his executioners, if they were willing to accept it.

The attitude we propose does not evade justice, rather it opens the way for justice to flow. Fraternity does not consist of passive and inert resignation. It points out the dangers of isolation and revenge in order to encourage repeated reconciliations. It seeks the coming together of all Ecuadorians in order to serve our common homeland.

We note that public works are presently being carried out and that production is increasing. But better distribution channels are necessary in order to disarm the mechanisms of exploitation and marginalization, and to move effectively toward a more just and fraternal society that takes away from violence its source of nourishment. On the other hand, considering the importance of the communications media, we strongly want them to make an effort to eliminate messages that in some way constitute an inducement to violence. On our part, we commit ourselves to a campaign of pacification of spirits, not as an evasion of reality, but rather as a fundamental basis of an environment in which truth, peace and justice, mutual respect, liberty, and fraternity can be cultivated, in order to undertake the building of the civilization of love.

The Foreign Debt

Among our most difficult problems, we find the growing indebtedness, which leads peoples to oppressive situations and endangers the real sovereignty of nations.

We are pleased by the efforts made to improve the conditions of debt service, without imposing excessive and discouraging sacrifices upon society. But our principal concern at the moment is directed toward the conditions that make getting into debt morally acceptable.

With respect to this, we note that the use of resources obtained by means of credit is unacceptable if used for superfluous, dangerous, or harmful expenses, such as those related to the arms race or to investment in projects that are lavish or simply disproportionate with respect to the nation's capacity, with the possibility that the nation be led to the edge of bankruptcy.

It is equally to be condemned when the credit does not benefit all levels of society but only a few. If some preference is admissible, it must be a preference for attention to the neediest sectors.

It seems prudent that the weight of the debt not be allowed to grow excessive for present or future generations. An excessive indebtedness might take away the necessary incentive to work and produce, or take away the nation's freedom to decide for itself about its own affairs. The future should be taken adequately into account out of a sense of patriotic responsibility, and we should not try to mend just the present urgent financial emergencies.

On the other hand, the problem of the debt involves the international community. It appears, according to the recent speech given by John Paul II at the United Nations, like "a problem of political cooperation and economic ethics," in which "justice and the interests of all demand a worldwide confrontation of the problem in all of its dimensions: not just the economic and monetarist dimensions, but also the social, political, and human ones." On the international level, the way must be made for criteria of greater justice and equity, in order to guarantee interest rates and installments supportable for the debtor nations. A new system, with greater participation and shared responsibility, imbued with greater respect for the dignity of persons and nations, should reformulate the relations between creditors and debtors. It should apply just, corrective measures with respect to compensation for work performed and the setting of prices of products and raw materials, as well as other aspects of the trade of goods and services. All of this implies decisive action on the part of Ecuador in the international forum, through its diplomacy, its intellectuals, and its journalists, in order to contribute to the formation of a new awareness and of more equitable relations.

The Development of Underground Resources

We are aware of the steps that have been taken to stimulate mining production and of the alluring perspectives presented by this new economic activity. We appreciate the fact that the government receives a high proportion of benefits within the framework of the current system of hydrocarbon production. It is because of this that the majority of the government's revenues come from what the subsoil produces, a fact that is known by the public. It is because of all of this that the decisions about these matters cause repercussions of such transcendence that they must be made while keeping in clear sight the service of the common good.

In this sense, the individuals, organisms, and institutions that direct petroleum policy should make a special effort to keep away from any type of exclusivity, sectarianism, and monopolization. They should also stay out of short-term political power plays and calculations since these can lead easily to dangerous injustices. For example, a rational rate should be set for petroleum production in order to prevent the premature exhaustion of oil reserves.

At the same time, those who have the responsibility to distribute the resources that come from these sources of wealth (in which we recognize the best opportunity Providence has given our country) should designate these funds toward goals with the greatest social benefit. That is to say, these resources should be destined toward preferential attention for the neediest and most oppressed in such a way as to make excessive social inequality disappear, instead of increasing. These resources should not be allowed to be used to create new, unjust—and some even dishonest—fortunes in the hands of a few.

This supposes a distribution that responds to the present and the future of the whole variety of the nation's geographic sectors. Special attention should be given to those who live in the oil-production centers, and the diverse range of occupations and socioeconomic levels should be taken into consideration.

Given the fact that it is a question of nonrenewable, limited resources, it is necessary to foresee their substitution in order to sustain a growing economic development. Thus, it is necessary to dedicate something to the development of alternative energy sources, mineral prospecting, and to obtaining technology. But, above all, this providential wealth should be taken advantage of to create abundant jobs, duly protected from exploitation by intermediaries and subcontractors. Production should also be diversified with an eye toward lessening dependence abroad.

Coming to the aid of our population's most urgent needs supposes intensifying efforts to provide every family with its own sufficient and affordable housing, even to the point of subsidising it with the greatest possible generosity. In addition, it supposes extension of basic services to those many places without roads, drinkable water, sewage, communications, electricity, and transportation.

Now then, given that one of the known consequences of the so-called petroleum boom is the abandonment of agricultural work, it seems to us that the master policy for investing petroleum resources should consist in strengthening Ecuador's fundamental agricultural vocation. The unfavorable treatment given to agriculture in relation to other branches of economic activity, whether these be industry, commerce, or services, must be ended. The public authorities cannot but adequately confront the unfortunate combination of farm-worker exodus and urban crowding, with the extremely serious problems that these bring in their wake. We propose, then, a "return to the countryside," understood as a significant shifting of all instruments available to the government toward the energetic promotion of the agricultural sector. We wish to dedicate the last section of our exposition to this point.

The Land

In our country, and especially with respect to native communities, it is true that the importance of landholding and cultivation goes far beyond a set of economic factors. Indeed, one of the characteristics that distinguishes the native cultures is born of their special relationship with "mother earth," which, as a community, the natives love dearly. As John Paul II said in Latacunga, "Your culture is linked to an effective and dignified possession of the land." For many native communities with roots in agrarian life, the land constitutes a factor of identity whose loss would constitute a true ethnicide, the ethnicide of those who first inhabited our land.

Therefore, a revision and serious evaluation should be undertaken of the ambiguous process followed by agrarian reform during the last twenty years. We must say that, in terms of a positive realization of liberty and dignity, what has been done to date is still insufficient. The countryside needs not only the basic structure we already mentioned, but also an atmosphere of peace and security; the stimulation of social and educational development; provision of medical and sanitary care; the extension and raising of social security benefits; and a just salary policy. Other requirements include promotion of production and commercialization associations, which permit direct entry of producers in consumer markets; lending technical assistance and offering credit with conditions that take into account rural activity (interests, paperwork, guarantees, etc.); sensitivity and justice with respect to setting product prices, through systems of storage, distribution, and export; extension of the amount of irrigated land, which can often be obtained through small, though numerous, projects that combine the efforts of public entities and the community. A reconsideration, always in the context of freedom and dignity, that might improve the traditional forms of productive association would not be bad. It would also be good to get the forest plan under way, rationalizing lumbering in order to avoid deforestation and urging an immediate halt to the cutting down of mangroves.

The problems we have noted here are of special importance for the eastern region. We want to point out the need to reconcile preexistent rights with the new economic activities on the rise in the region. The needs of persons should be taken into account over and above purely economic factors. Deplorable conflicts between new settlers and established native communities have already arisen. The native communities, without a doubt, have a right to a communitarian land reserve to assure that the communities continue to exist now and in the future in their own habitat. This right must be protected adequately by means of property titles duly and rapidly recognized. The lands the settlers have acquired justly should also be respected, while new colonization should be duly programmed and directed toward truly vacant lands. Land concessions for agroindustrial business should be realized with the land that is left over, respecting the rights mentioned above and taking care of the ecological conditions.

In a brief, the nation and its government have every right to obtain better production from the East, but only while always giving due attention to the rights of those who were there previously. When it is absolutely necessary to infringe upon these rights, an appropriate indemnification must be given.

In any case, the present circumstances demand coordinated action on the part of public authorities in order to make the way for lasting and just solutions. In this sense, the bishops' conference reiterates its willingness to collaborate in the search for these solutions, such as it demonstrated recently at the request of the native communities of the Amazon.

A Call to Hope

This review of our nation's problems, while necessarily incomplete, could give the impression of a certain disenchantment, given that the goals seem so distant and difficult to achieve. But no Christian, no person of good will should fall into this temptation. Rather, the seriousness of the problems obliges us to strengthen our spirit in order to work with tenaciousness and hope. Thanks to God, our people's spiritual reserves are immense and they are fed continually by the faith we have received as God's greatest gift to us. Providence has also given our country sufficient resources so as to provide a dignified life for all of God's children. Let us unite, each one contributing his or her part in the exercise of personal rights and the fulfillment of obligations. Better days are to come if God so wills.

Dominican Republic
Message to the Dominican People
(1985)

Since 1965, when civil war broke out and U.S. Marines intervened, leaders and citizens of the Dominican Republic have been struggling to achieve national unity. Through the years, as evidenced in the pastoral letter, the bishops have urged dialogue at all levels.

Despite considerable progress in renewing the Church and extending lay participation, the bishops call attention to two major problems: "moral decline and the growing deterioration of our life in common as a country."

The bishops point out a number of aspects to the moral decline as it occurs in the country. The worsening economic situation of the country has led to many complaints: "In such an atmosphere, it is therefore quite understandable that people from one side or the other continue to attack, justly and injustly, past and present rulers and blame our problems primarily on lack of foresight, incompetence, or an easygoing attitude. It is also easy to make international bodies primarily responsible for our present distress as though we were not the primary ones responsible, and that for well-known reasons."

The bishops point out the consequences: "By not controlling our emotions, we are killing the possibility of a sincere social dialogue, the utterly irreplaceable instrument for national understanding, progress, and peace." The episcopal conference dedicates the bulk of the letter to showing the conditions, some of the issues, and the agents of social dialogue.

1. We bishops of the Dominican Republic met during the first few days of the year with all of us in attendance. As pastors, we considered the present situation and the experience of our people at the beginning of 1985. We now want to share our reflections with you.

2. Among many problems, there are two that most concern us: moral decline and the growing deterioration of our life in common as a nation.

I. Moral Decline

3. Instead of making us reflect so as to lead us to repent and be converted to God and neighbor, and especially to the neediest, the seriousness of the situation in our nation has aggravated selfishness and has awakened evil passions in many people.

Three idols of our age—wealth, power, and pleasure—seem to dominate us, so much so that some people will go over any barriers, no matter what, as long as they can attain those idols.

4. Robbery, both common thievery and the kind that is disguised under cover of commissions or other such cunning schemes, is increasing every day; the "business" of prostitution, both open and disguised, is on the rise; there is also a rise in new entertainment centers, a clear expression of wastefulness, as well as in new kinds of dirty business and shady deals; prices for different items, especially those most necessary, are going up inordinately; too much is spent on legal gambling, and illegal gambling is spreading on all sides; economic parasitism seems to be on the rise as people do not do the work they should on their job, or simply because they are not needed in the position they occupy; there is an increase in acts of disrespect and contempt for one another; in the breaking of the marriage bond; in instances of marital infidelity; and in negligence and abandonment of the duty and responsibility that people have assumed. We are dismayed at the traces of cruel violence that occur periodically in Dominican society.

We could summarize this quick and incomplete diagnosis by quoting a passage from the pastoral letter we addressed to the Dominican people on March 25, 1983, when we said:

> Under that influence [the action of the Holy Spirit], we who are redeemed, liberated in Christ, vivified in the Holy Spirit can and must make a most opportune and effective contribution toward the solution of the grave problems that today are affecting humanity and, specifically, the people of the Dominican Republic: problems of moral perversion; of manifold kinds of coercion; of errors that are spread under the guise of science; of injustice that is approved and institutionalized; of lacerating inequality; of ignorance and handicaps; of negligence and irresponsibility in production; of passivity and lack of creativity; of aggravated selfishness; of disunity, antagonism, and continual struggles.

5. We repeat, all indications are that many people's motto is to get what they are after—wealth, power, and pleasure—without considering whether the means are licit or illicit. Indeed, they systematically make use of illicit means. As we witness this sad situation, we cannot but think that a growing number among us are bent on a lawless life, deaf to the voice of conscience, with backs turned away from the Father in heaven. It would be unfair to ignore the fact that, alongside such individuals, there are men and women in our populace who, every day, desire to be more faithful to God and others, especially to the poorest; who are more obedient to the dictates of their consciences and; above all, who are spurred by the criteria of the gospel and by the effort to bring light and life in Christ to their world.

6.   The paths of sin are not, and cannot be, those we Dominicans should follow if we desire to straighten out the present situation and effect the transformations we all demand and say we are seeking. It is from moral uprightness, which is sometimes heroic, and especially from the Lord's grace that there will emerge the personal and social order and the positive, effective, and hope-giving influence of God over us. "Unless the Lord build the house, they labor in vain who build it. Unless the Lord guard the city, in vain does the guard keep vigil" (Ps 127:1).

7.   Let us allow ourselves to be challenged by our conscience, which is the voice of God, and by God himself within us, and let us be really converted to the Lord, from the outset of this new year, which promises to be so decisive for our country. Let us sincerely seek, in the conversion of our lives, the beginning of the solution to all our ills.

II. Dialogue as an Element of Our Common Life as a Nation

8.   We now want to treat a point that we regard as being of capital importance: dialogue as an element in our common life as a nation— a common life that has been deteriorating more and more.

We are going to pause over some previously mentioned themes that will help us to understand better the need for dialogue at all levels within the Dominican population.

9.   On the one hand, it is the poor, that is, most Dominicans, who experience more directly in their lives the consequences of the scarcity of basic goods, the lack of jobs, and minimum levels of income. It should come as no surprise when they want to give angry expression to their despair over the worsening economic situation of our country.

10.   On the other hand, alongside their voice, one can hear other voices, the voices of many people who, bedazzled by the mirage of a world of affluence, enjoyment, and fun, which was out of joint with the limited resources of our country, now find themselves frustrated and upset and feel overwhelmed by the meaninglessness of their lives.

11.   In such an atmosphere, it is therefore quite understandable that

people from one side or the other continue to attack, justly and injustly, past and present rulers and blame our problems primarily on lack of foresight, incompetence, or an easygoing attitude. It is also easy to make international bodies primarily responsible for our present distress as though we ourselves were not the primary ones responsible, and that for well-known reasons.

However, this phenomenon is not exclusively ours. It is common throughout Latin America and throughout many other countries of the world as well.

In the light of this situation, which is almost worldwide, we would have to assume that most of the solution to our economic, social, and political problems is largely beyond the control of the authorities of any single country.

12.   Despite this real aspect of our situation, it is also clear that the growing need and anguish of many people, the frustration of others, and a certain political and intellectual oversimplifying to which we are reduced by the narrowing of our economic prospects are leading the nation toward a very grave and dangerous mutual aggressiveness and intolerance.

The impassioned accusations of some social and political groups against others—many of them against the government—and the responses provoked by such accusations are an indication that we are losing the reasonable control over our feelings, our thinking, and our speaking and acting. By not controlling our emotions, we are killing the possibility of a sincere social dialogue, the utterly irreplaceable instrument for national understanding, progress, and peace. When such dialogue is suppressed, passion, violence, and the response of harsh repression can reach the point of destroying everything. Let us not be blind. The atmosphere of tolerance and respect, which has taken the Dominican Republic such a long time to build up, is under serious threat.

13.   In such circumstances, it is the duty of the Dominican bishops to address some brief thoughts on national dialogue to all people of good will, no matter what their beliefs. That is the demand of the present situation, which requires of all Dominicans a unity in basic aims: unity of decision and common responsibility; and unity in efforts and sacrifices.

Conditions for Any Social Dialogue

14.   First of all, we are going to lay down several suppositions that are utterly necessary for bringing about true dialogue among us.

a) As John Paul II said in his *1983 World Day of Peace Message:* "Dialogue for peace is the urgent need for our age." We must be sincerely convinced of this. It lies in the depths of human nature and convinced of this. It lies in the depths of human nature and that is how our people experience it, when in their wisdom they say that "by talking, folks come to an understanding."

b) Along with John Paul II, we recall

- that this kind of dialogue will assume that what is sought is the true, the good, and the just for every human being . . . and that it especially demands openness and receptivity . . .;
- that dialogue assumes that each one accepts what is different and specific in the other . . .;
- and that true dialogue is the search for the good through peaceful means. . . .

We cannot resist quoting, in all its breadth, a passage from that Message of John Paul II, because we believe it is extraordinarily relevant for us:

> Dialogue is, at the same time, the search for what is and *what remains* common to people, even in the midst of tensions, oppositions, and conflicts. In this sense, it is to make the other party a neighbor. It is to accept its contribution. It is to share with it responsibility before truth and justice. It is to suggest and to study all the possible formulas for honest reconciliation, while being able to link to the just defense of the interests and honor of the party that one represents the no less just understanding and respect for the reasons of the other party, as well as the demands of the general good, which is common to both.

We must never offer in explanation reasons that are nothing but our own personal or group interests. It is often quite legitimate to pursue such interests, but they can scarcely constitute a satisfactory explanation for problems.

15.   *The first moral rule for social dialogue is to want to seek the true reason, the explanation for the facts.* Such an explanation or reason is not likely to be the fact that our interests have not been taken into account. This is an important point, and we should keep it in mind.

16.   *A second norm, which follows from the first, is that of being ready to present and clarify our explanations to anyone who disagrees with us.* Social dialogue demands that we give up presenting our own solutions and explanations as definitive. Before holding firmly to our own judgments and way of seeing things, we must listen to the viewpoint of others and weigh the differences.

On the other hand, there is no point in speaking with other persons if they simply repeat their explanation, and they do not try to defend it and explain it step by step to those who put forth another vision of things. One should explain one's opinions, and others should explain their own, with the aim of coming to an agreement.

17.   *A third norm is that one not seek to deceive others.* If one speaks to another with half truths and hides important facts or emotionally exaggerates opinions or feelings in order to disqualify or confuse such a person, one is morally wounding the fruitful possibility of human communication. Dialogue is fundamentally based on mutual trust, and it should not be confused with advertising or propaganda. As Paul VI said, dialogue "excludes pretending, enmity, deceit, and treachery" (*Ecclesiam suam*, AAS 56, [1964], p. 654).

Since we are speaking to Dominicans, we must say that our native astuteness has damaged mutual credibility. We almost always begin to dialogue with the assumption that, if I let my guard down, the other person will deceive me. This deepens social mistrust and and hinders dialogue.

18.   *A fourth norm, intimately linked to the previous one, is that, in speaking, the parties in dialogue must give up positions of power.* By way of example, such positions of power are expressed as follows: "That is the way it is because as an employee or beneficiary of the state you are dependent on me." "Someone like you cannot contradict me since I am more cultured, more wealthy, and more influential." Such an attitude destroys the root of dialogue.

Because of a series of historical circumstances, Dominicans are very skillful at surviving. They avoid head-on conflict, but they remain careful, suspicious, and as the saying goes, "keeping things to themselves."

Dialogue also becomes impossible or very difficult when each side threatens the other with a specific evil consequence if that side does not give in: strikes, firings, violence, and so forth.

It is also necessary that every person and social minority with serious objections (not mere self-interest) about a decision be confident of being able to maintain their behavior, their belief, and their activism, even when the agreement reached through dialogue goes against them on nonfundamental points. The basic rights of every social minority must be faithfully respected.

19.   *The fifth and last norm is to keep in mind that, in practice, the different parties do not always arrive at a total and final agreement.* In this sense, the important thing is to continue to come to partial agreements that all sides can accept with complete honesty.

Social dialogue, especially in a society that is so interdependent and complex in its parts as is our society today, is in fact a long process, and it will not always be possible to have quick and final results.

Nevertheless, this attitude does not mean that one must always remain content with what has been achieved. Nor should one be deeply disillusioned with dialogue when results do not reach the level of one's aspirations. It is no small thing to arrive at sincere areas of agreement on basic points, even when these points are still a long way from the desired final result.

III. Some Issues for Social Dialogue

20. Without exhausting the list, we see the following issues as important:

- the need for national objectives and goals that are above parties;
- both short- and long-range defense of the interests of the poor classes in social agreements;
- the delineation of the major goals and the principal means for a new approach to economic and social policy more in accord with our possibilities and the possibilities of an outside world that is in the midst of a grave crisis;
- basic traits of a new style of life that place more emphasis and make more room for the meaning of life and that would not be based on formulas that simply aim at cushioning the effects of an economic process that is accepted as inevitable;
- security with regard to laws promulgated and an assurance that laws will not have retroactive effects without just compensation.

IV. Agents of Social Dialogue

21. We hope that all will accept the high ideal that we have laid down of continually and tirelessly coming to social decisions through a procedure that is so human, as is dialogue. In that regard, we have presented some elementary norms based on common sense and on the human experience of an institution with roots so deep as the Church.

22. Let us promote dialogue in all fields of social life. Even children in their dealings with their parents and friends should already be introduced into observing the principles we have set forth. Saint Paul wrote to the community in Ephesus, "Do not exasperate by giving orders without listening." Let adults practice the criteria we have set forth in their professional world, in their community relations, in their efforts with political parties, in the world of work in the different branches of the state. The atmosphere of the nation is created and interconnected at the basic levels of society. Whether what prevails will be arbitrariness or social understanding will depend largely on the daily practice of our speaking and acting.

23. It is not superfluous to recall that this dialogue should be an ongoing effort. This is the way along which we should facilitate and make viable the solution for the problems that beset all democratic life. It would be strange and harmful to reserve dialogue for situations that are so closed and conflictive that they are threatening to degenerate into crisis.

24.   On the other hand, our dialogue must go beyond national boundaries and extend to the great Latin American homeland and to all humankind. We Dominican bishops certainly reinforce this dialogue with our brother bishops in the particular churches in other countries, as well as with Christian communities that are animated by an ecumenical spirit, and indeed with all persons of good will. That is what the international character of the present crisis demands.

25.   We are also presuming to call on the media to take on as their own unique role this pedagogy and practice of dialogue. Together with John Paul II in the previously mentioned Message, we say to you:

> Now, as those responsible for radio and television broadcasts and for the press, you have an evermore preponderant role in this sphere; I encourage you to weigh your responsibility and to show with greatest objectivity the rights, the problems, and the attitudes of each of the parties in order to promote understanding and dialogue among groups, countries, and civilizations.

26.   In what we have said about dialogue, it has not been our intention to minimize the seriousness of the sharp economic crisis, which has a harsh impact on everyone, and especially on those who are the poorest. Nevertheless, just as serious as this crisis, and indeed even more serious, is the human and social deterioration that is taking place in our midst. The fruit and reflection of it are the growing rifts in our common life as a nation and the presence of so much divisiveness and so many clashes. Hence, let us begin to recover national unity, which is so necessary, by means of a dialogue at all levels.

27.   With Pope John Paul II, in the Message we have been quoting, we proclaim, "Dialogue is a wager *upon the social nature of people,* upon their calling to go forward together, with continuity, by a converging meeting of minds, wills, hearts, toward the goal the Creator has fixed for them. This goal is to make the world a place for everybody to live in and worthy of everybody."

V. Call to Hope

28.   Sometimes, we are depressed and discouraged and feel that we are impotent and that our economic problems are overwhelming. That would be, and will be, the case if we trust only in our own efforts and connections. However, our hope is the Lord, "for the Lord will not cast off his people, nor abandon his inheritance" (Ps 94:14). "He only is my rock and my salvation, my stronghold; I shall not be disturbed at all" (Ps 62:3). "For from him comes my hope" (Ps 62:6). That is why we strongly encourage you with the psalm "Trust in him at all times, O my people! Pour out your hearts before him: God is our refuge!" (Ps 62:9). If he feeds the birds of the air and clothes the flowers of the field, how much more will he do the same for us, men and women of little faith?

29.   On the other hand, we who by God's grace bear the sublime dignity of being Christians have an immense and urgent responsibility in these present moments. Through our lives, judgments, activities, and apostolic daring, we must make present the living Christ, who wants to act in our history in this period. We are not light in Christ in order to block or hide that light. Quite the contrary: it is in order to make transformations by means of the utter security of the irrepressible action of the power of the risen Christ.

30.   It is precisely with regard to the urgent challenge of dialogue in the life of the Dominican people that we Christians have a special commitment. We have at our disposal the vigor of grace and the power of the faith that can move mountains, with the gifts of the Spirit of Christ, which has been poured into us, and with the effective intercession of the Virgin of Altagracia. We can call on the invincible power of prayer, and our vital task is that of encountering and loving every person, no matter who or in what condition that person may be.

31.   We urge Christians and people of good will to recite every day the prayer for peace of Saint Francis of Assisi, "Lord, make me and instrument of your peace. . . ."

Santo Domingo
January 21, 1985
Feast of Our Lady of Altagracia

Costa Rica
United in Hope
(1981)

Considered the most stable country of Central America, Costa Rica found itself facing uncommon crises in the 1980s. Shortages of food and other necessities caused long lines and severe problems for the poor. Salaries for many retained only a fourth of their previous value. However, many other Costa Ricans continued to enjoy a life of luxury. Some were even amassing immense fortunes.

The bishops attempted to identify causes of the extent of the crisis. One cause that they cite may surprise North American readers: little or no aid from friendly countries. (Costa Rica was causing no security problem and, thus, received little help from the United States.) Another reason they mention is the geographical location of being a neighbor to Nicaragua and, thus, suffering indirectly the instabilities and crises of the region.

The bishops propose concrete steps to be taken, beginning with a census of each parish to determine the presence of the unemployed and others in need. In an imaginative strategy, they call for a "work exchange," where those without work can meet those who need services. The heart of their message, though, is that each parish should work with one objective: parish community members, from their own resources, should attend to persons in need in their communities. The bishops elaborate other measures, as well.

We bishops of Costa Rica, aware of the difficult situation our country is undergoing, are submitting this pastoral letter to our people. With it, we intend to make a contribution toward assuring that love, justice, and peace—precious gifts that our divine Savior brought us from Heaven—not be dashed to pieces in our country, but rather be strengthened day by day for the benefit of all Costa Ricans.

If our pastoral duty obliges us to present a rather somber picture to our people, Christian hope enables us to affirm that, with the aid of God, the support of Mary, and the generous willingness of our citizenry, we will happily be able to overcome the problems that burden us today, and we will march securely toward better days for everyone.

There are three parts to our Christmas message: situations that concern us; the causes that produce them; and the solutions that we propose for dealing with them.

1. Situations that Concern Us

Because of the serious threat that they represent to our social peace, we single out the following factors:

1.1. As the press has noted recently, Costa Rica is the Central American country that shows the most serious shortage of basic food items. This news seems to be confirmed by the endless lines in front of stores selling basic goods; the fact that one cannot find certain essential articles, even with money in hand, or at least one cannot acquire the amount one needs; and the fact that it has now become established in many stores that certain articles are not sold unless one buys others, something that many poor people cannot do for lack of means.

1.2. This year, inflation in Costa Rica is 54 percent, the highest figure in Central America. Even more ominous, the figure has risen 36 percent in one year, since the International Monetary Fund has stated that in 1980 it was 18 percent. As is clear to all of us, it is the poor whom inflation hits hardest, and hence, we bishops ask that everything necessary be done to halt this runaway rise in inflation.

1.3. Sixty-five percent of wage earners in the country earn less than 3,000 colones a month. If we take into account the exchange rate with the dollar in recent months, this figure means that salaries have gone down to barely a fourth of their former value. How can a father pay rent, light and water bills, feed his children, and provide health care and education for them with such salaries?

1.4. If unemployment is already serious, since it affects tens of thousands of our fellow citizens, it will be even more serious in the next few weeks when the coffee harvest is over.

1.5. Despite the difficult situation, large numbers of Costa Ricans, belonging to all social levels, continue to spend money recklessly, perhaps now more than ever. Proof of that can be found in the fact that, at a recent soccer match held on an ordinary weekday, thousands of people not only did not go to work but they paid more than a half million colones to see the match. Three days later, at another match, ticket sales were more than six hundred thousand colones. There is a similar squandering on motels, night clubs, movies, and bars. Some people, whose motives are unclear, say that the reason is that people are seeking relief and want to forget about the bad situation. This is utterly false, since it is not only the poor who are squandering like this, but also the rich. We believe that the fault lies in an astonishing irresponsibility, and that this way will only lead us to chaos.

1.6.   Among those involved in the political life of the nation at all levels, there are some who succumb to pressure from partisan groups as well as from other sectors, which place their own interests above those of our homeland, which belongs to everyone.

1.7.   In this difficult situation, some bad Costa Ricans have taken advantage of things and piled up huge fortunes overnight. That is the case of those who speculate with dollars and, thus, bring about the impoverishment of the vast majorities because of the rising cost of living that such speculation produces.

2. Causes of the Present Situation

With no intention of being exhaustive, we here indicate some of the causes that seem most important to us:

2.1.   *Lack of stimulus for agricultural activity.* Those who work small- and medium-sized farms cannot get ahead. They are crucified by the sky-high prices they have to pay for supplies; by extremely high bank interest rates; and by traders who think only of their own profit, sacrificing producers and consumers alike.

We bishops of Costa Rica ask for justice and incentives for our farmers. We are absolutely convinced that that is the only way our country will have enough food for its population and also for export. What makes us certain is the noble character of our farmers, which is manifest in their amply demonstrated love for work.

2.2.   *Unjust relations in foreign trade.* The injustice is to be found in the low price paid for what we export and in the high price we have to pay for what we import. We will find a solution to this problem only by joining with so many other nations of the world who are in the same situation, in order to demand of the developed nations that they move from good intentions and fine words to a just and respectful way of treating developing nations. This question is vitally important in the so-called North-South dialogues.

2.3.   *Little help from friendly nations.* It is in moments of affliction and need that we know who our friends are. We are now undergoing one of those moments, and quite reasonably, we hope that we will be helped, not as though we were beggars, but as though we need this aid in order to exploit our own resources and, through the efforts of our own people, get out of the mud and start forward again. So far, we have received little help, and that truly saddens us. We urge friendly governments, the banks that have extended credit to us, and the International Monetary Fund to provide Costa Rica with effective help. We are certain that our country will not disappoint them.

2.4. *Negative impact of what is happening in Central America.* Given our country's geographic and political position within the Central American isthmus, it is inconceivable that the social convulsions affecting several countries in our area not affect us in many ways. Problems such as that of political exiles, refugees, ideological penetration, and arms trafficking have been further aggravating the crisis we are suffering.

2.5. *Frequent labor conflicts.* When all of us should be making every effort to help our country produce all it can, it is quite regretable that frequent labor conflicts should lead to the opposite effect, thus impoverishing us even more. We ask management and labor leaders to show patriotic good will so that, while always safeguarding justice, they may encourage harmonious relationships so as to prevent the loss of even an hour of work due to such conflicts.

3. Remedies We Propose

Faced with the grave situation we have described, the Catholic Church cannot remain indifferent, nor will it be content with mere denunciations, such as those so customary with demagogues. The Church proposes solutions and offers important aid to those who who might find themselves most affected by the crisis.

As Church, called to have compassion on the multitudes, following Christ's example, we will do our utmost to prevent any Costa Rican from undergoing hunger. We will do so in order to fulfill joyfully the supreme command of love for neighbor. We will also do so to prevent agitators, who are never lacking in hard times, from seeking to exploit the situation for their own political or ideological purposes. Once more, the Church will do everything possible to save the society in which it is incarnate and to preserve its best values. In order to achieve an objective so important, we lay down the following dispositions:

3.1. Every parish, using people from its own community, is to carry out a census of the unemployed and all those who are in need due to the economic crisis we are undergoing.

3.2. Every parish will also set up what we could call a job bank, which will enable those who are out of work and those who need services to come together. This can make a notable contribution to lessening the dreadful effects of unemployment.

3.3. Each and every parish in the country will strive energetically to accomplish this objective: to take care of its needy faithful by its own means. Pastors and other priests will organize their communities, both in the center of town and in outlying areas, so that, by means of a true Christian communion in goods, those who have a great deal can aid those who have less. Toward this end, they will set up a central commission and as many subcommissions as necessary in order to collect money, food, clothing, medicine, and so forth, so as to provide aid to the needy.

3.4.   *Caritas* of Costa Rica must move into action so that, with its own resources and international aid, it can support those parishes that cannot take care of all their own needy by themselves.

3.5.   From this moment on, we authorize all building committees, parish councils, and other church bodies that have their own funds to dedicate a portion of those funds to aiding the needy.

3.6.   We appeal to the Christian sentiments of our faithful so that they will receive our call with enthusiasm and contribute generously. Thus, we will keep Costa Rica free of the violence that hunger could provoke, with disastrous consequences for everyone.

3.7.   We urgently encourage other Christian churches, municipal governments, business groups, labor unions, associations, neighborhood committees, and so forth, to take measures similar to the ones we are proposing, so that within their own areas, they may contribute to mitigating the effects of the crisis we are suffering. In order to avoid abuses, it will be very necessary that all these bodies coordinate their efforts among themselves.

3.8.   We ask the central government and the autonomous state institutions in the midst of this urgent situation to give absolute priority to serving the needs of the population. Other projects that are not utterly indispensable can be postponed until times improve.

3.9.   We fervently implore all Costa Ricans to celebrate Christmas in a holy and austere manner; to make the best possible use of their bonuses; to refrain from spending money on unnecessary and even superfluous things; and to save all they can for the difficult months still ahead of us.

3.10.   Finally, we issue an urgent call to Costa Ricans holding capital to be willing to pay higher taxes for the sake of a more just distribution of the national income. Everyone should understand that Costa Rica's greatest wealth is its institutional stability, its democracy, and its peace. No price will be too high when what is at stake is safeguarding such fundamental values. May God not allow it to happen that because of selfishness, indifference, and lack of foresight on the part of some, the situation should become even worse, with violence breaking out, chaos taking over, and the country going under.

May the divine Jesus, whose birth fills our spirit with joy these days, illuminate with heavenly splendors the minds and hearts of our rulers, our politicians, our business people, and all those who can do so much to improve our present situation. Thus, they will contribute to assuring that the peace he brought us from the bosom of his Father

may continue to be the radiant star that shines over our homeland and the way that leads it to fulfill its destiny to the utmost.
We ask all priests to read and comment on this pastoral letter in all masses celebrated the Sunday after they receive it.

San José
December 1, 1981

Roman Arrieta Villalobos
Archbishop of San José

President of the Bishops'
Conference

Ignacio Trejos Picado
Bishop of San Isidro
de El General

José Rafael Barquero Arce
Bishop of Alajuela

Hector Morera Vega
Bishop of Tilarán

Alfonso Coto Monge
Apostolic Vicar of Limón

Antonio Troyo Calderón
Auxiliary Bishop of San José
Secretary of the Bishops'
Conference

Cuba
Christmas Message
(1987)

The Cuban bishops reflect on notable changes that have taken place in Cuban society and in the Cuban Church. An increasing ease of relations between the Church and the government facilitated a release of prisoners who had been in jail for many years. Together with the National Conference of Catholic Bishops (USA), the Cuban bishops arranged the release of several hundred prisoners who, along with their families, have been allowed to emigrate to the United States.

The bishops take up much larger questions of migration. They argue for the possibility of definitive return for those Cubans who wish to return to live and die in their country. This they see as a right that is not currently allowed by the Cuban government.

With new possibilities for persons and families living in Cuba to leave their country, the bishops take up the extremely delicate question: Should Cubans leave? The bishops state that it is understandable that, in some cases, individuals may wish to join their larger family living in another country. But in general, the bishops urge Catholics to stay in Cuba, citing the National Ecclesial Encounter: "We Catholics of Cuba recognize the right to emigrate from our country, especially for compelling personal reasons, but we do not judge this the best way for living out the evangelizing demands of our faith nor for contributing to the common good of our country."

Dear Brothers and Sisters and Friends:

Along with a good portion of the human race, this coming December 25 we Cuban Christians celebrate a new anniversary of the birth of Jesus of Nazareth "who went about doing good" (Acts 10:38) and whom we confess to be Son of God and Redeemer of human beings.

Every year Christmas, the feast of an "infant wrapped in swaddling clothes and laid in a manger" (Lk 2:2), brings us back to the essence of our faith and of life itself: "God so loved the world that he gave his only Son" (Jn 3:16). The familiar scene of the infant Jesus under the loving gaze of Mary and Joseph, endlessly repeated on a thousand holy cards and paintings and sung in popular carols, is the call to a love that is first of all tenderness, the love of our childhood that made us human and able to love, love without conditions, the love for which humankind unquestionably thirsts today.

Christmas is always yearning. A yearning because we are not like children, able to look at life with simplicity and, thereby, belong fully to the kingdom of God. A yearning for the silence of Bethlehem, beyond the reach of the sound of the weapons of war or of meaningless words. A yearning finally for peace, which on the blessed night of Christmas the angels proclaimed to the lowly shepherds "over all those whom God loves" (Lk 2:14).

This is the peace that we have not yet been able to establish on earth because the causes that overwhelm it have not been removed: hatred, ambition, injustice, dire poverty, falsehood. Nevertheless, some encouraging signs, like sparks of hope, brighten this 1987 Christmas. The grateful world has just witnessed the two greatest powers sign an agreement to place some limits on the huge nuclear arsenal that, in a few seconds, could destroy any vestige of civilization. The preparation and signing of this agreement seem to indicate that a climate of dialogue has opened up between the two most powerful states in the world.

There also seem to be efforts to resolve, through reconciliation and dialogue, some of the regional conflicts in Kampuchea, Afghanistan, and in nearby Central America. This is certainly consoling, especially when we consider how long these peoples have suffered.

Unfortunately, other conflict situations such as the one in Southern Africa, horribly marked by racism, with which we are so concerned because of the presence of Cuban combatants in Angola, presently do not seem to be moving toward a quick solution but, rather, are becoming more exacerbated. During this Christmas season, our prayer becomes urgent for our families, whose children, spouses, or brothers are far away and exposed to risk. We also have them very much in mind as we pray to Jesus, Prince of Peace, entreating him that this conflict, which like others preoccupies families and peoples, quickly come to a just and acceptable solution.

As we turn our gaze to this Caribbean region, we also see some factors that indicate a slow relaxation of tension, although in nearby Haiti political instability and violence are mounting on top of a desperate economic situation, thus hindering the yearnings for peace, development, and freedom in this sister nation. In our Christmas prayer, we stand in solidarity with the hopes of the Haitian people.

With regard to our own country, we Cuban bishops, in collaboration with the National Conference of Catholic Bishops in the United States, and in the framework of an effort to improve relationships between our countries, have made sustained efforts so that some prisoners who have been in Cuban jails for a long time, might receive visas from the United States government in order to go there to live. These humanitarian efforts have enabled a certain number of families to find stability and peace. For we are all obliged to seek not only macropeace but also that peace that is somewhat more within our reach, which can bring spiritual tranquility to many hearts.

Looking at things from this angle, we are pleased to see that migration agreements between Cuba and the United States have gone into effect to the point where separated families can be reunited and a great deal of anxiety and anguish can end. In addition, this agreement is a way of enabling people to exercise the right to emigrate. Nevertheless, we believe that a complete migration agreement would have to include the possibility that those Cubans who want to return and live in their country could come back to stay. We bishops of Cuba occasionally receive requests of this nature from Cubans living in various countries, including the United States.

We also believe that, in the future, the condition of finality of every departure from Cuba so far should be removed. A good deal of this emigration is due to economic motives, which are in themselves transitory or circumstantial. Moreover, there are other motivations whose nature is psychological, emotional, humanitarian, and so forth, which are serious enough so that, when leaving Cuba, a person would not rule out returning sometime to his or her country. Actually, many of our brothers and sisters deeply regret it when they leave the land where they were born and where they would have liked to live and die. As an agreement of this nature is being put into practice, along with the right to emigrate, there also ought to be clear emphasis on the right of every man or woman to live in his or her homeland.

Although we are satisfied with the humanitarian reasons already put forth, we Cuban bishops cannot simply take pleasure in the significance and overall scope of the present migration agreement. A large number of Cubans are now living outside their country, particularly in the United States. If a substantial number of citizens continue to leave Cuba each year, this number, which is already quite high, will grow, often without ending the pain of family separation but, rather, increasing it due to new splits that will take place in the normal course of events.

Moreover, during his trip to Australia, that is the very question that Pope John Paul II posed to a group of Polish emigres who greeted him enthusiastically: "Why have you left?" he asked them in a painful tone. "Why do you want to leave?" we are now asking, not without sadness. We believe that all of us Cubans are obliged to ask this question very seriously, whatever we think and whatever we personally intend to do in the future. The search for an adequate and honest answer to this question would lead us all to a deep and necessary thinking that could open the way to new humane and realistic approaches.

By making it easy for families to get together as their members make visits in one direction or the other, and by regularizing telephone communication and improving mail service, a gradual normalization of relations between Cubans living outside their country and relatives living in Cuba would make much more bearable the separation of loved ones and would thus make it humane. It is clear to us that family ties, which are very strong among us, are at the root of the desire of many Cubans to emigrate.

We Cuban bishops desire and hope that, for humanitarian reason, these migration agreements may be only the first step in overcoming the painful consequences of family separation, which to one extent or another affects a good portion of our population.

With regard to Christians active in our communities, we bishops fully appreciate and thank the Lord for the option many of them made some time ago to remain in our country, as they rose above economic attractions and the pull of family, even while they were experiencing that their presence and activity in society were not fully accepted because they were believers. In this decision, they have known how to integrate their loyalty to the Church and to their country with deep faith in God.

With regard to future decisions of this nature, we especially draw attention to what was said so clearly in the *Final Document* of the ENEC:

> . . . we Catholics in Cuba believe that although the right to emigrate exists it is not the best way to live out the evangelizing demands of our faith nor to contribute to the good of our country, except where there are serious personal reasons (para. 1114).

We bishops of Cuba appeal to Catholics to dismiss easy or selfish reasons for any intention to emigrate, for we believe that, in itself, emigration is often mistaken and is always painful for families and peoples. We are speaking not only as pastors of a Church that must announce the gospel here, but also as Cubans speaking to Cubans in order to remind them that love for our country sometimes demands efforts and sacrifices of us. We Christians must also give witness in this area.

Beloved Brothers and Sisters: As is traditional, the Catholic Church celebrates the first day of the New Year with a World Day of Prayer for Peace, whose theme this time is "Free to invoke God in order to live peace." On this occasion, Pope John Paul II wants us to think about the importance of religious freedom as a key factor for peace. When a human group feels that its exercising of its religion is hindered or limited by another religion or by the state, the result is instability and conflicts, which impede the consolidation of genuine peace, not only between countries but within nations as well. Also in this field, we Catholics in Cuba, and particularly after ENEC, have advanced steadily on the path of dialogue in order to overcome old tensions and be able to carry out our mission in peace.

This Christmas and New Year, as we wish you every sort of happiness and especially God's peace in your hearts, we bishops of Cuba implore the Lord to maintain and strengthen in 1988 the process of improvement of the situation of Christians within society and to continue to widen the Church's evangelizing space among us.

We are certain that, in the coming year, you, beloved Christian faithful, will strive to fill your personal and family life with the light of the gospel and will participate with renewed effort in the endeavors to promote ethical values in our society through daily work carried out with love and in a spirit of service to our people. In that way, you will cooperate with the progress of our homeland with a Christian sense of self-denial and sacrifice, ever inspired by him whose birth we celebrate this Christmas and who came not "to be served but to serve" (Mt 20:28), Jesus Christ our Lord, in whose name we bless you from our hearts.

The Cuban Bishops
Havana
November 26, 1987

Puerto Rico
The Political Situation of the Country
(1983)

The attempt to define Puerto Rico's future has caused intense debate for many years. The bishops of Puerto Rico add to a "responsible and serene dialogue." The bishops begin by saying that none of the three alternatives—statehood, free-state status, or independence—has any special backing from Scriptures and that persons are free to choose their political preference.

Concretely, the bishops charge the political parties with contributing to a "climate of confusion and inertia," working largely for their own interests and creating grotesque caricatures of their adversaries. Nor is it wise, they say, to believe that all the alternatives are equally valid and legitimate.

Catholics and persons of good will can find in Christian social teaching principles that will help guide the discussion. They name several transcendental values that should be used as criteria: dignity of the human person; integrity of family life; priority of the common good and of spiritual realities; preferential option for the poor; respect for life; service to the truth, to justice, and to freedom; love for country and for culture; peace and international solidarity. The bishops also touch on the consequences of neocolonialism.

1. We members of the Catholic Bishops' Conference of Puerto Rico, concerned for the political situation of the island, are presenting this message as a contribution to the responsible and serene dialogue of a community striving to define its destiny. The Church, mother and teacher, alert to the signs of the times, and a responsible component of our society, wishes to contribute to this dialogue of discernment within history.

2. The country's Catholic hierarchy knows that the "status" issue [whether Puerto Rico should be independent; become a state of the United States; or continue in its present "commonwealth" relationship] is highly controversial, and that ideological and economic connections hinder the development of a deep, objective, and impartial analysis of the question.

In taking a stand on temporal issues, which is a right and a duty, the Church does not act with the aim of imposing its criteria on public life. Indeed, Pope John Paul II has several times insisted on separating the clergy and religious communities from any activity in the field of party politics. This does not mean that Christians give up their social right with regard to injustice and oppression. The same pope has denounced situations in which justice and freedom are in jeopardy.

3.   That said, our starting premise is that there is a Christian public order on the local and the international levels. Christian spirituality and morality have a great deal to offer for political proposals and dilemmas. That is why we are proposing some guidelines, with the aim of shedding light on the sensitive process of the fundamental political option for Puerto Rico.

Here at the outset, we clearly posit that none of the three political alternatives—statehood, commonwealth, or independence—is inherently at odds with the gospel. "Different ideas on political questions can honestly and legitimately be spread throughout their proper sphere. The Church in no way condemns political tendencies as long as they are not against religion and social justice" (*Cum Multa*, 3).

4.   On the other hand, we are convinced that the political direction of the Island goes beyond the framework of the activity of political parties. In fact, although they express the ideals of a particular group of individuals, political parties are human instruments whose aim is the common good. But they are relative entities, and the measure of their goodness is the extent to which they promote the great values of humanity and social progress. Here we are speaking of a social progress that goes beyond mere economic development. As Pope John XXIII said in the encyclical *Mater et Magistra*, true progress transcends material progress so as to offer complete happiness to every human being.

5.   Unfortunately, in Puerto Rico, a climate of confusion and inertia has built up among both leaders and electorate with regard to the status question. Instead of furthering a rational and mature encounter in order to deal with the most serious needs of the country, each party works mainly for its own interests, seizing the political alternatives for itself and creating a grotesque caricature of its adversary. Pope Pius XI wisely warned us that the passion for domination tends to lead parties to harsh civil struggles that undermind the dignity of individuals and communities (cf. *Ubi Arcano*, 19).

6.   Certainly, political parties are means of democratic expression, and it is their legitimate right to struggle for the cause they have laid out for themselves. Nevertheless, political groups do not encompass the whole population nor the wealth of all nuances of ideology; furthermore, they bear the imprint of different interests, resentments, and suspicions. Moreover, when consensus is lacking, citizens will naturally organize in some fashion to promote the ideals they favor.

7. Both those who are members of political parties and those who are not involved in partisan politics must use solid criteria for justifying their decision in the face of the challenges of the present situation. To say that all the alternatives are equally valid and legitimate is not an adequate way of clarifying the confusing political panorama of the Island. One must know in which sense the options are equally valid or not. Otherwise, we may succumb to contradictory and demagogical opinions or remain fixed in our starting point.

8. This is even more valid in a society in which modern methods and media make public opinion very fickle and fluctuating in all areas of national life. The lack of truthfulness "today seems to be turned into a system, raised to the level of strategy, where lying, the distortion of words and of facts, and deceit have become classic offensive weapons, which some use masterfully, proud of their skill to the point where obliviousness to any moral sense is so much an inherent part of the modern technique for forming public opinion, guiding it, and making it serve their policies, determined as they are to triumph at any cost in the struggles over interests, opinion, teaching, and hegemony" (Pius XII, *La Festività*, 10).

9. Catholics and people of good will, will find in the sources of Christian social thought a profound framework for examining the progress of a community and opting for social and political alternatives. Christian criteria and principles judge the ideologies and political structures set forth along the paths of history on the basis of certain transcendental values: the dignity of the human person; the integrity of family life; the priority of the common good and of spiritual realities; the preferential option for the poor; respect for life; service to truth, to justice, and to freedom; love for country and for culture; peace; and international solidarity.

10. In the light of Christian principles, we Puerto Ricans have the right to aspire to optimum material conditions, without sacrificing spiritual serenity; psychic and ecological equilibrium; moral, cultural, and religious values—in a word, our *soul*. Christians who have a good knowledge of the thinking of the Church—based on the gospel, the social situation of the country, the programs and action of political organizations—have a reasonable parameter for making a wise and responsible decision in the public sphere. Such a decision entails seriousness and commitment, given the political, social, economic, cultural, and religious repercussions of public discussion in Puerto Rico.

11. Hence, the basic solutions that seek to do away with the status issue should meet at least two criteria: the options should be *worthy* and *workable*. It goes without saying that we believe that practical reasons are subject to considerations of principle: "One does not live on bread alone . . ." (Mt 4:4). Nevertheless, any political project, no matter how noble in theory, must convince the people that what it proposes is viable and show just what concrete benefits are supposed to be achieved. Citizens who place their confidence in a particular formula do not do so with the idea of signing a blank check or betting on the lottery. Rather, it is a reasonable risk for individual and common welfare. In other words, the traditional alternatives represent potential paths for the history of the country, but in themselves, they bear no infallible guarantee that will magically whisk away Puerto Rico's serious social and economic problems. In disputable matters, and in political questions, there can be an honest diversity of opinion.

12.   Even acknowledging this importance of the practical dimension of the political order, we must insist that the functional aspect is not the determining factor when the time comes for a community to opt for its destiny. There are other criteria, such as the criterion of dignity, which invites us to ask to what extent material factors (e.g., natural resources, international disputes, economic interests, migratory movements, strategic advantages) can condition the spiritual liberty and the enlightened conscience that demand a fundamental political option. Above any partisan consideration, the Church also must reject openly those initiatives that advocate violence, materialism, and atheism as a system for life in community. We must warn equally against the canons of materialistic and inhuman capitalism, which with its merchandising mechanisms grinds down the human heart (cf. QA, 105–109).

13.   In the perspective of the criteria related to dignity, the words of Pope Paul VI are relevant. He often said, "the most important duty in the realm of justice is to allow each country to promote its own development, within the framework of a cooperation free from any spirit of domination, whether economic or political" (OA, 43). Whatever the decision of our political community, it is extremely important that we safeguard our own personality, for "there will soon no longer exist a world divided into people who rule others and peoples who are subject to others. . . . There is no longer any community that wishes to be subject to domination by another" (John XXIII, *Pacem in Terris*, 42–43). If it is true that today self-determination is relative, it is also true that nations are moving toward an interdependence among equals that respects the particular characteristics of each people and rejects cultural uniformity.

14.   In this connection, Pope John Paul II noted the consequences of economic and ideological neocolonialism as he spoke to nations that had, in fact, already worked out their political status: "Political independence and national sovereignty demand, as a necessary corollary, that there also be economic independence and freedom from ideological domination. The situation of some nations may be profoundly conditioned by decisions taken by other powers, including the great world powers. Moreover, there may exist the subtle threat of a certain ideological interference that, in the realm of human dignity, could cause effects that are more damaging than any other kind of subjection" (*Speech to the Diplomatic Corps*, Kenya, May 6, 1982). With regard to cultural life, there must be recognized and safeguarded a wider space of freedom and independence for culture, given existing risks of manipulation through interests foreign to its nature, or of attitudes closed to the very dynamism of culture. "In every group or nation, there is an ever-increasing number of men and women who are conscious that they themselves are the artisans and the authors of the culture of their community" (GS, 55; cf. *Puebla*, 427).

15.   Finally, we must add that we are aware not only of the political and economic implications of the status question but also of the cultural and pastoral repercussions. We must take into account the cultural and religious values of our people, and we must cast our lot on the side of the conservation and enrichment of this historic inheritance. To some extent, a political option presupposes a cultural and religious option. A step of this kind may even have an influence on the identity and the juridical constitution of the ecclesiastical institution.

16.   The seriousness of this situation alerts us to the quality of citizen participation and the importance of social education: "Today, on all sides, the life of nations is fractured by the blind worship of numbers. The citizen is a voter. But as such, the citizen is really nothing more than a mere unit that, when added to others, is a majority or a minority, which can be reversed by the shift of a few votes or perhaps of a single vote" (Pius XII, *Tres Sensible*, 6).

17.   The status issue unquestionably brings into play all the material and spiritual resources of Puerto Rican society. The topic is too serious to be left in the hands of just one sector of the community or at the mercy of interests foreign to the aims of Puerto Rico. Optimum conditions for guaranteeing a wise and prudent decision must be established. And it is absolutely essential that such a decision be respected juridically in our nation, our continent, and throughout the world.

We have presented briefly some critical points relating to the situation of Puerto Rico. The Catholic Bishops' Conference of Puerto Rico wishes to shed light, without pressuring; to present its viewpoint; to clarify its role; and to be present in this historic moment, in this tropical spot, where it has been its lot to evangelize for five centuries. We pray the Lord that the celebration of the Fifth Centenary of the discovery of our island may find us united in charity, linked in solidarity with justice, and harmonious in peace.

San Juan
March 23, 1983

Bishop Juan Fremiot Torres Oliver
Bishop of Ponce
President
Catholic Bishops' Conference
of Puerto Rico

Bishop Héctor Manuel Rivera Pérez
Auxiliary Bishop of San Juan
Secretary
Catholic Bishops' Conference
of Puerto Rico

Cardinal Luis Aponte Martínez
Archbishop of San Juan

Bishop Ricardo Antonio Suriñach Carreras
Auxiliary Bishop of Ponce

Bishop Juan de Dios López Vitoria
Auxiliary Bishop of San Juan

Bishop Miguel Rodríguez Rodríguez, CSSR
Bishop of Arecibo

Bishop Ulises Aurelio Casiano Vargas
Bishop of Mayaguez

Bishop Enrique Hernández Rivera
Bishop of Caguas

Bishop Hermín Negrón Santana
Auxiliary Bishop of San Juan

Bishop Rafael Grovas
Bishop Emeritus of Caguas

Antilles
*True Freedom and Development
in the Caribbean*
(1982)

*The Catholic bishops of the largely English-speaking
part of the Caribbean took a leading role in the region
with their 1975 pastoral letter* Justice and Peace in the
New Caribbean. *The bishops expressed the social teaching of the Church, as applied to the region. The document
was widely disseminated and discussed.*

In 1982, the bishops issued another careful study True
Freedom and Development in the Caribbean, *which
examines the human and social conditions of the Caribbean in the 1980s. The bishops note the progress that
has been made in the seven intervening years, but they
detect certain problems that have grown much worse.*

*As part of the larger world economic system, the Carib-
bean is moved and shaped, in part, by forces that are, to
some considerable extent, beyond its control. Inflation
and decreased prices for its products buffet the small
Caribbean countries.*

*As if to foreshadow the conflicts that were to be fought
out in Grenada, the bishops reject both Marxism and
exploitative capitalism as "alien to the strong religious
and social sentiments of our people."*

*Where some would restrict the Church to other-worldly
matters, the bishops respond that "the Church is not
willing to restrict her mission solely to the religious field
and to dissociate herself from people's temporal problems.
Neither can she restrict her message simply to temporal
problems."*

I. Introduction

1. We Roman Catholic bishops of the Antilles Episcopal Conference
want once again to speak to all Roman Catholics in the territories of
our conference and, indeed, to all men and women in the Caribbean

247

who share our desire for the full human development and authentic liberation of our Caribbean people.

2.   Many of you recall that in 1975, when we bishops met in Martinique, we issued a pastoral letter entitled *Justice and Peace in the New Caribbean*. That letter was well received. It has been widely read, reprinted several times in the Caribbean, and translated into French, Dutch, and Spanish. It is still read and used as a most useful introduction to Catholic social teaching, which is so important and also as much neglected, and we trust it will continue to be of value.

3.   But we realize that in the past seven years, new situations have developed and new problems have arisen in our region. In addition, new emphasis has come about in Catholic social teaching. It is on this account that, wishing to continue the dialogue we began, we now speak to you again.

II. The Caribbean Today

Improvements

4.   Since *Justice and Peace* was published, we are glad to note that there has been some political advance as well as some improvements in the quality of life in the Caribbean.

5.   Dominica, Saint Lucia, Saint Vincent, Belize, and Antigua and Barbuda have all taken their places in the community of nations, and one result of Caribbean nations attaining independence has been that they have been able to make their voices heard, in union with those of other developing countries, and have been able to obtain benefits, restricted though these may still be (e.g., those of the LOME Convention between the European community and the ACP [African, Caribbean, and Pacific] countries). It was, in fact, this Convention that led to special grants being made to countries severely hit by hurricanes (cf. LE, 17).

6.   There has been a continuous growth in the level of aspirations of Caribbean peoples towards dignity and human worth. Despite serious political and economic problems facing the regional integration movement, Caribbean peoples at the grass-roots level have drawn closer together. The generosity and concern of the region as a whole in face of hurricane and volcanic devastation in several Caribbean islands is but one manifestation of this fraternal spirit, with its deep Christian roots. However, it is urgent that we intensify the level of cooperation between our countries in the Caribbean.

We welcome the formation of the Organization of Eastern Caribbean States, and we look forward to frequent meetings of Caricom Heads of Government.

7. Despite many difficulties, some progress has been made in the search for social and economic betterment, in some countries more than in others. Tourism has made considerable progress in some places. This not only aids the economy but can help to broaden the world view of our people. However, it is a precarious industry. Moreover, it brings with it not only economic and cultural benefits but moral and social ills as well. There has been some development in industrialization, but if it is to be significant, massive investment is still required. Efforts are continuing, also, to advance along the long road to improved agriculture and land reform.

Disappointments

8. On the other hand, there have been acute disappointment and frustration in the region because many of the hopes for better social and economic life have not been realized. Poverty and the wide gap between rich and poor continue to be a serious source of disharmony and challenge to the message and witness of Christ, in view of the preferential option the Church should have for the poor and oppressed. Special emphasis was laid on this by the bishops of Latin America and the Caribbean who met at Puebla (cf. *Puebla*, 1134 sequ.).

We are grieved to see that so many in our region are still living in degrading poverty and in miserable housing conditions, uncertain where their next meal is to come from. Many children are still suffering from malnutrition while many women have to carry an appalling burden with little or no support from the fathers; they have to care for a house and children while at the same time having to go out to work in order to support themselves and those dependent upon them.

9. As developing nations, we have been particularly hard hit by the problems of inflation and especially by the increased cost of oil products. Though attempts have been made to secure less unjust trading conditions from developed countries, what has been secured still falls far short of justice, and we remain the victims of distorted world monetary and trading systems that favor international capitalism. For example, the price we receive for our exports is out of all proportion to what we have to pay for the manufactured goods we import (cf. LE, 17).

10. The decrease in the possibility of emigration for the less advanced in society and the move away from agriculture to the towns have led to increased unemployment, with its frustrating and degrading consequence. Many of our young people, especially, find it impossible to find work, and some have recourse to marijuana as a form of escape. Young girls are tempted to prostitution in an effort to support themselves, and some women who seek employment find that jobs are offered dependent upon sexual favors granted to employers. It is

scarcely surprising that many react against society as they experience it. But unfortunately, a number adopt an alternative mode of life that puts them at odds with other people.

Abuses

11.   In some of our countries, as in other parts of the world, the powers of government are being abused. Governments favor certain sections and groups; human rights are denied; bribery and corruption have become all too easily accepted as a norm in public and professional life; deep divisions have led to hatred, violence, and even murder.

12.   Strong attempts continue to be made to subject our region to harmful foreign influences that threaten our peace. Politically, there are efforts to involve our territories in the international power struggle. Economically, there is a constant drive to promote the consumer mentality and to make luxuries appear as necessities. This emphasizes purely materialistic goals, fosters a competitive and aggressive spirit, and distracts our people's minds from humanizing, spiritual, and eternal values.

13.   In addition, attempts are being made to impose upon our people ideology of atheistic Marxism as well as the harmful influence of exploitative capitalism. We wish to emphasize that both are alien to the strong religious and social sentiments of our people.

III. The Task of the Church

14.   Paul VI wrote in his apostolic exhortation *On Evangelization in the Modern World:* "There is no true evangelization if the name, the teaching, the life, the promises, the Kingdom and the mystery of Jesus of Nazareth, Son of God, are not proclaimed" (EN, 22). It is the task of the Church and, therefore, in a special way ours as bishops, to proclaim the message brought by Jesus Christ, her Founder: the good news that he offers us liberation from the effects of sin and the promise of eternal life. But as Paul VI tells us later in the same exhortation: "Between evangelization and human advancement—development and liberation—there are in fact profound links. . . . [God's plan of salvation] touches the very concrete situations of injustice to be combatted and of justice to be restored. . . . How in fact can one proclaim the new commandment [of charity] without promoting, in justice and peace, the true, authentic advancement of man?" (EN, 31).

15.   Faced, then, by the many injustices and examples of human degradation that we have noted above, we feel it is important for us to supplement the points we made in our earlier letter on *Justice and Peace* in 1975, and to outline more clearly relevant points in the social teaching of the Church as sound and positive guidelines for following God's will today.

Liberation from . . . for . . .

16.   Let us stress most insistently how dynamic a process is "Christian liberation." Christ came to liberate mankind from all forms of bondage: *from* personal and social sinfulness, and *from* everything that tears apart the human individual and society (cf. Lk 4:18). But this liberation from evil is also a liberation *for* progressive growth through a new relationship with God and with other human beings. This reaches its culmination in the perfect communion of heaven, when God is all in all (cf. *Puebla,* 482).

17.   Much of the evil in this world is the result of sin, the result of human greed for wealth and power, the result of cruel disregard for other human beings. Indeed, our very society has become so infected with immoral principles that it becomes hard to shake ourselves free from them and avoid their consequences. We must, therefore, root out sin, not only that men may attain eternal happiness with God, but also to make this world the kind of place Christ wishes it to be, a place where justice and Christian love prevail. We destroy the meaning of the liberation Christ won for us on the cross if we forget that the very center of the gospel teaching on liberation is that it should transform men and women into active subjects of their own development, both as individuals and as members of a Christian community. It is equally destructive of Christian liberation to disregard dependence and the forms of bondage that violate the basic rights that come from God our Creator and Father (cf. *Puebla,* 485).

18.   To sum up, like Christ, the Church is not willing to restrict her mission solely to the religious field and to dissociate herself from man's temporal problems (cf. Mt 25:35). Neither can she restrict her message simply to purely temporal problems. She reaffirms the primacy of her spiritual vocation and insists that her contribution to liberation is incomplete if she neglects to proclaim salvation in Christ. It is through following out the salvation won by Christ, and all that this means, that true liberation is to be achieved (cf. EN, 32, 34).

IV. The Dignity and Rights of the Human Person

19.   Sacred Scripture teaches that men and women were created "in the image of God," that they are capable of knowing and loving their

Creator, and that they are appointed by God to be master of the things of creation, so that they may subdue them and use them for God's glory (cf. Gn 1:26; LE, 4, 25).

20.   Again, Christ by his manifestation of the Father and of his love gives man a full revelation of what he really is and to what sublime heights he is called. He who is "the image of the invisible God" (Col 1:15) is himself the perfect man. To the sons and daughters of Adam he has restored the divine likeness, which has been disfigured from the first sin onwards. For since his incarnation, the Son of God has united himself in some fashion with every man and woman. He worked with human hands; he thought with a human mind, acted by his human choice, and loved with a human heart. Born of the Virgin Mary, he has truly been made one of us, like us in all things except sin (cf. GS, 22).

21.   But this is not all. Those who have been baptized have been "born again" of water and the Holy Spirit (cf. Jn 3). They have come to have the life brought by Christ (cf. Jn 6;10;15). By becoming brothers and sisters of Christ, who is the Son of God, they have become themselves the adopted children of God, members of the family of God, heirs of God and co-heirs with Christ (cf. Rom 8). Indeed, they come to share in the divine nature (cf. 2 Pt 1:4).

22.   In his first encyclical, *Redemptor Hominis,* John Paul II makes this striking statement:

> How precious must man be in the eyes of the Creator, if he "gained so great a Redeemer" (*Exultet* at the Easter Vigil), and if God gave his only Son in order that man should not perish but have eternal life (cf. Jn 3:16).

And these words give full meaning to another statement by the pope:

> Society is made for men. . . . The human person may never be sacrificed for political interests, national or international, whatever they may be. . . . The principle to follow is not that of allowing economic, social and political forces to prevail over man, but for the dignity of the human person to be put above everything else.

Human Rights

23.   We have stressed the dignity of every man and woman, each with an immortal soul endowed with freedom. But precisely because of this dignity and power, each one has the duty freely to serve God and to follow the path asked of him or her by God as well as the God-given right to the conditions necessary to achieve this. Therefore, when a person is deliberately and unlawfully deprived of these conditions, there is injustice.

John Paul II writes:

> It is necessary to call by their name injustice, the exploitation of man by man, or the exploitation of man by the State, institutions, mechanisms or systems and regimes which sometimes operate without sensitivity. It is necessary to call by name every social injustice, discrimination, violence, inflicted on man against the body, against the spirit, against his conscience and against his convictions. Christ teaches us a special sensitivity for man, for the dignity of the human person, for human life, for the human spirit and body (*Address*, February 21, 1979).

The bishops of Latin America and the Caribbean, meeting at Puebla, stated emphatically in their final document: "Every attack on human dignity is simultaneously an attack on God himself, whose image the human being is" (*Puebla*, 306).

24.   Denial or neglect of the dignity and rights of individual men and women lies at the root of many of our problems today. The rights of women, in particular, are often set aside. But there is also another problem: the tragedy that so many fail not only to recognize the human dignity of others but also to appreciate sufficiently their own worth. Lack of self-appreciation and the underrating of local culture and products remain a sad legacy of slavery and colonialism.

V. Right to Share in the Works of Creation

25.   An important right of every human being is to share in the works of creation. The *Puebla Document* insists:

> By virtue of their origin and nature, by the will of the Creator, worldly goods and riches are meant to serve the utility and progress of each and every human being and people. Thus each and every one enjoys a primary, fundamental, and absolutely inviolable right to share in the use of these goods, insofar as that is necessary for the worthy fulfillment of the human person. All other rights, including the right of property and free trade, are subordinate to that right. As John Paul II teaches: "There is a social mortgage on all private property" (OPA:III, 4). To be compatible with primordial human rights, the right of ownership must be primarily a right of use and administration; and though this does not rule out ownership and control, it does not make these absolute or unlimited. Ownership should be a source of freedom for all, but never a source of domination or special privilege. We have a grave and pressing duty to restore this right to its original use and primary aim (PP:23) (*Puebla*, 492; cf. LE, 14, 19).

Just Wages

26.   In practice, if there is to be an equitable distribution of the work of creation, justice demands that a man who works hard should be able to earn a wage sufficient to ensure a truly human life and to face up to his family responsibilities with dignity (cf. LE, 19). This means that he should be able to put aside something in savings or in the purchase of land or other property or in improving his professional skill. Women should receive a wage equal to that of men for similar work (MM, 71; cf. LE, 10, 19).

27.   While investors should obtain a fair return for their investment, often the fruit of hard-earned savings, the problem can be that they demand a return in accord with a high rate of interest in the money market, and this may prevent the payment of a just wage.

28.   In most of our countries, the level of wages is being left to negotiations between trade unions and employers. Too often, such negotiations are conducted in a spirit of strife and bitterness. There is need in employer-employee relations for a mutual respect for each other's human dignity (cf. LE, 8); for a due respect by employers for the natural right of the employees to a decent standard of living in return for honest work (cf. LE, 7); and for an understanding by trade unions of the limitations imposed by the economic state of the country. The unions should also bear in mind not only the benefit of their own members but also that their demands for their members may have a damaging effect upon other fellow workers and the nation (cf. LE, 20). Where necessary, it is important that governments should intervene with legislation to fix a minimum wage and also to control prices.

29.   When socioeconomic disputes arise, efforts should be made to come to a speedy settlement by negotiation. A strike can be the necessary, though always ultimate, means for the defense of the workers' own rights and the fulfillment of their just demands. Because a strike can cause so much inconvenience, and even suffering to many innocent people, justice demands that it be used only as a last resort in matters of grave concern. It can be a wise provision that strikes should only take place after a secret ballot by the workers (cf. RN, 31; GS, 68; LE, 20). Workers on strike do have the right to publicize their protest and to seek support of others by use of the picket line; but they do not have the right to prevent entrance to the workplace by the use of violence.

The Farmers

30.   One group of workers who play a major part in developing the riches of creation are the farmers (cf. LE, 5, 21). Yet, they are often quite unjustly looked down upon, and they often receive a very poor return for their arduous work. Such failure to improve the lot of rural workers has led to an increase in the trek to the towns and aggravated the problems of urbanization. It will be well, then, to recall some of the points made by Pope John XXIII in his 1961 letter *Mater et Magistra*

(MM, 123–127). He stressed the need to develop adequately essential public services in rural areas including good roads, transportation, and means of communication, as well as religious, medical, educational, recreational, and buying facilities. He also noted the need for a government to develop a prudent agricultural policy including special economic help, price protection, taxation proportionate to the capacity to pay, and appropriate insurance (cf. GS, 66).

Consumerism

31. Justice suffers if those who work honestly do not have a sufficiency. Yet, there is the danger of another lamentable extreme when people make an idol of riches. Urged on by high-pressure advertising and a desire to keep up with, or to excel, their next-door neighbors, they make the acquisition of material possessions the be-all and end-all of their lives. It is important, therefore, to remember that the present-day spirit of consumerism is opposed to the spirit of Christ. We recall the parable of the rich man who heard the words, "thou fool, this night do they require your soul of you" (Lk 12:20) and also the words, "you cannot give yourself to God and to money" (Lk 16:13). The relentless pursuit of material possessions also leads to another sad situation, namely, the cruel contrast that arises between luxurious wealth, sometimes increased by corrupt practices, and extreme poverty.

VI. Exploitative Capitalism and Marxist Collectivism

32. The bishops at Puebla noted how the idolatry of wealth is concretized in two opposite forms that have a common root. "One is liberal capitalism [i.e., that kind of exploitative capitalism that seeks profit relentlessly and rejects any outside control]. The other, a reaction against liberal capitalism, is Marxist collectivism [a form of socialism that is atheistic, which denies the God-given rights of the individual and calls for the nationalization of all the means of production]. Both are forms of what can be called institutionalized injustice" (*Puebla*, 495; cf. LE, 11).

33. In describing exploitative capitalism, the bishops call it the idolatrous worship of wealth in *individualistic* terms, and they go on to use the same quotation from the letter of Paul VI *On the Development of Peoples,* which we ourselves used in our letter *Justice and Peace in the New Caribbean:* "It considers profit as the key motive for economic progress, competition as the supreme law of economics, and private ownership of the means of production as an absolute right that has no limits and carries no corresponding social obligation" (JP, 26; *Puebla*, 542).

It is true that in many countries of the world, efforts have been made, with some success, to bring under control those who cling to an exploitative capitalist outlook, but the fact remains that this outlook still exists and its power and damaging effects are being experienced in our region.

34.   Speaking of Marxist collectivism, the *Puebla Document* says: "With materialistic presuppositions, it leads to the idolatrous worship of wealth, but in collectivist terms" (543). "The driving force behind its dialectic is class struggle. Its objective is classless society, which is to be achieved by the dictatorship of the proletariat, but in the last analysis this really sets up the dictatorship of the party" (544).

35.   Both exploitative capitalism and Marxist collectivism look upon human beings merely as means of production—as hands or cogs—and, on this accord, they are both equally destructive of human dignity. Indeed, it is the deliberate policy of Marxist collectivism to foment discord and class war, which inevitably cause human suffering.

36.   The bishops at Puebla conclude by repeating what was said at the earlier Conference of Latin America Bishops at Medellín in 1968:

> The system of liberal capitalism and the temptation of the Marxist system would appear to exhaust the possibilities of transforming the economic structures of our continent. Both systems militate against the dignity of the human person. One takes for granted the primacy of capital, its power, and its indiscriminatory utilization in the function of profit making. The other, although it ideologically supports a kind of humanism, is more concerned with collective humanity, and in practice becomes a totalitarian concentration of state power (*Puebla*, 550).

In his latest encyclical, Pope John Paul II strongly stressed the primacy of labor over capital because only the individual is a person and capital is a collection of things subject to man: "Everything contained in the concept of capital in the strict sense is only a collection of things. Man, as the subject of work and independent of the work he does—man alone is a person. This truth has important and decisive consequences" (LE, 12).

37.   In the face of this situation, the Church rejects both these opposing systems in order to opt solely for the human being. What is at stake is not just economic development and the amassing of material wealth but what is called "integral human development" (i.e., that every person should have the means and the freedom for full development).

As Paul VI wrote: "Development cannot be limited to mere economic growth. In order to be authentic, it must be complete and integral, that is, it has to promote the good of every man and of the whole man" (PP, 14). Each must have an opportunity for human fulfillment, that is, to develop personal talents and to follow out the duty of living his or her life in accordance with God's will (cf. PP, 15 sequ.).

The "either/or" Mentality

38. One of the problems that faces us in the Caribbean is what may be called the "either/or" mentality. As a result, many see the choice as either exploitative capitalism or extreme Marxist collectivism, and this polarization is being encouraged by international influences and developments. Fear of Marxism keeps many from facing up to the oppressive reality of exploitative capitalism. "One could say that some people, faced with the danger of one clearly sinful system, forget to denounce and combat the established reality of another equally sinful system" (John Paul II, *Homily in Zapopan*). And it is particularly sad that often those who take the side of the poor and fight for justice are, quite unjustly, labeled communists.

39. While it is for each nation to determine its own policy within the limits of justice, we recall what we made clear in our previous letter: "exploitative capitalism and Marxist communism are not the only options" (JP, 26; cf. LE, 14). It is possible totally to reject uncontrolled exploitative capitalism with all the injustice to which it leads while accepting private-sector enterprise with proper legislative control as well as systems that allow for, and actually encourage, men and women to work to help themselves and to develop fully their powers.

Worker Participation

40. The Second Vatican Council urged that active participation of everyone in running the enterprise should be promoted and companies exist where workers share not only in the profits but also in the management and ownership of the undertaking. Pope John Paul II treats this especially in his encyclical *Laborem Exercens* (cf. GS, 68; LE, 14). Again, in the agricultural sector, men are more satisfied and work all the harder when they themselves own the land that they sow, reap, and develop.

Government Control

41. On the other hand, it is possible totally to reject atheistic Marxism and complete collectivism (i.e., a complete nationalization of the means of production), which destroy human liberty, while accepting a policy that, in this region, is sometimes called socialist (cf. JP, 31). So it is possible to opt for a measure of government control in industrial matters; indeed, such control is today very generally accepted. It is possible too, and sometimes desirable, to opt for nationalization of certain key industries and public utilities. Pius XI wrote, in *Quadragesimo Anno:* "It is rightly contended that certain forms of property must be reserved to the state since they carry with them a power too great to be left to private individuals without injury to the community at large" (QA, 114; cf. GS, 71).

42. In our own region, many governments provide extensive social service for education, health services, and community developments financed by a system of heavy taxation on industry and commercial enterprises and the well-to-do. They also enforce labor legislation and price and currency control. This curbs what might be the abuses of exploitative capitalism and helps to make the distribution of wealth less inequitable. We may note that such control is especially necessary in regard to transnational corporations that, though they may develop industry, are too often extremely self-centered in their activities (cf. LE, 17).

VII. Governments and Human Rights

43. We have spoken of how human rights can be destroyed by exploitation, capitalism, and by atheistic Marxist collectivism. We now turn to the true role of governments and note the harm that comes from the unjust use of the powers of government.

44. Individuals, families, and various groups cannot just live independently without some form of properly constituted authority. It is, therefore, obvious that the political community and public authority are based upon human nature and hence a part of God's plan for mankind. Love of country and our fellow countrymen should therefore encourage all to work for the common good and to take account of the needs and legitimate aspirations of others and of the general welfare (cf. GS, 26).

But there is clearly the need for the government to promote and protect the common good and to safeguard the rights of all the citizens. There can be a need for balance, and care must be taken to see that individual needs and aspirations are provided for, especially in the case of those who are less able to fend for themselves, such as women, children, and the less well-off (cf. GS, 74).

45. Today, governments are expected not only to provide social services and infrastructure but also to stimulate economic growth. Indeed, the responsibility of a government is so great that the happiness and well-being of the citizens will depend very largely on the dedication, efficiency, and high standard of integrity of those elected to office.

46.   Governments then have an all-important function and important responsibilities. They have the right and duty to exercise their authority, but they must be guided by certain principles:

a) A properly constituted government derives its authority ultimately from God and is bound to rule in accordance with the law of God, the Supreme Law-giver. It cannot, therefore, rightfully claim authority for enactments that are in defiance of God's law (cf. GS, 74). Also, to be authentic, a government must have the substantial support of the people.

b) The duty of those in power is to serve the community, not to seek self-aggrandizement and personal gain. They must work for the common good, not just for the interests of themselves or of their party.

c) The state exists for the benefit of the individual person and family; not the individual and family for the benefit of the state.

d) Too often, human rights are seen as something conceded by the state. This is not so. As we have explained above (sec. IV), every individual human being by his very nature has rights that come from God, and it is the duty of governments to respect these rights. A government that overrides these God-given rights is defying God and loses its claim to authenticity.

e) Today, in the actual sociopolitical situation in the world, in order to exercise power, a government must have a mandate from the people and must rule not only in accordance with the law of God, but also in conformity with the expressed will of the people. The most effective form of government is one in which the people know that they themselves have a share because they are actually given an opportunity freely to express their views on current issues and know that attention will be given to what they say (cf. GS, 75).

f) The mandate of a government should be ratified by the holding of properly conducted elections at prescribed intervals and should be sustained by constant and widespread consultation with the people. When a government clings to power in defiance of the popular will, it creates misery and frustration and is destructive of the national spirit.

g) The existence of an impartial, independent, and fearless judiciary is clearly essential for the well-being of any country.

h) In accordance with the important principle of "subsidiarity," the central government should avoid overcentralization and monopoly of control and give due scope to lesser bodies and private initiatives (cf. QA, 79; LE, 18).

47.   It is clearly no easy thing for a Caribbean government to carry out a task today in view of the social and economic problems that have to be faced, and we commend those who have given dedicated political service to their countries in face of great odds. These are true servants of their countries, worthy of the highest praise.

48.   But, unfortunately, too many of those who have entered politics have been far more intent on personal gain than on serving the people. Consequently, a number of politicians have fallen far short of what we expected of them, causing great damage to their countries. We have clear examples in the region of those who exercise the role of government, riding roughshod over humanity. There are ministers who cling to political power when they have lost the confidence of the people. They monopolize and pervert the means of communication, reject criticism, and limit employment to party members and favorites. Some governments even encourage or connive at violence. Indeed, violence has assumed such proportions in our region that we shall presently treat this especially.

49.   We also note with concern that, in some countries of the Caribbean, national security is being given an absolute value. This results in human rights and basic freedoms of individuals and of whole sections of the community being restricted and even denied. We therefore draw attention to the words of Pope John Paul II during his visit to the Philippines:

> Legitimate concern for the security of a nation, as demanded by the common good, could lead to the temptation of subjugating to the state the human being and his or her dignity and rights. Any apparent conflict between the exigencies of security and of the citizens' basic rights must be resolved according to the fundamental principle—upheld always by the Church—that social organization exists only for the service of man and for the protection of his dignity, and that it cannot claim to serve the common good when human rights are not safeguarded (*L'Osservatore Romano* [English Edition] 2/23/81).

VIII. Political Intolerance and Violence

50.   Political action should aim at the advancement of a nation. It calls for the contribution of the ablest members of the community and also for national unity and cooperation.

51.   We wish, therefore, to warn against the tendency for political parties or systems to require a blind loyalty from their supporters and for people to agree to such a demand. This leads to individuals becoming uncritical and passive. But it can also lead to intolerance, divisiveness, and even hatred. In some of our countries, politics has become debased by being associated with physical violence, leading to the senseless loss of many lives. In addition, degrading and inhuman treatment has become a matter of concern in the region. There have been increasing reports of police brutality and of detention of prisoners without charge or trial. Governments have maintained themselves in power by postponing elections or by manipulating the electoral process and muzzling a free press. In addition, there has been the growth of the phenomenon of structural violence and of exploitative systems using the powers of government to suppress human rights.

52.   In the face of these disturbing trends, in which so many of our people have suffered unjustly, let us recall this statement from the *Puebla Document:*

> Faced with the deplorable reality of violence in Latin America, we wish to express our view clearly. Condemnation is always the proper judgment on physical or psychological torture, kidnapping, the persecution of political dissidents or suspect persons, and the exclusion of people from public life because of their ideas. If these crimes are committed by the authorities entrusted with the task of safeguarding the common good, then they defile those who practice them, notwithstanding any reasons offered (*Puebla,* 531).

53.   "The Church is just as decisive in rejecting terrorist and guerilla violence, which becomes cruel and uncontrollable when it is unleashed. Criminal acts can in no way be justified as the way to liberation. Violence inexorably engenders new forms of oppression and bondage, which usually prove to be more serious than the ones from which people are allegedly being liberated. But more important, violence is an attack on life, which depends on the Creator alone. And we must also stress that when an ideology appeals to violence, it thereby admits its own weakness and inadequacy" (*Puebla,* 532).

54.   "Our responsibility as Christians is to use all possible means to promote the implementation of nonviolent tactics in the effort to re-establish justice in economic and sociopolitical relations. This is in accordance with the teaching of Vatican II, which applies to both national and international life:

> We cannot fail to praise those who renounce the use of violence in the vindication of their rights, and who resort to methods of defense which are otherwise available to weaker parties too, provided that this can be done without injury to the rights and duties of others or of the community (GS, 78) (*Puebla,* 533).

Here we may recall how much was achieved for human liberation and development through the active, nonviolent programs of Mahatma Ghandi and Martin Luther King.

IX. Political Coups

55. In several of our countries, there have recently been successful or attempted coups, and some of our countries can easily be vulnerable to such action.

56. We think it well, then, to set forth some general principles. First of all, we wish to recall how strongly Pope Paul VI condemned violence as a means to effect changes of government. Speaking in Bogota in 1968, he said:

> We must say and reaffirm that violence is not in accord with the gospel; that it is not Christian; and that sudden or violent changes of structures would be deceitful, ineffective in themselves, and certainly not in accord with the dignity of the people.

And in 1975, he wrote:

> The Church cannot accept violence, especially the force of arms—which is uncontrollable once it is let loose—and indiscriminate death as the path to liberation, because she knows that violence always provokes violence and irresistibly engenders new forms of oppression and enslavement, which are often harder to bear than those from which they claimed to bring freedom (EN, 37).

57. How serious, therefore, is the responsibility in conscience of those who, faced by circumstances of great tyranny, would have recourse to violence to effect a change of government. For, besides the almost inevitable loss of life and human suffering that would ensue, violence is likely to provoke a reaction of violence. And how often has a political coup simply replaced one tyranny by another!

58. In the interests of public order, a political coup may lead to the acceptance of those who come to power as a *de facto* government (i.e., a government that is accepted as having actual control). But a coup, as such, does not give legitimacy to the new government. Might is not to be identified with right. Genuine legitimacy can only come from the free support of the people and from respect by the government for the rights of the people. The obligation, therefore, remains for the new government to enlist the genuine participation of the people and to restore their rights and not simply those sectors of the population that may favor them.

59. The traditional means of peaceful political change through free and fair elections has come under assault in the Caribbean. Such elections, however, remain the well-tested model and a recognized right, even though they do not always guarantee good government.

X. Personal Violence

60. What has been said about violence can be applied to the sad deterioration of interpersonal relations, found in some places. Envy, jealousy, and political divisions have led to hatred and to a disregard for the value of human life, which has not stopped short of murder.

Again, we insist on the value of each human person; on the right to life of each one, including that of the unborn; on the right to live peacefully without oppression; on each one's right to hold and express his or her personal opinion; and on the duty of others to respect this right, just as they would wish others to respect their own right to do the same. Violence tends to provoke retaliation, and those who have recourse to violence bear guilt not only for the evil they do but also for the evil they may provoke in turn. Serious blame lies, also, with those who make arms available. Without such a supply of arms, the violence we have come to know would never have been possible.

XI. Conclusion

61. No one who considers the situation in the Caribbean can deny how serious are the problems that face us:

- how much need there is for the influence of Christ to become really effective among us;

- how much need there is for men and women to be liberated from personal sinfulness and from the devastating effects of sin;

- how much need there is for all men and women of good will to be more united and to work for a more just and prosperous society in which all will share in the benefits, and in which the dignity of every human person will be respected and all will enjoy a decent standard of living;

- how much need for our people to live in happiness and harmony, instead of being divided by hatred and enmity;

- how much need for governments to rule in accordance with the law of God and in active consultation with their people;

- how much need for them to work together with governments of other developing countries to present our case and secure at least some of the benefits that we justly demand; and

- how much need for them to work together in matters concerning the Caribbean, especially in making it a zone of peace.

Our Role as Christians

62.   Every Christian is sent to be an apostle of unity, of hope, and of salvation. As bishops, we have set out the Christian principles we consider particularly relevant to the situation. It will be largely for the laity to make effective plans to have these basic principles accepted and put into practice, and if all of us who call ourselves Christian really put our Christian principles into practice, the effect will be stupendous. We bishops wish to assure our laity that we realize that it is not easy to stand up for what is right and to work for justice. We know that you are vulnerable to ridicule and rejection. We also know that, in some territories of the Caribbean, you expose yourselves to the danger of loss of employment, loss of protection for yourselves and your families. We wish to express our solidarity with you and to offer you all the support and protection that we can give you.

63.   There is a danger that many will ask: "What can I do?" But if only members of the Church—both as individuals and in cooperation with others—would stand up for Christian principles, practicing and insisting upon justice, practicing the self-sacrificing love Christ asked of us, denouncing corruption and partiality, it would be amazing how much would be achieved.

64.   In our previous letter, we stressed the need for persons of integrity and high religious motivation to be active members of a political party, of a trade union, or of some other group or organization dedicated to the welfare of the community. We now wish to reiterate this call. What some of our countries lack is good government, and good government will never come as long as involvement in politics is shunned by those who by their integrity could contribute to transform political life (cf. JP, 10, 11).

The Power of the Spirit

65.   It is at once the weakness and the strength of Christianity that it relies on moral influence. Compliance with Christian principles is not brought about by force, but by high motivation and commitment. It is by the Christian community uniting in power of the Spirit to make the world the kind of place Christ wanted it to be that the world will be renewed. With increasing devotion to Christ, with love for all men, especially the most deprived, for His sake, with a deep desire for justice, in a spirit of willing self-sacrifice aided by the prayers of Mary, our Mother, let us go forward together.

Let us be mindful of the words of Scripture: "In him who is the source of my strength I have strength for everything" (Phil 4:13); "Everyone begotten of God conquers the world, and the power that has conquered the world is this faith of ours" (1 Jn 5:4).

In You, O Lord, and in your power, we put our trust. We know that our trust will not be in vain.

Dominica
February 2, 1982
Feast of the Presentation
of our Lord

Anthony Pantin
Archbishop of Port-of-Spain
President, A.E.C.

Arnold Boghaert, CSSR
Bishop of Roseau
Vice President, A.E.C.

Samuel Carter, SJ
Archbishop of Kingston

Kelvin Felix
Archbishop of Castries

Lawrence Burke, SJ
Bishop of Nassau

Sydney Charles
Bishop of St. George's in
Grenada

Edgerton Clarke
Bishop of Montego Bay

Antoine Demets
Titular Bishop of Cadossia

Willem Ellis
Bishop of Willemstad

Anthony Dickson
Bishop of Bridgetown-Kingstown

Richard Lester Guilly, SJ
Former Bishop of Georgetown

Brian Hennessy, CR
Bishop of Hamilton, Bermuda

Robert Hodapp, SJ
Bishop of Belize

Donald Reece
Bishop of St. John's-Basseterre

Benedict Singh
Bishop of Georgetown

Aloysius Zichem, CSSR
Bishop of Paramaribo

Peru
Liberation and the Gospel
(1984)

Brazilian and Peruvian churches have taken leadership positions in the development of the theology of liberation. Dialogue between these churches and the Vatican has gone on at an unusual and rapid pace. Not only individual theologians respond to queries from the Vatican about their writings but also entire national episcopates are expected to (or expect to) be part of the process of definition and clarification.

The Congregation for the Doctrine of the Faith issued two instructions on the theology of liberation. The first, The Instruction on Certain Aspects of the Theology of Liberation, *received extensive responses and commentaries from Latin America and other parts of the world. Foremost of these responses, in the minds of many observers, is that of the Peruvian bishops, in part because liberation "was born" in Peru.*

The bishops first give full and unanimous assent to the instruction. They then present a detailed characterization of the Church in Peru that "has achieved a significant place" in Peruvian society, "as a sign of hope and salvation, especially among the poorest and most marginated sectors." The letter goes on to analyze various issues, including the role of theologians.

1. We want to begin this document by making known our full and unanimous assent to the *Instruction on Certain Aspects of the "Theology of Liberation,"* published September 3, 1984, by the Sacred Congregation for the Doctrine of the Faith, with the expressed approval of the Holy Father.

2. The instruction to which we refer will facilitate the work the Peruvian bishops have been doing these last years because it deals with the same theme, one that touches us closely. It wants to provide the guidelines that are absolutely necessary for our own society.

3. The instruction affirms that "the expression 'theology of liberation' is a thoroughly valid term" (III, 4) that "refers first of all to a special

267

concern for the poor and the victims of oppression, which in turn begets a commitment to justice" (III, 3). For that, it must be understood "in light of the specific message of Revelation, authentically interpreted by the Magisterium of the Church" (III, 4).

4.   At the same time, the instruction points out that there are "deviations, and risks of deviation, damaging to the faith and to Christian living, that are brought about by certain forms of liberation theology" (Intro., para. 5).

5.   Following these directives, we confirm among ourselves the just aspiration for freedom and liberation that has brought to birth ecclesial movements in search of a commitment to justice "for the poor and the victims of oppression" (III, 3).

6.   In this regard, the saving ministry of Jesus is the constant theme in the gospel, which affirms this aspiration. The privileged ones are the poor (cf. Lk 6:21–26), to the point that Jesus made himself poor in order that the poor might become rich (cf. 2 Cor 8:9), and to identify himself with the poor. A constantly emphasized sign of Christ's messiahship is that *the poor are evangelized* (cf. Mt 11:5; Lk 7:22). When Jesus stated his mission in Nazareth, he did so by citing the Old Testament (Is 61:1ff), which he applied to himself (cf. Lk 4:18): He is the evangelizer of the poor.

7.   "And in the figure of the poor, we are led to recognize the mysterious presence of the Son of Man, who became poor himself for love of us. This is the foundation of the inexhaustible words of Jesus on the judgment in Matthew 25:31–46. Our Lord is one with all in distress; every distress is marked by his presence" (IV, 9).

8.   We find the essence of liberation throughout Holy Scripture, from Genesis and Exodus on, but its full understanding must be illuminated by the liberating and redeeming action of good through Jesus Christ in the Holy Spirit, who saves people from sin, from death, and from all slavery. Therefore, the center of the biblical message is the death and resurrection of the Lord because (his death and resurrection) are the fulfillment of the paschal mystery (cf. Rom 4:25; 7:25).

9.   Paul VI, in the apostolic exhortation *Evangelii Nuntiandi;* John Paul II, in the opening address in Puebla and in his subsequent comments in February 1979 (and more recently in Canada); and the Latin American episcopacy, in Medellín and Puebla, have given concrete and precise guidance about how the meaning of liberation in the Scriptures ought to be interpreted. The pastoral application of liberation is an ongoing task in the continent's present situation.

Liberation ought always to lead to unity and never in any way to confrontation between persons. Still more, it ought to guard and deepen the unity of the Church: "That all may be one as you, Father, are in me, and I in you; I pray that they may be one in us, that the world may believe that you sent me" (Jn 17:21).

10.   In recent years, this message of liberation has inspired the life of the Church in Peru. It has also inspired many pastoral documents from the episcopacy—the episcopacy being the source for the deepening of spiritual life. The Church has achieved a significant place in the whole of society as a sign of hope and salvation, especially in the poorest and most marginated sectors.

The Harsh Peruvian Reality

A. Cry for Justice

11.   Every day our pastoral work provides us with the opportunity to verify the various ways in which the situation of inhuman poverty continuously worsens: extremely low salaries; lack of stable employment; malnutrition with irreversible future consequences; increase in infant deaths; outbreak of illnesses that had been thought eliminated. . . . And to this panorama must be added a notable decadence in public morality and private behavior such as badly constituted homes, instability in marriages, abandonment of families, alcoholism, and so forth.

12.   The problem of violence has recently arisen in Peru, presumably as a response to this situation. It is a violence that has particular impact on youth under the influence of extreme ideologies that do not respect the fundamental value of life and human dignity. It is a violence that at times merges with disproportionate and indiscriminate repression that, instead of correcting evil, results in an atmosphere of vengeance that is unacceptable among Christians. Not removed from this sorrowful picture is the introduction of drug traffic in our country that simultaneously becomes a tool of violence and of corruption of our people.

13.   We cannot do less than reject these outrages, whatever their origin must be, since they truly constitute "the most devastating and humiliating kind of scourge" (*Puebla,* 29). Seen from the point of view of faith, it is "a scandal and a contradiction to Christian existence" (*Puebla,* 28).

14.   The roots of this state of affairs are deep, and the causes are personal, structural, economic, political, and social. In the last instance, this comes from a concept of the human person and of society that is marked by selfishness, the desire for power and wealth, the priority of material things over persons (cf. LE, 13) that makes people insensible to the suffering of our weaker sisters and brothers. It is a very grave situation of sin with all its personal, family, and social dimensions.

B. Challenge to the Faith

15.   Christian faith is not indifferent to this situation. Moreover, it feels itself questioned by it. In Peru, "undoubtedly, situations of injustice and acute poverty are an indictment in themselves, indicating that the faith was not strong enough to affect the criteria and the decisions of those responsible for ideological leadership and the organization of our people's socioeconomic life together" (*Puebla,* 437).
16.   All this constitutes a serious challenge for the Church's task of evangelization. In effect, the ecclesial community has as its specific mission to announce the good news of redemption in every place and every historical moment. This assumes that the Church ought to be attentive to the signs of the times and that it knows how to retrieve the fears of all people, especially the most scorned and oppressed, and that it gives full meaning to their justified longings for liberation (EN, 34).

C. The Path of a Church

17.   Faced with today's painful and often tragic situation, we see the Church in Latin America, strongly motivated by the Second Vatican Council and the conferences of Medellín and Puebla, making an effort for renewal and searching to find answers to the concrete demands of our countries. Without a doubt, our Church in Peru has achieved a significant place in the entire society as a sign of hope and salvation, especially among the poorest and most marginated sectors.
18.   Within this ecclesial dynamic of the people of God, we discover many forms of spirituality: movements centered in the following of Jesus Christ and in the encounter with God through the poor neighbor in whose "very concrete faces" are recognized "the suffering features of Christ the Lord, who questions and challenges us" (*Puebla,* 31); movements that put the emphasis on personal conversion as the condition for complete structural transformation; others who seek to secure the values of the family in a dehumanizing society; prayer movements that underline the value of that which is spiritual in the face of a world that each day becomes more materialistic; groups that meet to hear and comment on the word of God; greater participation in the eucharistic celebrations; and vigorous and generous youth movements.
19.   As fruit of what has just been mentioned, we affirm with joy the resurgence of priestly and religious vocations as a reaffirmation of an ecclesial commitment on the part of numerous lay people in the city and in the rural areas.
20.   Sensing the need to accompany this journey in the faith and the commitment of believing people, our Church has responded to the

renewing inspiration of Vatican II, and of Medellín and Puebla. It is here that originate the attempts to reflect, in the light of the word of God and the magisterium, about the meaning of so many efforts, including their achievements and their failures. One of these efforts, indubitably a significant one in our Church's process, is what is called "theology of liberation," which was born in our country and has spread and taken root in other neighboring countries.

21.   This process has led, at times, to positions that are not always coincident when it comes time to assume the evangelizing commitment of the Church in the present moment.

22.   This situation concerns us. We see the need for clear discernment that must result in practical guidance as we fulfill our obligation as teachers and pastors. We must seek to foster unity in the spirit of ecclesial communion and in filial loyalty to the vicar of Christ and in agreement with magisterium of the Church.

23.   In 1973, in our document regarding evangelization, we said: "On the other hand, there are also tensions among us because of different ways of understanding and carrying out the mission of the Church. The difficulty of a balance between immanence and transcendence, between present history and eschatology, between human history and the kingdom of God is today more noticeable. At times, it would seem that these tensions were going to be resolved by opting for one of the poles. The solution will be the determination of everyone to arrive at a true synthesis of the vertical and the horizontal, of the divine and the human; in all of this, we will move in the shadow and within the limits that the cross marks out for us" (cf. *Evangelization*, 2, 4, 2).

24.   With Paul VI, we recognize that, in order to maintain the integrity of the message and the unity of the Church, there is a "legitimate pluralism of research and thought that investigates and expounds dogma in various forms but without eliminating its authentic, objective meaning; this is a natural component of catholicity" (*Reconciliation within the Church*, 4). For this reason, the magisterium of the Church "is determinant for whatever refers to the faith of all people. It serves them also as a guarantee against the subjective criteria of whatever interpretation is different from it" (ibid).

D. *Constructors of Peace*

25.   In fulfillment of our obligation to be the sign of, as well as the constructors of, the unity at the center of this our society, in which many conflicts exist, and as defenders and promoters of human dignity in this same society, in which human rights are frequently not respected, we want to announce the gospel of peace and "to give reason for our hope" (1 Pt 3:15).

26. Through faith, we receive the peace of God in Christ, who is our peace and the Prince of Peace (cf. Eph 2:14; Is 9:5).

27. But where unjust social, political, economic, and cultural disparities are found, there is negation of the gift of peace from God. Even more, there is rejection of God himself (cf. Mt 25:31–46; *Medellín*, Peace, 14).

28. Isaiah reminded his fellow citizens that peace is the fruit of justice (cf. Is 32:17), and in the history of our people, a civilization of love can only be constructed on a foundation of justice. But we want to leave it clearly stated that structural changes will not be worth anything if the hearts of men and women are not changed. As John Paul II recently told us (World Day of Peace, 1984), peace sprouts from the heart of the new person. Only the new heart will be capable of renewing the world that surrounds it because only the new heart rejects sin and all its consequences and is open to a new life of grace with the strength to transform personal, family, community, and social matters.

E. Present Social Doctrine of the Church

29. One of the most outstanding points in the *Puebla Document* and in John Paul II's inaugural address at that meeting was the insistence on the social teachings of the Church. Before Puebla, in some sectors of the Church, there were unjust criticisms about the social doctrine; some judged it to be static and even ahistorical. In contrast, the final document from Puebla emphasized the strict tie that exists between the doctrine and the task of evangelization, human promotion, and integral liberation.

30. In order that these social teachings of the Church have credibility and are accepted, "they must effectively respond to the serious challenges and problems arising out of the reality of Latin America" (*Puebla*, 476). Recognizing the profound timeliness of the social doctrine of the Church, the Peruvian episcopacy, inspired by the publication of the encyclical *Laborem Exercens*, prepared a document that it applied to the present sociopolitical situation in Peru. In the document of the magisterium of John Paul II, we discovered the totality of the road that ought to be taken by the Church in the world of work and of the whole social structure that surrounds it.

31. Along this same line, a short time before the appearance of the document from our episcopacy, the social action department of CELAM edited the document *Christian Faith and Social Commitment*, which, without a doubt, greatly assists Christians who want to commit themselves to social tasks, to understand the harmoniously developed social teaching of the magisterium of the Church. We feel that in the difficult times that the country is presently experiencing, and in the face of the disorientation that some sectors of the Church are undergoing as they are influenced by diverse ideologies and theological currents, by reading this document they will find the necessary clarifications for good discernment and critical judgment about the responsibilities that they ought to assume in these circumstances.

32.   In this regard, we remind everyone of the words of the instruction that "the concern for the purity of the faith demands giving the answer of effective witness in the service of one's neighbor, the poor and the oppressed in particular, in an integral theological fashion" (XI, 18).

33.   As pastors, we ought to be vigilant about the formation of Christians so that they be mature in their faith, deeply living the gospel, and that they be capable of presenting with integrity the message of salvation and the imperatives of true Christian liberation. Generous persons will thereby avoid making simplifications or false interpretations of the revealed message, without critical judgment and adequate preparation.

The Need for Discernment

34.   As a consequence of becoming aware of the situation of misery in which so many people live in our country, with the resultant awakening of a longing for liberation, the Church in Peru is experiencing a greater desire for commitment to the poor, as we have pointed out elsewhere in this document.

35.   This commitment was not just made on a practical level but was also made in theological reflections that sought to illumine this commitment in the light of faith. The diverse currents of the theology of liberation should be put within this context of reflection. Some of these currents, in their attempt to better understand the socioeconomic reality of Latin America, have turned to the social sciences and have also used some elements of Marxist analysis as tools to interpret the social reality.

36.   Faced with these and other theological-pastoral currents that exist among us—currents that have made valuable contributions as well as having run the risk of deformations—it is worthwhile also to make careful discernment, based on the magisterium of the Church and, concretely, on the instruction to which we have been referring since the beginning of this document. The issue is broad and requires many nuances. Nevertheless, within the confines of this document, it is advantageous to make some considerations about three important themes for our reflection as Christians and pastors.

37.   The first is the view of history and of society; the second is the relation between praxis and truth; the third between the kingdom of

God and human action in history. We want the reflections that follow to serve the faithful as basic criteria for discerning these matters now, as well as in the future.

A. History and Society

38.   One of the aspects to which we refer in regard to the Marxist analysis is the concept of history as determined by the class struggle: the attempt to overcome the struggle of the classes through the suppression of capitalism (identified as private ownership of the means of production) and the introduction of socialism (interpreted as the collective appropriation of those same means of production). According to this way of thinking, private property necessarily divides the society into opposing classes and brings about the exploitation of the workers by the owners.

39.   Above all else, we must recognize not only the existence of social conflicts but also the structural nature of many of them since they arise out of the existence of opposing interests (cf. LE, 11). In fact, we can take for granted that these conflicts will never be resolved definitively as long as these conflicts of interest exist. But such conflicts and antagonisms are not essentially irreconcilable. Even less can we accept that they be deliberately exacerbated. We believe rather that by correctly applying distributive justice and establishing institutions and structures that truly embody that justice, those conflicts can be overcome.

40.   It is clear that good will is not enough; it is necessary to reach, through dialogue, a certain balance of power between those sectors. The poor sectors need unity and a clearer awareness of their own dignity and rights as much as of their political and economic realities (cf. LE, 8). There exists the real danger that unscrupulous leaders will attempt to take advantage of the efforts of the poor to unite and inform themselves. Nevertheless, if the desired dialogue is to occur with harmony and fraternal solidarity instead of catastrophic confrontation, both sides must be able to count on conditions that will permit them to be treated as truly free and equal in dignity. On the other hand, we cannot place our hope principally in the balance of strength. Only Christ's love is capable of overcoming the humanly unsavable dialectics of opposition.

41.   Although the common good should not be sacrificed for individual interests, a type of society in which all that is personal is sacrificed for the collective benefit is not acceptable either. The antagonisms cannot be resolved by the suppression of the parties in conflict. Nor is the denial of private property acceptable. And here we must remember the constant pontifical teaching about social issues: property or its equivalent rights are indispensable in order to guarantee an environment of freedom and dignity for each person. In this regard, one must also remember the blending of meanings that the *Puebla Document* pointed out when it stressed especially the "mortgage" that this right imposes. But it must also be pointed out that it is not the existence of property that is evil but rather the fact that it has not become the patrimony of all people. It ought, therefore, to be universalized. True community is only possible among people who are in control of their own lives and who freely give of themselves in reciprocity. By giving of themselves, they share common goods and burdens.

42.   We Christians believe that each person has been created by God as a free being, called to give his or her own personal response to grace, thereby becoming united to God and to one's brothers and sisters. A person is not simply a member of the human species but rather is part of all people and part of each person.

B. Praxis and Truth

43.   Another aspect of Marxist thought is the primacy of praxis from which truth arises or which becomes a fundamental criterion for truth. Admitting that thought should be the critical reflect on praxis, in this way of thinking, the origin of the criteria of criticisms is not clear unless it is out of that very praxis itself. We accept that all reflection is based on lived reality. We also accept that thought that is not converted into action and commitment is sterile. In the field of religion, the sincerity of our faith should be manifested by our behavior, which is true to that faith. Nonetheless, we must recall that the human person has an inalienable contemplative dimension, which results in an interest to know the truth as such, independent of their projects to transform the world through action. In the religious area, it must be understood that faith is not only the justification for what is moral.

44.   Another aspect of the relation between praxis and truth comes to us from verification. In effect, many times, action changes our first mental propositions with which we tried to represent for ourselves the real world. We learn from lived experiences. But this is valid only in the field of technical and experimental sciences. In spite of the fact that in ethical and religious matters the fruits of our actions can lead us to question our convictions and our practical decisions, no experience can be constructed into a source of basic principles in ethical and religious matters. For Christians, the supreme criteria of truth in these matters are found in revelation, interpreted by those who can legitimately do so. All theology should have its basis in revelation, in the *depositum fidei*. It is from this context that one can reflect on any reality whatever, including praxis, which always remains subordinate to revelation.

45. In certain currents of modern thought, among which Marxism is found, it is affirmed that people create themselves through their activities directed at transforming the world. Such is the power of praxis. We recognize that human persons have as a sign of their glory the ability to fulfill themselves through their action, to direct themselves to a particular goal by their moral decisions, and to contribute by their work to the perfection of the creation. But, for Christians, reality as such is the creation of God. People receive from God their existence and their nature, along with the moral law that must guide them. People act within physical conditions and moral norms that are given them, which they neither invent nor choose. Their creativity, which is part of being the "image of God," is exercised over all things as a search for and in obedience to the truth that comes from God. Their greatest glory is to enter into the plan of their Father God.

46. Marxist thought not only puts praxis first, but also considers praxis fundamental; the revolutionary praxis is considered to be the nerve center of history. A Christian cannot and should not think this way, nor begin to say that the truth is only to be grasped when one makes a class option and enters into the revolutionary praxis.

47. It is true that no one can truly come to understand how harsh the fate of the poor and their struggle to maintain and better their existence really are unless one sufficiently shares their situation with them. It is also certain that people really only live their convictions when their lives are consistent with their convictions. But to affirm that one should begin by choosing sides is to already falsify thought and to remove from it the possibility of being objective. To affirm beforehand that the reasons that are contrary to one's own explanations of things are invalid (due to excessive idealism or out of defense of class interests), deprives people of any possible corrective to their way of looking at the world. Dialogue becomes impossible, and that which is real is systematically seen through prejudices that deform things and facts. Thought becomes only an instrument of militant action or a corrective of strategies themselves, beginning with the practical problems that are encountered. One falls into true dogmatism and his or her option takes on the conviction of religious faith.

48. Christians who adopt the principle of the need to make a class option in order to arrive at the truth could be led to a distorted, radical reinterpretation of their faith. The Scriptures, the figure and person of Christ, the nature and function of the Church, worship and the sacraments, and spirituality would all be reinterpreted in a political key, in a dimension that would remain absolutized. The Church would also remain so, irreconcilably divided according to political criteria: those who are for and those who are opposed to the system that claims to save (neutrality or a third way being impossible), those who look and live their faith from one or the other side, in confrontation.

49.   Christ cannot be reduced to a fighter who was put to death for being a subversive. Nor can it be said that the Church that is born within a people is brought forth from the people. As to the Eucharist, it cannot be converted into simply a celebration of the people's serious attempts at liberation.

C. *The Kingdom of God and Human Action*

50.   In healthy reaction to an inadequate concept of faith that is limited to interior piety, to salvation after death, and to morality between persons, many Christians have been led to affirm strongly the social and historical consequences of the gospel and its impact on the world. This reaction is not exempt from danger and should not lead us to a practical denial of the transcendental nature of faith and of the priority of the eternal salvation of each person.

51.   We find ourselves faced with affirmations about concepts—such as that of the uniqueness of history—that are, at the least, ambiguous. Is the history of the efforts of people to better their situation now sacred history, the history of salvation? Is progress part of the arrival of the kingdom? If by salvation history we understand not only those activities that are properly divine, such as creation, incarnation, and redemption, but also the activities of people insofar as they are in response to the initiatives of God, be they accepted or rejected, there is effectively only one history; the vacillating efforts of humans are written within the divine plan, whether they wish it or not, whether they know it or not. Christ, the Son of God made man, has given the perfect response, but all people are called to participate in this response. This supernaturalism and gratuitousness of the order of grace cannot be denied. It is a question, then, of making clear distinctions without making separations. *Gaudium et Spes* (39) said it very well: "Earthly progress must be carefully distinguished from the growth of Christ's kingdom. Nevertheless, to the extent that the former can contribute to the better ordering of human society, it is of vital concern to the kingdom of God." If this distinction is not made, grace will be absorbed by nature, God by history, Christ will remain reduced to a moral teacher or a social leader, and the Church will be seen as a human institution. Or, the temporal realities of history, the people, and revolution will be made divine or messianic. Eschatology will be diluted in the revolutionary process of history, and the reign of God will be achieved only through the efforts of people.

52.   On the other hand, if the unity between the two dimensions is not maintained, the reality of our faith is denied: creation, incarnation, redemption, and grace. Immanent messianism cannot be allowed to lead to bitter disillusions; but to renounce all hope of improving this world from now on is to negate the saving power of the Lord. The struggle against evil in this world is the responsibility of human beings, assisted by grace, but the definitive triumph against death and evil is the gift we await from God. It is for him to put an end to history, as it was he who began history.

53.   Thus, it is a matter of affirming the implication of the gospel in all of life, the world and the history of humanity and the ineradicable distinction between the natural order and the order of grace. It is a difficult position but an indispensable one for our faith.

Pastoral Guidelines

54.   In agreement with the preceding reflections, concerned about our obligations as pastors and guides of the people of God and inspired by the instruction from the Sacred Congregation for the Doctrine of the Faith and by the discourse that the Holy Father gave October 4, 1984, when he received the plenary assembly of the Peruvian bishops in an audience and exhorted them "to discern realistically and objectively the doctrinal and pastoral situation of the different local situations so that priest, religious, and faithful lay people do not lack timely and necessary guidance," we want to give the following concrete pastoral guidelines:

   In the first place, we transcribe the content of canon 823 of the recently promulgated religious code in which this right and obligation of the bishops is supported:

55.   "§1. In order for the integrity of the truths of the faith and morals to be preserved, the pastors of the Church have the duty and the right to be vigilant lest harm be done to the faith or morals of the Christian faithful through writings or the use of instruments of social communication; . . . they also have the duty and right to denounce writings which harm correct faith or good morals.

56.   "§2. The bishops as individuals or gathered in particular councils or conferences of bishops have the duty and the right mentioned in §1 with regard to the Christian faithful committed to their care; the supreme authority of the Church has this duty and right in regard to the whole of God."

A. Publications

57.   We assign what follows for the entire territory of Peru, but always with due recognition for the jurisdictional authority of bishops of local dioceses.

58.   a) According to its regulations, and in coordination with the respective local ordinary, the episcopal conference will oversee with

special care the publication of written material and audiovisuals that touch on or expound doctrinal or pastoral subjects whose influence would be on a national level.

59. b) Attention is drawn to the fact that publications that lack the proper authorization (cf. c. 827:2) and are already in circulation cannot be used as textbooks for teaching nor can they be sold in churches or oratories (cf. c. 827:4).

B. Religious Formation

60. a) Canon 812 specifies that "it is necessary that those who teach theological disciplines in any institute of higher studies have a mandate from the competent ecclesiastical authority."

61. b) With respect to Catholic universities, canon 810 states: "§1. It is the responsibility of the authority who is competent in accord with the statutes to provide for the appointment of teachers to Catholic universities who besides their scientific and pedagogical suitability are also outstanding in their integrity of doctrine and probity of life; when those requisite qualities are lacking, they are to be removed from their positions in accord with the procedure set forth in the statutes.

62. "§2. The conference of bishops and the diocesan bishops concerned have the duty and the right of being vigilant that in these universities the principles of Catholic doctrine are faithfully observed."

63. c) The proper formation of catechists is entrusted by canon law especially to the diocesan bishops as part of their mission (cf. c. 780). The same canon law recommends that theological courses for the formation of lay people be established (cf. c. 811); and, in the same sense, canon 821 exhorts the episcopal conferences and all the bishops that Christian formation and evangelization are under their vigilance, as the pope reminded us in his discourse of October 4; that "evangelization must be systematic, explicit, and profound so that the faithful can also overcome the harassment of groups with different leanings that want to wrench from them the treasure of their Christian faith."

64. d) It is also opportune to remember the need to be faithful to the liturgical norms that the statutes of the Church set, and the adaptations that were granted by petition of our episcopal conference, both in the celebration of the Eucharist as well as in the other sacraments and for which is appropriate in preaching. Also concerning this matter, the Holy Father told us (October 4): "The liturgy celebrated according to the norms of the Church and actively participated in guarantees the most authentic instruction in the words and in the holy symbols to which faithful people are so sensitive. And, as the liturgy is essentially the task of the Church and cannot be monopolized by any group in the way that it is celebrated, it must be the mirror of an active ecclesial community, united to its pastor, committed to living that which it celebrates by carrying the grace of the preached word, shared prayer, and communion with Christ and with sisters and brothers in the Eucharist into daily lives."

C. Organizations

65.   a) Organizations of priests or of the faithful that have religious or ecclesial objectives (cf. c. 305:1,2) or that affect pastoral work are under the vigilance and eventually the approval of the competent authority.

66.   b) Likewise, the episcopal conference commends to the episcopal commission of bishops and religious and to the Peruvian Conference of Religious the study of the instruction, with a view to its application to the pastoral activity of religious and to the consecrated life, in accord with the special guidelines that the Holy Father gave us in his message during the October 4 audience.

67.   c) The episcopal conference requests the different episcopal commissions to study the instruction from the Sacred Congregation for the Doctrine of the Faith in order to apply it to our society and to propose corresponding pastoral actions.

D. Theologians

68.   We petition the different theological and pastoral currents in our midst—we do this at the same time that we manifest our appreciation for their work—and commend the following tasks to them:

69.   a) We bear in mind the just liberty that canon law points out to theologians, within the conditions of canon 218: "Those who are engaged in the sacred disciplines enjoy a lawful freedom of inquiry and of prudently expressing their opinions on matters in which they have expertise, while observing a due respect for the magisterium of the Church."

70.   b) "Aware of the ecclesial character of their vocation, theologians will collaborate loyally and in a spirit of dialogue with the Magisterium of the Church. They will be able to recognize in the Magisterium a gift of Christ to His Church and will welcome its word and its directives with filial respect" (XI, 4).

71.   c) "A theology of liberation correctly understood constitutes an invitation to theologians to deepen certain essential biblical themes with a concern for the grave and urgent questions which the contemporary yearning for liberation, and those movements which more or less faithfully echo it, pose for the Church. We dare not forget for a single instant the situations of acute distress which issue such a dramatic call to theologians" (IV, 1).

72. d) We urgently appeal to theologians to help us discern clearly, as the instruction invites us to do, between an authentic theology of liberation and those that are not authentic.

73. e) We invite particularly those who are dedicated to the theology of liberation to make an evaluation of their own studies and publications in light of the said instruction and of this document. And after communicating it to the episcopal conference, and after its approval, to make it public in the spirit of communication and ecclesial service.

74. f) We also ask theologians to help our faithful to shape solid, critical opinions about ideologies such as capitalist liberalism and Marxism, which have influence in our midst.

75. g) Finally, we ask them to be attentive always to the repercussions that their theological work can have on pastoral work.

E. Special Application of the Instruction

76. a) The episcopal conference plans to prepare a manual that will provide guidelines for the practical application of the subjects dealt with in the document from the Sacred Congregation for the Doctrine of the Faith, to which we have been referring.

77. b) We find the fundamental orientations that this manual ought to contain in the document itself, particularly in section XI, 17:

78. c) "It is proper to emphasize those essential aspects which the 'theologies of liberation' especially tend to misunderstand or to eliminate, namely: the transcendence and gratuity of liberation in Jesus Christ, true God and true man; the sovereignty of grace; and the true nature of the means of salvation, especially of the Church and the sacraments. One should also keep in mind the true meaning of ethics, in which the distinction between good and evil is not relativized; the real meaning of sin, the necessity for conversion, and the universality of the law of fraternal love.

d) "One needs to be on guard against the politicization of existence which, misunderstanding the entire meaning of the kingdom of God and the transcendence of the person, begins to sacralize politics and betray the religion of the people in favor of the projects of the revolution."

79. e) It seems opportune to highlight the following guidelines:

"The warning against the serious deviations of some 'theologies of liberation' must not at all be taken as some kind of approval, even indirect, of those who keep the poor in misery, who profit from the misery, who notice it while doing nothing about it or who remain indifferent to it. The Church, guided by the Gospel of mercy and by the love for mankind, hears the cry for justice and intends to respond to it with all her might" (XI, 1).

80. And as the instruction tells us, "with boldness and courage, with farsightedness and prudence [the Church ought to follow] with zeal and strength of spirit, with a love for the poor which demands sacrifice (XI, 2). And "all priests, religious, and lay people [will work in this sense] in communion with their bishop and with the Church, each in accord with his or her own specific ecclesial vocation" (XI, 3).

F. Formation for Moral Responsibility

81. a) In relation to the situation that presently exists in the country concerning the crisis of ethical values in our society and the need to guide the commitment of faithful lay people who have the responsibility of Christian influence in the temporal order: "It is generally the function of their well-formed Christian conscience to see that the divine law is inscribed in the life of the earthly city" (GS, 43; AA, 7). The episcopal conference also proposes to create a program of social ethics which can, at the same time, serve to help in the development of the course in civic education in school education. It can be further disseminated through the communications media so that through that means it will reach the major part of the population that is suffering from this crisis of values.

82. b) We also judge it to be necessary to disseminate what is explicit in the *Code of Canon Law* in reference to the liberty and responsibility that correspond to the lay person in the performance of his or her civic activities. Canon 227 says: "Lay Christian faithful have the right to have recognized that freedom in the affairs of the earthly city which belongs to all citizens; when they exercise such freedom, however, they are to take care that their actions are imbued with the spirit of the gospel and take into account the doctrine set forth by the magisterium of the Church; but they are to avoid proposing their own opinions as the teachings of the Church in questions that are open to various opinions."

83. c) Although the principal motivation explicit in the theology of liberation has been the proximity, in the faith and in charity, to the circumstances of the poverty of our people, and while reaffirming that we reject the intent of many who want to protect the gospel in order to defend their own selfish interests, we want to state that it is not just to attribute love and defense of the poor exclusively to one line of theology. All healthy theology ought to be inspired by the gospel, which manifests a predilection for the poor and leads necessarily to liberation from sin, the root of all evil and injustice. It is what the documents *Evangelii Nuntiandi* and *Puebla* call "integral liberation."

Final Exhortation

84.   Let us all together seek the path for the restoration of justice, as St. Paul exhorts, writing to the Ephesians: "Let us profess the truth in love" (Eph 4:15) so that our Church in Peru acquires that unity that Jesus, in his prayer to the Father, sought as an effective sign so that all the world will believe that the Father had sent him (cf. Jn 17:21). In this way, let us begin to make real the phrase that has been chosen as the motto in preparation for the forthcoming visit of the Holy Father to Peru—"The people of God on the way with John Paul, the pilgrim"—indicating that all of us are on the way to revitalizing the faith that we received as the heritage of our fathers.

85.   Our heritage has its roots in the holiness of the saints: Toribio de Mogrovejo, Rosa, Martin, Francisco Solano, Juan Macias, and the venerable Ana de los Angeles. It ought to help us discover the love necessary to live as brothers and sisters, under the protection of Mary, Queen of Peace, and protectress of our country.

Southern Andes, Peru
Witnesses to the Resurrection
(1987)

Terrorism and turbulence have disrupted the lives of many farm families in the southern highlands of Peru. The bishops of that region here reflect on "a situation of permanent threat to the life of the people." Beyond the violence of guerrillas and of indiscriminate response by government forces that often injures the innocent, the bishops look for more lasting solutions "to our ancestral problems," especially in the distribution of land.

As objectives, the bishops choose first "to accompany our people who live in a permanent situation of emergency, a people who have always been crushed." Then the bishops hope to "contribute to the earth becoming a way to peace and life." Land distribution by the government has begun, but the process has been uneven, slow, and autocratic. Further, the bishops express concern for the observance of human rights and note that they have established Vicariates for Solidarity for this purpose. Lastly, the bishops have as an objective "to encourage the exercise of democracy and an appreciation of the identity of the Andean people."

1. As witnesses of the resurrection of Jesus Christ, Lord of Life and conqueror of death, we, the pastors of the Church of the Southern Peruvian Highlands, have accompanied our people, encouraging, through gestures and words, their struggle for life and their incessant search for peace in this region and in the country.

2. In this paschal time, in which the Church celebrates in Jesus the triumph of life over death, we turn anew to the women and the men of this part of the Andes to express to them our desire to renew and strengthen our mission and our fidelity.

In the Year of Evangelization

3. This same desire led us, at the beginning of 1987, to declare a Year of Evangelization in the ecclesiastical jurisdictions commended to us with the theme of "Evangelize: Sow Life to Harvest Peace."

4. Evangelization is the task of the Church. To announce the gospel, message of liberty and strength of liberation,[1] is to announce the Good News of the kingdom of God, kingdom of life, kingdom of justice and peace.

5. To announce the kingdom of the God of life here, in the South Andean Highlands, in a situation of permanent threat to the life of the people, has meant and means for us to sow life, gift of God, which every person ought to care for and defend as the most precious seed of our fields.

6. Those who sow with tears, harvest with joy (Ps 126:5), says the psalmist. Convinced of that, we await, along with our people, the time and the days of the fullness of justice among us, unequivocal sign that we will be able to harvest peace.

7. To accomplish this urgent task, we need to mobilize all the energy, all the good will, all the capacity willing to work for a radical option for life and peace, above all, now that "we are living in Peruvian society and especially in the rural areas, a climate both of frustration and of immense expectation of finally discovering solutions to our ancestral problems."[2]

Orientations for the Sowing of Peace

8. As humble followers of Him who came so that we might all have life and life in abundance (cf. Jn 10:10), we convoke the people of God—the communities of the Church, pastoral agents, and, in general, all Christians—to a renewal of their efforts in the field of life. That our seed not be blown away by the wind or fall on rocky ground, we invite them to work following these orientations, which are meant to be concrete, adapting them to the specific conditions in each of our jurisdictions and pastoral teams:

● *Accompany our people who live in a permanent situation of emergency.*

9. In our pastoral work, many times we have asked: How are we to announce the God of Life to men and women who, as a consequence

---

[1] Vatican, Sacred Congregation for the Doctrine of Faith, *Instruction on Certain Aspects of Theology of Liberation* (1984).

[2] Bishops of the South Andes Church, *Sow Life to Reap Peace*. Statement on the Proposed Laws for Peasant Communities (February 1987).

of different forms of historic and geographic violence, live in a permanent situation of emergency?

10.   In fact, our work as Church is carried out in the midst of a people who, in a phrase we gather from the document *Accompanying Our People,* "has always been crushed," as a result of the disregard, the plundering, and the exclusion to which our region has been submitted for centuries.

11.   The life of the people of the South Andes Highlands is also conditioned by the hardness and the hostility of the geographic environment that limits the productivity of the soil and restricts the possibilities for a return on the harsh labor of the rural family. On the other hand, there are the droughts and floods that cyclically impose hunger, desolation, and death on our population. In many areas of the region, the drought is once again destroying fields and crops. It is the responsibility of the authorities to declare these areas in a state of emergency, thus helping maintain, albeit precariously, the life of our people.

12.   In this unjust situation, armed groups also present themselves. They believe in irrational violence as the only solution to the present situation. They have been met with a violent repressive response that has not always discriminated between the guilty and the innocent. We see with sorrow how in our region the leaders of the people are persecuted and imprisoned, accusing them of being terrorists. Our own priests and pastoral agents are not free from threats. And there have recently been attacks, which we strongly condemn.

13.   So, the spiral of various forms of violence continues; the same that destroys, causes suffering and draws us all into a painfully tragic reality. The exercise of violence on the part of groups with different insignia continues to produce in the region repeated attempts against human life and has fomented a climate of suspicion, fear, and terror.

14.   To announce the God of life in this reality marked by death will mean from now on redoubling our efforts to accompany our people, reaffirming, as Church of the South Andes, our preferential option for the poor.

15.   To sow life, pastoral work must contribute to the personal and collective search for justice, an effective path to solve the old problems of the South Andean region, and especially the problem of land and overcentralization.

16.   We also affirm the urgency of facing and closing the path to various forms of violence because "the use of violence, whatever the cause it defends, is an attack against life. It dehumanizes, engenders cruelty, vengeance, and more violence and, besides, is not a path to resolve the true problems of our people."[3] As pastors, we do not tire of defending life because it is precious in the eyes of God from the very moment of conception in the mother's womb. It is necessary, as an inevitable pastoral task, to create instances that make possible spiritual climate of mutual respect, of tolerance, of confidence, and of solidarity.

- *Contribute to the earth becoming a way to peace and life.*

17. As we celebrate, in the mystery of the resurrection, the triumph of life over death and remember the events that occurred in the following of Jesus among us, we note that this is also the path of our South Andean people to achieve land, an indispensable requirement for a dignified life and, in the words of Bishop Luis Dalle, "the place of communitarian fraternity."

18. It is a journey of hard labors, pains, demands, and struggles that has made it possible for a part of the lands of some of the associative enterprises of Puno to be returned into the hands of the rural communities. The promulgation of the decree on the *Restructuring of the Associative Enterprises* has contributed to this and is a motive for joy for us, insofar as it gathers up the just aspirations of the Andean rural population. Still, at the moment of getting the process of restructuring underway, the lack of participation of the rural communities and their organizations in the decisions that affect them has produced a series of tensions and conflicts. The rural peasants themselves express it in this way:

- "They have given the same land to two communities. Between neighbors we now have problems."

- "The lands they have given are far away. Are we going to be able to go up to the tops of the mountains to sow or to pasture our little animals?"

- "It is the same old story as always. Once again they want to corral us into pure stones, just like the old hacienda owners. Don't we *comuneros* [members of traditional rural communities] have a right to better lands?"

- "They tell us we have to give up our lands next to the lake. Why? In spite of the floods and everything, it is our place. What we want is more land."

---

[3] Bishops of the South Andes Church, *Following Christ*. Pastoral Letter (March 1986).

- "Some of the large land owners now say they are a community. Are they going to be the only ones to get land?"

- "They never consult us peasants. It was the same thing when they had the agrarian reform."

19.   Important sectors of the peasants today continue to demand, in different ways, this gift of God, right of the people, as we said when we referred to the land in our pastoral document of March 1986.

20.   A process of restructuring of the land has been started, over-coming a multitude of resistances and, with successes and errors, is creating a new moment in the South Andean rural Highlands.

21.   We are witnesses that the land makes possible the rediscovery of the disperse community, unifies it and revitalizes it. We are confident that the creativity of our people, so many times tested by adversity of every kind, contributes, in this new situation that is dawning, to recreate life and the cultural values of the Andean world.

22.   All this presents us with new possibilities and new challenges: to reorganize for production, to make possible communal and regional development, demands from each and all of us that our capacities and the responsibilities we have undertaken produce in service and benefit the entire community.

23.   So that the land be really a path to peace and life for everyone, we also want to make a contribution so that the peasants still in need of land reflect on the experience of those who have already achieved it, and think about the way to proceed, taking into account the necessary differences in each case.

24.   We do not want to fail to call on those responsible for the agrarian policies to accompany this new process they have opened with new measures and new attitudes. It would be good that they activate the communal enterprises and the development of the region. In this respect, we demand once more: a policy of price regulation that will benefit the producer; loans of the Agrarian Bank, given with greater amplitude and not laden with prior "conditions" as has occurred at times; channels of commercialization placed under the responsibility and control of the peasants themselves. The technical support should take into account the customs and technical traditions of the Andean region. In addition, they should encourage a process of industrialization that will engender sources of work and alternatives for the poorest of our region.

25.   As we are preparing this pastoral letter, we have been informed of the promulgation of the laws regarding the "Demarcation and Title of the Rural Communities" and the "General Law of Rural Communities." These laws, long awaited by the rural population of the country, will play an important role in the future of the communities. In what concerns the norms, we want to reaffirm once more what we have already said in the document *Sow Life to Harvest Peace:* "We also demand that the elaboration of the law and its norms include the participation of the rural communities through its organizations, giving them in this way an authentic democratic meaning."[4]

26.   In the midst of this reality, fraught with difficulties and possibilities, we wish to invite our whole Southern Andean Church to celebrate our faith in the God of Life. He is revealed to us in the advance of our people, which has suffered blows so often and in so many ways, but always keeps the hope of the resurrection, a hope that leads us toward a new society where right, justice, and fraternity dwell. For that reason, we openly say to all our pastoral agents: "to accompany and encourage the people in their urgent desires and just claims for land is part of the evangelizing task and a sign of the kingdom announced by Jesus."

- *The defense and promotion of human rights is a just aspiration of the people.*

27.   Part of our deepest faith in Jesus Christ is the conviction that the authentic criterion of our behavior toward God is our behavior toward the poor (see Mt 25:31–46). Both in the practice and word of this Southern Andean Church, there is a long experience in defense of the dispossessed, of those who are deprived of the most elementary rights. This forms part of its evangelizing identity: "the Church takes on the defense of human rights and joins in solidarity with those who champion them" (*Puebla,* 146).

28.   However, today we again feel compelled to raise our voice in defense of the dignity and human rights we see threatened in the overall population, but especially among the very poorest. The pastoral orientations contained in this letter are meant in this sense.

29.   As Church, we are happy to be able to say that in our ecclesiastical jurisdictions we have created Vicariates for Solidarity so as to accomplish this task more effectively.

30.   However, no one should feel excluded from assuming this commitment with conviction. Therefore, we propose the following challenges to all the people in our region:

- To know our rights: the universal rights, the rights of women, of the child, of the sick, of students, of prisoners. . . . To know the legal rights and make them known massively in our area.

---

[4] *Sow Life to Reap Peace,* no. 6.

- To detect and denounce the chief causes that make the people victims of constant violations that transgress the sacred right to a full life.

- To undertake, in an organized and permanent manner, the conquest and defense of the rights of all people, no matter who they are, because we are all brothers and sisters; to do it creatively, insistently, and valiantly.

31.   Finally, we consider the defense of life and human rights a permanent task and responsibility of all those who wish to sow life so as to reap peace.

- *Encourage the exercise of democracy and an appreciation of the identity of the Andean people.*

32.   Through our pastoral experience, we know that within the rural community there is an exercise of democracy by means of which the decisions of interest to the whole community are made by all its members. This experience is frequently reproduced in the urban world, especially where there are people's organizations concerned for the common good.

33.   The election of leaders, the best use of the land, what is going to be produced or done as a community, the norms that regulate how the rural community functions—all require the participation of every community member. The same often holds true in many quarters of our cities.

34.   We know that this is also a common experience, not exempt from difficulties. However, an appreciation of how this works brings us to what we could call an aspiration of this same people to participate in the overall life of the country. They have a complete right to do so.

35.   So, it is a question of understanding democracy in the context of the recognition of the dignity of all persons, the men and women of the country, as well as their organizations. The fact of being of rural or common extraction or poor should never be a reason for excluding anyone from national life.

36.   Here, we have a reason for serious concern. There are organizations, in the country and in the city, that have been created by the people in their struggle for life. In some cases, their rights to participate in the life of their locality or region are not recognized. In other cases, they are pressured to give up their autonomy by denying them support or forming parallel organizations that only foster confrontations among different groups of the popular sector.

37.   The high priority the government has given to the Southern

Andean area is a challenge for the development and well-being of this region, to be won while consolidating the people's conscientious, autonomously organized participation. In this sense, it seems completely valid for us to recall the commitment we assumed some time ago to support the organizations that, springing from the people and not imposed on them, favor access to a greater dignity.[5]

38.   We think that the real guarantee for the democratic life of the country, as well as what is meant by the defense of national interests, resides in the organized rural and urban poor.

39.   Our faith helps us to understand this. When God wished to constitute the people of Israel as a people, God did not do it starting with the powerful, but with the poor who were suffering oppression. God gave a law of freedom that demanded the consensus and participation of all, so that the relations of injustice, margination, and oppression lived in Egypt, the land of slavery, would not be repeated.

40.   This exercise of democracy should also mean for the people themselves an affirmation of their own identity, so often denied and scorned. When the people value and insist on respect for their history, their race, their culture, their tongue, their celebrations, their ancestral ways of relating to God and among themselves, and their organizations, they make up a people that can receive and support with their own resources the country as a whole. They are prepared to welcome the call of the Lord to the struggle for life and the conquest of peace.

41.   "The Church believes in democracy and aspires to it."[6]

42.   We are aware that this process of democratic development challenges all of society and also seriously challenges the life of the Church.

43.   Understood in this way, the exercise of democracy and the appreciation of the identity of the Andean people should be encouraged as part of the pastoral labor of our times.

A People of God, an Agent of Evangelization, and an Artisan of Peace

44.   To build the Church as a people of God according to the perspective of the Second Vatican Council constitutes, even today, a challenge for all of us. We recognize from our experience that there

---

[5] Bishops of the South Andes Church, Regional Episcopal Assembly at Abancay (1975).

[6] Pius XII, *Christmas Allocution*, no. 9 (1944).

have been small successes in that process, and we hope that putting into practice these orientations will permit us to advance a little more.

45.   The poor in our region have gradually become aware of being Church, the people of God. In their struggle for life, confronting different forms of violence, they have shown themselves to be artisans of peace. They will also become continually more active subjects of evangelization to the extent that they make their own the task of "sowing life to reap the peace."

46.   The community celebration of the Eucharist, where the effective love of Christ is made manifest, occupies a fundamental place in this task. "Love which is stronger than death."[7] Thus, we wish to remind the whole Christian people that "the Eucharist strongly encourages us to cultivate 'social' love, through which we place the common good before the private good, we make the cause of the whole community, the universal Church, our own, and we extend love to the whole world."[8]

47.   Our people have wisely known how to interpret this manifestation of love, when they sing in their own tongue:

Qanmi Dios kanki, yuraq Hostia Santa, qonqor sayaspa chunca much'aycuyki, uyarillaway, Apu Jesucristo, Dios wakchaq khuyaq. (My God, Holy white Host, on my knees I implore you and adore you. Hear me, God Jesus Christ, God who takes compassion on the poor.)

48.   We pray that the parishes, communities and Christian groups, movements, pastoral coordinations . . . place themselves at the service of this process.

49.   As for ourselves, in honor of the Year of Evangelization and as a preparation for the Bolivarian Eucharistic Congress, we believed it opportune to convoke all the Christian people to a Eucharistic-Theological Congress, which will bear as its motto: "to evangelize: sow life to reap peace."

50.   This congress will take place in all our ecclesiastical jurisdictions. The central dates will be September 5–6, in the city of Puno.

51.   In this congress, we want to bear witness to our evangelizing experience of the God of Life and renew our efforts by celebrating together the mystery of the death and resurrection of Jesus Christ, the Eucharist, the true Christian celebration of solidarity, life, and hope.

---

[7] Cf. John Paul II, *Easter Message* (April 19, 1987).

[8] Paul VI, *Mysterium Fidei* (*On the Holy Eucharist*). Papal Encyclical (1965).

Final Words

52.   Brothers and Sisters: In closing, we wish to recall Bishop Albert Koenigsknecht when he called us to bear the Good News with the valor and courage that the Lord demands of all disciples and friends, and to do it fearlessly.

53.   Along with Saint Paul, we remind you: "What we cultivate is what we will reap . . . therefore, let us not tire of doing good so that, if we do not weaken, in time we will reap a harvest" (Gal 6:7,9).

May 10, 1988.

Southern Pacific Coast, Mexico
The Gospel and Temporal Goods
(1985)

Latin American bishops seldom devote a whole pastoral letter to middle- and upper-class members. The bishops of the Southern Pacific region provide an exception in The Gospel and Temporal Goods. *In doing so, they also provide the majority of North American Christians with a biblically based reflection.*

The states of Oaxaca and Chiapas, where the seven dioceses are located, have the highest population of Indians in Mexico, and it was to Oaxaca that John Paul II went in a bold move of solidarity with the impoverished Indians. The area also has the highest number of political prisoners and kidnappings in the country.

The bishops have seen violence and turbulence first-hand. For helping small farmers claim their legal land titles, priests and bishops have received death threats. Gunmen shot at Bishop Antonio Lona Reyes and badly wounded a local priest the bishop was visiting. The bishops have also witnessed the results of violence in Guatemala and El Salvador in the large number of refugees from those countries in their dioceses.

1. *We have always spoken from an option.* We have been addressing the people of God in our South Pacific Pastoral Region for many years through letters, messages, and documents. As servants of the gospel, we have spoken to all (see Mt 28:18ff), seeking and revealing the way of salvation. Following the example of Christ, our primary preoccupation has been the poor (see Mt 11:2–5), and among them the poorest of the poor (see *Puebla*, 34–35), the indigenous peoples and farm workers. We wished to accompany them in their faith.

2. *Today, we speak to a particular sector of the population.* Because our love and pastoral responsibility embrace the whole people of God, and so that all in the Church may live the option to which the gospel and the Church itself call us (see *Puebla*, 1134–1165), following the model of Christ, we want the good news to reach in a special way those who enjoy a middle- or upper-class socioeconomic situation.

We also want it to reach those who aspire to greater economic goods, so as to point out to them God's plan. In this way, their riches may help them to build the kingdom of God, act in fraternal solidarity with the poor, and attain eternal life.

3. *We are all called to serve in the Church.* We are writing this letter because, in the Church, we are all responsible for others. We are all one another's servants out of love (see Gal 5:13). We also write because some well-to-do persons have expressed their preoccupation. We have shared this preoccupation with groups and individuals of different socioeconomic strata in order to understand the Christian experience in relation to temporal goods and riches. All have expressed sincere and comprehensive feelings on the subject, knowing that meant a greater commitment to the rest of their brothers and sisters. We unite our voice with theirs, hoping it may be of service pastorally.

I. The Situation of Christians and Temporal Goods

4. *Sincere worries.* Many who possess economic resources and are conscious of the unjust structures of our society are interested in helping the poor in different ways; they want to find ways to live the call of the gospel to justice and fraternity. They are asking themselves what their role should be in today's society so as to make the decisions and accept the responsibilities that, as Church, are essential to living out their faith in Christ. They are like the group of women with resources who followed the Lord closely and helped out with his and his apostles' expenses (see Lk 8:3). They take Jesus more into account than they do their riches. With all those who use their possessions in a Christian manner, we share the convictions of our faith on the subject of riches, so that we may all give reason for the hope we have as those who believe in the Lord Jesus (see 1 Pt 3:15), and we try to bring about his kingdom of justice.

5. *Services that people with resources perform.* There are well-to-do people who help the needy with their money by giving alms. Some do this constantly, helping poor friends they know well so their situation might be less painful. There are also groups in the middle and upper classes who succour the poor through religious organizations with that specific aim. Others assist good works developed by priests or religious in marginated areas. Some give to the Church and other institutions so that they can carry out social works. There are also those who use their resources to generate jobs. The Church appreciates all that and esteems the persons who give generously of what they have to works of mercy.

6. *Professional talents at the service of the poor.* We know communities and individuals who have benefitted from the services of professionals who, by their counsel and advice, have bettered their agricultural techniques, their organization, their diet, their health, and their education. This indicates how those professionals place their own talents, a cultural and intellectual wealth, at the service of the most needy.

7.   *The Church's recognition of Christian example.* This reality of support and solidarity for the poor on the part of those who have material or spiritual riches is not something new. Throughout the history of the Church, there have been many cases of middle or upper class people who lived Christian fraternity and used their possessions to show their faith and their commitment to others, either by using their riches in a Christian manner or totally renouncing them for the kingdom. The Church has canonized several of them as examples of Christian life. Among them there are educators such as Thomas Aquinas, Charles Borromeo, John Baptist de la Salle; there are philosophers and theologians, such as Augustine, Albert the Great, Cyril of Alexandria; there are members of government, such as Isabel of Hungry, Thomas a Beckett, the Emperor Henry, Thomas Moore, and other politicians. Saint Francis of Assisi reached such a radical rejection of riches that he is called the "Poor Little One of Assisi." The Church raised all of these to her altars, not for their riches, but because they used their riches and power in an ethical manner and according to the gospel.

8.   *There is ostentation and waste.* In spite of the fact that our country is suffering one of its worst economic crises, it appears some are living a reality of prosperity. They make long, expensive trips; they buy the latest luxury cars. At the same time, we see that many persons cannot even pay the high prices of urban and interurban transportation. The factories introduce superfluous items in their products, whether what they produce be things, vehicles, or tools; meanwhile, many rural people cannot even replace or repair the few indispensable tools they have for their work. Houses are built with expensive materials, with luxurious finishings and furniture, in sharp contrast to the poverty and lack of hygienic conditions in the majority of the houses and slum dwellings. Everywhere there are exclusive stores that specialize in clothes and rich foods for customers prepared to pay very high prices for what they consume. Meanwhile, the rural communities have to go through mounds of paperwork and appointments just to have stores stocked with popular foods. They carry home little food, and even that is often of poor quality. There are those who enjoy enormous credit ratings, while the majority cannot even continue farming until harvest time for lack of credit. The communications media assure us that some people in this now impoverished Mexico yearly export millions of dollars to their private foreign accounts. Because of the massive information media in our consumer society, poor people

sometimes even waste their few resources in useless or superfluous things. So there is a general social preoccupation that, faced with a crisis and the poverty of the vast majority, those who do have economic resources waste them.

9. *The danger of some middle classes disappearing.* A middle class of professionals and specialized workers has been forming in Mexico for many years. It struggled to rise from poverty through the production of goods or services. It began to consume, act, and think like the social sectors with more resources. For that reason, on occasions it has lost communications and solidarity with the poor. Now, as all prices have risen beyond the increase of salaries, the middle class, paying more, has had to decrease its consumption. This, Pope John Paul II denounced as "the ever-increasing wealth of the rich at the expense of the ever-increasing poverty of the poor." (*Puebla*, "Inaugural Address," III, 4). Besides, we are told that seventy percent of the salaries of the majority are spent just to buy food. At the same time, the prices of rent and services have risen considerably. Thus, the middle classes live in anguish because they cannot maintain their standard of living; they try to afford a house, clothing, and transportation, but they have to cut back on their budget for food, education, and recreation. The way things are going, the middle classes could disappear in a short time.

10. *The poverty of the majority.* We are aware there is a continual increase in the poverty of the region. There is terrible want. In the towns and in the belts surrounding our cities, the markets are not kept supplied as they were previously. One feels the hunger spreading through the communities. In some places, people have starved to death. Many wear ragged and dirty clothes because they do not even have soap to wash them. We have reached extremely high levels of unemployment, which, besides producing all that has already been mentioned, also generated personal and social frustration. Thousands upon thousands cry for a job, which could certainly be created if capital were reinvested instead of fleeing the country. It is unjust to oblige Mexico to reduce salaries and jobs in these moments of crisis. This situation of poverty, as the bishops meeting in Puebla declared, "is a palpable seal stamped" on the vast majorities of this region (see 1129ff) and is a scandalous reality (see 1154) that threatens to spread even further.

11. *The social problems of the poorest sector of the population.* We have frequently pointed out that there are those who, taking advantage of and manipulating the poverty of the indigenous people and farm workers, strip them of their lands, exploit them as day laborers, and cheat them or force them to grow narcotics. In addition, many workers and farm laborers keep the law by asking for an increase in salaries through the established channels, only to see that in the majority of cases the decision goes in favor of management. Thus, they are left without social arbiters to protect their rights. They say that the official arbitrators benefit only capital to the prejudice of labor. According to our faith, as Pope John Paul II has affirmed, this goes against the will of God since labor has priority over capital (see LE, 12).

This creates a tense social situation where hunger forces people to have recourse to theft, assaults, and even prostitution to survive. Often, these "criminal acts" can be interpreted more as part of the struggle for life than a form of deliberate delinquency. Thus, social pressure grows and could reach levels where it might set loose situations of violence and social repression, which no one wants (see our position on violence in *Living Our Political Commitment in a Christian Manner*, 112–120).

12.   *Some Christians exploit their brothers and sisters.* In short, our preoccupation as pastors is that everything we have pointed out indicates that some Christians are exploiting their brothers and sisters. And this exploitation occurs not only because at times personal decisions are taken in that sense, but above all because we live in a society that calls itself Christian but, contrary to what it proclaims, depends on an unjust social system that causes some to take advantage of their social position, their better preparation, their relationship with power groups, as well as structures and institutions so as to maintain their domination and exploitation of others. Basically, this presents us with a radical problem of evangelization. And it demands a response because the anguish of the poor and afflicted is the anguish of the servants of Christ (see GS, 1). Both those who benefit from this situation and those who suffer from it in the midst of their poverty and misery draw near to the Church. How can the Church serve both groups pastorally?

We have often spoken of the situation of the poor and their evangelization. In this letter, we address principally those who have goods and riches. Our initiative is a consequence of the preferential option for the poor, which we are attempting to live out in the pastoral ministry of this region. Our option is neither exclusive nor excluding but, rather, calls all to fraternal solidarity by saying, "the Church is deeply committed to this cause because it considers it as its mission, its service, as a proof of its fidelity to Christ, in order to be truly the 'Church of the Poor'" (LE, 8; see also the principal speeches of John Paul II in his recent visit to Central and South America and the Caribbean). "God is the God of all, but he grants his first mercy to the dispossessed of this world" (John Paul II, *Homily* at the Santo Domingo Race Track, 5).

II. Goods and Riches in God's Plan

13. *The first temporal good is creation.* Good and riches have always been seen in profound relationship with persons. Thus, to speak of economic goods and riches is a moral and theological matter. Further, according to faith, material things are intimately bound up with God and his salvific plan.

He created all things (see Gn 1–2) and made them "very good" (see Gn 1:31). In other words, all material things have their origin in God, who gave them to persons (see Gn 1:28) to fulfill his will by using them and mastering them (see Gn 1:29–30). One who accepts the Word of the Lord takes on the attitude of Job, who used riches to free the poor man when he called out; he acted justly and righteously, becoming eyes for the blind, feet for the lame, and father of the poor; snatching the poor from the jaws of the wicked (see Jb 29:12–17). Thus, we should value and appreciate things because they are a reflection of the will of God and contain the Word of him who created them. The respectful or unjust attitude that we believers have toward created things and riches is measured in relation to our brothers and sisters, who are flesh of our flesh and bone of our bone (see Gn 2:23); in that integral relationship we clearly show our attitude toward God. In many places, the Bible tells us that when we also place our goods at the service of our brother according to God's plan, those goods are turned into a blessing, which God himself gives to those who fulfill his Word (see Gn 13:2–5; Jb 1:1ff; Ps 112:1,3). We read that Abraham was rich in cattle, gold, and silver; and Job, being rich, held everything as a good belonging to God. In praying, the community of believers said that he who possessed riches was blessed and his justice remained forever (see Gn 13:2ff; Jb 1:1ff; Ps 112:1ff).

14. *The purpose of goods in God's plan.* Thus, in the temporal order, creation is the greatest value. But goods do not have intrinsic value. As we have seen, the appreciation we have for things derives from their relationship to their Author, because they have a purpose in God's plan, and because they pertain very closely to persons.

In the Book of Genesis, we read that God made man and woman (1:26) so as to use all things, master the land, and thus feed themselves and live (1:26–31). For that reason, man and woman have the right and the obligation from God to work so that the purpose God gave to all goods might be accomplished. That is to say, in working the land, in changing it, in converting natural resources into goods, in using those goods, we are fulfilling the purpose God gave them. But, as John Paul II reminds us, in carrying this out, we must not go contrary to the other purpose: that goods should serve all persons, giving them life and food, and in such a way that all can truly benefit from them (see LE, 14). To realize this purpose, God wanted his people, as a people, to have all these things in the image and reality of a Promised Land where no one would lack for anything (see Ex 3:17).

Thus, only the person who honors creation and respects its common destiny for people really considers God his creator. The opposite of this, using resources and goods badly, or hoarding them and harming others, is a betrayal of the plan of God, who gave everything to everyone out of love. God's plan is for us to live as brothers and sisters. Goods are an indispensable condition for our growth and realization.

15.   *All goods belong to God.* As has been said, no one with faith can use riches and goods in an arbitrary manner or hoard them in a way that prejudices others. This contradicts the will of God. Only he who arranges his affairs so that all his collaborators and workers benefit with Christian justice from the goods that they all produce from his businesses and industries can say as David did: "Lord, all that exists in heaven and earth is yours" (1 Chr 29:12). God demands that when we use material goods others may also benefit because those things are his, and he wished them to be used in this way (see LE, 4).

16.   *The value of goods and personal riches.* The Sacred Scriptures warn us that riches are not an end in themselves, but a means we should use to realize the history of God's plan for his people. There are frequent scriptural texts that speak ironically of riches, which did not permit their owners to practice the justice that they should have showed with them. Thus, the holy Job says, "Why do the wicked still live on, their power increasing with their age?" (21:7). The wisdom of God led the psalmist to say, "Those who trust in their wealth behave like fools; they will not redeem their soul, and will leave their fortunes to others" (Ps 49:6,11). The Word of God accuses those who create riches and do not remember that with them they also have to do the will of God.

17.   *Injustice perverts goods and riches.* If God created all natural resources and gave us the commandment to master them and transform them into goods and riches, why then does Holy Scripture criticize those persons who become rich? What creates the situation where riches and their owners do not fulfill in a just manner the purpose God gave them? The reason (for the criticism in Holy Scripture) is that the riches, in many cases, are unjustly accumulated or are used in such a way that others are prevented from obtaining them. Thus, an injustice against creation is committed because we frustrate their universal purpose; an injustice against persons is committed because we deprive them of the right to work creatively and participate in the goods created; and an injustice against God is committed because, in this case, we place the goods in God's place. We fall into the grave sin of idolatry, which does not consist only in rendering cult to idols and statues (see Is 40:12–20). It is also idolatry to overvalue one's own works and possessions (see Wis 13–14). Isaiah prophesied that those who are filled with silver, gold, and riches fill the earth with idols (see 2:6–8); and finally, for that reason, Saint Paul would say in all clarity that covetousness is idolatry (see Col 3:5; Eph 5:5).

18.   *The judgment of God on the injustice of riches evilly acquired or evilly used.* This injustice or idolatry often consists in the fact that riches are acquired at the expense of employees, customers, workers, the resources of others, or on the basis of iniquitous laws and social systems that permit riches to be generated from poverty and misery. Whoever prospers at the cost of committing injustices is called "unholy," lacking in piety toward others and toward God." For that reason, the rich person is also called "wicked," "a nightmare," "greedy," and "dammed" (see Jb 20:5,8,21,29). Already in the Old Testament, it is affirmed that for the rich to become rich, they abuse the poor and the miserable. The rich do not give the poor what is owing to them; they spy on them and treat them arrogantly. Yahweh will see that the unjust person remains sterile, perishes, or is exterminated—both him and his descendants (see Ps 37). Such harsh words explain why, in the spirituality of the Old Testament, to trample on the poor is to commit many rebellious acts against God (see Am 5:11–13; Prv 14:31.17:5; Eccl 34:18–22).

19.   *The justice of God despoils the unjust.* Frequently, the judgments and punishments of God were carried out in a very crude way each time that some, unjustly accumulating possessions, prevented others from living with dignity. Thus, this injustice finally overflows the patience of those who suffer it. For example, we see that God despoils the unjust, and in the same act does justice to the weak: Yahweh had promised to judge the Egyptians who exploited and impoverished the Hebrews (see Gn 15:14.45:20). This he did when the Israelites despoiled the Egyptians before their departure and liberation (see Ex 12:35–36). God's justice acts in us as persons and in our society; it gives with full hands to the poor and remains always (see 2 Cor 9:9).

III. Jesus and the Early Church concerning Riches

20.   *Some of Jesus' experiences with those who possessed goods and with the poor.* The New Testament clarifies for us the attitude of faith toward riches, through the words and actions of Jesus concerning these things. In the light of Christ's experience with the humble and the well-off, the first communities rethought Jewish wisdom and spirituality.

21. a) *Christ was a poor person.* Jesus was born poor by his own choice (see Phil 2:6; Lk 2:1–7). The Lord begins his mission by proclaiming their liberation to the poor (see Lk 4:16–19), and to bring it about, he frequently contrasts the reality of the humble with that of the powerful. Starting from the poor and their just cause, he announces to both of them the message of salvation in different but closely related ways.

22. b) *The conflict between poverty and riches as lived by the Virgin Mary.* Mary, the mother of Jesus, expressed very dramatically this spiritual and social dilemma: "My soul proclaims the greatness of the Lord. . . . The hungry he has filled with good things; the rich sent empty away" (Lk 1:46, 53).

23. c) *The life of Jesus in the midst of poverty and riches.* Christ lived the most important moments of his mission involved in the situation of the poor and the rich: He is born poor (see Lk 2:7), but is adored by wise men whom tradition treats as kings (see Mt 2:11); before beginning his work of evangelization, he is tempted by the possession of riches and power (see Mt 4:1ff); in his first talk he proclaims the Beatitudes concerning the poor (see Mt 5:1ff) which, according to Saint Luke, are followed by curses against the rich and powerful (see Mt 6:24–26); at the core of this talk, he defines the attitudes of the rich before God (see Mt 6:24) and of the humble believer before divine providence (see Mt 6:25–34).

24. d) *The mission and commitment of Christ to alleviate poverty.* Jesus proclaims that he was sent to announce the good news to the poor (see Lk 4:16ff); his gospel service to the poor is a proof of his divinity, and he says, "Happy is the man who does not lose faith in me" (Mt 11:6). In sending off his disciples, he prophecies that they will be handed over to the courts (see Mt 10:16–20). He blesses God because he hides his will from the wise but reveals it to the little ones (see Mt 11:25). His commitment to the poor shows that he himself is the "Poor of Yahweh" (see Mt 12:15–21), but at the same time, he compares the kingdom of God to a treasure (see Mt 13:44–46). In the midst of the greatest scarcity, he performs the multiplication of the loaves (see Mt 14:13–21). He compares the kingdom of God to a king who pardons his administrator but then sends him to the torturers for not having mercy on the poor (see Mt 18:23–35).

25. e) *Christ dialogues with the rich.* Jesus finds a rich man who keeps the commandments but cannot accept a commitment to the poor; on that occasion, he gives his most serious teaching on the danger of riches (see Mt 19:16–29). In the parable of Lazarus and the glutton, he explains that when riches are an obstacle to recognizing and establishing solidarity with the poor, those riches are a cause of damnation (see Lk 16:19–31). On the other hand, in the passage on

Zacchaeus, the gospel tells us about the initiative of a rich administrator who is converted and uses his money to practice justice (see Lk 19:1–10).

26. f) *Jesus accuses the rich and identifies with the poor.* On another occasion, Christ calls the merchants and moneylenders in the temple of Jerusalem bandits (see Mt 21:12–13) and acts violently toward them (Jn 2:13–17). To explain God's judgment at the end of the world, he uses the example of a faithful administrator, who serves his servants, and an unfaithful administrator, who mistreats them (see Mt 24:45–51). He gave important teachings on the occasion he spent with the tax collectors (see Lk 5:29–32). Before his betrayal, he outlines the meaning of his teachings and the actions of his mission thus: "Insofar as you did this to one of the least of these brothers of mine, you did it to me" (see Mt 25:31–40); and by "least" he understood the starving, the ragged, the jailed, the homeless. As we see, during the evangelization carried out by Jesus, there is frequent reference to persons with economic resources. Thus, it is necessary to point out some of the principal themes.

27. *Riches as a rejection of the kingdom of God.* The parable of the kingdom of God as a banquet points out that those who rejected the invitation possessed lands, were traders or assassins (see Mt 22:5–6); they do not go to the banquet of the kingdom because taking care of their occupations and businesses is more important to them than the kingdom of God. On another occasion, Jesus complained, "If then you cannot be trusted with money, that tainted thing, who will trust you with genuine riches?" (see Lk 16:9–12). Thus, so as to be able to live our faith and accept the risks and commitments of the kingdom, the Lord warns us: "Be on your guard against avarice of any kind" (Lk 12:15) because greed makes us prefer riches to what is really important for the believer: "Do not store up treasures for yourselves on earth, where moths and woodworms destroy them and thieves can break in and steal. But store up treasures for yourselves in heaven, where neither moth nor woodworms destroy them and thieves cannot break in and steal" (Mt 6:19–21).

Whoever is drawn to riches truly rejects the gospel. Whoever has as the goal of life the search for riches always commits injustices. On the other hand, whoever has faith and accepts the faith experience in the kingdom uses all his capabilities, including his riches, to make over this society according to the kingdom of God: The kingdom of heaven is like a treasure hidden in a field; he who desires it goes and sells everything he owns and buys that field (see Mt 13:44), because "What gain is it to win the whole world and ruin one's life?" (Mk 8:36). Christ himself was tempted by the devil, with power and riches, not to fulfill the mission his Father had given him: The devil

". . . showed him all the kingdoms of the world and their splendor, promising: 'I will give you all these . . . if you fall at my feet and worship me'" (Mt 4:9).

28.   *Riches separate us from the poor and from salvation.* The parable of the rich man and the poor man, Lazarus (see Lk 16:19–31), tells us that one lived in opulence and the other in misery. Both died; the poor was taken in to the bosom of Abraham, while the rich man was subjected to terrible torments. The rich man was worried about the salvation of his brothers and asked Lazarus to warn them so they would not go to the same place of suffering. The gospel does not tell us that the rich man was evil. It simply points out that he had not noticed the existence of the poor man nor had mercy on him by using his riches to remedy his situation. Riches had placed an abyss between them, and that abyss between them in life was the same abyss that exists between salvation and damnation; an insurmountable abyss. For that reason, Lazarus could not go to warn the rich man's brothers. Riches can keep us from listening to the Word of God and from seeing the poor in a fraternal way. In this parable, Jesus clearly teaches that if riches are not to be unjust or become a reason for damnation, they must also be placed at the service of the poor.

29.   *Riches as a rejection of God.* We opt for riches and reject God himself, either because we surrender to the malignant one or give in to dominant culture, which has as its idol power, possessions, and pleasure. By trusting in riches, one gradually begins to lose confidence in the will of God and reject God himself. Jesus said this very clearly: "No one can be the slave of two masters: he will either hate the first and love the second, or treat the first with respect and the second with scorn. You cannot be the slave both of God and of money" (Mt 6:24). When the magisterium of the Church proclaims evangelical truth, some well-to-do persons even reach the point of also rejecting the Church, disqualifying its ministers as communists and subversives. On occasion, this rejection of Christ, because of money, can show itself very concretely: Judas went to the high priests, Jesus' enemies, and asked, "'What are you prepared to give me if I hand him over to you?' They paid him thirty pieces of silver" (Mt 26:15), which was the value of a slave.

30.   *A rich young man seeks Jesus.* The first three evangelists tell us of a rich young man who was seeking Jesus (see Mt 19:16–26; Mk 10:17–22; Lk 18:18–23). It is a most beautiful passage, full of experience and teachings. Saint Mark presents us with a personage not very clearly defined, simply saying he was "a man" (see 10:17); Saint Matthew says more clearly that he was "a young man of great wealth" (see 19:22); Saint Luke, more concretely, says that he was "one of the leading families . . . very rich" (see 18:18–23). All agree that he took the initiative in meeting Jesus: "And there was a man who came to him and put this question to him" (see Mt 19:16; Mk 10:17; Lk 18:18). This was the same attitude the rich functionary, Zacchaeus, had (see Lk 19:2–4). We also have the experience of knowing rich persons, who, like the young man or Zacchaeus, anxiously desire to know the Lord.

31. *The rich man worries about doing good.* The first thing the young man asked Jesus was: "Master, what good deed must I do to possess eternal life?" (Mt 19:16). This certainly means that he was worried about doing good and finding a way to salvation. The cultures, the religions, and the laws of any society ordinarily seek the common good of its members; but, as we see in this passage, some persons who have fortunes in possessions see that the gospel and Christ are the way to eternal life. Jesus reminds us that the true believer must go beyond the purely moral and legal; he should reach evangelical good, conversion, the justice of God, God himself. For that reason, he told him: "Why do you ask me about what is good? There is one alone who is good" (Mt 19:17). If one wants to be good, it is enough to fulfill the laws, not to kill, or rob, or defraud, or cheat, to respect your parents; things that the commandments also ask of us. For that reason, the Lord also answered him saying that to be a good person and save himself he should "keep the commandments" (Mt 19:17). And it happens that the rich young man had fulfilled all that for a long time (see Mt 19:20); for that reason, Christ "looked steadily at him and loved him" (Mk 10:21). In the same way, today, the Church esteems greatly those persons who, enjoying a comfortable economic and social situation, fulfill the commandments.

32. *What is lacking to the good rich man.* The rich young man sensed that to believe in the Lord demanded more than to be good. For that reason, he also asked him: "What more do I need to do?" (Mt 19:20). Jesus answers him that the person who is already good but, beyond that, wishes to commit himself to gospel justice "is still lacking one thing" (Mk 10:21). In all religions and in every place, there are good persons, but there are not persons who really live the gospel everywhere. To really live faith in Christ one must be "perfect" (see Mt 19:21). For Christ, to be perfect means "you must therefore be perfect just as your heavenly Father is perfect" (Mt 5:48), and that means accepting the commitment to practice the justice, the love, and the peace of the kingdom of God. The believer can only be perfect if he is like the Father, if he does what God the Father wants, which is his kingdom. Thus, Jesus tells the young man that if he wishes to be perfect, that is, if he wishes to collaborate in creating the kingdom, he must take another step: "If you wish to be perfect, go and sell what you own and give the money to the poor, and you will have treasure in heaven; then come, follow me" (Mt 19:21). According to Christ, one must rid himself of attachment to riches because, as we have already seen clearly, riches are a danger for the believer and, when placed as ends in themselves, proceed from injustice and are the fruit of sin (see Mk 10:23–27; Lk 18:24–27). God himself, sent Jesus to carry out the redemption and become incarnate: "though his state was divine, yet he did not cling to his equality with God but emptied himself" (see Phil 2:6–7) to become as we are, though without sin (see Heb 4:15). For that reason, he had affirmed: "In the same way, none of you can be my disciple unless he gives up all his possessions" (Lk 14:33).

33.   *To be perfect.* Often we think that to be good Christians the only thing Christ asks of us is to observe the commandments; as we said in no. 31 above: "not to kill, or rob, or defraud, or cheat. . . ." But society and the law also demand the same thing from us for us to be persons and to live in respect for one another. We also think frequently that the call to "be perfect" and to shed our riches is directed only to those with a religious vocation among the people of God. However, we see clearly in the gospel that Jesus requires all his disciples, all his followers, all believers, "to be perfect." In the Sermon on the Mount, he speaks to the "masses" (see Mt 5:1) and tells them that to be sons of God they must be perfect as his Heavenly Father is perfect (see Mt 5:43–48). That is to say, what Jesus asks of the rich young man is, in fact, a requirement for all. The perfection the Lord speaks of is attained not only by shedding the attachment to riches: "go and sell all that you have," but basically by placing riches at the service of the needy: "and give it to the poor" (see Mt 19:21).

34.   *Do justice to the poor just as Christ did.* When Jesus invites the rich man to have faith in the gospel, "sell all and give it to the poor," he is inviting him to the same mission he himself received from his Father and was carrying out with the power of the Spirit: "The Spirit of the Lord has been given to me; for he has anointed me. He has sent me to bring the good news to the poor, to proclaim liberty to captives, to set the downtrodden free, to proclaim liberty the Lord's year of favor" (Lk 4:16–19). Christ asks for and demands this option for the poor of anyone who wishes to be his apostle and disciple (see Mt 19:29). But this "give to the poor" is not a giving in just any sense; it is to give as brothers and sisters, in a respectful, dignified, serving manner, that is to say, in the perspective of the construction of the kingdom of God and in the same way that Jesus did it. For that reason, he says to the young man: "Come back and follow me" (Mt 19:21). This attitude of giving oneself to the poor as brothers and sisters is an attitude of Christian love. It is a love greater than our attachment to riches or even to ourselves.

35.   *The serious obstacle placed by riches.* The Lord's call to the rich man is short and clear. The young man who heard it was a good man, fulfilled the commandments, knew Jesus personally; the Lord loves him for his moral conduct and invites him to build with him the gospel of the poor. But the rich man did not want to and was profoundly disturbed. There was an obstacle—the riches: "The young man went away sad, for his possessions were many" (Mt 19:22). Saint Mark writes that the young man's "face fell" and he went away (see 10:22); on the contrary, Saint Luke assures us that the publican, Zacchaeus, said: "I give half of my belongings, Lord, to the poor. If I have defrauded anyone in the least, I pay him back fourfold" (Lk 19:8).

With the young man, Christ could only confirm what the spirituality of his people, and he himself, had experienced: "I assure you, only with difficulty will a rich man enter into the kingdom of God" (Mt 19:23). In the passage on Zacchaeus, who was truly converted, Jesus tells him: "Today salvation has come to this house" (Lk 19:9). Thus, the Word of God makes us understand very clearly that with riches one can follow either of two roads: one is the road of attachment to riches, which distances one from the gospel and Christ, as happened to the young man. The other is the road of conversion, which means to accept Jesus' invitation, enter into solidarity with the poor, and restore justice, as the publican Zacchaeus did.

36. *The first communities and riches.* In the Acts of the Apostles, it appears there were not many conversions of the well-to-do during the early years. The apostle James wrote a few years later: "As for you, you rich, weep and wail. . . . Here, crying aloud, are the wages you withheld from the farmhands who harvested your fields. The cries of the harvesters have reached the ears of the Lord of hosts" (Jas 5:1,4). Even more forcefully, he said that the rich continued to oppress the poor and drag them to the courts, blaspheming (see Jas 2:6–7). The poor communities, in order to practice the fraternity and love that Jesus had lived and taught, shared their bread and lives in brotherly communion (see Acts 2:42). They missed the commitment of those with many resources but believed that the Lord could bring about their conversion, which seemed humanly impossible, since "everything is possible with God" (Mk 10:27).

37. *From the Beatitudes of the poor.* We believe that Christ's program of Beatitudes for the poor should become a reality. God is with the poor to make it a reality, and the rich who wish to follow the Lord should cooperate so that the poor will be truly blessed because they take possession of the earth (see Mt 5:4); because they are consoled (see 5:5); because full justice is done them (see 5:6); because there is a great effort of all believers, beginning now, for the kingdom of God to be theirs (see 5:1). For the Beatitudes to become a reality, it is also essential for those who enjoy a middle- or upper-class economic situation to make the option for the poor theirs and practice the Beatitudes in solidarity with the poor, so that all of us can live together the good news of the gospel. The rich should live the first Beatitude, stripping themselves of all attachment to riches and entering into a solidarity with the poor. Only by becoming "poor in spirit" can the kingdom be theirs. Thus, the Word of the Lord, when he spoke of the great difficulty the rich have in being saved, will be fulfilled: "For man it is impossible; but for God all things are possible" (Mt 19:26).

38.   *The poor of spirit.* According to biblical spirituality and religiosity, the Spirit is creator (see Gn 1:2); is life (see Gn 2:7), is wisdom (see Dt 34:9); is a blessing (see Is 44:3); is renewal (see Ps 104:30); is prophetic accusation (see Mi 3:8); is service to the people (see Nm 27:18,23); is convocation (see Jgs 6:33–35); is fearlessness (see Jgs 11:29ff); is strength (see Is 11:2); is liberation (see Is 61:1; Lk 4:16ff); and is love (see Is 11:2).

At times committed to the poor, at times sinners in the use of possessions, we believe profoundly in the presence of the Spirit in his people today. Thus, we believe that the Lord will give his Spirit to those who seek it, so that creatively, in a vital manner, with wisdom, by means of a profound renewal of prophetic attitudes, serving the people with fearlessness and courage, we may, through the strength of love, bring about the liberation and evangelization of those who possess riches, so they use them justly according to the will of God. In that way, the first Beatitude of the Sermon on the Mount will apply equally to the poor and the rich: "How happy are the poor in spirit; theirs is the kingdom of heaven" (Mt 5:3). On the one hand, the poor have to change their situation, making a reality of the justice of the kingdom; on the other hand, those who possess material, professional, or cultural goods have to be converted so that their goods and they themselves may serve to change that same reality and make it new.

IV. Pastoral Guidelines

39.   *On the evangelical use of riches.* All of us who perform some hierarchical ministry in the Church are obliged to give pastoral service by also announcing the good news to those who are well-off, who possess resources, so that their riches may play their proper role in strengthening the conversion and evangelization of the people of God. But, as the way we use money and the concepts we have concerning riches normally come to us through our social and cultural experience, and our way of handling possessions derives from the cultural and social values of our environment, it is clear that lay people have a special vocation to Christianize those realities and resources and give them the purpose our faith demands (see GS, 43).

40. *Understanding the origin and use of riches in our society.* It is essential to know exactly what the mechanisms and concrete situations are that give rise to personal and family riches if we are to respond to riches in a committed manner, with evangelical efficacy. But, above all, we must see clearly what are the mechanisms of labor, production, market, and distribution, as well as the juridical and institutional mechanisms; also, what are the social, economic, and political structures (see *Puebla*, 30) that create riches and the situation where many poor who labor in the creation of those riches are kept marginated and deprived of them, because capital appropriates almost the totality of the economic gain (see MM, 76; LE, 12–13) so that the workers always remain poor or even find that their poverty keeps getting worse.

Generally, we are not conscious of all these factors because our education and environment do not help us find possibilities of change in this situation (see *Puebla*, 1014), and we consider it normal that some become rich and others poor. This situation, as we have seen is in reality a product of sin (see *Puebla*, 70) and radically contradicts God's creative plan and the gospel spirit.

41. *The "justification" of riches and a change of social structures.* Frequently, for cultural reasons or for reasons of convenience, we Christians also accept this justification. We live in social structures that reinforce an individualistic vision of people and are tempted to justify our riches by considering them a good that God has granted us, even though we know that these riches have been acquired by trampling on justice. This shows the ease with which riches become idols and urges us to examine them and our conduct toward the poor, so as to be able to unmask the sin these riches contain and give them the purpose they ought to have in building fraternity.

The social mechanisms that generate riches and distribute them badly are unjust and should be courageously denounced (see *Puebla*, 1160). And as those who have a solid economic position also have the capacity to influence institutions and structures, if they accept the gospel challenge and act with energetic faith, they can make decisions within their own social environment that will rapidly be effective in bringing signs of change. Basically, this is a task that involves denouncing the inhumaneness and sinfulness of society (see *Puebla*, 310–312) and converting the social structures that contradict the gospel (see EN, 19).

42. *The necessity of mercy and charity.* Only the Spirit of Christ can sustain the decision, conviction, and commitments required to work toward change in social structures. Those unavoidable efforts toward change do not dispense us, on the other hand, from sharing through direct, immediate actions of aid, charity, and mercy (see OA, 16). But it should never consist in giving what we do not need or our crumbs. We must distribute liberally (see OA, 51) for reasons of justice and in joint actions that clearly lead to justice (see John Paul II, *Address to the Indigenous Peoples and Farm Workers in Cuilapan*). Today, to love is to practice justice (see *Puebla*, 327).

43.   *The gift of oneself in the service of others.* It would be a still greater act of mercy for those who have possessions and technical or other capabilities to coordinate their resources, efforts, and their own persons to carry out economic, social, cultural, and religious projects to benefit the poor. They should not consider the poor as simply passive receptacles of our aid. Basically, this would give the stamp of approval to an unjust system on which we have already given our moral judgment many times. Rather, the rich should accompany the poor, using a methodology by which they themselves deliberate, decide, and bring about their own integral, evangelizing liberation (see *Puebla*, 487). That example of persons giving themselves to the integral, evangelical service of the poor witnesses to the fact that for us the poor person is the most vital presence of the Lord (see John Paul II, *Address to the Poor in the Minas Suburb in Santo Domingo*).

44.   *We are the administrators, not owners, of all goods.* What we have suggested as the Christian commitment—to give riches a purpose in accordance with our faith—can only become a reality if we begin to live in practice what the Church has traditionally taught us: that we are in no way the absolute owners of the goods and riches we possess, but only the administrators (see *Summa Theologica* 2–2, Q.32, a.5, ad.2). Goods should be available to all under the guidance of justice and love (see GS, 69). For that reason, all of us as believers, each according to his possibilities, should participate with determination in politics so as to bring about an economic and social structure that protects the true right that everyone has to possess goods, which will permit them to live a material and spiritual life worthy of an image and child of God (see John XXIII, *Pacem in Terra*, 146). Even personal goods and talents, innate or acquired, are gifts of God, granted for the common good; they are not just a personal talent nor should we use them exclusively for our own benefit.

45.   *The purpose of goods is not only personal but communitarian.* We make these commitments considering that, because of their origins, natural goods and resources should serve first the community and only secondly the individual. The same should be said of other goods and riches created by those resources. That is, the product of work, technical advance, financial services, and all human productivity, including cultural goods, should benefit all the members of the community and society. Thus, on the level of relationships between groups and larger societies, they should benefit principally and primarily the local communities or the national community. As the Church has traditionally held, the right to private goods includes the real, effective responsibility of service to society (see MM, 119). It is not licit or

Christian to possess goods in abundance and waste them, when the majority of the population lacks even the most elementary goods and services. For that reason, John Paul II reminded the indigenous peoples and farm workers in Cuilapan that, in these circumstances, they have the right to recur to the expropriation of property. The social conflicts taking place today, and the even graver ones that could take place if we do not act accordingly, can only be checked if everyone has the real possibility of possessing adequate and worthy goods to meet their necessities, since all have the right to these goods in recompense for their labor and their salary. This is the ancient and present doctrine of the Church (see RN, 33; GS, 69; LE, 14).

46.   *The natural and divine right of all persons to possess goods.* We maintain the principle that all have the natural and divine right to possess goods and to have their human dignity respected, so that Christian fraternity might be a reality. We call this to mind and insist on its being put into practice. As we have seen in section II of this document, all have a divine right to a share in the goods and riches available. John XXIII and the Second Vatican Council both taught this (see MM, 119; GS, 63). This is the preoccupation of Christ in the Beatitudes and in his gospel conversations with the rich, as we have already seen.

47.   *The creation of jobs.* The vicious circle of high prices reduces demand, then reduces production; it can be broken only by creating jobs that generate goods and services really needed by society. The latter process will increase the buying capacity of the people and, consequently, the growth of productivity leading to a real social benefit. By assuming this commitment, we will make it easier to keep God's command: "Be fertile and multiply; fill the earth and subdue it" (Gn 1:28). We make it possible for all to have the right to work and to be the image of God, the first worker: He made all things, and besides "the Lord God planted a garden in Eden, which is in the east, and there he put the man he had fashioned" (Gn 2:8).

48.   *Social justice as a dynamic of change and conversion.* In everything, we have said it is not just a question of attaining distributive justice of goods, nor even true participation in goods according to the efforts each one makes in serving the community. What the magisterium of the Church proposes is a just participation in resources, goods, talents, capabilities, and culture at a highly social level. That is, the whole of society should benefit from all the goods available, without excluding persons or groups (see LE, 15ff). It is a distribution of goods and riches as made by the early Christians, who "divided everything on the basis of each one's need" (Acts 2:45).

49.   *The Christian commitment under any system of holding property so that it may be in accord with evangelical justice.* The commitments we have pointed out can never be sincere if they do not really touch, concretely, the system of holding property we live under, when it is unjust and produces injustices. We should ask ourselves serious questions on the subject. For the believer, it is not a question of having legally, on paper, a good system of holding property. It is a question of implementing a system that truly produces gospel justice, given the fact, as the Church has always sustained, that goods should first be at the disposition of the needy (see MM, 120). And today, as we know, the needy cannot in any real or legal way find solutions to their crushing needs.

50.   *The preferential option for the poor.* To live sincerely and integrally the demands of the gospel, one must make the "preferential option for the poor" (see the document we published in 1977: *Our Christian Commitment with the Indigenous Peoples and Farm Workers of the Southern Pacific Region*; and the *Puebla Document*). The Church demands this option for the socially poor (see *Puebla*, 1135 with footnote 2) "no matter what moral or personal situation they are in" (*Puebla*, 1142). Otherwise, it is impossible to really practice, here and now, what we believe and hope. How can we share? How can we to do justice? How can we seek the participation of all? How can we bring about change in existing structures, if we do not have a preferential love, not exclusive or excluding but including those who are really suffering from those structures? Without this option, would not the desire for change merely be a desire to change structures for the sake of change? The conversions we want as Christians have a historical subject, the poor, destined by the liberation of Christ to form part of the new people of God and to inherit the kingdom.

This option, as the *Puebla Document* states, gives many biblical and theological reasons (see 1141–1152) that assure us that by serving the poor, seeing that he or she also attains the goods that we already enjoy to a greater or lesser degree, we are doing a service to Christ, who identified himself fully with the poor by his incarnation, by his redemptive action, and by his resurrection. Without this option, no one can say he has opted for Christ, since Jesus himself was poor and identified completely with the poor (see Mt 25).

51.   *The new civilization of love.* Authentic evangelization and Christian commitment cause all material, technical, and cultural goods, as well as religious values, to be placed justly and wholly at the service of the social, political, cultural, and religious life of everyone. Those who have riches and other goods are people who have displayed a lot of talent to obtain them. Those same capabilities, purified and converted, should be placed at the service of the faith to accomplish the enormous, magnificent project that the Church called the "New Civilization of Love" (see *Puebla*, 1118). Thus, all those who enjoy middle- or upper-class goods and resources are called by the Church, not simply to a passive shedding of their riches, but to active participation in the construction of that New Civilization of Love.

Venezuela
The Church Speaks for the Unemployed
(1986)

The Venezuelan Church, largely unknown by other national Churches, made a striking statement that speaks for the unemployed.

Venezuelans found their economic hopes turned around. Salaries and wages had increased dramatically in the early 1970s because of bountiful petroleum resources, priced higher than ever. When oil prices dropped, Venezuela's economy sagged. Widespread unemployment, well known in other Latin American countries, now touched a large percentage of Venezuelans (33 percent) and left many others further impoverished.

The Venezuelan Church depends on the government for a substantial part of its income and exists in a society noted for its anticlericalism. Despite its disadvantageous position, the Venezuelan bishops responded strongly to the crisis, calling attention to the extent of the problem and proposing governmental, church, and private initiatives.

One year after the unforgetable visit of our Holy Father, John Paul II, we, the bishops of Venezuela, address all Venezuelans in order to share with you a problem that weighs heavily upon our hearts as pastors.

The gospel tells us that Jesus, seeing the multitude that followed him, suffering from many ills, "took pity on them because they were like sheep without a shepherd, and he set himself to teach them at some length" (Mk 6:34); he "healed the sick" (Mt 14:14) and worked the miracle of the multiplication of the bread and fishes to feed them.

We, as pastors of the Church, have walked with the Venezuelan social process, and we have made reference to it in recent documents and pastoral letters. In the light of the gospel and the social teaching of the Church, we have analyzed the crisis we are suffering and its moral roots, and we have called for the correction of one of the nation's urgent social problems.

In the permanent mission that is now beginning, we have chosen

313

the social apostolate for a new society as one of the areas of priority. As a consequence of this decision, we now turn to the conscience of the Venezuelans, calling their attention to the alarming growth of unemployed. We want to be in solidarity with these unemployed people and encourage all Venezuelans to look not only for middle- and long-term solutions for this serious problem, but also urgently to find ways of alleviating the desperate situation in which so many of our brothers and sisters live.

A. Interpretation of the Situation

We invite all Venezuelans of good will, and very especially our brothers and sisters in faith and in the following of Jesus Christ, to see and to judge this lamentable situation that affects millions of our fellow citizens, and to act with decision and effectiveness to alleviate this situation and find the means for its solution.

1. The Drama of the Unemployed and Their Families

In thinking of the many thousands of unemployed in Venezuela, it hurts us to contemplate their numerous and exhausting trips to knock on the doors of factories and possible work places, only to return home at the end of the day frustrated, exhausted, and humiliated. We see their defenselessness and pain before the questioning and needful gaze of their loved ones, whose most elemental welfare depends on the job that is never found.

We know that for a mother or father that anguish means that day by day their psychological resistance is undermined until they are pushed to the edge of desperation. This can lead to violence.

Unemployment today increasingly affects young workers and professionals, including those who have completed long years of university studies. One-fourth of the youth between fifteen and twenty-four years of age are without work. A youth without work is a youth whose ideals and hope are threatened with collapse. His or her expectations of life and plans for starting a home are blocked. A youth without work, hope, or ideals is a youth who has been spiritually mutilated by society and for society. Thus, it is not strange that they feel tempted to give themselves over to all kinds of degrading conduct: drugs, stealing, alcohol, sex without true love, and an aggressiveness toward a society that attacks and takes away their expectations of life and hope.

We know that this situation of unemployment, which is not limited to Venezuela, is experienced in our society with special helplessness because we lack legislation to protect and establish concrete supports to alleviate its consequences. And, on the other hand, we consider it a temptation to shield ourselves behind the fact that there is unemployment in all countries.

Behind the alarming number of unemployed, there is a greater number of underemployed who lack the income necessary to live with dignity as human beings. We feel we are brothers to all of these persons.

2. The Problem of Underemployment

To the serious problem of unemployment, we must add the anguish of *under*employment. In today's Venezuela, a considerable number of working-age people are engaged in activities considered to be underemployment. In this way, they receive incomes that are far below that needed to cover their needs. They enjoy no social benefits and live in continuous insecurity. All of this means that approximately half of the country's economically active population is disconnected from the productive apparatus and lacks opportunities to obtain an adequate income from their work.

3. Irritating Differences

Together with the serious problems mentioned, there are many public and private institutions whose upper-level functionaries receive exorbitantly high salaries, or others who hold several paid positions simultaneously.

In addition to this irritating disparity, the families who suffer the effects of unemployment become discouraged in face of the uncontrolled and lavish spending of official entities and private persons (e.g., on trips, weddings, birthdays, etc.), some of whom even go so far as to display their ostentation in the communication media.

4. The Fall of the Bolivar

The problem of unemployment and underemployment is exacerbated by the loss of buying power of the bolivar. This implies an alarming drop in real income. Serious and responsible studies inform us that in 1985, the real value of income received by Venezuelans was less than that in 1978. Although workers nominally earn more than in times past, this increase is less than the increase in prices of the goods and services they need to acquire.

5. Consequences

As a result, we see that together unemployment, underemployment, and the deterioration of the real buying power of wages cause hunger and a lack of elemental necessities in the countryside and poor neighborhoods of Venezuela.

Underemployment is also a factor that hinders all social dynamism and economic recuperation. As the buying power of the majority of Venezuelans drops, the companies that produce basic goods lose their capacity to grow and generate employment, and this causes the country to grow poorer.

6. Is a Solution Possible?

We are aware that today Venezuela is in a position to begin solving this extremely serious problem, if all of us take it up as our own with firmness and correct criteria.

There are several facts that support this affirmation:

- It is said that there are around U.S. $35 billion deposited in foreign banks that belong to Venezuelans. In bolivars this would be 500 billion, equivalent to the nation's foreign debt. There is no doubt that this flight of capital is directly related to unemployment and the lack of investment in Venezuela. The decision as to the use of this capital is not now, nor was it ever, free from moral obligations. This money, if repatriated, could open up many sources of jobs and stimulate the production of goods and services.

- There is the fact that in Venezuela agriculture, as well as industry, is in a very incipient stage of production of the goods required by the country. On the other hand, the reduction of foreign currency would force a reduction in imports, making farming and industrial production a national challenge. This would, in turn, be a source of employment.

- The capital invested in Venezuelan industry is functioning at much below its production and employment capacities. In sectors such as construction, this situation is especially serious.

- The state, despite the reduction in petroleum income, still has enough dollars and bolivars to stimulate economic development so that the Venezuelan people would have the possibility of creative work that dignifies them. What is necessary, above all, are determined policies of honest, intelligent, and diligent authorities and administrations who do not give in to unjust pressures to pay the foreign debt. Proof of this (capacity of the state to generate development) is found in the high level of the present national budget.

- There is a lack of confidence on the part of private investment due to the lack of continuity in economic policies. Their money, their capital, is safely invested abroad. An exaggeratedly capitalistic criterion is also seen in our businessmen. They say that their earnings should reach more than 50 percent of what they invest. This scheme favors lack of investment and, ultimately, unemployment.

- It is also common knowledge that the private banks have much greater financial resources than they invest. There is a lack of productive activity to create goods and services that would put these resources to work.

- The greater part of the national territory and natural resources are waiting for the talent that puts in the capital and work necessary to convert them to the service of human persons.

B. The Word of God Questions Us

As pastors called to take up this painful human situation, we would like to invite you to judge it in the light of the gospel and the social teaching of the Church. Faced with this situation, we affirm first of all the dignity of human work.

Human beings, as the image and likeness of God, participate in the creative act of God and grow closer to him by working. John Paul II rightly tells us that "work is a good of mankind—it is a good of humanity—because not only is nature transformed by work, adapting it to each one's needs, but also because each one is fulfilled as a person by working. What is more, in a certain sense, each one is 'made more of a person'" (LE, 9).

So, one can understand why the denial of work experienced by unemployed Venezuelans constitutes an attack on their dignity and the possibilities of their human fulfillment. And (one can understand) why, with the dimensions the problem has today, unemploymnent becomes a "true social calamity" (LE, 18). Unemployment wounds the person in his or her very identity and, consequently, constitutes a threat to peace and social harmony.

Those kinds of employment that deny workers just remuneration for their work also turn out to be prejudicial for human dignity and social harmony. In these cases, it is God himself who comes forth to defend the dispossessed, as the New Testament reminds us: "Laborers mowed your fields, and you cheated them—listen to the wages that you kept back, calling out: realize that the cries of the reapers have reached the ears of the Lord of Hosts" (Jas 5:4). Thus, all indifference toward the unemployed and all capital management and economic

decisions that fail to take into account the generation of employmen
are incompatible with true Christian faith.

The problem of unemployment is humiliating for everyone, espe
cially for the government and for the owners of large private businesses who have not figured out how to use their extensive resource
to promote the dignity of all Venezuelans and their fundamental righ
to work.

C. Invitation to Action

Without trying to enter into technical aspects that are beyond ou
competence, we want to invite all Venezuelans to weigh the seriousness of this situation. We are convinced of the great importance o
the problem of unemployment and of workers' low incomes. Thi
problem is so important that, if the entire nation were to become
aware of its seriousness and take action together to solve it, thi
initiative would be decisive not only for the persons directly affected
but also for the whole national economy, and so for the achievemen
of peace and justice in the country. Likewise, we are convinced that,
despite the crisis, we have the necessary natural, economic, and human resources.

1. A Call to the Nation

We energetically invite the national government, private enterprise
and federated union leaders, research centers specialized in these
problems, and centers of university studies to design a competent,
rapid, and determined plan of action oriented toward the resolution
of the problem of unemployment and deteriorating workers' incomes.
Today in Venezuela, we have two concrete pressing needs:

1.1.   The obligation to subsidize in some way the unemployed for
their own subsistence and that of their families. This is ". . . an obligation that springs from the fundamental moral principle in this
area, that is, the principle of the common use of goods or, to speak
in an even simpler way, the right to life and to subsistence" (LE, 18).

1.2.   The obligation to provide for planning that guarantees the availability of work for all. This overall planning should include a profound
reorientation of the educational system so as to prepare young people
who will be capable of assuming productive activity and appreciating
the dignity of manual work, in the rural areas as well as in the city.

2. A Call to Solidarity

While these urgent and positive programs are being put into action
and achieve the desired effect, a more profound and effective solidarity

with the unemployed and their families is necessary. This cannot be postponed. In their reception of John Paul II during his recent visit (a friendly reception befitting a son) the Venezuelan people gave public testimony to their Christian faith. Basing ourselves on this fundamental identity, we dare to make a call to the deepest fiber of faith in our people: let us be brothers in solidarity with the unemployed. If this desire springs from the depth of our hearts, and aware that whoever becomes a brother or sister to the needy becomes a brother or sister to Christ, we are sure that many initiatives will come forth that open paths of hope and solution for the unemployed. This must be done without humiliating the unemployed, without making them feel like objects of charity, but rather as persons fraternally receiving what is rightfully theirs.

This solidarity should be shown in two ways:

a) *Solidarity among the workers themselves.* It is understandable that, in situations of growing unemployment, those who have jobs feel tempted to forget those who do not, and even consider them potential rivals. Even the unions can fall into this temptation and forget their duty to the nonunionized and unemployed workers.

b) *Solidarity on the part of the Christian community.*
The Christian community, as such, is called by Christ, present in the needy of today, to awaken this cordial and effective solidarity with the unemployed. "It is the touchstone of its fidelity to Christ."

The Christian Community is varied, but the commitment with our brothers obliges all of us: those Christians who live on their income as workers and those who, being owners of the means of production, make decisions on which, in part, the generation of employment or unemployment depends. People in government and professional experts also participate in the Christian community. All should show this commitment through their talents, decisions, and disposition to shared sacrifice.

3. Immediate Concrete Actions

Desirous of making the Venezuelan Church's preferential option for the poor real by announcing, denouncing, and serving, as we insist upon in the *Permanent Mission Plan*, we, as pastors, invite you to develop a process that would inspire a variety of concrete initiatives during all of 1986.

Besides the individual initiatives that might arise, we invite all pastors; religious superiors; leaders of communities, educational centers, and other groups to study this pastoral letter, to undertake activities to help the unemployed and their families, and to press for the generation of more employment.

Concretely, we propose the use of the 1986 Lenten "Sharing" Campaign to begin a reflexion and action process:

- On the second Sunday of Lent, this message will be read, and all parishes and Christian communities will begin in light of the Word: "Is not this the sort of fast that pleases me—it is the Lord who speaks—to break unjust fetters and undo the thongs of the yoke, to let the oppressed go free, and break every yoke, to share your bread with the hungry, and shelter the homeless poor, to clothe the one you see to be naked and not turn from your own kin?" (Is 58:6–7). In this process, we will examine our personal and social sins that carry the Lord to the cross and cause his death. Let us do so as a response to God who asks us: Where is your unemployed brother? What have you done for him?

- During all of Lent the parish community will study initiatives looking for ways of expressing solidarity and support for the unemployed, under the guidance of the pastor and those who carry responsibility, and in accordance with the orientation of the diocesan curia.

- On the Fifth Sunday of Lent (March 16) the traditional "Sharing" Collection will take place, in solidarity with our unemployed brothers and sisters. That Sunday's Collection will be used to alleviate extreme situations of the families of unemployed in the parish, or in more needy parishes, under the organization decided upon in each parish and with the approval of the bishop.

D. Final Exhortation

May our common Father, who listens to our trusting prayer as we ask for "our daily bread," and the example of Mary our Mother, a humble worker's wife who knew the anguish of poverty, exile, and the pain of not being able to find a place where her son might be born, give us the strength necessary to reconquer for humanity our dignity as children of God, to build justice and peace, and to reestablish the society of love.

Receive our blessing, as a demonstration of our closeness to you and as inspiration and encouragement for the work that awaits all of us.

The Bishops of Venezuela
Caracas
January 11, 1986

Venezuela

They Will Build Their Houses and
Live in Them
(1987)

Housing has become a major issue of this decade and will continue to be an issue in the 1990s. The bishops use the occasion of the International Year for Suitable Housing to examine the situation in Venezuela. They note great changes in their society, which has become 84 percent urban—a major shift over time.

While recognizing efforts at helping to provide housing by the state, Church, and individuals, the bishops find that six million (of a population of eighteen million) Venezuelans suffer overcrowding, lack of security and public services, and unsanitary conditions.

Their judgment of the situation is severe: "The utilization of space in Venezuela is totally inadequate. . . . Great vacant areas, presently completely empty, await the humanizing, productive presence of human labor." The bishops are especially concerned about impoverished housing because of the bad moral effects such housing fosters.

The bishops call for a change in housing policy, for rethinking of priorities in land use, for rethinking the role of private enterprise, and for the involvement of all citizens.

A house is a basic necessity and a basic family right. During this International Year for Suitable Housing, under the motto, "A Roof for the Homeless," the Venezuelan bishops wish to draw near to all those families suffering for lack of adequate housing. We also wish to unite our voices and our influence with those of so many Christians, as well as men and women of good will, who are doing everything possible so that Venezuelan families may satisfy with complete justice their need for space for family intimacy, where children and young people can grow up in an atmosphere of love and security. After studying the overall picture of housing in Venezuela, where the great contrasts and situations of extreme necessity are very clear, we bishops, as shepherds of the Church, feel obligated to share our concern with all Venezuelans and invite them to reflect on desired and possible solutions.

1. The Present Realty

1.1. A Country in the Midst of Change

During the last half century, Venezuela has undergone great changes. Not only has there been great internal demographic growth, but also the majority of the population has ceased to be rural and has become urban, as indeed is the case throughout the world. In fact, today, 84 percent of all Venezuelans live in the cities, and half of the present urban dwellers have migrated or are direct descendants of those who, for different reasons, had to abandon their land and their home in search of a new environment and new housing.

Added to the internal migration, a large number of our brothers and sisters have been forced, over the last fifty years, to come to Venezuela. This has been due to war, poverty, political intolerance, and persecution in their countries or simply the search for a job and a new place to live. For them, Venezuela has been a land of sacrifice and great effort, but also a land of progress, hope, and freedom.

This rapid process of demographic growth, migrations, and urbanization has created a very serious lack of adequate and humane housing for millions of our brothers and sisters.

1.2. Some Praiseworthy Efforts, though Insufficient

It would be unjust to deny that, during these five decades, immense efforts have been made to give each Venezuelan family its own home. The state has done a lot through initiatives such as the Institute for People's Housing, the Workers' Bank, INAVI, the Institute for Rural Housing, Malariologia, and other organizations, as well as through the subsidy for the construction and acquiring of housing built to satisfy social needs. There have also been private institutions and business enterprises as well as the Church involved in contributions for housing through foundations, credit, cooperatives, and so forth. Individual citizens have also used their imagination and capacity for hard work in creating their own housing, even if it is only an improvised shack.

But the severity of the situation has surpassed all the efforts made, and there are more than six million Venezuelans suffering overcrowding, lack of security and public services, and unsanitary conditions in the marginal areas. Many must also be satisfied with apartments of minimum size, in the poor urbanized areas, often built without sufficient planning, and lacking the space needed for community activities.

Thus, while recognizing all that has been done, we believe there must be a new and greater drive in the development of a housing policy so that every Venezuelan family may have its own home, suitable for the needs of a life with dignity.

1.3. Vacant Land and Overpopulated Cities

The utilization of space in Venezuela is totally inadequate. While in the cities, especially Caracas, the population lives in inhumane, crowded conditions and the costs of a transportation system are multiplied, great vacant areas, presently completely empty, await the humanizing, productive presence of human labor. Besides this, the neglect suffered by rural populations and small towns is generally known. All this forces people to find a solution in the unjust, questionable exodus to the cities.

The whole population suffers the negative results of this distorting contrast, but especially those sectors with the least resources. There are millions of work hours lost each year with people caught up in traffic and waiting for transportation. There is a lack of personal security and of contact with one's family. There are the ever-higher costs of public services and the construction of schools, churches, public squares, recreational areas, and so forth. The space, or lack of it, prevents communication and fraternal encounter with neighbors. This lack becomes more acute, and even dramatic, because of the living conditions in the home.

1.4. Improvised Housing and the Marginal Residential Areas

The phenomenon of improvised housing (*el rancho*) and marginal residential areas (*barriadas*) graphically demonstrates the whole housing drama in Venezuela. When former farm workers, now urban dwellers, look at the past from the perspective of an improvised shack stuck on the side of a hill, they see progress and place all their hope in the future of their children. In spite of moments of desperation and discouragement at not finding employment, food, and a roof, confidence in self and in God has always prevailed. In the midst of their deprivations, the simplest people have felt themselves accompanied by God and our Mother, the Blessed Virgin Mary. And they have been faithful to that confidence. Hurriedly building their shacks on marginal urban land, they did not consider themselves firmly established until they had received the blessing of the priest and raised the cross, their Patron, on a hill and built a chapel with the labor of their own hands. These are expressions of confidence in a God who is near to them ("He lived among us"), who shares their hopes and sufferings.

The hundreds of such poor residential areas that surround our cities, besides being an accusing crown of thorns, are at the same time the concrete realization of an admirable effort on the part of their inhabitants. It represents their initiative, talent, labor, tenacity, savings, and sacrifice, along with the solidarity of their relatives and neighbors. However, the inadequacy of the land, often unstable and dangerous; the lack of easy access; the distance from work centers; the lack of streets, squares, and recreational areas always make that effort seem temporary and inadequate.

That is how the improvised housing shows up a contradiction and is a denunciation of our social reality. It is the fruit of the creative effort of Venezuelans with few resources available for housing and a first step toward the hope of something better. But it is also an accusing finger pointed at a social system that condemns the majority to unjust and inadequate income and, therefore, to precarious housing that does not have the facilities necessary for the authentic development of family life. Last of all, we cannot avoid mentioning that this situation of injustice has often been manipulated by politicians without scruples to foment the invasion of zones that do not guarantee a minimum of suitable living conditions.

1.5. Prices Compared with Salaries

One factor that has traditionally influenced the serious lack of housing among us has been the high cost, that is, the lack of proportion between the cost and the salaries of the majority of the population. This makes it impossible for a great number of Venezuelans to exercise the right to housing guaranteed in Article 73 of the National Constitution. In spite of rising wages and salaries over the last several years, the possibility of acquiring suitable housing daily grows more distant for the majority of families.

In this context, it is also painful to recognize that many of our brothers and sisters suffer personal defects, which make it much more difficult to find solutions, or which make it necessary to postpone them. These complications include the lack of an attitude of saving; lack of constancy in work; careless spending habits that often border on sinful waste; and, in some cases, irresponsible parenthood, which produces incomplete and abandoned families without any possibility of adequate economic support.

Besides these obstacles, recent years have brought the growing deterioration of the national economy due to the fall in oil prices, the foreign debt, the devaluation of our currency, and inflation, with the resulting loss of buying power of wages and salaries.

The Venezuelan bishops note with concern that the situation of 72 percent of the population with a family income of less than 5,000 bolivars is gradually worsening. With that kind of income, they cannot possibly set aside anything for housing. Even in sectors of the middle class, many young couples have no way of acquiring their own home and must live with their parents.

Besides all this, we run the danger—and there are already visible indicators—that anarchistic or violent reactions will become more common when faced with the impossibility of satisfying vital necessities. As is obvious, a healthy family life is impossible in an inhospitable environment, where the families live in promiscuity, where even minimum conditions for true humane living do not exist, as is the case in the improvised housing existing in our cities and in the countryside. Such housing, as well as the mini-apartments in some of our badly planned poor residential areas, cannot promote the harmonious development of the family, the couple, the children, and the young people, who often flee in search of better surroundings.

1.6. The Manipulation of Neighborhood Associations

In the case of the cities, a housing unit is not isolated, but is rather one part of an overall residential complex where the people's lives take place. We are pleased to see how the inhabitants have taken the initiative in many places to organize neighborhood "boards" or "associations." In the poor urbanized areas, as well as the marginal zones, there are flourishing activities that we hope will draw an increasing participation by everyone. However, we want to warn against the danger of the manipulation of these initiatives for personal or party interests. There is a need for sincere, direct, nonpaternalistic dialogue between government authorities and the neighborhood associations and a healthy independence from specific political parties so as to better the public services and increase cooperation and coexistence, as well as a neighborly, fraternal spirit in these residential areas.

2. In Search of Solutions

2.1. A Change of Policy

As we have seen, the housing problem is very serious and complex. One must consider not only the walls that make up the home, but also the totality of the services that influence family and neighborhood living. Faced with this situation, there is a need for decided action by the state, private enterprise, and the citizens themselves. There must be an energetic reaction and the promotion of effective solutions for the drama that afflicts so many of our brothers and sisters.

As we are aware that it is not our job to offer technical solutions, we cordially invite all persons of good will to use their talents and initiatives, to orient their activities and the institutions they belong to in a determined effort to make the right to a worthy home possible for all those who lack it today. In this context, we dare suggest some lines of action.

2.2. The State's Task

2.2.1. A Broad Housing Policy

We know that the Venezuelan state has carried out many housing initiatives during the last half century, but much more is hoped for. We think that a broad housing policy should be implemented, intensifying such actions as those that follow. The state should make available to private enterprise greater economic resources than those foreseen up until now for the construction of socially oriented housing. It should increase subsidies for the construction and acquisition of this housing. It should increase the work of such organizations as INAVI and the Institute for Rural Housing. It should continue the task of consolidating what already exists in marginal areas, located in zones that are not dangerous or clearly inadequate for housing. It should continue and increase support for families building their own homes. It should avoid speculation in urban land.

2.2.2. A Rethinking of Priorities in Land Use

These elements, which, along with others, could make up a broad housing policy, should be accompanied by a serious and bold effort at rethinking priorities in land use. There is a need for decisive, energetic, systematic planning of how land is to be used, looking to the future. In that way, the population will be distributed nationally in a more balanced and productive manner.

This planning would include fostering the growth of intermediate-sized cities located south of the present huge concentrations of people. For that to be feasible, there must be jobs and adequate living conditions. In this context, we support all the efforts made to promote the inhabiting of our frontiers.

2.2.3. Improving Rural Living Conditions

Along with all this, there must be increased effort at providing for roads; facilities for fulfilling health, religious, educational, and cultural needs to the existing farm workers and rural towns; and in assuring jobs that permit the inhabitants a better standard of living. At the same time, the exodus toward the large cities should be slowed down.

2.2.4. Economic Policy

On the other hand, without an economic policy that guarantees a profit and stability for prices of agricultural products, as well as salaries that are just and adequate to the growing cost of living, all this effort would be useless. Thus, there is a need for coherent economic measures that assure increasing democracy of economic power and the redistribution of the buying power of all Venezuelans.

2.3. Private Enterprise

We recognize the generosity and good will of some business people who have produced initiatives such as foundations that help their workers obtain housing, credit for their employees, and so forth. This is an example that should continue and be expanded, especially through setting aside a part of business profit for the construction and financing of social interest housing. However, besides all this, we believe it is necessary for financial institutions to devote a greater percentage of their available funds as preferred credit for housing. On the other hand, investment in housing must be stimulated while, at the same time, having a generous social criterion for calculating the profits. These who manage the construction industry must also see their activity not just as a legitimate way of making a profit but also as a contribution to the solution of this serious human problem. We also remind all business people of the need for considering social justice in calculating wages, salaries, and worker benefits, thus giving the people greater buying power.

2.4. All Citizens

Feeling ourselves very close to our brothers and sisters who suffer the lack of housing worthy of the name, we invite you to keep up your hope and keep struggling for better housing. In this context, we support all the initiatives in building your own homes and bettering the services in stable zones, and we denounce unjust, arbitrary evictions. At the same time, we ask all those who have benefited from state housing programs to pay for and keep their houses and apartments in good condition, as well as working for better relationships, more fraternity and bettering the conditions of the neighborhood. We also strongly insist that constancy in work and in saving are an absolutely indispensable necessity for the construction of a better future.

2.5. The Church

Some years ago, Cardinal Jose Humberto Quintero, then archbishop of Caracas, used funds given him for his own housing to create an urban neighborhood for the poor, which took the name of Juan XXIII. It was a living, concrete example of the generosity and concern of a shepherd for the housing of his people. There have been and still are many initiatives by priests and religious who have fostered the creation of housing cooperatives. However, it is not the task of the Church itself to construct housing, nor does it have the means to do so. The Church is present wherever its people are. And even among the very poorest, there are many priests, religious, and lay people. In their countless marginal and urbanized residential areas, they share the destiny of those new neighborhoods, living and proclaiming the Lord's word and accompanying them in the construction of God's kingdom. Even when the accompaniment may be numerically inadequate, the Church continues with its efforts at creating chapels, free schools, clinics, and formation centers. It promotes and organizes cooperatives, associations, prayer groups, basic ecclesial communities, and the formation of catechists and church leaders.

Thus, we want to remind the state authorities and private developers of the need for including, in the plans for new developments, land for churches, chapels, and community centers.

3. Conclusion

Housing is a great challenge for Venezuela. We dare to say that not to take this challenge up today and confront it responsibly will make any future solution impossible. Improvised housing will continue to proliferate; the social reactions will become more violent and repressive responses will begin. There will be no progress in the true situation of our people.

For that reason, during this International Year for Suitable Housing, and within the framework of the social pastoral care of the permanent mission that the Church is presently developing in Venezuela, we renew our call for increased boldness, decision, and generosity in all that concerns the national housing policy. This includes the contribution of those affected, the state and private enterprise, the talent and technical ability of universities and professionals, and the good will of all.

We make our own the words addressed by the Holy Father to the inhabitants of the urban slum, *Dos Alagados,* in San Salvador de Bahia, Brazil, on July 7, 1980:

> You have a great sense of solidarity in helping one another when it is necessary. . . . You must struggle for life and do everything possible to better the conditions under which you live. This is a sacred duty because it is also the will of God. Do not say it is God's will that you remain in a situation of poverty, sickness, insalubrious housing, often contrary to your dignity as human persons. Do not say "God wants it." I know that this does not depend only on you. I am not ignorant of the fact that others should do a great deal to put an end to these evil conditions that afflict you, or at least to better them. But you should be the first to try to better your life in every way, to wish to overcome the bad conditions, to help out one another—all together—so that better days may come. These are some of the important steps in your journey.

As shepherds of the Church, we encourage all communities not only to read and reflect on this pastoral letter, but also to take a positive stance on the subject under discussion, each contributing according to his or her possibilities in the creation of a collective conscience, leading to effective solutions.

During this Marian Year, we turn our eyes toward the Holy Family of Nazareth, which knew how to convert their humble home into a space for unity and family love, for constructive labor, and of welcome for all those who entered there.

Caracas
July 13, 1987

Cuba
External Debt and the New International Economic Order
(1986)

For the first time in twenty-five years, the Catholic Church took part in an international meeting called by the Cuban government. That the Church was invited and that it accepted surpised many; that the Church's first participation was on a topic of external debt also was a surprise to some.

Bishop Adolfo Rodriguez Herrera, president of the episcopal conference, explains why the Church participated and why the bishops were interested in the topic. Although the presentation was made in his own name, the episcopal conference then adopted the document as its own.

The topic has become a major concern of most of the episcopates of Latin America. They were probably the group that most influenced John Paul II to initiate and to endorse the study on external debt, which was published by the Holy See in 1987, through the Pontifical Commission on Justice and Peace.

Christian Presence at the Conference on the Foreign Debt

The fact that, for the first time in twenty-five years, the Church was invited to a meeting convened by the government of our country, that the Cuban Bishops' Conference accepted the meeting, and that the agenda of the conference was a topic seemingly so remote from the Church's mission as the foreign debt, cannot but surprise a good many Catholics, make many happy, fill most people with hope, and perhaps worry some here or there.

It is true that the President of the Council of State and of the government, Commandante Fidel Castro, personally invited the Archbishop of Havana and both the secretary and president of the bishops' conference to attend this conference on the foreign debt, held in Havana from July 30 to August 3 [1985]. By a prior arrangement, there were to be no conclusions or agreements. The two bishops and the rest of our bishops' conference appreciated this invitation, and the church was represented in this Havana conference, which took place in an atmosphere of openness, dialogue, pluralism, diversity, and freedom of expression. No one was forced to speak and no one was prohibited from speaking. We bishops did not go up to the speakers' platform since none of the Cubans present did so.

All the meetings were plenary assemblies. The speakers dealt with the issues of the foreign debt, Latin American integration, and the need for a New International Economic Order, which are obviously interconnected. Taking part were more than 1,200 Latin Americans from the political, economic, business, military, artistic, and religious spheres. The Christian presence was especially noteworthy, not only because of the high number of Christians (more than 100 priests and a vast majority of believers), but also because of the serenity with which they professed their Christian faith when speaking from the podium.

A Moral Basis

In accepting this invitation, we thought that although the issue of the foreign debt is financial, technical, political, and proper to experts, this problem nevertheless has an underlying moral, ethical, and human basis, and the Church cannot be totally indifferent to it, as indeed it never has been. Clearly, it is not a problem that exhausts all the problems of our region, but everyone agrees that it is one of the most grave and urgent on the horizon of our Latin American peoples.

The Church is not an expert in economics and is not competent in this area. That is not the mission Jesus entrusted to it. Nor does the Church have the sole responsibility for justice in the world. It is not its task to outline policies and economic programs; it is not up to the Church to do away with the International Monetary Fund with a stroke of the pen, nor to draw up legislation on a country's exports and imports, nor to close the World Bank and put its employees out of work, nor to fix prices. Jesus did not bring a detailed list of concrete solutions for each concrete situation in the life of human beings in society but, rather, a gospel of moral activities for every concrete situation in human life.

Indeed, because this problem of the foreign debt is a problem of moral responsibility, the Church cannot remain neutral, as though if it did so, the issue would thereby not be moral. The fact is that the Church has not remained neutral with regard to this problem, even during the period when the foreign debt as such did not exist, except in embryo, when it was only a danger. Everything related to the moral order is also related to the Church's mission; it is not an expert in economics, but it is an expert in humanity. The Church has taught that behind an unjust system there are always unjust persons; behind bad laws there are always bad individuals; behind a sin there is always a sinner. Prior to being structural, sins are personal; systems, laws, mechanisms are consequences before they are causes. The root is in free and responsible persons, in selfish human nature. The blind forces of nature, such as cyclones, droughts, floods, or earthquakes, may worsen matters, but they are not the root; they occur, but they are not always the cause. Injustices are produced by human beings, and human beings can and must correct them.

The foreign debt is a complex phenomenon brought about by economic dependence: by international aid, when it comes in the form of credit, and by foreign investment. Any aid that creates dependence does not liberate but rather subjects, humiliates, insults, and impoverishes. Those who lend, often do so with very onerous conditions. For these reasons, and because of poor investment practices and internal management, the debtor countries have become increasingly indebted, reaching astronomical levels of monies owed, and now they are unable to reduce the principle or pay the high interest rates. In an interrelated and self-reinforcing way, there have appeared mechanisms that John Paul II calls "mechanisms that generate greater poverty" and which we know as inflation, protectionist policies, dumping, capital flight, and so forth.

Opinion of the Magisterium

Everyone believes that Latin America has come to its worst economic crisis in this century. It is impossible to develop a country under these conditions. People cannot be happy with things the way they are. Inequality is on the rise; the gap between rich and poor countries is growing ever wider; North-South tensions are hardening; areas of dire poverty are spreading; and the whole continent has become, as John Paul II, says, a giant mirror reflecting "the unfolding of the parable of the rich glutton and the poor Lazarus," who are separated by an enormous chasm.

It is precisely at this point that the mission, interest, and concern of the Church are to be found, and we would include the responsibility and competence of the Church. There is no reason to be surprised that the Church's message on one or other of the three topics of the Havana conference, or on all of them at once, goes back a long way, for the dust of those days was a harbinger of the mud of today. This

s not a latecomer's zeal on the part of the Church, which could be
questioned as opportunistic. In former times, the official teaching
authority of the Church raised its voice not to advise the poor to be
content with their poverty as the rich were content with their wealth,
but to denounce the unjust causes of poverty and to proclaim the
gospel attitudes that might avoid the consequences. Let us examine
only a few landmarks along this progression of the ecclesiastical mag-
sterium.

1.   In 1891, almost a hundred years ago, Pope Leo XIII published the
encyclical *Rerum Novarum*, which has unanimously been regarded as
"the magna carta of the new economic and social order," (MM, 26).

In 1931, Pius XI in *Quadragesimo Anno*, with words that are aston-
ishingly up to date, denounces "economic dictatorship . . . the desire
for profit . . . the economy which has become terribly harsh, implac-
able and cruel"; "despotic economic arrogance"; and the "wretched
internationalism of capital." Pius XI urges that the economy be linked
to the moral order; that individual interests be subordinated to the
common good; that the social order be rebuilt through the creation
of international bodies of an economic and professional nature; and
he blames liberal capitalism for foreign economic aggression and the
creation of what he calls, the "international imperialism of money,
whose homeland is wherever it does well."

2.   There is not enough space to mention the extensive teaching
activity of Pius XII, nor to quote the great John XXIII, especially his
two encyclicals *Mater et Magistra* (1961) and *Pacem in Terris* (1963), in
which we find teachings on gradual and harmonious development of
the whole world economic order that are clear and even more up to
date.

The Council's Prophetic Voice

3.   1962 marks the opening of the Second Vatican Council which, in
addition to many other passing references, specifically devotes chapters III, IV, and V of part II of the *Constitution on the Church in the
Modern World* (*Gaudium et Spes*) to this issue. With a prophetic voice,
the Council begins the chapter on economic life by saying that "reasons
for anxiety . . . are not lacking (63) and denounces "excessive inequalities and . . . undue dependence" (85) and "economic inequalities
and . . . exessive slowness in applying the needed remedies" (83).
These chapters must be reread in their entirety. The Council urges
that the human being become "the source, the center, and the purpose
of all socioeconomic life" (63). It calls for a change in mentality and
customs, based on the principles of justice both in the order of individual life and in international life (see 85); a change in the way

world trade is organized; another way for rich countries to "aid" poor countries (see 86); just investment and monetary policies (see 70); and finally, it calls for a new International Economic Order (see 83–86).

Countries Overwhelmed by Debt

4.   In his speeches, in his visit to the U.N., in his apostolic letters and encyclicals, Paul VI deals with these issues with an almost obsessive persistence. An inexhaustible source of light from the gospel is provided by his encyclicals *Ecclesiam Suam* (1964), *Octogesima Adveniens* (1971), *Evangelii Nuntiandi* (1975), and especially by *Populorum Progressio* (1967), in which he proposes moral norms so that "developing countries will . . . no longer risk being overwhelmed by debts whose repayment swallows up the greater part of their gains" (54). In 1967, Paul VI warns of the possibility that the foreign debt might become overwhelming: "it is unacceptable that citizens with abundant incomes from the resources and activity of their country should transfer a considerable part of this income abroad," (24). He speaks about interest rates and payment schedules (see 54); on the use of "two systems of weights and measures" (61); on unequal terms of trade (see 56 and 59); on the need for grant aid, for loans without interest or very low interest; and on the efficient use of loans (see 54). He condemns neocolonialism disguised as financial aid or technical assistance or political pressure whose purpose is to gain a dominant hegemony (see 52); and he once more earnestly calls on the governments of the world to do what he had asked in his 1964 *Message to the World:* to create a World Fund, partly made up of money that would have gone for military spending (see 51, 52), in order to aid poor countries, to whom it happens, as he says, that "[what is] given them with one hand . . . [is] . . . taken away with the other" (56).

Dramatic Levels in Latin America

5.   The Second General Conference of CELAM was held in Medellín in 1968, a number of years before the foreign debt reached the dramatic levels we see today throughout Latin America. We must carefully reread the conclusions of the *Medellín Document* that focus on "Justice" (ch. 1) and especially on "Peace" (ch. 2), in which Medellín criticizes uneven terms of trade:

> Because of the relative depreciation of the terms of exchange, the value of raw materials is increasingly less in relation to the cost of manufactured

products. This means that the countries that produce raw materials—especially if they are dependent upon one major export—always remain poor, while the industrialized countries enrich themselves. This injustice, clearly denounced by *Populorum Progressio*, nullifies the eventual positive effect of external aid and constitutes a permanent menace against peace, because our countries sense that "one hand takes away what the other hand gives (PP, 56)" (*Medellín*, 2:9a).

Back in 1968, Medellín denounces the flight of capital that does not return to its point of origin; tax evasion by foreign companies; international monopolies; the international imperialism of money; the arms race; economic dependence; and "the risk of encumbering ourselves with debts whose payment absorbs the greater part of our profits (PP, 54)" (*Medellín*, 2:9d).

6.   In 1971, the Synod of Bishops was convened in Rome to discuss the topic of "Justice in the World." This synod once more took positions on the problems of a world marked by the sin of injustice. It spoke in favor of "the transfer of a determined percentage of the annual income of the richer countries to the developing nations; fairer prices for raw materials; the opening of the markets of the richer nations; and, in some fields, preferential treatment for exports of manufactured goods from the developing nations" (66). The Synod on Justice calls to mind the Pontifical Commission for Justice and Peace whose active efforts and publications are too numerous to mention.

7.   Thus, we come to the pontificate of John Paul II, at the height of the world crisis that could have been avoided if the voices of his predecessors had been heeded. John Paul II is unsparing in trips throughout the world, speeches, letters, encyclicals, visiting the United Nations—all for the sake of arousing people's consciences. Especially noteworthy are his speeches on trips through Latin America. Also noteworthy is his first encyclical, *Redemptor Hominis*, (1979) as well as *Laborem Exercens* (1981); both must be reread, especially chapters 15 and 16 of *Redemptor Hominis*. There, John Paul II says that "today, humankind seems to be threatened by what it produces" (15). He speaks of inflation as a "fever"; strikes as a "plague"; the present situation as an "overwhelming burden"; and production mechanisms as a "manipulation." He denounces the arms race, unequal commercial exchange, the poor distribution of wealth, and the lack of control. At Edmonton, Canada, referring specifically to our continent, John Paul II said, "This impoverished South will judge the wealthy North, and the poor peoples will judge the rich nations . . . they will judge those who seize their wealth and accumulate for themselves an imperialist economic monopoly and political supremacy at the expense of everyone else."

8.   In 1979, the Third General Conference of CELAM was held in

Puebla. The conference opens with a "Message to the Peoples of Latin America," in which our continent is described as a spectacle in which "there is an ever-increasing distance between the many who have little and the few who have much" (*Puebla*, 2). Without ignoring any of the situations of injustice that Latin America is experiencing, Puebla provides gospel-inspired paths toward solutions in its documents.

CELAM, which convened Puebla, has published many serious studies on the situation in Latin America. We especially draw attention to *Fe Cristiana y Compromiso Social* (*Christian Faith and Social Commitment*) (1981) and more recently, *Brecha entre ricos y pobres* (*Gap between Rich and Poor*), in which CELAM's Department of Social Pastoral Work "recognizes that Latin America's debt cannot be paid as it is currently scheduled" (p. 22). CELAM has repeatedly stated that no solution is acceptable if it makes those already poor poorer and makes those who are already suffering suffer more. Through its Department of Social Pastoral Work, CELAM urges "a dialogue of pastors with economists, politicians, business and professional people, and so forth, on ethical aspects of the human being and the economy." That is precisely what our Cuban government's initiative is about (*Brecha*, 3:15, p. 110).

Economic Conscience of Solidarity

Both debtors and creditors are seeking a way out of this complex problem in Latin America, which CELAM describes as "being trapped." Various approaches to solutions are discussed, such as renegotiation; moratorium; a debtors' strike; erasing and starting over; a grace period; a sabbath year; it-must-be-paid; it-need-not-be-paid; it-cannot-be-paid; it-must-not-be-paid; change-the-payment-schedule. Everyone rejects the solutions proposed by the International Monetary Fund because they consist of sharp adjustments, which moreover are unfair since they fall exclusively on the backs of the debtors and not on the creditors: monetary devaluation, reduced public spending, higher taxes, reduced imports, increasing exports.

As a religious and hierarchical community, the Church is not competent to define specific solutions, but each Christian is free to take the option his or her conscience dictates on the basis of what the gospel demands. Christians are not free to take a "couldn't-care-less" attitude. The Church's magisterium teaches that economics cannot be separated from morality because, in that case, it becomes inhuman; that the economy should be at the service of human beings and not human beings at the service of the economy; that there must be an awakening of an economic conscience of solidarity between societies; that ethics is above technology, and spirit above matter; that economic liberation is not the only kind of liberation that the human being needs. Finally, for a long time, the Church has been urging that there be a new economic order, on both national and international levels, under a just, guiding principle so as to to regulate the economy.

Commitment between Faith and Life

At the conference held in Havana one could observe a consensus that the crisis caused by the foreign debt is very serious and immediate; that the debt cannot be paid under present conditions; that the IMF's solutions must be rejected; that Latin America must be integrated; and that there is an urgent need for a new International Economic Order. Even though the conference did not seek to come to a general agreement, it was significant that the letter from Cardinal Paulo Evaristo Arns, archbishop of São Paulo, Brazil, became something like a tacit consensus when the whole assembly unanimously arose to give it warm applause.

Another significant fact about the conference was the temporal commitment of so many Latin American Christians attending the meeting. It is sometimes said that faith alienates, evades, and prevents people from being committed; that faith destroys their responsibility for history and turns them toward a nonexistent world; that religion is antiscience; and that it is a private affair. These Christians, however, showed us that in their very faith—and out of their very faith—they find an internal drive and further motivation for their commitment to humankind and to society; that without compromising their conscience, their dignity, and autonomy, they make faith in God the ultimate basis for this very conscience, autonomy, and dignity. As Radomiro Tomic said in his speech: "What I want to highlight is this phenomenon, which is new in its massive expression, though not new in its basic perspective, that of the growing commitment between faith and life being made by believers."

Approval and Support of the Cuban Church

Personally, I am quite grateful to the priests, religious brothers and sisters, and lay people for the sincere expressions of approval, support, and encouragement they have given their Church. I served as the unworthy representative of this Church at the conference, to which we were invited and in which we took part. I express this gratitude especially to the young people of the diocese, with whom I had the opportunity to speak on this topic at the recent Diocesan Youth Conference in response to their request. I am here expressing, in a simple manner, the same ideas I expressed there.

I share with all the hope that is nourished by this gesture of our government toward our Church, and I also share the joy of a pastor on having once more seen proof that the lay people of our diocese are not indifferent or insensitive toward this problem or toward any other human problem. My other joy—just as great—is that of seeing proof that you Cuban lay people in your work, study, and professions, through your commitment and example, are in no way different from those Christians whom we met and got to know during the conference.

Bishop Adolfo Rodríguez Herrera of Camagüey
President
Cuban Bishops' Conference

Mexico
At the Service of the Human Community
An Ethical Consideration of the International Debt
(1987)

*Mexico assumed one of the world's largest debts mainly
on the basis of favorable prices for petroleum. When these
prices declined drastically, Mexico and its debtors found
themselves faced with a grave crisis. Following the lead
of the major statement on international debt by the Pontifical Commission on Justice and Peace (January 1987),
the Mexican bishops here search for an adequate description of and ethical guidelines for a discussion of the Mexican situation that produced a burden reaching "intolerable
limits for our people."*

*The bishops focus first on the country itself, recognizing that "we are the persons and groups of our country
. . . who have produced this intense and grave crisis."
Further, "the essential and necessary link of politics and
economics with morality has not been respected." The
bishops maintain that a healthy attitude entails recognizing responsibilities: "[while] there are causes that can
be laid to external mechanisms [this] gives no license to
disclaim personal responsibilities."*

*The bishops then stress shared responsibility: "Both
those who loan and those who ask for the loan have a
mutual responsibility in the advantages and in the errors
of good will" and " in the negative consequences of an
error committed by both parties. It would be unjust to
make the burden of error fall only on the debtor." The
bishops conclude with considerations of responsibilities
for the present and future.*

1. The Mexican bishops present these reflections as an instrument
to communicate and apply to our country the ethical consideration
of the international debt, which the Pontifical Commission on Justice
and Peace published on January 27, 1987.
2. As Mexicans, we search with sincerity for the good of our country;
we offer the profound convictions that give us our faith and the

certainty that they are a solid basis for a solution to the current situation. As pastors, we fulfill the mission given to us by Christ himself: to allow the light of the gospel to reach the conscience and the centers where the economic and political decisions that affect national life are made, so that those decisions are enriched with the humanitarian criteria contained in the gospel. We do not pretend to criticize in this situation. In this way, we fulfill our duty to promote human dignity and, consistent with that, to judge the social, economic, and political life of human beings in order to help them grow in the dignity with which God has created them.

I. It Is Necessary to See Reality

3.   Our Mexican reality, with all its values and problems, cannot be reduced simply to economic factors; nor can these be reduced to the internal and external debt. The crisis we find ourselves in is complex and consists of many diverse and interdependent elements that combine personal, social, economic, political, technical, and educational factors—all of which are related to ethical-religious elements that penetrate the whole of human reality and constitute their deepest meaning. We are the persons and groups of our country—with our formation or deformation, with our values and antivalues, with our integrity or unworthy fears, with our way of thinking and our conduct—who have produced this intense and severe crisis.

4.   A crisis is a decisive moment or period in the life of a person or of a society in which the decisions and the actions that will affect the future are played out, and consequently, they will condition ways of living and of being. There is a crisis of convalescence and recuperation, and there are also those of decline and agony. Thus, a crisis is the moment to give a new direction to our way of acting and of living. It is the time to correct with energy what is going badly.

5.   The crisis is revealed principally as economic and political, and its cause is to be found in the fact that the essential and necessary link of politics and economics with morality has not been respected, nor is it presently respected. When this rupture takes place, politics is reduced to a technique of power, of domination, and of oppression, and the economy is converted into a strategy of avarice. Then, both are transformed into dreadfully effective factors of crisis and decadence because they produce injustice, lack of love, and the negation of solidarity. The present situation is the natural and explainable result of a profound and extensive moral collapse.

6.   For our people, the crisis has meant a drastic reduction in the standard of living because of inflation and unemployment; it has also promoted a growing discontent and it is not clear what the required remedy is, in whose implementation we could all collaborate mutually and freely.

7.   The present situation makes the burden reach intolerable limits for our people. The internal effort to adjust the economy is having a high social cost and, judging by the facts, has not, until now, permitted definitive measures to correct the situation, but only attempts to avoid an even worse deterioration.

8.   Although there are many gloomy facts in the panorama of our country, they should not lead us to forget that we also count on transcendent values that are a basis for solid hope. With these, we should form our conscience in these difficult times and promote solidarity and a spirit of service in our conduct.

9.   The proper formation of conscience demands recognition of the efforts made to negotiate the debt. We cannot affirm that the failure to overcome the crisis is due only to poor handling.

II. We Have to Examine the Causes and Recognize Responsibilities

10.   A healthy attitude in face of the problems—above all the most complex—is that of recognizing responsibilities; if not, the attitude of blaming others and excusing one's self from all guilt serves no purpose and rather complicates the problem. Evidently, in the critical situation of our country, there are causes that can be laid to global mechanisms that appear to escape all control. But it is also clear that this gives no license to disclaim personal responsibilities, which exist to varying degrees and in different forms.

11.   "The sectors that hold power in the developed countries should accept that their comportment and their eventual responsibilities in the indebtedness of their countries be clarified: negligence in the establishment of adequate structures or abuse of the existing structures (monetary fraud, corruption, monetary speculation, flight of private capital, 'perks' in international contracts . . .). This duty of transparency and of truthfulness would help to establish better the responsibilities of each and to avoid unjustified suspicions as well as propose adequate and necessary reforms as much for the institutions as for the procedures" (Pontifical Commission on Justice and Peace, *At the service of the Human Community: An Ethical Consideration of the International Debt*, 198, III, 2).

12.   Mexico's external debt was generated at a point when the price of petroleum appeared to guarantee our capacity for payment. But the fall in prices in the petroleum market, the rise in interest rates, the inadequate response of the industrialized nations to the international crisis, and the short-term financing arrangements have led

to a moment in which it is excessively difficult to complete the commitments undertaken.

13.   On the other hand, the desire to achieve rapidly a progress so long dreamed of, but excessively based on external resources and without having executed the necessary reforms in social life and in the economic and political structures, led us in the end to become aware of the illusion involved in getting rich quickly.

14.   Besides, the inequality in international relations—evident above all in the setting of interest rates, in protectionist measures, and in economic policies, which the industrialized countries put in practice to reactivate their economic growth—has a negative influence on our country's possibility of payment.

15.   Public opinion continually presents its suspicion and, in some cases, its certainty that there is a connection between corruption and Mexico's debt. It is important that clear information be given regarding the unexplainable fortunes of people in the public and private sector. The crisis of moral values grows worse when these preoccupations are left without a reply since there arises spontaneously the conviction that there is complicity and that, in our society, robbing the state is encouraged. No one is unaware that an important place in the deterioration of our national life is occupied by the practice of corruption.

16.   The problems planted by the external debt fund an obstacle for their solution in the flight of capital and in contraband. These vices expose the enormous egoism of those who love their country only for their own interests and do little or nothing for the good of all.

17.   The external debt is oriented to what is outside the country and favors the creditors who are not residents of Mexico. The internal debt, on the other hand, points to the internal sphere and refers to creditors who reside in Mexico. The internal debt tries to reduce the problems imposed by the service of the external debt with the resources available in Mexico. If the limits of justice are lowered, the government decision to capture resources runs the risk of making private and public economic activity impossible.

III. Ethical Principles

18.   The natural finality of a debt generated by a loan is to satisfy the human necessities of the one who is asking and to compensate equitable the one who makes the loan. In fact, a debt that corresponds to an authentic finality begins when the money is requested in quantities adequate to satisfy the necessities of consumption or of investment that cannot be covered by personal resources. Prudently and with foresight, one hopes to be able to respond to the obligation of returning the loan and, in each case, pay the interest either with income generated by the productively invested loan or with income independent of the loan, which was not available when the loan was made.

19.   To this natural finality of a debt, people can oppose unacceptable goals. For example, the debtor could have the intention of not paying, or the creditor could try to subject the debtor through impossible or abnormally difficult obligations that prolong the debt indefinitely. In both cases, the rights of one of the parties are injured and the natural goal of the debt is corrupted.

20.   In becoming indebted through a loan, both those who loan and those who ask for the loan have a mutual responsibility in the advantages and in the errors of good will. In the case of Mexico, neither our government nor its creditors were unaware or hid the fact that the possibility of paying the debt depended basically on the favorable prices of petroleum. The mutual responsibility in the cause—for not having paid attention to decisive factors—is one of the foundations of the obligation to share mutually and equitably the negative consequences of an error committed by both parts. It would be unjust to make the burden of this error fall only on the debtor. This mutual responsibility does not exclude either ways of relieving the debt service or the possibility of radical solutions when the subsistence of an enormous percentage of the population is at stake. The establishment of these mechanisms avoids putting money ahead of the vital necessities of human beings.

21.   Given that the debt has as its natural goal that of favoring equitably both the debtor and the creditor, all payment—partial, punctual, or late—should be applied in just proportion to the payment of interest and to the payment of capital, without permitting any contrary agreement. The application of payments exclusively to the balance of interest, as long as these have not been fully covered, destroys the rationale and the only moral justification for a debt generated by a loan because it tends to submit the debtor to serfdom, prolonging indefinitely his debt, progressively weakening his ability to pay, and seriously diminishing the standard of living of the most needy. According to reliable statistics, Mexico has paid the equivalent of half of the capital it borrowed, and yet the principal has not diminished; on the contrary, it has grown and with it the debt service.

22.   To pay the debt, no country is obliged to destroy or to compromise seriously its own fundamental economic levels of subsistence, its growth, and its social peace. If a country, having proceeded with honor in the fulfillment of its obligations, comes to a point at which its people are seriously compromised, the creditors and the debtor should correct the agreements in a spirit of solidarity and of sharing the burdens, and program the payments with justice and technical expertise. But if the honorable effort of a country to fulfill its obligations runs into the impossibility of doing so, a radical, joint and shared international remedy is required, which does not exclude either the total or partial forgiveness of the debt, nor the acceptance of delays that assist the debtor country to recover its solvency.

23.   Countries become indebted through the mediation of their governments. Governments contract debts that the people pay. To the question that has been asked whether the people have the obligation of being responsible for debts contracted by their governments, even when these have not acted fully in representation of the people, we reply that the social doctrine of the Church considers that the obligations of life in society have their foundation in the objective demands of the common good and, therefore, people ought to be responsible for the commitments made by their governments in the measure indicated by those demands.

24.   The same common good demands that the burden and consequences of the debt be distributed in different degrees and in proportion to the economic capacity of the different persons and groups. It would not be just for the heaviest burden to be placed on the shoulders of the weakest sector of the population, nor (would it be just) to fail to demand greater responsibility of those who most benefited from the crisis.

25.   The obligation to pay taxes, which is an important way of sharing the burden of the crisis, has its foundation in the obligation of contributing to the common good. The common good arises from simply being a member of a society. For that reason, the thinking that proposes the evasion of taxes is not valid if these are just, under the pretext of their bad use and theft by corrupt officials. This does not mean that citizens, while paying their taxes, should fail to demand good use of the funds given for the common good.

26.   An elemental moral principle is that what is stolen must be restored. And against this principle, there can be no appeal to the principle of banking or business protection that, while it has its reason for existing and should be respected when the activity is within licit bounds, nevertheless, in no way can be utilized to hide larceny without making one's self an accomplice of the theft.

IV. The Responsibilities Today and in the Future

27.   Our country, as a moral union of persons and groups for the realization of the common good, will not be able to overcome the crisis or progress in justice and peace without taking into account the moral values that are at play in this situation. One the other hand, Mexico needs the ideas, the good will, the affection, and the action of everyone united and converging on the truth and on fundamental ethical values. Without this profound unity and solidarity, it is impossible to respond adequately to the situation.

28.   We are made for solidarity. The foundation of solidarity is love of neighbor, whose first manifestation is justice. Solidarity has to be realized both at the level of persons and groups and also at the national and international levels. It is time to create new solidarities and to overcome the egoism that isolates us. Those who feel more stricken by the crisis should get together. We have to establish organizations of solidarity with them. A national movement of authentic solidarity is lacking. Consequently, in trying to resolve our problems, we cannot look out only for our own welfare, but rather, we must harmonize it with that of the rest—above all, with the most needy.

29.   Within the framework of international solidarity, we need to think about reanimating international economic growth from which those countries like our own, who need that growth for the subsistence of many of our people, would not be excluded. The task of resolving our problems belongs to Mexicans, but we need to find in international solidarity a health environment and apt structures for the fulfillment of our commitments.

30.   International solidarity, which we should all promote, demands that the fluctuations in interest rates take into account not only the interests of those depositing money in the creditor countries, but also the immediate necessities of the debtor countries. It must be admitted that a large portion of the present problem arises from the instability of and the drastic rise in interest rates of the current loans in comparison with those originally contracted.

31.   The principle of the universal destiny of goods and the solidarity of nations imposes special obligations on the rich countries, above all when some sectors of the poorest countries live in extreme need. This is now not just a theoretical possibility remote from most Mexicans, but rather a reality evermore present. The rich countries should not make decisions favoring their interests without taking into account the repercussions they will have on the economies of the weak. For this reason, protectionist measures that selfishly favor them should not be implemented when they cause a deterioration of the exports of developing countries.

32.   Authentic relations are based on mutual confidence. On the international plane, our country needs to enjoy the confidence of other nations and this, in a special way, at a time when we are encountering serious difficulties in meeting our commitments. Confidence is given to persons and societies for their loyalty and their effort, independently of the circumstances that temporarily affect the fulfillment of their obligation.

33.   On the national level, relations of confidence are no less important. To establish a solidarity that would better our society, it is indispensable to offer solid motives for confidence through a coherence between positive talk and just action.

34.   Technical resources and organizations are necessary in attending to the present crisis; but this is not sufficient to produce the radical changes that the gravity of the situation requires. Also indispensable are the moral resources and among these, in a special way, ethical-religious conversion: radical liberation from sin by the power of the death and resurrection of Jesus Christ. This profound liberation is absolutely necessary for a true political, social, economic, and cultural liberation that will not be complete if it does not lead to a Christian sharing of goods.

35.   Nevertheless, systematic opposition to the moral education of Catholicism in our country has left many citizens without a firm basis for living ethically their social, political, and economic life. There are people who are afraid that a stronger link between religion and human activity would damage the autonomy of society. To link social life to morality is a universal requirement of human nature and does not diminish or limit the people's freedom. For the good and the integration of the country, it is necessary, at this point, to abandon old prejudices that keep our minds tied to the past and only produce evils for the nation.

36.   The moral renovation that our homeland needs can only become a reality when it is accepted from the heart. If it remains only as a penal threat for those who are caught violating the law, we will never achieve a public morality. There is an urgent and vital demand to struggle and finally to overcome corruption. Let us put an end to the vice of offering and receiving graft and of receiving abusive profits in offering services or in the sale of merchandise!

37.   In Mexico, we need radically to eliminate convenient opportunisms and abuse of power. This abuse occurs both in families and groups, as well as in private and public institutions. In this task, the first steps fall to each of us, without waiting for Mexico to change before individually deciding on personal change.

38.   Egoistic speculation should be eliminated; it is unacceptable for citizens who have achieved abundant income in national life to transfer their capital outside the country for their exclusive personal benefit, thus causing serious damage to the country, above all when Mexico has a great need for capital.

39.   It is inhuman and unchristian to consider business protection to be an absolute good that ought to take priority over any other human good—including life itself—over minimum levels of survival, and over basic economic conditions for social peace. When, in banks or companies, there exist funds stolen from individuals or from the country, they must be restored to their legitimate owners. The intervention and restitution should be accomplished by licit means.

40. The crisis we are experiencing, with its inflation rate and its high interest rates, has opened a chasm between the rich and the poor. This indicates that the burden of the crisis is largely being carried by the most dispossessed. Solidarity and justice demand that those who are in better conditions accept the responsibility of a fuller and more committed participation. It is not fair that the consequences of inflation be attributed to the rise in wages and that there be no mention of the arbitrary increase in every sort of utility as a cause of inflation. The generalized alliance between greed and fear is a decisive factor in inflation.

41. There are certainly business people worthy of recognition who, in spite of the difficult circumstances of the market for their product, have decided not to close their businesses, so that their workers and employees might continue working. There are also workers, exemplary for their solidarity, who have agreed with their companions and with their employers to take a loss in wages, to work less so that no one will be fired. Authentic solidarity possesses great creativity because it springs from hearts that love their neighbors.

42. But certainly, there is no lack of business persons who, far from having in mind a national project, only think selfishly of increasing their personal wealth. At another level, the same mentality is shared by those workers who do not value the importance for the country of their personal work and the quality of what they produce nor do they measure the negative consequences of their absenteeism. The moral obligation to be productive falls on everyone, business and labor, public functionaries and private employees.

43. There is a variety of proposals for concrete formulas that would allow a mitigation, and later a resolution, of the problem of the debt. But they all require a process of development as a condition for their realization. Although the external circumstances today indicate that it would be difficult to achieve a rhythm of growth that would permit payment (of the debt) without a major impoverishment, we should renew our hope since, if we take up the path of real development with enthusiasm and hope, we will manage to achieve our own solution through our own effort.

44. Authentic development is integral. Every area of human existence should be attended to, educated, and pressed into service in order to achieve it. Development is not just economic growth alone; rather, it reaches into our heart and, at the same time, starts there. Love and justice as well as an integral recognition of the dignity of the human person both in conscience and in conduct are the irreplaceable foundation for every positive change in personal and social life. Mexico cannot progress on the basis of a systematic and generalized negation of human dignity.

45. There are many topics related to the crisis in our country and to the external debt. They require study and action. We encourage the specialists and especially the Catholics to cooperate with their knowledge to produce those studies that will propose solutions to the crisis with a well-founded hope in our possibilities for change.

46. Let us make of this crisis an opportune moment for real development. Let us not allow ourselves to be led into a new form of decadence. Whatever measures are taken to get out of the crises without achieving solidarity will turn back into degenerating factors. If, on the contrary, we construct a solidarity founded on love of neighbor, we will achieve respect for human dignity, and we will lay the foundations for an authentic recovery.

47. Faith in God, the power of Jesus Christ, and the guidance that the Holy Spirit gives us, will provide the necessary ability to achieve a solidarity based on love of neighbor. God wants us to overcome this situation that has laid us low and to construct a civilization of love. God wants it; consequently, it is possible with God's power and our decision.

48. Certain that we are heard, we pray and invite you to pray to God with the prayer of the liturgy of December 12: "God of mercy, who has placed your people under the special protection of the ever Virgin Mary of Guadalupe, Mother of your Son, grant us, by your intercession, to deepen our faith and search for the progress of our homeland along the paths of justice and peace. Through Christ our Lord."

Brazil
The Church and the Problem of Land
(1980)

The price the Brazilian Church has paid for making the struggle over land one of its priorities has been high. In 1986 alone, fifty church workers, including priests, were murdered over the issue. The house of Cardinal Aloisio Lorscheider was bombed and gunmen barely missed shooting Bishop Marcelo Carvatheira, wounding instead a priest standing next to him at a meeting of small farmers. Many rural families in Brazil have worked plots of land for decades, even centuries, without having to concern themselves with land titles. But their claims, being undocumented, can be questioned. When entrepreneurs seek large plots of land for mass cultivation, government officials eager for agribusiness (and often a profit of their own) begin evicting these families from the land. Estimates for Brazil put 5,000 entrepreneurs as owning or controlling 50 percent of the arable land.

The Church has actively supported the rural poor by means of agrarian leagues, advocacy before the government, and publicizing outrageous situations to larger audiences to gain public support. Selections from a key document are presented here.

19. Financial incentive policies deviate the money that belongs to all for the use of a minority, without regard for the demands of the common good. Rather than being utilized on projects to serve the public, this money is made available for large companies to use as their own. Nevertheless, even the government acknowledges that most of the food in our country comes from small producers, who thus far have not been favored by any tax or fiscal policies. This policy thrust shows that the state is committed to serving the interests of the large economic groups.

20. The policy of providing incentives in the Amazon region has not increased productivity on large cattle ranches, whose land usage is less intensive than that of small producers. The conclusion can be drawn that, for the present, the large economic groups are simply trying to reap the benefits of fiscal incentives.

21.   Moreover, in the Amazon, large companies are invading the rivers with fishing boats equipped with cold storage. By intensifying predatory fishing, they are causing hunger in the riverbank settlements of people who fish by hand to complement their poor diet.
22.   People fishing by hand along costal areas also suffer the effects of tourism projects and industrial waste dumping.

The Issue of the Lands Belonging to Indigenous Peoples

23.   No native community in contact with our national society has been free from assaults on its lands.
24.   Despite the fact that the the Indian Statute is in effect, conflicts in indigenous areas are becoming increasingly violent and widespread. Such conflicts are connected to the following factors: the fact that their lands are not surveyed; the invasion of their lands after they have been surveyed; the fact that FUNAI [government agency for indigenous peoples] takes over and commercializes the natural resources of those lands; the prejudice against Indians, seeing them as an obstacle to development; the failure to recognize that their lands belong to them by right as peoples; ignorance of the specific requirements that flow from the relation of Indians to their land, in accordance with their culture, their practices, customs, and historic memory; in sum, the fact that the Indians are completely excluded from the policy toward indigenous peoples, both in its formulation and in its execution.

Migrations and Violence in the Countryside

28.   All kinds of violence are committed against these people (settlers and Indians) in order to push them off the land. In these instances of violence, it has been abundantly proven that those involved range from professional killers and gunslingers to government agents and even judges. It is not a rare sight to observe for one's self the gravest irregularity of hired killers and police joining forces to carry out sentences of land seizure. . . .

Responsibility for the Situation

33.   The responsibility is not God's, even though some people convey that impression when they say, "things are like this because God wills

it." It is not God's will that the people suffer and live in misery.
34.   It may be that working people are responsible for not being more united and better organized. However, the people have been prevented from participating and deciding the fate of our country.
35.   The greatest responsibility falls on those who impose and maintain in Brazil a way of life and work that makes some wealthy at the cost of the poverty or misery of the majority. . . .
36.   This occurs when property is an absolute good and is used as an instrument of exploitation. This situation has become exacerbated in the path that economic development is taking in our country, chosen without popular participation. . . .

Concentration of Capital and Concentration of Power

38.   As a result of the unrestrained quest for profit, the goods produced by the work of all are concentrated in the hands of a few. Goods, capital, and ownership of the land and the resources in it are concentrated; political power is even more concentrated, in a process of accumulation that results from the exploitation of labor and the social and political marginalization of most of our people.
39.   We are witnessing a broad process in which economic groups are expropriating the peasants and farm workers. Unfortunately, the very definition of the government's policies with regard to land problems is based on an ideal of social development that is unacceptable to a humanist and Christian vision of society. . . .
42.   Because of the scarcity of land and exorbitant prices for it in their own areas, these farmers are unable to broaden their own chances to find work and to guarantee for their children a chance to continue working as they grow up and form their own families. Their only alternative is to migrate. . . .
44.   Another factor that discourages peasants is their utter inability to sell their products commercially and the ridiculous sum they receive for their work. . . .
46.   Nor can we ignore a certain perverse character in the price mechanisms of agricultural food products. Food that the urban consumer regards as expensive and that the peasant regards as cheap and not sufficiently remunerated by the buyer, benefits another economic category. In reality, the cost of the food that the urban worker consumes is expensive in comparison with their low salaries; it is cheap for those who employ their labor. What is missing in the payment made to peasants for the products produced by their labor in fact surfaces as a form of cheap labor in the accounting and profits of national and multinational businesses. When peasants buy something produced

by industry—fertilizer, insecticides, clothes, shoes, or medicines—
they pay a great deal in comparison with what they earn. When they
sell their products, which will be consumed in the city, they can only
sell them cheaply in comparison to the profits made by large industry,
which can take advantage of the lowered costs of the labor force. What
we observe is a clear transference of income from small farms, which
produce most of our foods, to large capital. . . .

Accumulation and Degradation

48.   Those who do not manage to resist the various pressures and
assaults cannot continue as settlers, sharecroppers, renters, inhabitants; thus, they become proletarians, workers looking for work not
only in the countryside but also in the city.

49.   The situation of laborers in the Amazon territory is even worse.
They are landless workers, recruited when they are hooked up to a
labor contractor in Goaias, in the the Northeast, and even in São
Paulo, and then sold to contractors like an item of merchandise. . . .

51.   The fact that peasants are sold is justified on the grounds of
the debts they must contract for food and transportation on their
way to the job. The debt is transferred from the one who first
hooked them to the contractor, who uses that debt to enslave the
worker as needed. The police, storeowners, and the owners of
boarding houses in the towns of the *sertão* [arid interior of northern Brazil] are almost always involved in this trafficking in human
beings. When the worker tries to flee, he is almost always pun-
ished or murdered, with the excuse that, in principle, he is a thief;
he is trying to run off with something that now belongs to the one
who contracted him: his labor power. . . .

Doctrinal Foundation
The Land Is God's Gift for All People

56.   In this doctrinal section, in which we seek to discover criteria so
as to discern our pastoral options starting from the situation described
above, our intention obviously is not to elaborate an exhaustive treatise
on the whole of the biblical and doctrinal message of the Christian
tradition, which the Church has received, enriched, and faithfully
preserved for us. We only want to recall some themes and draw out
some ideas that can help us understand the problem of the possession
and use of the land within a vision that is Christian, socially just, and
more family-spirited. . . .

61.   As Creator, the Lord God has the power to define the use and destiny of the land. From the beginning, God has entrusted it to human beings so that they can subject it and draw their sustenance from it (cf. Gn 1:23–30). . . .

65.   The whole New Testament, the new alliance of God with his children, Jesus' brothers and sisters, guides us toward participation and the practice of justice in the distribution of material goods, as a necessary condition for the brotherhood and sisterhood of children of the same Father, in accordance with the teaching of the Sermon on the Mount (cf. Mt 5:7). . . .

68.   In working out its teaching today, the Church seeks to learn from the experience of the saintly fathers, who tried to translate the lessons of Sacred Scripture for their societies.

69.   "It was greed that distributed the rights to ownership that people claimed were theirs. . . . The earth was given to all, not just to the rich" (St. Ambrose).

70.   "It was through positive law that property distinctions and the system of servitude were set up. Nevertheless, through natural law what prevailed was ownership common to all and the same freedom for all" (Gratian). This text is especially eloquent since it links individual appropriation to the system of servitude. Due to selfishness, the strong take for themselves not only things but persons, those who are weakest.

71.   Saint Thomas tends to regard individual property as one of the ways whereby goods reach their social destiny of serving all. That is what he brings out with greater precision in this text: "With regard to the faculty of administering and directing, it is licit that human beings possess things as their own; with regard to use, human beings should not have external things as their own, but in common, that is, so as to share them with others." . . .

74.   Pius XII also says, "Capital rushes in to take over land . . . which then becomes no longer something loved but something for cold speculation."

75.   [The] "overall supply of goods is assigned, first of all, that all men may lead a decent life" (John XXIII, MM, 119). . . .

77.   Paul VI insists on the principle that "private property does not constitute for anyone an absolute and unconditioned right" (PP, 23). . . .

79.   John Paul II says, "There is a social mortgage on all private property."

80.   A mortgage is a guarantee that obligations taken on will be fulfilled. From what the Holy Father says, it can be concluded that all private property is to some extent impounded, committed to its social destiny. . . .

Land for Exploitation and Land for Work

82.   A great number of our rural workers have this message of God vividly in their minds. The settlers express it when they struggle for the "possession and use" of the land, rather than for its "ownership." Property, in many cases, is represented by large ranchers and the big agricultural and agroindustrial companies. They "wheel and deal with the land" that God has entrusted to all human beings.

83.   This mindset of the people alerts us to the distinction between two ways of appropriating the land, which deserve our attention: land for exploitation, which our peasants call land as a business; and land for work. Nevertheless, this distinction does not ignore the existence of land as productive, rural property that respects the right of workers, in accordance with the demands of the Church's social teaching.

84.   Land for exploitation is land that capital appropriates so it may continue to grow, so as to constantly generate new and ever-greater profits. Such profit may derive either from the work of those who have lost their land and means of work, or from those who never had access to it, or from speculation that enables some to get rich at the cost of the whole society.

85.   Land for work is land held by the one who works it. It is not land for exploiting others nor for speculating. In our country, the notion of land to be worked is strongly present in the people's law or right to family, tribal, and community property and in the right to "possession" [cf. next paragraph]. These forms of property, which are alternatives to capitalist exploitation, clearly open a broad avenue that makes viable a community way of working, even in extensive areas, and the utilization of adequate technology that will not require the exploitation of other people's labor.

86.   In our country, two kinds of property systems stand in sharp opposition: on the one hand, the system that makes matters conflictive for peasants and rural workers, which is capitalist property; on the other hand, the alternative property systems mentioned above, which are being destroyed or mutilated by capital: family property, such as that of small farmers in the south and elsewhere; "possession," in which land is regarded as the property of all and the fruits go to the family working it—a system spread throughout country, especially in what is called the Amazon territory; and tribal and community property of the indigenous peoples and some rural communities. . . .

91.   "Land is a gift from God." It is a natural good that belongs to everyone and not the result of work. However, it is work, more than anything else, that legitimizes the possession of land. That is how the settlers understand things when they claim the right to take possession of lands that are free, unoccupied, or unworked, since it is their understanding that land is a common patrimony and, as long as they are working it, they cannot be expelled.

92.   Finally, we should not forget land on which to live, an especially distressing problem on the outskirts of cities, where families are forced to live in inhumane conditions of overcrowding and insecurity, and from which they are often expelled, even violently, to serve the interests of real estate companies or to expand the cities.

93.   Such expulsions from housing land is all the more unjust and inhumane since these families are left utterly helpless and abandoned.

Our Pastoral Commitment

94.   God continues to watch over the people. . . . And God challenges us: How can we bring it about that the earth may belong to all? How can we assure that the dignity of the human person be respected? How can we bring it about that Brazilian society overcome institutionalized injustice and reject political options opposed to the gospel? We believe the challenges here formulated are positive. However, we are aware that without concrete actions to respond to these challenges, the Church will not be a sign of God's love for human beings. Hence:

95.   (1) As a first gesture, we want to place the problem of the possession and use of the Church's property under scrutiny and reexamine constantly its pastoral and social purpose, avoiding speculation in real estate and respecting the rights of those who work on the land.

96.   (2) We commit ourselves to denounce patently unjust situations and the violence perpetrated in the areas of our dioceses and prelatures and to combat the causes that produce such injustices and violence, in fidelity to the Puebla commitments (see *Puebla*, 1160).

97.   (3) We reaffirm our support for the just initiatives and organizations of workers, placing our energies and our means at the service of their cause, in conformity with those same commitments (see *Puebla*, 1162). Without replacing the people's initiatives, our pastoral activity will stimulate conscious and critical participation by workers in unions, associations, and commissions, as well as other kinds of cooperation, so that their organizations may be really independent and free, defending the interests and coordinating the demands of their members and their whole class.

98.   (4) We support the efforts of rural people for a genuine Agrarian Reform, which we have already defined on several occasions, one that will permit access to land and conditions that favor working it. In order to make such agrarian reform effective, we want to esteem, defend, and promote property systems based on family, "possession," the tribal property of native peoples, and community property in which land is regarded as an instrument of work. We also support the organizing efforts of workers to demand the application and/or or reformulation of existing laws as well as to achieve agrarian, labor, and social security policies in accordance with the aspirations of the population. We also support the creation of Yanomami Park, in the form that avoids a reduction or fragmentation of that tribal land, and we insist that it is urgent that the remaining indigenous reserves be surveyed and marked off, including those in the border regions of our country. . . .

102.   (7) We renew our commitment to deepen the way the gospel is lived within our church communities, both rural and urban, as an effective way for the Church to contribute to the cause of the workers— for we are convinced of its transforming power.

103.   As we take on a serious commitment to the workers, we need to nourish their courage and our own, their hope and our own, especially in moments of hardship and persecution. Thus, continually reencouraged by the recollection of the promise and certainty of the liberation brought by the Lord, lived in community, and celebrated in the mystery of the Eucharist, Christians will carry out their mission of being leaven, salt, and light in the midst of their working brothers and sisters.

104.   In this manner, the Church will contribute to building up the new human being, the basis for a new society.

Conclusion

105.   We are making this statement today precisely when agriculture is being called on to accept the serious responsibility of meeting the demands for alternate energy sources and for increasing our exports.

106.   We fear that the discharging of these tasks will serve as a new pretext for trampling on the rights of those humble people in whose defense we are committing ourselves as pastors. This concern is not imaginary. Today, among the kinds of neocolonialism denounced by John Paul II, there looms the way the international economy is organized so as to assign to Brazil and other underdeveloped nations the role of providing foods and agriculturally derived raw materials for the nations that control that economy. In this context, overall capital-intensive strategies would reinforce the Brazilian economy's dependent condition and would tend to accelerate the process of proletarization of our rural people.

107.   It is our understanding that the issues facing rural and urban workers and the issues around land will be truly solved only if there is a change in both the attitude and structure within which our society functions. As long as the politicoeconomic system favors the profit of a small number of capitalists, and the educational model is an instrument for maintaining this system, even by discouraging rural life and its values, there will be no true solution for the situation of injustice and the exploitation of the labor of the majority.

108. However, we recognize that the experience and creativity of our people who work the land can indicate new directions for taking advantage of alternative technologies and new community and co-operative ways of using the instruments of work.

109. This society will be built up through the efforts of all, through the utterly essential participation of young people, through the unity and organization of the weak—those for whom the world has contempt and whom God has chosen to confound and judge the powerful (cf. 1 Cor 1:26ff).

110. Finally, we express our special support and encouragement to all those community leaders, pastoral agents, and members of church bodies and groups that in recent years have been working in pastoral work concerning land, indigenous pastoral work, working-class pastoral work, and other kinds of pastoral work with the outcast. We also join our work to that of other Christian Churches, who are united by the same ideal.

111. We pray the Lord to enlighten us and to give us strength and courage to put into practice the commitments we are making.

Itaicí
February 22–28, 1980.

Brazil
The Use of Urban Land and Pastoral Action
(1982)

Following their statement of the problem of rural land struggles, one that received widespread attention, the Brazilian bishops addressed an equally pressing problem: the use of urban land.

Throughout Latin America, persons and families have left their rural homes for a variety of reasons and have sought employment and shelter in cities. Residents of Mexico City, São Paulo, Lima, Santiago, or other large cities have seen their population almost double in fifteen years. Sometimes, peasants "invade" unused land and attempt to work out a "modus vivendi" with governments. Often, these squatter settlements begin with clandestine occupations; of those that surround São Paulo, 70 percent are believed to exist without legal basis.

Often, speculators hold unused land for future investment. Thirty percent of usable urban land in Brazil is withheld from the market, aggravating the problem. Given the length of the document, selections are presented here.

1. Sent by Jesus Christ to evangelize the world, the Church carries out its mission within the concrete reality of human history, sharing the hopes and fears of peoples.
2. It is for this reason that we bishops of Brazil frequently study the serious problems that challenge the Church's pastoral activity in our country. . . .
4. The National Conference of Bishops of Brazil (CNBB) realizes that this complex challenge includes technical aspects that are beyond its competence. It strongly urges specialists in the field to make their own contributions. At the same time, we know that even the poorest of our people are aware of the major options available for solving the problem that afflicts them. . . .

Urban Land-Use in Brazil

9.   In 1940, only 31 percent of the Brazilian population lived in cities. Today, that figure has risen to 67 percent—more than 80 million citizens. Brazil now has ten cities with more than a million residents and five metropolitan areas with more than two million. In 1940, barely 8 percent of the population lived in cities of over a million people. Today, 32 percent of the total population, representing half the urban population, dwells in thirteen densely populated urban zones. Obviously, problems are especially great in the largest metropolitan areas such as greater São Paulo, with 13 million residents, or greater Rio de Janeiro with 8 million.

10.   In the 1970s, for the first time in Brazilian history, there was a decrease in rural population. There was a decline, in absolute terms, of more than 2 million people compared to the 1960 census. During that decade, the city of São Paulo experienced faster demographic growth than did the entire Amazon region. In the same period, 16 million Brazilians migrated from the countryside to the city. . . .

12.   The problem of urban land-use is, in large part, the result of countryside-to-city migration. The problems created are aggravated by social factors within the cities themselves.

13.   To suggest the need for a controlled pattern of urban growth is not to decry all migrations from the country to the city. What must be questioned is the intense rate of influx, caused by the accelerated loss of jobs in rural areas and by expectations for a better life in the city created by the communications media. . . .

15.   Migration to urban centers coincides with a rapid increase in land values due to intense real estate speculation. Large numbers of empty lots are held for this reason. They amount to about one-third of the space suitable for construction in Brazilian cities.

16.   The increase in value of urban land since the mid-1960s is alarming: on the average, the real price of land has tripled in twenty years. . . .

18.   By inflating the price of land, real estate speculation aggravates the country's housing situation. A basic characteristic of urban land-use for housing is the unequal distribution among different social strata.

19–20.   Patterns of urban land ownership reflect the disparity of income levels in Brazil. Today, the income gap grows ever wider, threatening the country with a social and economic explosion. While 37.9 percent of total income is concentrated in the hands of the wealthiest 5 percent of the population, scarcely 12.6 percent of the national income is distributed among the poorest 50 percent. . . .

26.   Much urban land is owned by the middle- and upper-sectors of Brazilian society, most of whom live in residential areas that quickly receive basic services and infrastructure. When realtors designate lots for the construction of luxury housing, water, electricity, sewage, and sanitation services arrive with amazing rapidity. This stands in shocking contrast to the neighborhoods where most people live, which have been deprived of those services for many years. In theory, the urban service infrastructure ought to be installed simultaneously with the developing of urban land because such services are essential to city life.

27.   It is in the city, which by its very nature ought to be a place where human beings live together in harmony, that the market economy has revealed the worst fruits of the egoism that is its hallmark. It is there that a system of radical injustice is institutionalized, violating the fundamental rights of vast sectors of the population. . . .

34.   Because of rapid urban growth, unbridled real estate speculation not only keeps a large proportion of lots outside the marketplace—thus, contracting the supply of urban land and increasing demand for the little land available—but it also misallocates national resources that should be invested in urban infrastructure and services and increases overall production costs in the economy as a whole. It also could be otherwise invested more productively. . . .

38–39.   The Brazilian economy is affected by the cycles of recession and recovery prevailing in the international market. These cycles have a strong impact on our country's economy, which is heavily export-oriented and rests on a fragile internal base. Production tends to be oriented toward a middle- and upper-income market. Thus, real estate speculation is favored to the detriment of productive investment. . . .

41.   In recent decades, lack of state investment in public services (schools, nurseries, health-care centers, etc.) has created enormous deficits in these service areas, which have been financed almost exclusively by the poor people of the cities.

42.   Large urban landowners are, apparently, the beneficiaries of this process, be they actual persons, firms, or institutions. Speculative profits are enormous, and the whole nation is suffering because such speculation reduces the overall wealth of the country. It is the poor, however, who bear the heaviest burden as a result of this speculation. . . .

Control of Urban Land-Use

49.   Given the insecurity of their earnings, very poor people generally prefer to have a lot where they can build their home over a number of years with their own hands, usually with some sort of community support. . . .

51. The state does not exercise effective control over urban development. It permits many legal irregularities and tolerates gross disorganization in the urban system. To correct this will require immense financial and social investment.

Grass-Roots Initiatives

52. Because of rapid urban growth, public control over the process was given over to avid real estate speculation while increasing numbers of people with scarce resources were abandoned by the state, which did not address their housing needs.

53. Housing is a necessity for every person or family group. The poor are forced to seek one of the following expedients to satisfy this need: occupation of abandoned lands; rental of precarious dwellings far from their place of work; or the purchase of cheap lots on the city's outskirts. . . .

55. Pressured by this stark reality and, at times, lead by interested third parties, hundreds and even thousands of persons have carried out urban land occupations. These occupations are called "invasions."

56. Many fail to realize that land occupation by the migrant population . . . is the only solution possible for the impasse in which they find themselves.

57. For many families, the situation is aggravated by a constant increase in rental costs, which results in the gradual proletarianization of Brazil's small middle class.

58. In the large urban centers, urban space is divided up unfairly. In Rio de Janeiro, for example, urban land occupied by the *favelas* (shantytowns) amounts to less than 10 percent of the city's total land mass. But in that 10 percent, lives 35 percent of Rio's entire population.

59. In 1950, the population of the *favelas* of Rio de Janeiro represented 7 percent of the city's entire population. From 1950 to 1980, the city's population doubled, while that of the *favelas* increased nearly ten times. In 1950, one in every fourteen inhabitants of Rio lived in a *favela*; today, the ratio is one in three, a total of almost 2 million people. . . .

62. It is important not to forget all the creativity, energy, struggle, and suffering that lie behind these statistics.

63. People with few resources have built real cities—some numbering over 100,000—within Brazil's large urban centers.

64. The difficulties those residents encountered and solved were enormous: they constructed their rustic dwellings on steep hills, on swamps, and over lakes, without relying on a material or service infrastructure. They carried all the needed construction materials on their shoulders or heads. Such effort required, without doubt, tremendous creativity.

65.   The struggle to construct a proper dwelling was often a community task that, together with the daily struggle for survival, contributed to the unity of the poor.

66.   If poor people could achieve so much by themselves and with so few resources, what could not they accomplish with the help and collaboration they are demanding? . . .

Social Consequences

69.   The quality of life in urban centers is deteriorating at an alarming rate. City life is being sacrificed to predatory real estate speculation on the one hand, and "invasions" of the poor in the city's outskirts on the other, thus keeping vast sectors of the population out of reach of land that they should be able to inhabit.

70.   As urban life deteriorates, crime, violence, and the drug traffic increase. Given these collective frustrations, a minor episode could spark a crisis with unforeseeable consequences.

71.   A special by-product of this unjust situation is the existence of thousands of abandoned children called "daytime orphans," who are shutup in a small space for long hours while their parents work.

72.   All of us must become aware of the seriousness of the situation described above and join in finding a solution. . . .

A Christian Vision of the City

74.   The Christian vision of the city is biblically inspired. The city is both the creation of God and the creation of human beings. The life of urban dwellers is not outside of the action of God's province: those human relationships produced by the densely populated environment of the city are not in themselves any less gospel-inspired than those that occur in rural areas. . . .

77.   To paraphrase what John Paul II says with regard to work in the encyclical *Laborem Exercens:* we believe that the city should exist for the human person, and not the human person for the sake of the city. When Christians affirm that the city should exist for the sake of the human person, they mean that it ought to be a place of mutual harmony for all who dwell there, a harmony that is the result of a common effort to make the city a more human place.

78.   In a certain sense, the city constitutes the beginnings of a natural community. People work to serve all the others who live in the city.

The ideal would be for all to be able to choose their professions and see their work as a call to serve their brothers and sisters in the community. All would work at tasks that would allow them to develop fully their natural gifts and, at the same time, respond to the real needs of society. . . .

86.   A system that distributes the wealth produced by the work of all and favors a wealthy minority, leaving the majority living in poverty, if not outright misery, is totally alien to the Christian ethic. All of the city's inhabitants should, by their labor, contribute to the prosperity of the community and, therefore, have a right to the goods and services the city provides. . . .

Right to Housing

88.   The right to make use of urban land to guarantee adequate housing is one of the primary conditions for creating a life that is authentically human. Therefore, when land occupations—or even land invasions—occur, legal judgments on property titles must begin with the right of all to adequate housing. All claims to private ownership must take second place to this basic need. . . .

94.   Bearing in mind the teaching of Pope John Paul II, that all private property carries with it a social responsibility, we conclude that the natural right to housing has priority over the law that governs land appropriation. A legal title to property can hardly be an absolute value in the face of the human need of people who have nowhere to make their home. . . .

Sociocultural Obstacles

97–99.   Evil structures have unjustly distributed wealth, giving everything to some and marginalizing others. . . . The Church does not want to judge persons indiscriminately, but condemns the structures that divide people and constantly calls human beings to be converted.

100.   Many believe that the poor have no right to land. This idea discourages poor people, victims of a long process of cultural marginalization, and prevents them from learning about their legal rights. They come to accept an evil situation and fail to struggle for their rights.

Socioeconomic Obstacles

101.   A disparity in economic conditions leads to disparity in the ownership of urban land. It is very difficult for those in need to make their right to housing a reality. They live in constant insecurity due to evictions, building collapses, floods, fear of unemployment, and anxiety over rent increases.

102.   However, city life is only possible thanks to the services rendered by these people. In order to survive, they take on the harshest jobs at wages set by those who benefit from their services. They prepare the food eaten in restaurants. They wash clothes and clean the streets. They transport passengers as well as consumer goods. They make up the work force for construction projects. They operate the machines of industry.

The injustice of inadequate housing for most of the population is a consequence of the country's economic structure. Many must work for insufficient salaries so that the privileges of the minority can be maintained. Often, the few benefits granted to the poor are conceded out of charity when they should be given as a right that is due them. . . .

Sociopolitical Obstacles

107.   Here, we touch upon the most sensitive point at issue. Many years of social and pastoral experience convince us that the obstacles to a humane solution arise mainly on the political level. A deliberate political decision is made that thwarts the legitimate interests of the people.

108.   In the eyes of the majority of the population, the issue of scarce resources has not been dealt with. They know about the cases of corruption, about the misuse of public funds, and about the use of vast resources for projects whose usefulness seems minimal in the face of their urgent needs. The issue here is: According to what model and what policy are resources developed and to benefit what sectors of the population? The question of political decision making is essential and becomes more obvious at election time, when there is a sudden increase in aid and emergency assistance projects in the *favelas, mocambos,* and *alagados* (hillside, central city, and waterfront slums). These projects are obviously useful, but they do not resolve the problem.

109.   Experience shows that no evil will be tolerated indefinitely when it affects everyone, even though it may not be easy to eradicate. If a certain social ill continues for decades, it is because its continuation is in the interest of some, or at least because some have no interest in eliminating it. . . .

Sociojuridical Obstacles

112.   The laws that govern the ownership and use of urban land are, in the light of current reality, profoundly inadequate. This inadequacy is based on an understanding of private property as an absolute right with no social responsibility attached to it.

113. This understanding of private property affirms the owner's absolute right to use, enjoy, and dispose of urban land as he or she pleases, protecting only his or her own interests. This conception legitimizes real estate speculation, allowing the socialization of its costs but the privatization of its benefits. . . .

117. It is not enough to condemn this situation. It must be transformed in the light of gospel principles and norms. In order to understand the urgency of this transformation, we must place ourselves in a position that permits us to see better the structural causes of injustice, that is, among the people who suffer most from injustice. . . .

Pastoral Action

131. We suggest a total consideration of large-scale urban renewal projects, which are becoming worthless. We favor short-term measures such as: regulation of areas to be occupied by housing; alternative types of urbanization; occupant or community construction projects; housing subsidies; zoning policies on housing for the poor, including the installation of services; and social-minded tax reform. . . .

143. With concern and with a great evangelizing effort, the Brazilian Church is accompanying the people in this chaotic process of urbanization. By virtue of its presence in the midst of the poor—proclaiming the gospel, catechizing, and celebrating its faith—the Church became aware of the problems involved in urban land-use.

144. The consequence of this evangelizing action has been the growing awareness on the people's part of their basic rights, especially of their right to the use of urban land. . . .

146. In the basic Christian communities, the people find a renewed Christian life, which leads them to believe in their dignity and calling. It moves them, inspired by the light of God's Word, to participate freely, responsibly, and communally in the construction of a new and more fraternal human community.

147. The Church grows more and more aware of the ability of the poor to resolve their own problems. It urges them to participate in all the decisions that affect their lives and supports various forms of organizing and popular movements, including neighborhood organizations. . . .

Some Proposals for Action

160. To commit the whole Church to the solution of the urban problem. It is important to raise consciousness about urban problems, and

especially about the tragic social sin of the *favelas*. All Christians must become aware of conditions in these shantytowns in order to become sensitized to the issue and to bring about a genuine conversion to justice and human community. . . .

164. To make known and to apply legal recourses on behalf of the poor; to condemn the propaganda that confuses the just struggle of the poor for ownership of urban land with subversion. . . .

166. To publicize the fact that the inability to obtain land or housing is intimately intertwined with insufficient wages, underemployment, and unemployment. . . .

Conclusions

168. The bettering of living conditions in the cities is not only a question of generosity, charity, or justice; it is a question of everyone's survival. . . .

170. We call upon all Catholics working in government and in influential national positions to become aware of this serious situation. They should use their influence to insist that those who suffer the most serious effects of these problems ought to be the primary agents in resolving them. We also call upon all Christians and persons of good will to work for a situation where the cities will no longer be centers of misery and suffering, but will rather become places in which individuals and families can gather in peace, justice, and harmony.

Paraguay
The Paraguayan Peasant and the Land
(1983)

The film The Mission *made vivid the centuries-old struggle of subsistence farmers in Paraguay. Many of the same problems continue today under the changing and more complex structures of the country and the wider world.*

In recent times, the Church has become increasingly involved in the lives of the majority of Paraguayans: the peasants. In doing so, bishops and priests have seen first-hand the severe problems small farmers suffer in Paraguay. There, as in many other Latin American countries, titles to land are elusive. The peasant culture, moreover, is not a "paper" culture; it is enough to live on and work the land for years and, in some cases, centuries.

To gain strength for peasants in the struggle, bishops, priests, and lay pastoral workers aided in the formation of peasant leagues. The Church has stood directly on the side of the powerless or has offered its assistance as mediators.

1. The Paraguayan Peasant and the Land

In recent years, the rapid and complex transformation that the rural areas of our country have experienced has been the object of deep concern for the Church. It is a dramatic problem whose roots are to be sought not only in the current socioeconomic development model, but also in the conception and implementation of a particular policy of land distribution and development.

This concern grows in intensity daily in the minds of the faithful and in our conscience as pastors. The problem has repercussions throughout the national society. It demands, therefore, urgent attention.

In recent decades, positive steps have been taken through the efforts of the Institute of Rural Welfare (IBR) in the distribution of land to peasants. This huge task can be measured: from 1955–1980, approximately 80,000 pieces of agricultural land were distributed. Thus, it was possible to relieve to a degree the congestion of the population that was, at that time, packed together in tiny farmsteads, by dispersing people into new settlements and thereby creating new centers of population. It should not be forgotten that the most recent Agrarian Law was promulgated in 1963. But, as positive as that law might be, it is necessary to reflect on the facts that show the depth of the problem and demand solutions much different from those that are being practiced.

1.1. The Development Model

In the *Plan de Pastoral Orgánica* (no. 71), one reads: "everything seems to indicate that the structural models continued in this process respond to the most gross capitalist, neoliberal plan, with the exclusive privilege of economic growth and luxury as the central dynamic, while forgetting social and humanitarian concerns."

If we compare it with other periods, we see that today's model continues to be an agroexport model, but it is marked by the establishment and predominance of capitalist enterprises to an extent previously unknown in Paraguay. Several of these companies are quite extensive and are owned by foreign capital. This phenomenon is not limited to the area of agricultural economy, but it is also found in other economic areas such as agroindustry, construction, finance, and, of course, it has repercussions in the political sphere as well.

1.2. Main Consequences

Among the principal consequences generated, it is important to list the following:

a) *Impoverishment of the peasant*. Certainly, this situation is not new. The peculiarity of the current process is the extent and severity of the impoverishment. Farmers, stimulated by economic modernization, tend to replace food production with farming for commercial markets. When this method does not produce the hoped-for results due to the lower prices received, the situation becomes dramatic. This is a painful reality being experienced by many peasants.

b) *Increase in wage earners*. As a consequence of the previous phenomenon, the option of salaried work becomes imperative and seems to be the only means to assure family subsistence. Coinciding with the decrease of emigration, the expansion of the rural and urban job market made possible the concretion of a wage-based employment market. Thus, for example, numerous peasants joined the job market opened by the construction of the Itaipú Dam and the growth of neighboring urban centers. A large part of this work force has been laid off. Those whose families were able to maintain their farms, returned to them; others who could not, stayed in the city, doing any kind of job, all of which were generally poorly paid. This situation generated an increase in unemployment and marginated neighborhoods in cities and towns.

c) *Land speculation.* This recent phenomenon is related to a rising tide of a new style of development. Land is considered a commodity item. As a result, people attempt to attain land and speculate with it. In many parts of the country, peasants—with or without land title— are selling their land or its improvements, expecting to reap a profit. These hopes are not always fulfilled.

d) *Cultural change.* It is obvious that important changes have taken place in the heart of the peasant culture. To the degree that their production methods are part of the dialectic of modern, capitalist economy, peasants are assuming individualistic criteria and values. Old practices of solidarity, such as the community work party (*minga*), tend to disappear. Unaware, the peasant abandons traditional life styles and assumes a life style instilled by the modern consumer society and encouraged by the social communications media such as radio, and, in part, television. This can be seen in the desire to obtain, on credit, items that are beyond their financial means; and in the changes in clothing, food, entertainment, and even in forms of religious expression, encouraged by a chain of exploiters. Of course, these changes are greater in those rural zones most directly influenced by the big cities.

1.3. The Problems of Ownership and Development of Land

We want to mention certain cases, clearly caused by projects designed to consolidate the modernization of the agrarian economy.

a) *The restoration of large estates.* The formation of large farms, incorporating the land distributed to some of the settlements, is common knowledge. The major stimulus for this stems from the favorable conditions opened up by the land market. These annexations are at times peaceful, but at other times, they result in eviction and violence.

b) *The handling of mortgages.* In some rural development programs, the property of the borrower (who cannot make his payments) passes directly to the bank, without prior judicial action. In this way, the land can be transferred and redistributed to larger units. Certainly, these practices are not new. What is new is the method used to recuperate the loans and to create circumstances that favor the reversion to large developments and estates.

c) *The takeover of communal lands.* Current agrarian legislation both favors and regulates the creation and use of communal lands. Unfortunately, it is not always possible to guarantee the establishment and utilization of these lands. In not a few cases, persons protected by influence or by their political or economic powers take over these lands. The loss of communal property causes serious consequences to the peasant community.

d) *Evictions.* Actual evictions and attempted evictions occur in two situations: (1) when the owner, old or new, wants to sell the land "free of occupants"; and (2) when the new owners, who acquire land that has occupants, disregard the latter's rights to residency and use agents of the government to evict the people. All of these issues are full of economic and political factors. The strength and violence that some use, supported by political backing, hangs as a permanent threat over many peasants.

1.4. Defects in the Administrative Institutions

The vicissitudes that many peasants have to endure in defense of their rights are not few. They begin to lose all hope for an effective response on the part of the responsible agencies. If to this is added the natural difficulties that they have in dealing with administrative and judicial proceedings, we can easily understand their disappointments and mistrust. Let us recall briefly the major conflicts produced by a bad, or even corrupt, administrative process:

a) *Double sales.* It does not seem possible, but there are cases—and not just a few—of double sales. Sometimes, a real estate company charges the farmers the value of their land and issues only a simple receipt; at the same time, it sells the same land to a third party. At other times, the very institution that has responsibility for implementing settlement programs, the Institute of Rural Welfare, because of lack of knowledge or error, issues more than one land title for the same parcel of land. The worst part is that the final solution to the problem is in the hands of those who are affected.

b) *Direct eviction.* Cases appear relatively frequently in which the property assigned to the peasant is repossessed because of overdue payments. They are replaced by someone who, in addition to being able to pay easily the current selling price in cash, tends to have backing or political pull. Of course, we cannot ignore the obligations contracted by the peasants who have been assigned land, but when land becomes a commodity and business item, no attention is given to the real reasons for nonpayment, and one must condemn the arbitrariness to which the peasants are subjected. A social problem is created that tends to produce anxiety for the humble workers.

c) *Problems of measurement and boundaries.* The lack of measurements properly carried out at the appropriate time results in unnecessary costs (new measurements) and, what is worse, alienation and even quarrels between neighbors. This type of problem appears predominantly in the older peasant settlements since it is in those areas where the demographic pressure is most acute.

d) *Eviction due to increases in land prices.* Pressure on the peasants to leave the land so that the price of the land can be increased is exerted mostly by private land speculators (companies or individuals) who, on one hand, ignore the tariffs of the Institute of Rural Welfare and, on the other hand, commit abuses with their price demands and payment schedules. Frequently, these speculators count on easy recourse to force in order to impose their demands.

e) *The role of justice.* This account of the problems that affect the peasant would not be complete if we did not mention the legal procedure. Once again, we must point out, painfully but clearly, the mistrust in the role of the judges. This mistrust is fully justified since there are innumerable examples of violations of rights that not only go unpunished, but are protected by decisions and sentences that are simply unjust.

1.5. The Paraguayan Attitude concerning Land

Obviously, the Paraguayan peasant can live for years and decades without worrying about his land title. It would seem that he has no interest in ownership nor in formal documents. And we wonder why many so easily sell their lands or hand over their right to occupy them after having paid for the improvements. Is this not in sharp contrast to their attachment to the soil, the village, the valley, so apparent at other times?

In general, it seems that the "civilization of paper" and the reliance on documents have not yet been accepted nor are they in effect in the peasant society of our country which, in great part, is still an oral culture. Few persons have their documents, and there is little concern about getting them. The lack of initiative in registering children in the civil register is also notable. Rural people have a deep conviction that, in relation to the land, their best titles have been and continue to be the occupation and working of the land.

Experience has taught the peasant that his work is the primary source of subsistence and welfare of the family. For this very reason, he believes he has every right to continue to use the land worked by his ancestors. Modern capitalist economy, on the other hand, transforms the land to a commodity and exerts pressure, through this model, on the peasant mentality.

We are barely drawing attention to a topic that deserves attention and study in order to understand fully the deep sense of the land belonging to the peasant and the peasant belonging to the land he works.

Undoubtedly, we should turn to the education of the rural people in relation to the importance and value of the documentation of the land they occupy. The best arrangement of the fruits of their labor will permit the peasants to make the payment on their land without fear or worry.

Our reflection should point out emphatically our trust in the rural people, trust born out of the awareness of their great capacity for work, sacrifice, and initiative. They have shown this innumerable times throughout history and during difficult circumstances. Their subsistence with dignity and honor, in such adverse situations and with so few resources, alone speaks clearly of the personal quality of the Paraguayan peasant.

1.6. Peasant Organizations

With the well-organized network of middlemen and exploiters of all types, peasants have little or no possibility of competing with their products nor can they hope for just payment. Thus, we see the fundamental importance of organizations that protect and guide the peasants in planning their work, production, and marketing. Many times, it is these middlemen who create difficulties or obstruct the effectiveness of those organizations. Neither do they hesitate to resort to dishonesty nor the use of intimidation and mistrust.

The Church's teaching, however, is different. We will limit ourselves to recent documents. Pope John Paul II said, "the right to work can be destroyed when the peasant is denied the right to free association, keeping in mind the just social, cultural, and economic development of the agricultural worker" (LE, 21). And even before this papal document, the Episcopal Conference of Paraguay, in its *Plan de Pastoral Orgánica,* indicated that one of its priorities was "a pastoral approach to land that supports the formation of peasant organizations and defends rural workers. . . ." This priority was also pointed out in the 1979 pastoral letter *The Moral Healing of the Nation,* the objective of which was the "reweaving of the national social fabric." In that same letter, the bishops asked that those responsible for the national public welfare recognize and support those so-called intervening bodies.

On the other hand, there are many positive experiences that have been carried out on the level of peasant organization and the integrated human development of the peasant. Some of these experiences have been supported by nonpeasants (e.g., public, social, and church-related individuals and institutions) and others, to a lesser degree, have been promoted by the peasants themselves. We can cite cooperatives, farm committees, and base communities as those of major significance.

2. The Christian View of Reality

2.1. Reality and Doctrine

Stopping to examine the reality does not mean looking for negative aspects to criticize nor does it mean limiting ourselves to enthusiastic approval of the positive aspects of the reality. Our objective is different. We believe it is necessary to know and to evaluate the reality in order to transform it in accordance with God's plan. The Lord does not want us simply to repeat gestures like automatons and even less does he want us passively to accept unjust and irritating situations. The bishops have the right and the obligation to illuminate reality with the light of faith. There is nothing worse than a mute and blind Church. More than once, those of us who are, by God's plan, designated as pastors and servants of this people have remembered this responsibility. Thus, the understanding of the Paraguayan peasant and his relationship to the land lead us to confront the present situation with the Word of God and with the teaching of the Church, which will shed light on the reality with its particular vision. We have discovered facts that do not correspond to the Word of God. We cannot be quiet nor do we wish to be quiet. We propose these reflections, therefore, as elements for judging the reality and as a firm base for effective pastoral work.

2.2. A Christian Perspective of the Problem

We offer, as a synthesis of the Christian doctrine on the domination of nature and on the destiny of resources for the use, benefit, and full development of all people, the teaching of Vatican II, which says in the *Pastoral Constitution on the Church in the Modern World:*

> God intended the earth and all that it contains for the use of every human being and people. Thus, as all men follow justice and unite in charity, created goods should abound for them on a reasonable basis. Whatever the forms of ownership may be, as adapted to the legitimate institutions of people according to diverse and changeable circumstances, attention must always be paid to the universal purpose for which created goods are meant. In using them, therefore, a man should regard his lawful possessions not merely as his own but also as common property in the sense that they should accrue to the benefit of not only himself but of others (GS, 69).

2.3. The Word of God

In the story of the beginning of the earth, in the first chapter of the Bible, we see that God the Father made man and woman from the mud of the earth, but "in his image and likeness" (Gn 1:26). God put them in the Garden of Eden in order that they work and care for it (Gn 1:26). People, all people, are the owners of the earth. On their own right, although subordinated to the absolute right of God, they can take possession of it by their understanding of reason and the strength of their hands. Every human being has the right to take from the surrounding world the means of existence, such as food, clothing, and other life resources.

This initial design of God that established such solidarity between people and the earth has continued, then, in spite of all the vicissitudes that human existence has endured. Since the original fall of Adam and Eve, the image of God imprinted on our nature has become clouded over by sin. The earth has also become difficult, producing thorns and resisting the efforts of labor. Consequently, the estimable relationship between people and the earth has suffered serious upsets and the rational and honest use of the gifts of the land has become very difficult. Temptations and overwhelming appetites of all kinds assault men and women. Sometimes, overcome by laziness or sloth, they abandon the land, leaving it unworked and deformed by infertility. More frequently, however, we see greed and avarice, people desiring the products of the earth, attempting to build up inordinate riches, committing violence, and setting snares to abuse the welfare and rights of others.

The prophets of the Old Testament were vehement spokesmen; with the Word of God, they denounced the iniquity of the rich and powerful who made use of the land to oppress the poor and exploit the humble. We hear, for example, Amos, the "prophet of social justice," tell us: "Jehovah says, 'I will be inflexible with Israel for its crimes. Because they sell the innocent for money and the destitute for a pair of shoes. They stomp the poor into the ground and make trouble for the humble'" (Am 2:6–7). The prophet Isaiah says, "Oh, you who join house to house and add field to field until you take up all the space, you will remain alone in the middle of the country" (Is 5:8).

Christ's coming into the world has once again transformed the violent condition of our relations to the land. The New Testament confirms the moral regulations of the Old Testament and raises them to an ethical level. The grace of Christ makes it possible to seek, own, and utilize the goods of the earth in justice and fraternal holiness. "You cannot serve God and wealth," says Jesus (Mt 6:24). And also: "Seek first the kingdom of God and its justice and the rest will be given to you besides" (Mt 6:33). Jesus does not condemn ownership nor the individual use of earthly goods, but he vehemently reminds us of the involvement and participation of all people, especially the poor, in these same resources that God the Father left for the subsistence and welfare of all. We can summarize New Testament doctrine on the possession and use of the goods of the earth by saying that it is *necessary* and *legitimate,* but we cannot nor should we ever convert these goods into absolute values. Jesus spoke clearly: "This is my commandment: love one another as I love you" (Jn 15:12) and also: "This I command you: love one another" (Jn 15:17). This is the new command of Jesus. From that time on, it is clear that the strength of Christian love is the only force that makes possible the practice of justice. Love is the heart of Christianity.

That is how the first Christian community understood it. "All believers lived together and held all things in common" (Acts 2:44). "There was no one needy among them because all who had fields or houses sold them, bringing the proceeds of the sale and putting it at the feet of the apostles; and they distributed to each one according to their needs" (Acts 4:34–35).

2.4. Tradition and Teaching of the Church

Those testimonies from the Scriptures were gathered with great zeal and explained by Christian thought. In the early centuries, the Church fathers closest to the origins of the gospels and more sensitive to the cries of the biblical prophets, left precious teachings about the meaning of ownership, the destiny of the land, the responsibilities of the rich, and the demands of justice. What stands out most is their insistence that God's initial intention was that all the goods of the earth were meant for all people. According to God's design and natural law, there are no human beings left out nor is there exclusive ownership. Thus, Saint Basil preached, "The earth was given in common to all people; no one should consider one's own that which is more than necessary." Saint John Chrysostom is more explicit and more vehement: "God never made some rich and some poor. He gave the same earth to all. All of the earth is the Lord's and the fruits thereof should be for everyone."

Throughout the centuries, concepts and language have become more precise. Saint Thomas Aquinas, master of Christian medieval thought, summed up the doctrines of the fathers in a composite, precise way. He taught that private ownership is permitted, but, when speaking of use, the goods are communal and whoever owns them should readily give them over to anyone who needs them (2:2 c 66, a 2). Then, we come to the modern age and the great changes in the cultural and socioeconomic order of recent centuries. The Church wants to be faithful to this long, doctrinal tradition and also to the serious demands of the times. It does not want to stop exercising its teachings on the so-called social questions. Principally, the Roman popes offer us an abundant source of teachings. Pius XII, in 1941, reaffirmed the natural right to private property but pointed out and demanded, at the same time, its social function. John XXIII, in his encyclical *Mater et Magistra*, affirmed that "the entirety of the earth's productivity is designated for the meritorious sustenance of all human beings." We have already mentioned the fundamental content of the teachings of Vatican II. Let us still mention Paul VI who, in *Populorum Progressio*, stated that "private property does not constitute for anyone an absolute and unconditioned right" (23). The same pope, in *Octogesima Adveniens*, calls attention to the serious threat inherent in the irrational exploitation of nature. Finally, let us remember the many doctrines of John Paul II that have particular and concrete resonance for having been delivered in Third World countries. "The Church defends the legitimate right to private ownership but teaches no less clearly that over all private property hangs a social mortgage so that the goods serve the general destiny for which God has given them" (*Address to Mexican Indians*, January 1979). In his first encyclical, *Redemptor Hominis*, he pointed out that "the exploitation of the earth, not only for industrial but also for military purposes, and the development of techniques that are neither controlled nor in harmony with a universal, authentically human plan frequently carry with them threats to the human environment and alienation and separation in their relationship to nature."

From all this plentiful doctrine, which the Church has given over the centuries, we can point out certain fundamental rules:

a) *The earth is a gift from God for all people.* This means the universal sharing of goods is a fundamental law that legitimizes and regulates their possession.

b) *Individual possession of the land is legitimate as long as it is not seen as an absolute right, without limit and immovable.* It is a true right but limited and relative, rational and congruent so that all human beings have sufficient access to the use and fruits of the land.

c) *Human work and the technical exploitation of nature to attain proper and respectable subsistence must be done rationally and morally.* Thus, the conservation and improvement of nature and the dignity of men and women remain intact while access to the ultimate values of existence remain open. It is worth more *to be* than *to have.* People can then exercise their freedom as sons and daughters of God and as citizens; their basic rights and obligations can be respected.

d) *All peasants have the natural right to possess a reasonable plot of land where they can establish their home, work for the subsistence of their family, and have the security of their existence.* This right (established in our own national constitution) should be guaranteed so that its practice will not be an illusion but rather a reality. This means that, in addition to title of ownership, the peasant should be able to depend on technical education, credit, insurance, and marketing.

2.5. The Moral Aspect of the Problem

The moral aspect of the Christian understanding of this problem deserves special consideration. In effect, the subject of the common good cannot be forgotten when one attempts to establish the moral demands of ownership. It is essentially a moral problem.

The search for the common good, in traditional Church doctrine, is so obligatory that no one can consider one's self exempt from this law. In our *End of the Year Message*, we recalled that it is "a duty that is incumbent on all citizens." We also said that the common good is the total of all conditions that permit individuals and communities to reach their own fulfillment. The participation of all citizens in the search for the common good is, therefore, a right and a duty. And this involvement is translated into the overcoming of a selfish concept of private property. Thus, the bringing together of goods can be achieved, not as the fruit of spoils or as gifts, but as the result of the active participation of citizens in production and national development.

Therefore, the presence of justice will be very important in this search and involvement, in the sharing of goods, in all things. Justice is an ongoing disposition to give to each person what is due to her or him. There are different forms of justice that are mentioned as aspects of a fundamental requirement. So, we speak of *social* justice as the obligation of all persons to contribute to the common good of humanity. In the private sphere, one speaks of *distributive* justice (just distribution of goods and responsibilities) and of *commutative* justice (the regulation of the interchange of goods). It is not possible, therefore, to forget the complex character of justice in a concrete situation. And, above all, it is not possible to not emphasize that all are obliged to contribute to the common good of all humanity.

It is not a question, finally, of dealing with social justice and individual justice; it is a question of understanding that social living together assumes the presence of love. Only love, authentic love, that which respects the dignity and rights of one's brother and sister, is capable of bringing about justice in the freedom of the spirit. And, in this freedom of the spirit, to seek, in the judicial code of society, the way to define the right to property in order to put it in harmony with the demands for the common good. The challenge of our time is to find the channels so that the many people who need the land for living and working can have access to property. If the answer is not easy, neither is it impossible. We only need to remember the words of Pope Paul VI, in his encyclical *Populorum Progressio,* as the synthesis of our reflection:

> If the world is made to furnish each individual with the means of livelihood and the instruments for his growth and progress, each man has, therefore, the right to find in the world what is necessary for himself. The recent Council reminded us of this: "God intended the earth and all that it contains for the use of every human being and people. Thus, as all men follow justice and unite in charity, created goods should abound for them on a reasonable basis." All other rights whatsoever, including those of property and free commerce, are to be subordinated to this principle. They should not hinder but, on the contrary, favor its application. It is a grave and urgent social duty to redirect them to their primary finality (PP, 22).

3. Pastoral Guidance

3.1. An Ecclesiastic Response

The knowledge that we have a land problem in Paraguay and the reflection that the Word of God and the teachings of the Church elicit lead us to formulate, in this last part of our work, these pastoral guidelines.

First of all, they express the commitment that the bishops assume in the name of the Church in Paraguay. Precisely because we consider ourselves members of the national community, do we want to give this proof of our concern about the welfare of the country.

But also, we propose goals and tasks that should be sought and undertaken by everyone. Those who govern and those who are governed, residents of the countryside and the cities—all must take part in the huge task of obtaining for our people a life that expresses the force of justice in a reign of genuine human and Christian love.

We will point out, for better understanding and order, some short-term and long-term tasks. Finally, we will explain the duties we believe correspond to us, the bishops.

3.2. Short-Term Tasks

a) In the first place, it is essential and urgent that we have a broader understanding and greater awareness of the Church's mission in today's world and, in particular, of the doctrine or social teachings of the Church. The Second Vatican Council, the papal encyclicals, the documents of the Latin American bishops who met at Medellín and Puebla, and our *Plan de Pastoral Orgánica* are the principal points of reference to meet this objective. All of this is in order to create and form conscience and a Christian criteria in personal, family, and social behavior, thus joining together faith and daily life.

b) As a consequence of the above, it is imperative to guide, promote, and accompany Christians in the living of the ecclesial reality, in communion and in participation with one another. Necessarily, this communion of life and participation in the mission of the Church are expressed in solidarity that helps people to grow and to be more fulfilled.

c) If the peasants should be the initiators of their own liberation and growth, the importance of an adequate education is unquestionable. And, of course, it is also necessary that they be provided with technical, financial, and legal assistance.

d) In today's circumstances, it is imperative to secure land to be worked. We offer the services of National and Diocesan Social Care in order that, through the offices of legal assistance, the solution to their problems might be facilitated.

e) We believe it worthwhile to be reminded, once more, that these tasks cannot be thoroughly carried out as long as the activities of the pastoral workers are not related—through education and in practice—to the concrete problems of Paraguayans. The aforementioned problems should be assumed not only in the specific tasks of social pastoral work, but also in all of the orders and dimensions of ecclesial activities, above all in the growth and maturation of Christian faith. We repeat our confidence in the efforts performed in this sense in catechetical, liturgical, youth, vocational, and pastoral works.

3.3. Long-Term Projects

a) We believe it is necessary to study a new model of appropriation, tenancy, and use of land; one that would not necessarily be individual but would respond to community guidelines of possession and development, making the best use of pieces of land and valuing the most reasonable agricultural work. All of this is certainly a challenge. It assumes an enormous amount of effort, study, prudent initiatives, and adequate organization. But it is worth it to take on this challenge. Remember that our country is not the first to have risen to the test.

b) With a resolute commitment to the common good, it is necessary to review carefully the existence of the large estates (*latifundios*), especially the nonproducing ones that are located on land suitable for agriculture near where numerous peasants are living without land or without sufficient land for the full development of human beings. A more equitable distribution of such properties ought to be sought.

c) Laws and regulation of this type ought to grant initiatives for the protection of the rural producer, both in regard to ownership and development of the land and in marketing of his products. More can be said of the ongoing assistance and accompaniment that the life and work of the farmers demand.

d) The political development model that we wish for Paraguay requires wide and careful study. It is a very important topic that demands attention to the natural conditions of the country, to the various circumstances and difficulties, both on a long and short term. Paraguay will become, in a very short time, a major producer of electrical energy. Its use should be sensible and at the service of all Paraguayans and should be studied well ahead of time.

e) Finally, let us emphasize that the defense and preservation of the natural surroundings and the environment constitute another element in this integrated project. Nature is a gift of God for our use and benefit. However, its use must not be destructive, but rather rational, proportionate, and humane. We still have time to preserve the wealth and beauty of our ecology. With our technical skills, we must save and improve this magnificent gift that is Paraguay, for Paraguayans.

3.4. Our Duties

a) We want to make efforts, resolutely and systematically, to provide doctrinal and pastoral guidance, in a personal as well as in an institutional way. This is our obligation as pastors of local churches and as members of the Episcopal Conference of Paraguay.

b) We also want to give clear testimony of the preferential option for the poor, solemnly proclaiming Puebla and ratifying the *Plan de Pastoral Orgánica* of the Paraguayan Church. Unquestionably, in our country, the peasant farmers are one of the most vivid examples of the poor.

c) We understand our commitment as bishops in terms of listening, being near, generating, and accompanying the whole process of growth and maturation in the integrated human welfare of those peasants who are assuming initiative and are taking on the defense of their legitimate rights so that they might be in a position to fulfill their corresponding responsibilities.

d) We vehemently call upon priests, brothers, sisters, catechists, leaders, and all responsible persons within communities, so many of whom know and feel the painful situation of our rural world. We urge all of them to echo our voice and pastoral commitment and to put into action, in an organized way, the many possibilities of service that these circumstances demand. We ask everyone for the necessary help for the Christian formation of people's consciences and to assume courageous positions in the face of genuine changes in accordance with the dignity of the human being, in the midst of a society ever more insensitive and selfish.

3.5. Our Final Word

Our vocation and position as Christians, our love of our brothers and sisters, should express themselves in effective solidarity and in the force of justice. There is much to study and to do. There is work for everyone. We ask that each one assume that part of the commitment that corresponds to him or her in order to extend the kingdom of God and his justice in our country.Beloved brothers and sisters, our pastoral letter comes at a most important moment. The drama of the floods has affected the entire nation. And it is the entire nation that, in solidarity and in exemplary ways, has demonstrated the capacity of Paraguayans. We ask God to help us overcome this painful test. We exhort everyone to continue in their generous assistance. And, looking to the good of the nation, we offer our reflection, our prayers, and our pastoral commitment.

The maternal protection of the Blessed Virgin of Caacapé and the example of the Blessed Roque Gonzalez of Santa Cruz will help us accomplish, with great anticipation, the plans that we have to make Paraguay the gift of God of all.

Episcopal Conference of Paraguay
Asuncion, Paraguay
June 12, 1983

Peru
Declaration of the Bishops of the Jungle Region
(1980)

From the beginning of its missionary work in Latin America, almost 500 years ago, the Church has faced the challenge of native and marginal cultures.

In preparing for the Roman Synod of Bishops on "Christian Family in the Contemporary World," the bishops of eastern Peru (Amazonian Region) believed that something new was expected of them. They attempt to examine as clearly as possible the situation of persons and families of their region. Changes that are taking place affect native societies, as well as riverbank, peasant, and urban lower-class societies.

For some years, Peru has attempted to fill its interior with colonizers. Some colonizers, and especially outsiders, exploit the resources of the area and move on, ignoring the rights of native communities by infringing on their lands and forests. They have indiscriminately depleted some resources, such as wood and fish.

Further, the bishops denouce the witholding or delay in granting titles to the lands their people have been holding since time immemorial while watching titles for exploitation of the lands and forests being given to national and foreign entrepreneurs.

1.   We bishops of the jungle, meeting in our Fifth Episcopal Assembly, along with priests, sisters, and lay delegates of our local churches, to study "The Mission of the Christian Family in the Contemporary World," the topic of the next Synod of Bishops in Rome, feel that the Lord expects something new from our Church in the jungle here and now.

Reflecting on the situation of the family in its sociocultural, economic, political, and religious context, we have noted how this complex reality deeply affects most of our families, and especially the families of native peoples, riverbank inhabitants, peasant families, and those of the popular sectors in the jungle cities, a situation that restricts them to a life of insecurity, anxiety, and poverty.

2. Therefore, we are fully convinced that, as pastors, we cannot ignore the cry of these families, living and suffering in this situation of injustice, struggling for a more just and family-spirited society, where it will be possible for families to develop and fulfill their Christian mission as community of life and love, open, and standing in solidarity.

3. "By virtue of their origin and nature, by the will of the Creator, worldly goods and riches are meant to serve the utility and progress of each and every human being and people. Thus, each and every one enjoys a primary, fundamental, and absolutely inviolable right to share in the use of these goods, insofar as that is necessary for the worthy fulfillment of the human person. All other rights, including the right of property and free trade, are subordinate to that right. As John Paul II teaches: 'There is a social mortgage on all private property' (OAP, III:4). To be compatible with primordial human rights, the right of ownership must be primarily a right of use and administration; and though this does not rule out ownership and control, it does not make these absolute or unlimited. Ownership should be a source of freedom for all, but never a source of domination or special privilege. We have a grave and pressing duty to restore this right to its original and primary aim (PP, 23)" (*Puebla, 492*).

4. From this perspective, and in fulfillment of our pastoral mission, we feel impelled to raise our voice with regard to very serious situations:

   a) The disregard, in practice, of the rights of many of our indigenous communities, especially with regard to their natural resources: lands, forests, wetlands.

   b) The indiscriminate exploitation of these resources, especially lumber and fish, which is despoiling our jungle and adjoining area, leading to economic and ecological damages to indigenous communities and the peoples of the Amazon. Most of the economic benefit from this exploitation goes to a very few.

   c) We are astonished to note the fact that, while many of our indigenous, riverbank, and peasant communities find that their requests to have the land they have occupied from time immemorial are denied or postponed, both national and foreign companies are receiving licenses to exploit lands and forests over vast areas. We cannot but protest this situation.

5. We therefore urge:

   a) Respect for, and compliance with, the Law for Native Communities and the Development of the Jungle and Adjoining Region, taking into account the environment and the cultural characteristics of native, riverbank, and/or peasant communities.

   b) That the surveying and titling of land of native communities and peasant families in the jungle and adjoining areas be hastened, in accordance with recent legal decisions.

c) That the natural resources of our brothers and sisters, the natives, riverbank inhabitants, and/or peasants be respected: lands, forests, wetlands, and rivers, thus safeguarding the basis of their subsistence.

6. The Joint Assembly of Bishops and Pastoral Agents has enabled us to recognize the human Christian values present in, and exemplified by, so many families in the jungle, even though they do not always reach the ideal that the gospel and the Church propose to the Christian family.

Above all else, however, we want to encourage and support the notable effort that families in the Amazon are making so as to embody fully and carry out the mission the Lord has entrusted to them, a mission to inspire the Christian community and transform society.

Lima
April 12, 1980

Bishop Miguel Irízar
Apostolic Vicar of Yurimaguas

Bishop Lorenzo Guibord
Apostolic Vicar of San José del Amazonas

Bishop Gustavo Prévost
Apostolic Vicar of Pucallpa

Bishop Luis M. Maestu
Apostolic Vicar of San Ramón

Bishop Gabino Peral
Apostolic Vicar of Iquitos

Bishop Venancio Orbe
Prelate of Moyobamba

Bishop Juan José Larrañeta
Auxiliary Bishop of Puerto Maldonado

Bishop Odorico Saiz
Apostolic Vicar of Requena

Bishop Augusto Vargas
Apostolic Vicar of San Francisco Javier

Southern Pacific Coast, Mexico
Statement on the Refugee Situation
(1982)

Among the first to call attention to the plight of Central American refugees were the bishops of the Southern Pacific zone of Mexico. To their pastoral areas, thousands of persons fled from the ravages of war, guerrilla activity, and repression under a military government in Guatemala.

As pastors, the bishops are mindful that they are to defend and promote the rights of the whole human person. They urge the formation of a large network of persons who will carry on alleviating the "terrible necessities" these refugees have. The bishops describe the conditions in which they find the refugees living, petition the Mexican government for assistance, and address their brother bishops in the neighboring dioceses of Guatemala.

Through the years following Vatican II, the bishops of bordering regions of both countries had met regularly to discuss common problems and pastoral strategies. Now, the Mexican bishops recall that Guatemalan bishops had spoken up "when no one dared to speak clearly nor to express themselves freely because they know that any expression could cost one his life."

In their petitions to the Mexican government, the bishops specifically ask for mechanisms to guarantee the security of the refugees, for a process that will not demand documents the refugees do not possess, and for administrative practices that will not be burdensome. The bishops also petition the government to grant free access to the refugee zones for "good-will" observers and journalists.

To our priests, men and women religious, and in general to all our pastoral agents, to all our faithful, and to all Christians and all people of good will.

With the arrival of thousands of Guatemalan peasants and Indians in the areas under our pastoral care, we feel we must address ourselves to you to tell you about the situation of these unfortunate brothers and sisters; to explain to you the measures of Christian charity we think we should take to help them; and, especially, to appeal to your virtues of generosity and hospitality toward them.

We are conscious that defending and promoting the rights of every human person is also an essential part of our pastoral ministry and that, in Puebla, we had already noted the phenomenon of migrations and of exiles in our countries. Hence, we trust that our word will be effective in arousing a wide net of humanitarian solidarity so as to alleviate the terrible needs that these refugees have communicated personally in our conversations with them in the regions where they have taken shelter.

In the Third General Conference of the Latin American bishops, we had already stated that "the Church takes up the defense of human rights and joins in solidarity with those who champion them" (*Puebla*, 146). "Sociopolitical imbalance on the national and international levels is creating many displaced people. Such, for example, are the emigrants, whose numbers can reach unexpected proportions in the near future. To them, we must add people who have been displaced for political reasons (e.g., those in political asylum, refugees, exiles, and all the various people lacking proper documentary identification)" (*Puebla*, 1266).

On that occasion, out of pastoral concern, we had also stressed that "the Church proclaims the necessity of the following rights, among others, and their implementation: . . . the right to life . . . to physical and psychic integrity, to legal protection, to religious freedom, to freedom of opinion . . . to fashioning one's own destiny . . . to work, to housing, to health . . ." (*Puebla*, 1270–1272).

Hence, just as on other occasions, we have addressed ourselves to you in a collegial fashion to give voice to your problems and to let you know about our criteria and pastoral directions; this time we are doing so as spokespersons for these unfortunate brothers and sisters—many of them Christians and pastorally committed in their own country—and we are making an urgent appeal to you so we may provide for them the Christian response they are demanding of us.

The season of Lent presents itself as a call for us to revitalize the penitential spirit to which we are called during these days, living it with the dimension of charity that it originally had: to give up something so as to share it. The day of charity that will be celebrated on the First Sunday of Lent also invites us to live the penitential spirit in this manner.

1. The Situation

Thousands of peasants and Indians from the neighboring country of Guatemala—with which we share more than 800 kilometers of border—are increasingly seeking refuge in our pastoral zone. There are men (especially old men), women, and children, and they arrive in pitiful physical condition, filled with horror and sadness over the conditions of aggression and persecution they say they are suffering in their own country. They often arrive sick, malnourished, without enough food, and suffering terrible psychological traumas. Many parents find themselves forced to give their children away among our peasants and fellow citizens, simply in order to safeguard their lives in such an emergency. When they arrive, many children are missing their parents or relatives.

They say they have been sent fleeing from their villages and settlements; that their relatives, neighbors, and acquaintances have been murdered and tortured; that their houses, belongings, and harvests have been burned; that for now, there is no safety for them in their country. Hence, they find themselves urgently needing to seek refuge temporarily on the Mexican side. They cannot return now, since many who have tried to do so in order to save a few of their scarce possessions or who have been forced to return have met their death or have disappeared.

Upon arriving in our country, they set up shelter in the hills and under the trees and share among themselves the little food they have been able to carry. They have encountered the hospitality and affection of our peasants, who share with them their scant resources. A good number of these refugees have kept up an ancient tie with some of our communities and even have family connections.

Needing work to supply their basic needs, some of them have found jobs on nearby ranches and farms, where unfortunately—as also happens with our own citizens—they have had to accept unjust pay. Despite the fact that they are struggling to set up minimum conditions of health while contending with the polluted waters of rivers, which often carry in their currents the bodies of fellow citizens, rotting and often eaten by vultures and buzzards, the situation is becoming desperate since the coffee and cotton harvests are coming to an end.

Therefore, what is needed from you is emergency first aid to provide them with the absolutely necessary food, clothing, medicine, and somewhere to stay. Since they themselves have the skills and qualities needed to be self-sustaining and to develop, they must be provided with tools for working. In addition to the generosity and mercy that we now think all Mexicans are called to practice toward them, it is possible to find in our country and elsewhere ways they can become organized economically so that the presence of these refugees among us will not lay even greater burdens on our poor peasants.

We firmly believe that the aid we are all obliged to give them should be absolutely disinterested, and not—as we know to have been the case elsewhere on other occasions—the chance to selfishly seek prestige or an occasion for ideological, political, and even economic manipulation by our own citizens or by foreigners. It is our intention to aid these unfortunate brothers and sisters, in a Christian manner, in all their needs. The fact that many of them profess Christianity and confidently approach us seeking help only motivates us more.

In a manner that is absolutely disinterested, we offer our collaboration and cooperation to other aid committees, whether national or foreign, official or unofficial, that have been set up or will be set up for this purpose.

Although for the refugees themselves, this situation is transitory and therefore our aid is simply to fill a need, and although we are convinced that we must respect their community ties and their geographical and cultural roots, we nevertheless believe that this situation will continue for some time. Through what our people have said, and through events reported by national and international press, we are aware of a military cordon that the Guatemalan authorities are extending along the whole border of our country. We also repeat that many of these Indians and peasants say that for now they would rather die from a bullet in Mexico, than return to be tortured, persecuted, and murdered in their own country. There they have neither security nor resources.

2. Petitions to the Mexican Government

We are very pleased to see that our country has been gaining international respect and sympathy from many people because of the way it has been defending the just principle of the free self-determination of peoples and nonintervention during such conflictive moments in history.

We made the same point ourselves at Puebla when we stated: "The right to a just form of international coexistence between nations, with full respect for their economic, political, social, and cultural self-determination" (*Puebla*, 1276).

We are also pleased that, despite all the self-serving misrepresentations, our country has proved capable of appealing to the ethical conscience of the world in the midst of various recent situations that cannot leave people's conscience indifferent.

In keeping with our people's traditional values, attitudes, and commitments of friendship and hospitality, Mexico has been able to serve as a transitory home for many of the world's exiles, especially from Latin America, and particularly during the most recent years of its history.

We should also keep in mind that, given the global nature of regional conflicts in the modern world, the eyes of many peoples are observing with both concern and hope the way we act with regard to the situation Central America is currently suffering.

We are also confident that—despite the ugly incidents we recently had to lament on our southern border—our authorities will try to be consistent with the demand we make that our own citizens be treated well and respectfully elsewhere, and that they will give the refugees for whom we now plead the safeguards and aid they are demanding.

The authorities of our country have the organization and experience needed to provide aid within our country to groups suffering misfortune, and they have been doing so worthily and efficiently under difficult circumstances. In that connection, we are pleased to note that the Intersecretarial Committee to Aid Central American Refugees has been set up and is now working, and that the United Nations High Commissioner for Refugees (UNHCR) has been warmly received. We see as a positive sign, the fact that this international institution has established an office in our country.

Nevertheless, we urge our civil authorities:

- to continue to implement all the juridical mechanisms necessary in order to guarantee fully the safety of these refugees in our country;

- to reevaluate, in view of the utterly exceptional circumstances of these people, the requirement of impossible paperwork;

- to ensure that the administrative structures that must be set up to aid these refugees—thus, enabling them to really exercise their rights—not be so burdensome and difficult as to further augment the anxiety and suffering they bring with them.

We emphatically beg those in authority to be on the alert so that these refugees not be subjected to extortion, mistreatment, or abuse by low-level civil authorities or by the country's security forces.

We are also aware that our country is not opposed to the presence of good-willed observers nor to national or international journalists, who by spreading the truth will be able to help defend the life and safety of these refugees, increase solidarity with them, and sustain the image of dignity and respect Mexico has been able to win in the concert of nations.

For ourselves, we reiterate that we are always ready to collaborate and cooperate, through authorized commissions, with international efforts recognized by our government or with both official and private bodies set up for that purpose.

---

3. Greetings to Our Brother Bishops of Guatemala

Being on the border with your country, we cannot forget to greet you, brother bishops of Guatemala, with whom our pastoral zone has long maintained very sincere bonds of friendship, arising out of our common pastoral concern for our peasant and Indian communities.

Oaxaca, San Cristóbal, Tehuantepec (Chetumal would have been included were it not for the earthquake that devastated our whole country) on the Mexican side, and Huehuetenango, Guatemala City, Solola, and El Quiche on the Guatemalan side were the main places in which a number of us met to reflect and plan our activities after the council. As Puebla noted with regard to the whole continent (cf. *Puebla*, 667), out of such meetings and conferences there has emerged a strong friendship among a number of us.

"To take on episcopal collegiality in all its dimensions and consequences on both the regional and universal levels" (702) was the commitment expressed at Puebla, which we now intend to carry out. This is all the more so, for besides suffering along with your people, who have been ravaged and decimated in a variety of ways, you have seen the elimination or disappearance of some of the best Christians; you have experienced a situation of persecution against the Church (as you yourselves stated in your April 8, 1981, letter and more emphatically, in a statement on August 6, 1981); you have felt in your own persons insecurity, snares, calumny, death threats; and you have felt impotent as your closest coworkers were tortured and murdered. Along with you, who are "witnesses to the pastoral work" of priests, religious, and catechists, "we praise and render a homage of admiration and thanksgiving for your silent and sacrificial surrender that, in . . . notable cases, has been sealed with your own blood." These examples are signposts along the path of a history of salvation, and they strengthen our Christian hope in the establishment of the kingdom of God.

Following the example of John Paul II, in his November 1, 1980, letter to you, we also want to show our admiration and solidarity for the effort with which you have accompanied and supported those who work apostolically on behalf of the poorest; because, as Church, you have set yourselves "in the line of the gospel and of its divine

Founder, who in his life showed a preferential love . . . for the dis-inherited of the earth"; because as responsible pastors, despite "ir-rational violence . . . [that] has led to the loss of freedom," and its replacement by "terror and fear," you have spoken when "no one dares to speak clearly nor to express freely his or her opinions . . . for they know that any expression can cost one's life" (*Pastoral Letter*, April 8, 1981). Your fortitude strengthens us.

Knowing that you and the pastoral agents still working with you are concerned about so many of the faithful who have had to leave, we assure you that we are sparing no effort to ensure that their lives are safe and that they have decent subsistence when they are forced to remain here. We are pleased that the Christian refugees can accept us as their pastors and brothers while they are in our midst, and we feel unworthy since in them we receive Christ needing bread, clothing, freedom, and human dignity.

---

4. Conclusion

We want to appeal to Christians and to all people of good will so that there may be a greater awareness of how urgently necessary it is that we help all refugees from Central America, and especially those from Guatemala because they are close to us, thus giving concrete proof of our traditional values of hospitality and making our Christian commitment something real in history. Our own diocesan churches want to become involved in this effort.

We also encourage all pastoral agents who have taken initiatives in our dioceses to continue to help our refugee brothers and sisters in communion and in mutual coordination. We offer our support for this work, which is exhausting and not free of risk.

In order to keep track of initiatives, suggestions, aid, and available personnel, and in order to channel them and put them to work, information and activity can be centralized in our various diocesan chancery offices and in the Solidarity Committee of the Diocese of San Cristóbal.

We exhort all believers to raise their hearts to the Lord, through his Son, who sent us the Spirit, who calls us to unity in love, so as to hasten the establishment of his kingdom. (We urge that, in cele-brating the Eucharist, priests in our zone use the text of the Mass for "Those Who Have Fled and Exiles," found in Masses *ad libitum* in the *Roman Missal*, when permitted by liturgical norms.) In these prayers, we know that Mary, the Mother of God, who with Joseph had to go to Egypt for the survival of her Son, whom Herod's fury made a political exile, will mediate for us before that Son. It is our firm hope that the Father will today call his Son out of Egypt so as to lead him to the promised land.

San Cristóbal de las Casas
Chiapas
February 27, 1982

Archbishop Bartolomé Carrasco
of Oaxaca

Bishop Samuel Ruíz Garcia
of San Cristóbal

Auxiliary Bishop Jesús C. Alba
of Oaxaca

Bishop Arturo Lona Reyes
of Tehuantepec

Bishop Hermenegildo Ramírez, M.J.
of Huautla

Colombia
Statement on Drug Addiction and Drug Trafficking
(1984)

Beyond the argument of who is to blame for the drug problem—users or producers—the Colombian bishops discuss the situation of drug addiction and trafficking in their country. Statistics are such that the bishops say only that drug consumption is "great or very great." They are thoroughly alarmed not only by the large numbers of drug users but also by the effects of drug consumption that last for generations, passed on from parent to child.

Though it is a problem that affects all the Americas— as was pointed out at the Puebla Conference—and the larger world, the bishops concentrate on the problem at home. They are appalled by a drug culture that includes terrorism and eroticism and by thousands of young persons whose minds and wills have been lost.

The bishops examine causes that range from loss of a sense of God to permissiveness and economic opportunities. They also point to coverups by powerful traffickers. In a "war without quarter," the bishops call for Colombians to save their country for today and tomorrow, suggesting action on several levels.

1. A Somber Picture

1.1. "The joys and the hopes, the griefs and the anxieties of the [people] of this age, especially those who are poor or in any way afflicted, these too are the joys and hopes, the griefs and anxieties of the followers of Christ," says Vatican Council II (GS, 1).

As pastors of the Church in Colombia, we make our own this cherished conciliar expression as we approach the somber picture presented to us by the alarming and incalculable use of drugs in our country and the criminal fact that drug trafficking has become big business. Growing the plants and preparing, distributing, and selling the drugs have

393

become a sinister enterprise. It is not joys and hopes but griefs and anxieties that we see in this scourge afflicting our country.

1.2.   When the bishops of the continent, meeting at the Puebla Conference, referred to the grave evils darkening the horizon in Latin America, they also referred—indeed, many times—to drug addiction and to the criminal activity of drug trafficking (cf. *Puebla*, 58, 577, 1267).

1.3.   There is something here that is hurting and threatening our nation. Hence, we feel it our duty to point it out and to offer enlightenment as heralds of the gospel.

2. Scope of the Problem

2.1.   Statistics on the real consumption level of mind-altering drugs in our country do not concur, but the discussion here centers on the question of whether the amount is large or *extremely* large. Information on drug consumption by young people is astonishing, and reports on adults—both men and women—are also alarming.

2.2.   Drug use of various kinds is unquestionably causing ravages in persons. The evils for the family and for society are very serious. We are aware of the struggle being waged against similar situations in other countries, where people are convinced that, unless the harmful advance of drugs is stopped, whole generations may be lost.

2.3.   Both these phenomena of drug addiction and drug trafficking and their influence on the suicidal mindset of our society, which has gone so far as to speak of a "drug culture," are so blatant that they cannot be ignored. However, in April of this year, the Holy Father, John Paul II, in one of his catecheses on the topic of youth, spoke rather of a "culture of death afflicting the world," which must be denounced, and which is based on "drugs, terrorism, eroticism, and other kinds of vice."

2.4.   Our young people are being destroyed by the use of drugs, goaded on by those true merchants of death, who are leading them on to a fearful physical and spiritual degradation. The damage done to the victims of these dreadful vices on their own person are obvious, often even leading them to lose their minds and wills. It deeply pains us to see many thousands of young people in these sad and pitiful circumstances.

3. Causes

3.1.   *Ignoring God and loss of moral values.* The primary cause of these evils and of their willing acceptance in various circles is now, as in the past, as Saint Paul noted, ignoring God and his law (cf. Rom 1:28–32). As a necessary consequence and as a new cause of tremendous wrongdoing, we find the reversal and even the loss of moral values. It should not be surprising that in a society that, even while it still calls itself "Christian," turns its back on God, and which, with an alarming permissiveness, shows disdain for the moral teachings of the Church, is opened to all kinds of vices and excesses that undermine the human family. Hence, there is an insatiable appetite for money and pleasure as ideals to live for, and drug users and traffickers become celebrities.

3.2. *Crisis of the family.* One very special circumstance, which gives rise to and aggravates the problem of drug addiction, is the crisis of the family. Young people and adults who feel unwelcomed at home, where there is neither love nor dialogue, fall into friendships and habits that lead them to sink frightfully into these evils. Those who contribute to the breakup of homes are also responsible for this drama of drug addiction and drug traffic.

3.3. *Bad example.* A very serious factor leading people to fall into these vices is the negative witness given in so many respects by those who should guide the community. When, for its own financial support, the Colombian government continues to advertise alcoholic beverages, which are also harmful, when many teachers destroy the minds of children and young people with their example or their teachings, when parents who severely admonish their drug-addicted children fall into drunkenness and other vices, the foundation for urgently needed campaigns is itself being undermined. We must overcome these inconsistencies if we want firm and effective results from these efforts to improve the situation.

3.4. *Social and economic circumstances.* There are other causes, such as social and economic ones, that lead people to seek the kind of escape produced by drugs or the income that motivates traffickers from the poorer classes. To this, we should add unemployment and, in both cities and villages, the lack of fitting means and environments for healthy recreation and suitable use of free time.

3.5. *Publicity that makes crime attractive.* A further cause tending to aggravate these problems is the publicity given to crime and criminals, through poor handling of news by the media. There are even some who lend themselves to publicity campaigns that attempt to minimize and even justify drug-related activities, through certain charitable works ostentatiously presented and paid for with money made in drug trafficking. Such news, presented suggestively, arouses the curiosity that for so many people has meant a one-way journey to the abyss of vice.

3.6. *Complacency.* The fact that society stands by in silent complacency, that there are no denunciations at opportune times, and that some persons accept gifts from those involved in these illicit activities has also had a hand in worsening the problem. Such situations are abetted when such traffickers, who persist in their crime and seek to cover it up with donations, encounter weak attitudes. When people do not undergo conversion, but rather seek ways to cover over situations of sin, in this case as in others, there must be enough courage to say, like the apostle Peter, "May you and your money rot . . . " (Acts 8:20).

---

4. Paths toward Overcoming the Problem

4.1. *Deep motivations.* Only when we are deeply motivated can we overcome the evil within ourselves. It is particularly through a total assent to Christ, to his law and his grace, that we can raise ourselves *from* life according to the flesh *to* life according to the Spirit, as the apostle Paul teaches (cf. Rom 8: 5–12). Hence, in response to the flight toward drugs, Pope John Paul II points to the need to lead people to live with "love, friendship, understanding, communication" (*Address,* September 21, 1980).

4.2. *Preventive measures.* Preventive campaigns must be stepped up decisively. Whatever is invested in such campaigns, when they are well conducted, is crucial for defending our people. Young people must be drawn away from the illusory pleasures of drugs. Peasants must be taught not to change their beneficial crops for the bewitching harvests of plants that will end up poisoning their children and the entire community. The state should promote activities that lead people in a healthy direction, rather than the evils brought by drugs. In agriculture, the state ought to aid food production and crop rotation. Destroying bad crops is not enough; good crops must be grown.

4.3. *Rehabilitation of those who have fallen.* Those who have fallen into the grip of these destructive vices must be provided help by the various members of the community and organizations that can provide serious and well-tested individual and group therapies. Everything done to extend a hand to pull them out of vice is a deeply Christian deed. Institutions that help drug addicts recover must be encouraged, and many more must be started for they are utterly necessary in these anguished times that our society is experiencing.

4.4. *Harsher laws.* Colombian laws to punish drug users, and particularly laws to punish drug traffickers, must be harsher and applied very firmly. Countries that have drawn up severe laws—or are in process of drawing them up—are doing the right thing. When persuasion does not produce the desired fruits, legitimate authority must be exercised with rigor.

5. Those Who Fashion and Carry Out Rescue Activity

5.1.   *All good citizens.* Forced into a war to the bitter end with these vices and crimes, committed to rescuing the Colombia of today and tomorrow from these great enemies that threaten to annihilate it, yearning for the definitive victory of good over evil, we call all citizens in solidarity to be artisans of a great victory.

5.2.   *The Church.* First of all, we pastors of the Church feel committed to work in this urgent salvific action. We witness the spiritual and material afflictions of individuals and families, and we will not remained unmoved. All members of the Church have to lend a hand in campaigns, initiatives, and actions to combat vice in its causes. We support the positive efforts being made in different parts of our country to seek the rehabilitation of those who have been prostrated by the vice of drug addiction. In preaching, through severe treatment in the confessional of those who are guilty, in newspapers and magazines, in religion classes, in all our pastoral activity, we must be clear about the seriousness of the problem and provide concrete solutions. We are pleased to note that among the activities of our Church have been institutions that effectively rehabilitate drug addicts.

5.3.   *Parents.* We turn our thoughts to parents because of their powerful influence in society and because of the primary nature of their position. As they fully take on their mission, their contribution will certainly be decisive in this great campaign. Let them think of their children and the other members of the family community rather than their material goods and their personal preferences and pleasures. When they do this, they are strengthening this primary bulwark of our society.

5.4.   *The government.* The state should continue to put its full energy into the struggle against drug traffic, a struggle undertaken more decisively after the death of a courageous minister. Let the Congress pass strong laws with sanctions that will serve as an example, together with all those laws that further harmonious progress in our country. Let the judicial branch apply the laws vigorously, and let the police act bravely and with dedication; let them both carry out their duties with unswervable rectitude. They should act without fear or timidity and without any hesitancy, despite any dalliances in this matter in the past, remaining firm because of the immense seriousness of the problem and of the ignominious crimes into which those involved in drug traffic may fall.

5.5.   *Teachers.* Teachers have an irreplaceable role in this patriotic campaign. Their witness; the formation and high ideals they provide to children and young people; their ongoing teaching of moral values; their timely presentation of the grave dangers involved in drugs—all are tasks incumbent on those who undertake teaching activity with an upright intention. In this educational labor, there should be a great openness to teaching religious and moral principles, as well as an openness to the diligent activity of chaplains, who can provide guidance to young people during this period in their life, which is so decisive, and may steer them away from the paths of corruption.

5.6.   *The media.* It is extremely important that the media, properly channeled, collaborate in all such campaigns. There are many technical and didactic resources for prodding and spreading ideas that are useful for both formation and information and for creating a healthy attitude. There are many opportunities for effective action in the major media, as well as in simple forms of communication, that can easily reach all circles. A contribution that people expect of communicators is that they manage the news sensitively and prudently.

5.7.   *Those rehabilitated.* Likewise, the very people who are directly affected by these evils and plunged into this agonizing slavery of vice are also called to help with their own effort. They are called to be co-authors of this great rescue endeavor. There are many cases of young people who, with exemplary effort, have managed to free themselves of these ills and recover their dignity and return to work. Young people should struggle to rise up from this abyss with courage and optimism.

5.8.   *Those who make full reparation.* And finally, let those who have been engaged in drug trafficking reflect before God and their country on the immense evil they have caused, let them no longer practice this most serious crime, and let them prove that they have repented and given up completely all such contemptible trafficking. A radical basic change in the behavior of such persons, reflected in an effective reparation for the damages they have caused, would be a very significant contribution to this great enterprise of redeeming a suffering country.

Conclusion

The picture of shadows and despair that we indicated at the outset can be transformed into horizons of peace and paths of joy. If other sister nations are struggling valiantly to eliminate evils as great, we can and must do the same. Let no one evade his or her own responsibility. May we all be one in the defense of those Christian values that are the firm foundation of our national identity. Thus, faithful to God and to our country, we will certainly see our sorrow turn into joy.

The Virgin of Chiquinquirá, Queen of Colombia, who has always exercised her maternal care over our nation, will be merciful and powerful in aiding us in this new and decisive campaign for the freedom of our country and for the triumph of the supreme Christian values.

The Bishops of Colombia
Bogotá
July 14, 1984

Honduras
Statement on War, Dialogue, and Reconciliation
(1983)

As early as 1982, while U.S. and Honduran leaders were denying that Honduras was being used as a staging base for the Nicaraguan contras, *the bishops' conference called attention to the situation. They saw the threat of an internationalization of the conflicts shaking Central America, which could involve Honduras "in a spiral of violence."*

They repeated an earlier message of John Paul II in Central America that war would only lead to further self-destruction, "to bring about war would be to once again crucify Jesus Christ." In a petition that foreshadowed the Arias Peace Plan, they plead for dialogue from which no one is excluded.

1.   On the occasion of our last plenary meeting, we, the bishops of Honduras, have once again verified the difficult situation that is hindering life in Central America in general, and in Honduras in particular. To the problems of poverty—characteristic of underdeveloped countries and already referred to in our pastoral letter of October 1982—have now been added border tensions and rumors of war. In our continual relationship with the people, we have been able to observe an increase of anxiety and insecurity in the face of the threat—so widely publicized—of an internationalization of the conflicts shaking Central America, which could involve Hondurans in the spiral of violence. Our people are aware that a war among Central American countries would be truly a fratricidal war. It would be a war in which, although the weapons might come from other countries, we would be the ones contributing the dead, and in much greater numbers than ever before because of the growing sophistication of the arms currently being used.

2.   We have also proven that our people neither seek nor want war, but rather have a great longing for peace. Honduras belongs to "those innocent peoples yearning for peace, who do not want division nor war nor hatred nor injustice," referred to by John Paul II at the beginning of his pilgrimage to Central America (*Address upon Arrival in Costa Rica*, March 2, 1983). We, the bishops of Honduras, want to reinforce, together with the Supreme Shepherd of the Church, "the heart-rending cry that arises from these lands and invokes peace" (ibid.). Although this outcry does not have such dramatic aspects in Honduras as in the neighboring countries torn apart by real internal wars, we are becoming an echo of it. Moreover, in a certain way, we feel urged on by the recent words of John Paul II, addressing himself with great emphasis to all Central American bishops: "Maintain, at all cost, the harmony among your nations. Permit nothing so lamentable and alarming as the slightest threat of war which would pull the countries into a battle and convert them into a sad scene of foreign interests" (*Address to the Central American Bishops*, Costa Rica, March 2, 1983).

3.   In the face of our advocacy for peace, we want to repeat with greater urgency the criteria that we stipulated in our pastoral message of October 22, 1982. At that time, we mentioned with concern the "accusations of warlike incidents"; the predictions and wagers over an "inevitable and imminent war" in which Honduras would find itself involved; and the news that "they also speak of a general arms increase that will also affect our nation." In the face of this reality, we stood clearly against the war, recalling the statement of John Paul II: "Nothing is lost by peace; everything can be lost in war" (*1982 World Day of Peace Message*). We added then that "war would not solve our problems but would increase and worsen them."

4.   Today, when the situation is even more serious than last October, and when the results of war could imply a severe blow to the lives and development of our people, we want to once again reaffirm the criteria that we expressed then, and now repeat, that all of us, as Christians, should be "builders of peace and harmony in the spirit of the Beatitudes . . . because only a profound reconciliation of our intentions will be able to overcome the spirit of dialectic, of enmity, of violence—be it hidden or open—and of war, which are the paths to self-destruction" (John Paul II in Leon, Nicaragua, March 4, 1983). We should remove obstacles that inhibit dialogue, exhaust all their possibilities, and remember that dialogue for peace demands major efforts, including sacrifice. What we said to the journalists last year, indicating to them that, if at some time they take sides, it be "always in the cause of peace," we repeat today to all in Honduras and Central America who have in their hands the tools for genuine negotiation and effective progress in the dialogue for peace. Participation in the international conferences presently underway to establish conditions for a pacification in our area, including the invitations for permanent observers from neutral nations in order to guarantee that there be no

belligerence on our borders, is part of the possible initiatives to pro-mote the climate of dialogue that our people long for and that the Church wants to bring about.

5.   In this same sense, we wish to join the pope in inviting to peace "those who, within or outside of this geographic area, wherever they may be, are taking advantage of, in one way or another, the ideo-logical, economic, or military tensions to impede the free development of those who so love peace, fellowship, and genuine human, spiritual, civic, and democratic progress" (John Paul II, *Address upon Arrival in Nicaragua,* March 4, 1983). We want peace, and we hope that the people, as well as those who govern them, make a deep and committed option in favor of that very peace. Only in that way will we be able to realize the wish of the Holy Father when he strongly repeated to the countries in the Central American region: "Let there be peace among your peoples. Let the borders be zones, not of tension, but rather of arms open to reconciliation" (*Homily in El Salvador,* March 6, 1983). In this task, both Honduran and foreign journalists have the great responsibility to present information in such a way that they do not produce hatred, fear, or unjustified alarm. They also have the duty and the difficult task of encouraging, by any honest means within their reach, the cause of peace and dialogue.

We all feel that to bring about war would be to once again crucify Jesus Christ.

6.   Conscious of the dangerous situation that is exacerbating our already anguished problems, understanding clearly that our people neither want nor seek war, and willing to utilize all honest means in our reach to construct peace, we realize that we cannot end our ex-hortations without strongly encouraging the use of the best means we have through our faith: prayer. Only prayer can bring us to an authentic conversion in which we discover God as Father and those around us, near and far, as true sisters and brothers. "To speak of conversion as the road to peace," said John Paul II, "is to advocate an artificial peace that hides the problems and ignores the worn-out tools that must be repaired. It is concerned with the peace, in truth, in justice, and in the integral recognition of the rights of the human person. It is peace for everyone, of all ages, situations, groups, origins, political preferences. No one should be excluded from the dialogue for peace" (*Address to the Bishops of El Salvador,* March 6, 1983). Only by recognizing themselves as children of the same God and brothers and sisters of all persons—a reality born of true conversion—will the growth of peace and justice in Central America be possible. Let us pray then, with all our strength, that God our Lord will reconcile our spirits and convert our hearts, especially of those who view violence as a valid recourse.

7. Let us take advantage of the celebration of the Holy Year of Reconciliation, whose main theme is the reconciliation with God and our brothers and sisters, to renew our strength and our prayers in favor of this peace that comes from God and for which we so deeply yearn. Let us pray that the spirit of the Lord inspire those who govern and all of those who have influence in Central America, so that, above and beyond human interests, a responsible consensus in the achievement of peace can be effected.

Tegucigalpa, Honduras
July 13, 1983

Central America and Panama
Message to Our People
(1984)

The bishops talk as Central Americans, not as citizens of neighboring countries, but as having a common identity. Perhaps, as one observer remarked, such "easy" identity gives one the basis for hoping there will be a peace plan deriving from the region itself.

The bishops characterize the situation in Central America in 1984, as "extremely dark. . . . We see the tragic signs of poverty, injustice, and violence over Central America, unleashed among brothers and encouraged by external forces." They readily admit internal causes for the conflict. But they also point to "the interference of the great powers . . . putting the peace of the region in constant danger."

Since 1970, the bishops have condemned human rights violations in Central America. The record grew much worse in ensuing years, and the martyrs' lists bear the names of Archbishop Oscar Romero and thousands of others, some with North American surnames. The bishops also discuss militarism, corruption, the family, and religious and ideological confusion.

Nonetheless, religious ferment has fostered "the extraordinary vigor of our Church, which has never seen as many vocations, joyfully committed to the Lord, among lay people, religious, and candidates for the priesthood, who fill almost all our seminaries.

1.   We bishops, pastors of the Church in the sister nations of Central America and Panama, meeting in ordinary session of the Secretariado Episcopal de America Central (SEDAC) in the Major Seminary of Our Lady of Suyapa in Tegucigalpa, Honduras, greet all of our brothers and sisters in the faith: bishops, priests, religious, laity, and all persons of good will who desire peace and prosperity for our peoples, the fruit of true justice and fraternity.

2.   This greeting and message of ours will be communicated to many communities of the isthmus in the Sunday Masses and newspapers of December 2, the First Sunday of Advent, the time of hope that

announces the coming of Jesus the Savior. We are pleased with this happy coincidence. The panorama of Central America is extremely dark. We see the tragic signs of poverty, injustice, and violence over Central America, unleashed among brothers and encouraged by external forces. Nevertheless, in the midst of so much pain and death, we sense an extraordinary force of redemption, of reconciliation, and of resurrection to a new life. We feel it in the extraordinary vigor of our Church, which has never seen so many vocations, joyfully committed to the Lord, among lay people, religious, and candidates for the priesthood who fill the spaces of almost all of our seminaries. We feel this force in the increasingly profound identification of our Church with the poor of our lands, who are becoming the protagonists and pastoral agents, inspired by the love of Christ, seeking not the death of brothers but their conversion and reconciliation with him.

3.   Almost fifteen years ago, in Antigua, Guatemala, the bishops of these nations—some of whom have already entered into the glory of the Lord—published a message that demanded the full recognition and observance of human rights in our nations. It would seem that that cry has fallen on deaf ears and on closed hearts. There have been and there continue to be so many violations of the most sacred rights of the human person.

4.   Nevertheless, the grace of the Lord is at work. Along the difficult way of the cross, a new light is dawning. Social changes required by justice, so long desired and so long postponed, as Pope John Paul II has recalled on various occasions, begin to be converted into reality. The necessary connection between faith and life in the social area and the struggle for justice is being evidenced more and more among many pastors, pastoral agents, and faithful.

5.   There is still a long way to go, but we continue on with our heads raised high because we are people of faith and of hope. The fundamental priority of the Church is and will continue to be *evangelization,* that is, the announcement of the gospel and the call to our personal genuine conversion to Christ, which must be manifest in the sacramental and interior life and in good works. This conversion must be social and communitarian in order effectively to impel us to be artisans of a just and fraternal society, the civilization of love, as an anticipation of the future kingdom that is to come.

6.   In the following points, we indicate some of the principal urgencies along this path.

I. Violence: War and Peace

7.   Armed violence has come to several of our republics and with it, the danger of turning into a regional conflict. This violence continues

to bear down on our countries, causing forced displacement of people within each country; the painful drama of refugees, widows, and orphans, whose number constantly grows; the abandonment of farming lands and the increase of unemployment; hunger, sickness, and the lack of doctors and medicines.

8.   Even though these conflicts have had internal causes, they have been strengthened by two external factors: the ideology, generally Marxist, on the part of the revolutionary groups and that of national security, which typically inspires repressive actions on the part of the armed forces; and the interference of the great powers, seeking to maintain their spheres of influence by feeding the arms race and militarization in the search for a precarious balance of forces, thus, putting the peace of the region in constant danger.

9.   We can do no less than to condemn the war and the related sending of arms to Central America, and we issue a fervent invitation to the dialogue for peace.

10.   In this connection, we offer our encouragement to our sister Church in El Salvador, which has struggled so that a dialogue might be achieved and has been accepted as moderator by both parties. We give our support also to the efforts of those countries that have sought effective measures to put an end to armed intervention in neighboring countries, to remove external forces from the region, and to allow Central Americans peacefully to settle their differences. We raise our voices equally so that those who make decisions at the geopolitical level may peacefully resolve their differences without continuing the useless shedding of blood in this region.

II. Militarism

11.   This situation of violence, among other evils, has generated an exaggerated role for the armed forces at every level of life in almost all our countries. Their members now form a privileged class, forgetting the specific role that the military has within society. They invade the civilian areas of life and frequently occupy the principal governmental positions dealing with the life of citizens, with certain exceptions in countries that are democratic or in a process of democratization.

12.   The accelerated growth of the military apparatus has involved an enormous expenditure of funds for the purchase of arms, taking these funds from budget items intended for more urgent needs of the population. This arms traffic dramatically increases the danger of a wider war in Central America.

13.   To maintain their hegemony, according to the ideology of national security, the armed forces exercise a dehumanizing control over the human person and all levels of civic life. In some nations, they have succeeded in putting thousands of citizens under strict military control through paramilitary bodies or patrols for "civilian self-defense." This has given rise to a destructive war-like spirit in large sectors of the population, especially among youth, with the foreseeable consequences of greater violence and loss of ethical values.

14.   We have hope that love of country and defense of its integrity and its most noble values may restrain group ambitions and the temptation of the armed forces to interfere in areas that are not theirs, to the harm and subjugation of the majority of the people of Central America.

III. Public and Private Corruption

15.   It is impossible to understand the wrenching drama of poverty without looking at the heavily dependent situation of the economies of our countries. On the one hand, the constant growth of our external debt reveals the cold and dehumanizing concept of the international economy, since the decisions regarding product value and quotas, loans and fuel prices, and so forth, are made outside our countries. On the other hand, our pastoral perspective sees the alarming reduction of the most urgent social services for the poor in the areas of health, work, housing, and education. Yet, measures of economic austerity imposed by the international organisms always hit hardest the poorest and most needy.

16.   Of very great concern to us is the high level of public and private corruption which, as it worsens the situation of our dependent economies even further, makes the solution of our internal problems still more difficult. Public corruption, such as the misappropriation of public funds, theft, bribery, venality, drug traffic, and arms commerce, has unfortunately become a fact, leaving those responsible with complete impunity while highly profiting from the international loans that are supposed to benefit all the citizens. To this public corruption, we must add also the corruption in the private sector, where tax evasion, illicit financial operations, the "sale" of jobs, contraband, and the hoarding of basic products are practiced—also with impressive impunity. All of this has led to a greater dependency and a greater impoverishment of our peoples, with the poor being the ones who suffer most the consequences of these moral disorders.

17.   The vices of the past and the present will only be eliminated finally when those responsible for them are sanctioned effectively and their impunity ended by the action of honest citizens and officials with a consciousness of their obligations.

IV. The Family

18.   All of the problems of our nation are felt within the family. It is Within the family that poverty, violence, war, and corruption make their effects felt. On the other hand, it is in the family where the moral social and cultural values have to begin. These values are requirements for a society if it is to achieve those fundamental goals of family and home such as personal formation, education in faith, and advancement of the community (cf. *Medellín*, "Family," 5–7).

19.   On a scale of values, the chief enemy of the family institution is without a doubt the commercialization of pleasure, entertainment, and vice purveyed by the merchants of the consumer society, which opposes or ridicules ever more openly the most sacred values of our culture related to the home. We refer especially to the constant commercialization of sex in the communications media, especially in movies and on television, where free love is celebrated; that is to say, love without any relation to responsibility between man and woman for marriage and the home. We recognize that in this problem there are internal factors such as the unstable makeup of the home, the large number of consensual unions, the large number of children born outside of marriage among our people, and so forth. But we recognize also the aggression of foreign cultural values, hostile to our faith, which are imposed upon us from outside.

20.   With equal concern, we have to mention the well-financed anti-natality campaigns carried on in our countries, often by the government or other institutions in favor of divorce, abortion, sterilization, and the indiscriminate distribution of birth control devices. These campaigns, often financed by foreign agencies and governments, represent a serious attack against the values and the rights of our peoples.

21.   The family is the first center of rights. Parental authority is a right and a duty toward children. It should be exercised as the first and the most sacred responsibility of the parents. The state, as well as the Church and the social institutions, should encourage, support, and esteem this parental responsibility and, for the same reason, respect it without trying to replace it. We must oppose and denounce every attempt by the state to inject itself between parents and their children in order to impose, through schooling or other means, its political or ideological point of view.

22.   In the face of this vast family problem, it is necessary for the Church, through its pastors, to defend the family in season and out, joining with all social forces to create the legal, economic, and other conditions favoring a more integral home. In order to increase the well-developed and effective efforts in this area, we recommend that each diocese, each parish, and each school give priority to the promotion of the family and that training courses for family promoters on all levels be established.

V. Religious and Ideological Confusion

23. Because we feel responsible for the doctrinal integrity of the faithful, we are greatly concerned about the religious confusion that, in the Central American community, has been generated by the many fundamentalist sects and by the ideological movement known as the "Popular Church."

24. In effect, there is an undeniable impact produced in our people by the aggressive and costly Evangelical propaganda which, responding frequently to hidden political motives, impedes every effort at integral human promotion, dividing and anesthetizing our communities with false spiritualisms and promises of easy salvation.

25. Faced with the proliferation of these religious sects, we urge that our people be offered a more complete and profound biblical and doctrinal formation; a greater consciousness of their belonging to the one Church founded by Christ; and a clear ecumenical sense that, respecting those who do not profess our religion, would have us reject the errors and uncover those whose exaggerated proselytism frustrates every effort to live in authentic ecumenism.

26. No less harmful is the divisive and conflictive work of the so-called Popular Church, which we should mention, even if briefly. It is not a question of a formally constituted entity in confrontation with the official or institutional Church, but rather of a movement seeking, under the appearance of a radical commitment to the poor, to instrumentalize the religious sense of the people in the service of particular political and ideological interests. The gospel is thus reduced, deprived of its undeniable transcendence, and Christ himself becomes but a human figure, a social leader, or just another revolutionary.

27. The Popular Church, conceived in this manner, ruptures the internal unity and cohesion of the Church, which is necessary for proclaiming the true message of the gospel according to the norms of tradition and the magisterium; it becomes one more sect by its juridical and doctrinal self-sufficiency and an instrument of whatever human ideology or political program.

28. Therefore, no Christian and, still less, no one specially consecrated in the Church should be responsible for breaking that unity, acting at the margin of or against the will of the bishops, "whom the Holy Spirit has placed to guide the Church of God" (John Paul II, *Homily in Managua*).

Conclusion

29.   In concluding this twenty-first regular meeting of SEDAC, we express thanks to the episcopal commission that produced the document *Christ Is Our Salvation*, which has served as a basis for our reflection in these days. With this message, we have wanted to emphasize certain aspects. We recommend to our priests, religious, and laity that they continue in this line of reflection and social action, firmly supported by the teaching of Pope John Paul II in Central America and in his recent addresses in Santo Domingo (October 11–12).

30.   If it seems surprising that, in this message, SEDAC addresses mainly themes of a social nature, it is not only because of the gravity of these questions. There is another reason, which we consider so important that we make it the object of our final point, namely, the limited effective presence of trained laity in secular structures. We would point out, in effect, that in all of our nations, as we mentioned earlier, there is a great revitalization of the internal life of the Church, as shown by the new structures of evangelization and especially by so many vocations of lay persons, religious, and priests committed to the Church.

31.   Through pastoral letters and messages, the episcopal teaching maintains a constant, careful presence in the social field, and we are quite often called upon to help resolve conflicts or problems of a social nature, which are of great importance for the good of the entire community.

32.   On the other hand, we often have to lament the absence of Catholic lay men and women who are sufficiently trained and committed to be of influence in professional and political fields, among workers and entrepreneurs, and so forth. This makes it difficult for problems that arise in these areas to find solutions in accord with the human values and rights that are based in the gospel.

33.   We believe that it is within the competence of the magisterium of the bishops, shared with our priests and other pastoral agents, to work for the formation of consciences that are more in agreement with the ethical and social teachings of the Church as regards the true understanding of politics and economy at the service of the common good. We must make greater efforts toward this goal.

34.   But it is also of great urgency that this social teaching of the Church be a truly constant part of all of our Christian formation, as Puebla emphasized (479), and that it be projected in very special and concrete ways in the various areas of human and common life (cf. *Puebla*, 1206ff). Only thus, with Christian laity truly converted to the Lord in their personal life and formed in the social doctrine of the

Church, can we hope for "the commitment of Christians to the elaboration of historical projects that meet the needs of a given moment and a given culture (*Puebla,* 553). It is clear that the faith does not directly offer political or socioeconomic models, nor can any one concrete model claim to be the representation of the faith, as the Second Vatican Council reminds us (cf. GS, 75). What is needed here is that within a democratic political pluralism, Christians should reflect upon the great problems of the community and take action in the light of faith.

Greetings and Blessings

From Tegucigalpa and under the protection of Our Lady of Suyapa, we renew the expression of our communion with and support for all priests, religious, and laity of our particular Churches. To all, we ask to be witnesses of hope in these difficult and conflictive moments in which we live. We trust in the grace of God; in the transforming force of the gospel; in the great human values of the Central American people; and in the true longing to achieve in our region a way of living together socially, firmly based in the justice and love that will give us the gift of peace.

Roman Arrieta Villalobos
Archbishop of San José
Outgoing President

Arturo Rivera y Damas
Archbishop of San Salvador
President

Antonio Troyo
Auxiliary Bishop of San José
Outgoing Secretary

Gregoria Rosa y Chavez
Auxiliary Bishop of San Salvador
Secretary

Central America, Panama, and the United States
Joint Statement by Central American and U.S. Bishops
(1987)

> *Ten bishops from the leadership of the Central American and Panamanian Bishops' Conference met with five bishop delegates from the National Conference of Catholic Bishops (USA). Profoundly concerned about the suffering that characterizes the lives of Central Americans, they agreed that "the solution of the conflicts that afflict Central America should be sought through political means. They were unanimous that the United States, in its relation with Central America, "should give clear priority to economic aid for development over military aid."*
>
> *The situation of Central American refugees in the United States occupied a central place in the bishops' discussions. They attempted to find "the best way of attending them spiritually and in every other way, including legal assistance."*

A group of ten bishops, members of the Council of the Presidency of the Central American and Panamanian Episcopal Secretariat (SEDAC), and a delegation of five U.S. bishops, representing the National Conference of Catholic Bishops, met in San José, Costa Rica, July 21–23, 1987. In our meeting, we examined the religious and sociopolitical situation of the Central American region, with special emphasis on the policy of the U.S. government toward the countries of the Isthmus, and the dramatic problem of the refugees and emigrants without documents from those countries, who have been forced to emigrate to the United States.

At the end of our reflection, carried out in an atmosphere of great fraternity, prayer, and communion, we are making public the following statement:

1. First of all, we want to emphasize our profound concern for the moving human suffering that characterizes, to a greater or lesser degree, the life of all the men and women who inhabit the countries of Central America. This suffering originates in the reality of poverty and in the complex problems that prevent these brothers and sisters of ours from living, according to their dignity, as children of God.

At the same time, we wish to express our hope for better days, given the extraordinary vitality of the churches in each of the Central American nations.

2.　We studied the problem of refugees from Central American countries who live under difficult conditions in neighboring countries. We wish to express our gratitude for the hospitality of those who have received them fraternally. However, as pastors, we have paid special attention to the hundreds of thousands of persons without documents from the Central American region who have been forced to travel to the United States because of the difficult living conditions in their respective countries. We did not exchange information on this situation, but rather studied the implications of the recent U.S. immigration law and the efforts of the Church in that nation to modify essential points of the law.

The most important moment (of our meeting) was a dialogue on the best way of attending them spiritually and in every other way, including legal assistance.

3.　As bishops of the United States and Central America meeting in San José, we have analyzed, from our point of view as pastors, the region's complex sociopolitical reality. After a frank and fraternal discussion, we agreed that the solution of the conflicts that afflict Central America should be sought through political means. This supposes an intense and persevering effort to reach a dialogue whose aim is peace at a national as well as a regional and international level.

We have also seen as a sign of hope the rise of democratic trends throughout Latin America, including Central America. We very decidedly encourage such trends but wish to stress that democracy is not limited to the political arena, but must also be social and economic.

We have also been unanimous in affirming that the United States, in its relationship with Central America, should give a clear priority to economic aid for development over military aid.

4.　The U.S. delegation, taking advantage of its presence in the capital of Costa Rica, managed to have a dialogue with President Arias, who explained to them in detail his plan for bringing peace to the region. In supporting this peace initiative and those presented earlier, such as that of Contadora and its Support Group, we pray for success in the meeting of the Presidents in Guatemala in the near future. (The meeting was, in fact, held in August 1987, and achieved a unanimous consensus on a concrete peace plan.)

5.　However, as true peace is not just the fruit of human effort but a "gift of God entrusted to us"—according to John Paul II's beautiful phrase—we exhort our people to ask the Lord for it in humble and persevering prayer. For that reason, we unite our hearts to the Day of Prayer that the Costa Rica Church has organized on the eve of the celebration of the Patroness of this nation, the Virgin of the Angels, to pray for the Presidential Summit in Guatemala. We hope that in the other nations we represent similar initiatives will be taken.

May Mary, pilgrim of faith, walk with us during this difficult stage of our history and obtain for us from her Son the precious gift of reconciliation and peace.

Puerto Rico
Peace among Human Beings
(1984)

The bishops of Puerto Rico join with the Synod of Bishops, which called for reconciliation, to overcome war-like aggression and to end the "scandalous" arms race. They also recall the recent "bloodying of Caribbean beaches" (presumably Grenada), and they hope to add their voices to those of the Holy Father and other bishops, concerning international peace.

The bishops acknowledge that political questions need political responses, but they insist that the arms race be considered from religious and ethical points of view as well. They trace the teachings of recent popes, especially of Paul VI, who termed the arms race an intolerable scandal.

Concerning Puerto Rico, their ethical-religious reflection leads to two issues: the degree of social and military vulnerability of the island, and Puerto Rico's contribution to harmony and universal communion. Given the strategic location of Puerto Rico and its heavy dependence on military spending, the bishops discourage arms stockpiling and encourage initiatives to exclude Puerto Rico from nuclear, biological, and chemical networks.

This will mean that Puerto Rico should begin to develop alternative economic strategies. The bishops favor a policy of multilateral disarmament that would be gradual and verifiable. They encourage Catholic educators to continue to foster Catholic social teaching in this regard.

The Conference of Catholic Bishops of Puerto Rico wishes to offer a message of peace and reconciliation in the last stage of the Holy Year convoked by His Holiness John Paul II. Still fresh in our minds are the words of the recent Synod of Bishops, words that call us to reconciliation and to overcoming belligerent aggression, the denial of human rights, and the scandalous commerce of arms. And we recall still the fratricidal conflicts that blooded the beaches of the Antilles archipelago and other parts of the world.

On this occasion, we only desire to unite our humble voice to the continuous and dramatic warnings of the Holy Father and to the declarations of so many brother bishops at the international level. We know that in recent times the theme of peace has been written about copiously and that there exist many organizations dedicated to promoting peace among brothers. We recognize equally that the theme is very sensitive and that we build toward a consensus regarding the necessity and the end of the arms race. Nonetheless, we perceive irrefutable facts, facts that are the source of profound preoccupation. So also, we base ourselves on the Catholic social thought that illuminates a correct understanding of such phenomena.

The first fact that comes to view is the precarious and illusive peace in which we live. Leaving aside the high degree of terrorism and delinquency that prevails on all continents, we note that the world witnesses dozens of belligerent conflicts: national wars, guerrilla actions, and civil wars. From the Second World War to present times, we have been witnesses of such great simultaneous and consecutive fratricidal occurrences that one can hardly point to even a brief period of general tranquillity.

In addition to that phenomenon, we must point out another equally ominous: the arms race. Here, we include not only the quantitative and qualitative development of the instruments of war, but also their sale and distribution. Though, for obvious reasons, the statistics about arms and military spending are not entirely believable, we know well that almost all countries, especially the great blocks of power, invest astronomical sums in military spending. The consequences are especially grave for less developed countries where vital necessities are less attended to because of the importation of arms.

But the economic aspect is not the only tragic angle from which to view the arms race. What especially preoccupies humanity is the real possibility that man is constructing his own destruction. Thus far, the great nations have accumulated a destructive force beyond proportion. It is not our intention to analyze these "storehouses of death" that threaten every part of the globe. Our judgment derives from religious and ethical concern. We believe sincerely that man has the right and the obligation to defend his ideals, his person, his community, his home. Nonetheless, this does not mean that man is condemned to annihilate his natural and historical heritage and to act in an irrational manner.

When we talk about the universal holocaust, we generally think of strategies of fateful nuclear extermination. So, there is the situation in which nuclear war leaves little or no hope of life thereafter. But, without minimizing those apocalyptic effects, we also emphasize the danger of biological, chemical, and conventional arms. The first two types can devastate life in all its manifestations and alter profoundly the ecological equilibrium of the world. The third type produces ever more abundant losses, brings in its wake a diplomacy of violence, and acts as an antecedent to nuclear war. As if the nuclear arsenal were insufficient, the great powers experiment with rays and other deathdealing means in outer space.

Evidently a complete inventory of military devices would take up innumerable pages. Although the affair is truly complicated, a general analysis reveals a determination to use whatever natural resources—physical, chemical, or biological—as adequate means to resolve any human conflict violently. From this comes what has been called the alphabet of terror: every bomb or military device has a letter or a euphemism, but at the base of this, we find science at the service of a political philosophy. A sign of the result of this alliance has already left its terrible imprint in some sectors of the globe and on testing grounds. Although the arms are now silent, we pay a terrible price in fear, poverty, and sickness.

Viewing such a picture, Christians and persons of good will face an inevitable question: Why do persons give themselves over to violence and allow the sword of full-scale war to hang over their heads rather than opening ways to peace? At first view, the reasons that motivate the aggressiveness of political or social groups are clear and simple: territorial expansion, ideological fights, economic crises, ethnic or religious discord, dispute about primary materials or world hegemony. Beyond these socioeconomic causes, scholars are accustomed to debating the primary cause of human violence. Some judge that it comes from a natural instinct, a heritage of evolution; others define it as a product of social living that makes vicious the pristine innocence of the human being.

Christians believe that God created us in original innocence, but our first fathers disobeyed and broke the fundamental harmony. That rupture, which altered the equilibrium of that positive relation with God, with our fellow human beings, and with nature, is known as original sin. That is the source of alienation, death, and egoism. Despite the fall that clouded over the dawn of humanity, hope prevailed through Jesus Christ, the Prince of Peace, who redeemed us from sin and death.

Men and women are free and are able to refuse this salvation. For this reason, scandal piles upon scandal, war upon war. And men and women walk, dragging a long chain of barbaric acts, in which conflicts are the causes and effects of other conflicts. We do not refer here only to individual sin but also to the structures of sin. We men and women have built towers of Babel, such dumbfounding structures of sin, as often as we weave a shady web of injustices that imprison men and women, that strangle their dignity and threaten their peace every day. The zeal for profit, the hunger for power, and many forms of materialism rush forward as roaming lions to devour millions of victims on all continents.

The Church, an expert in humanity, knows profoundly this situation and also has paid its quota of suffering in the martyred flesh of its faithful and its communities. From its foundation, it has proclaimed the ideal of its meek and humble Founder: blessed are the peacemakers. In the midst of historical ambiguity, it has proclaimed the supreme aspiration, the evangelical message: the kingdom of peace, justice, and love. For the Church, then, the work of peace is not a novelty or a passing fad; nor does she treat this as a political strategy in favor of one ideology or one block of power.

If the popes, the bishops, and Catholics in general have emphasized their statements about war in recent decades, this is due to the nature of the risk involving the survival of the present civilization. The classical arguments in favor of just war, particularly those dealing with just defense, require a careful examination at the present time to ponder the effects of a thermonuclear slaughter.

Naturally, we have to be realists and apply political methods to political problems. Nonetheless, it would be counterproductive to exclude ethical principles in favor of a realism more conformist and pragmatic. Some even have found in *Gaudium et Spes* an open justification for a system of deterrence:

> Scientific arms, to be sure, are not to be amassed solely for use in war. The defensive strength of any nation is considered to be dependent upon its capacity for immediate retaliation against an adversary. Hence this accumulation of arms, which increases each year, also serves, in a way heretofore unknown, as a deterrent to possible enemy attack. Many regard this state of affairs as the most effective way by which peace of a sort can be maintained between nations at the present time (81).

The last sentence of this citation does not represent support for the famous "equilibrium of terror," but rather, a simple statement of a thesis defended by many. The conciliar fathers transcended the politics of deterrence and exhorted men and women that they convince themselves

> that the arms race in which so many countries are engaged is not a safe way to preserve a steady peace. Nor is the so-called balance resulting from this race a sure and authentic peace. Rather than being eliminated thereby, the causes of war threaten to grow gradually stronger. While extravagant sums are being spent for the furnishing of ever new weapons, an adequate remedy cannot be provided for the multiple miseries afflicting the whole modern world. . . . Therefore, it must be said again: the arms race is an utterly treacherous trap for humanity, and one that injures the poor to an intolerable degree. It is much to be feared that if this race persists, it will eventually spawn all the lethal ruin whose path it is now making ready (ibid.).

Consequently, deterrence would be as a minimum or as a conditional step on the road to peace. It was so viewed by His Holiness John Paul II, in his *Message to the Second Special Session of the United Nations* in June 1982: "Under current conditions, deterrence based on balance—certainly not an end in itself but a stage on the way to progressive disarmament—can still be judged as morally acceptable."

The popes, always attentive to the signs of the times, had prophetized the moral advance of a slowed arms process. In effect, from September 30, 1954, Pope Pius XII observed to the World Health Association: "When, nonetheless, the use of these means brings with it an extension of evil which escapes totally from human control, its utilization must be rejected as immoral. One does not treat here of 'defense' against injustice and of the necessary 'safeguarding' of legitimate possessions, but of annihilation pure and simple of all human life within the radius of its effect. This cannot be permitted for whatever reason."

Pope John XXIII dedicated an entire encyclical, *Pacem in Terris*, to the establishment of peace, the supreme aspiration of humanity. In that encyclical, he became the spokesperson of justice, right reason, and a sense of human dignity, for urgently demanding the end to the arms race: simultaneous reduction of arms, prohibition of atomic arms, simultaneous disarmament, controlled by mutual and efficacious guarantees (see no. 112). Among his convictions about the present situation, Pope John XXIII emphasized that he rejected arms and promoted negotiations and agreements as means of resolving differences among peoples.

> We acknowledge that this conviction owes its origin chiefly to the terrifying destructive force of modern weapons. It arises from the fear of ghastly and catastrophic consequences of their use. Thus, in the age that boasts of its atomic power, it no longer makes sense to maintain that war is a fit instrument with which to repair the violation of justice (27).

The Holy Father laments that peoples are relegated to terror as a supreme law and they invest, for the same reason, great sums in military expenses. This does not place in doubt the motive for deterrence but insists on the priority of love in individual and international relations.

His Holiness Paul VI was no less categorical in his condemnation of the seeds of destruction. In his *Discourse to the United Nations Organization* (March 4, 1965), he affirmed that brotherhood and love are impossible as long as we fill our hands with guns. Even before bringing death and destruction, these terrible modern arms bring on nightmares, lack of confidence, and pessimism. The encyclical *Populorum Progressio* denounces the intolerable scandal of the whole arms race, of all national and personal ostentation, when so many peoples suffer hunger, misery, ignorance, sickness (see no. 53). We cite, finally, the words of Pope John Paul II in the encyclical *Redemptor Hominis* as a synthesis of his many pronouncements in favor of peace: "The Church, not having any weapons of its own, only those of the spirit . . . does not cease to implore each side of the two and to beg everybody in the name of God and in the name of man: Do not kill! Do not prepare destruction and extermination for men" (16).

All the aforesaid is but a demonstration of of the treasury of Christian peace that the Church conserves and enriches through the course of the ages. Many treatments exist that are designed for reflecting on the theological principles and practical implications of this sacred Catholic heritage. At all events, the Church does not pretend to offer technical remedies for political and military evils. Her mission is essentially ethical and religious. And it is precisely this ethical-religious preoccupation that leads us to ask ourselves about the repercussions of warmaking potential in Puerto Rico. Our preoccupation goes along two lines: the degree of social and military vulnerability of the island and the challenge to universal harmony and communion that this could engender.

Regarding the social and military vulnerability of Puerto Rico, history persuades us that the island has occupied a strategic place of great importance. The opinion prevails that this condition has affected adversely the social and cultural development of the country. Given the politico-military effervescence of the Caribbean region, it is possible that the military aspect of our economy might be accentuated, with the negative consequences that such a phenomenon brings. Without entering into the controversy about the presence of nuclear arms in Puerto Rico and the interpretation of the Treaty and Protocol of Tlatelolco, we have to discourage the arms race and encourage the initiatives begun to exclude Puerto Rico from the game of nuclear, biological, and chemical war.

It is necessary to revise seriously the strategies of economic development of Puerto Rico, in harmony with its natural resources, the situation of unemployment and spiritual tranquillity. Puerto Rico could become a center of hemispheric union, of peaceful enterprises. As we take for granted that we are a peaceful people, we bring something special to the effort for universal peace. May we be meek as doves and prudent as serpents. Meekness shields us from the scandal of being aggressive and of hypocrisy from those who expect peace and simplicity. Security will not permit others to take us as ingenuous nor allow others who come in sheep's clothing to deceive us.

Our greatest desires, surely, can be embodied in specific recommendations. Hence, we proceed to enumerate, by way of example, some suggestions that may contribute to the strengthening of peace.

We support, first, the mission of the United Nations. Its efforts dedicated to confer greater efficiency to its international authority are praiseworthy. We insist, as has the Church, in the urgency of establishing world government that would achieve a sane equilibrium among soverign nations and universal interdependency. This not being so, the very concept of a "United Nations" Organization would be a radical contradiction.

We argue also for a policy of disarmament that would be patiently realistic and courageously humanist. The process must be multilateral, organic, gradual, sincere, and verifiable. We believe that war is not something inevitable and that there is a factor more important than security of national space: security of the people, common security, security of the human race. This is the work of all, including the military sector, a group whose final goal consists in preserving peace. If we consign funds for defense, we support also economically works of peace, whether for the promotion of justice at the local or worldwide level or through organizations explicitly committed to a philosophy of peace.

To transform swords into plowshares also requires good educational projects in justice and peace. In Puerto Rico, Catholic education has taken some steps in this direction. We exhort Catholic educators at all levels and categories that they intensify investigation, teaching, and diffusion of Catholic social thought about this topic, which is so sensitive and important. In this way, we wish to join with our brother bishops of the United States episcopacy who have recommended educational programs and the formation of consciences as a pastoral response to the crisis of war in the contemporary world (see *The Challenge of Peace: God's Promise and Our Response* IV, B; Washington, D.C.: U.S. Catholic Conference Office of Publishing and Promotion Services, 1983).

In the same place cited above, the bishops of the United States propose three additional responses that we consider of great pastoral relevance: the respect for life, prayer, and penance. These "remedies" acquire a particular significance in a morally contaminated world where material progress contrasts sharply with spiritual underdevelopment. Peace requires a disarmament in the heart. If we accept human violence in all its manifestations, with what moral authority will we avail ourselves for rejecting war? If we take away life from the innocent by means of abortion, how will we expect that people will be opposed to the killing of civilians in a conflagration? We do not understand the philosophy of some who work for world peace and oppose any direct attack concerning abortion. The millions of abortions that are practiced in the world constitute a sordid and cruel war and are synonymous with a serious sickness of the human spirit.

Lastly, Christians bear the two arms of peace that are infallible:

prayer and penance. By prayer, we strengthen union with Jesus Christ, source of all peace, and with our brothers and sisters. As good sons and daughters, we have recourse to our Lady of Peace, who blesses us in union with all the saints, instruments of peace. Through contemplation, we live peace that the world cannot give, and we acquire the force of love that breaks all boundaries of hatreds and prejudices. The Church, sacrament of unity, reunites us in prayer, especially in the Eucharist. And, so that the embrace of peace be genuine and persevering, we are called to conversion, to penance. Penance is repentance, forgiveness, reparation for the damage of individual and collective violence. Especially in the Holy Year, the Church has wished to emphasize the importance of confession and reconciliation based on the redemption of our Savior and reparation for injustice (cf. Is 58:6–8).

Brothers and sisters, this is our message of peace. The theme of peace is very broad and complicated. We have only tried to touch upon certain aspects of the theme. Although we are a small island, we form part of the universe, of the Church. We must overcome any vision that is too closed or insular. We share the happiness and the hopes, the worries and sorrows of the world. Still peace continues to be the supreme aspiration of humanity. We ask our Lord that he convert us into apostles of peace and bless our efforts to work for peace among men and women. We hope that the Prince of Peace, born and crucified in humility, will give us a heart like his.

Puerto Rican Conference of Catholic Bishops
April 10, 1984

About the Editor

EDWARD L. CLEARY, OP, is professor and director of the Hispanic Ministry Program at Pontifical College Josephinum. He is also consultant to Latin American/North American Church Concerns, University of Notre Dame, and an associate, Center for Latin American Studies, University of Pittsburgh. He served as president of the Bolivian Institute of Social Study and Action and is editor of *Estudios Andinos*.

About the Translator

PHILLIP BERRYMAN has been involved in Latin American affairs for nearly twenty-five years. He worked in pastoral and humanitarian projects in Central America for nearly ten years. Since then, he has authored several books and magazine articles on Latin American themes. From his base in Philadelphia, he continues to research, lecture, and write on these issues.

Acknowlegments

Debts of gratitude for assistance in the completion of this work are extensive, owing to more that a year and a half of travels to Rome, Washington, New York, Princeton, and Cambridge, Massachusetts. To the technical specialists and librarians at the Pontifical Commission on Justice and Peace and Collegio Pio Latinoamericano, and to Fr. Arthur Brown and James O'Halloran of the Maryknoll Library, special thanks are owed. They not only responded to requests but generously sought out materials on their own initiative.

But the main acknowledgment of gratitude belongs to Pater Veracka, director of library; Eleanor Beyerly; Brenda Walker; Joan Oelgoetz; and Carnlyn Saffen of the Wehle Library, all of whom gave effective research assistance.

The creation of documentation centers in Latin America within the last twenty years have made possible great advances in researching the Church in Latin America. Among these centers, SIDEAT (Servicio de Información, Documentación, Estadistica y Asistencia Tecnica) of the Latin American Bishops Council (CELAM); SERV-I-R of the Latin American Conference of Men and Women Religious; CEP (Centro de Estudios y Publicaciones); and SELADOC (Seminario Latinoamericano Centro Documentación) rendered rapid assistance.

Bishop Ricardo Ramirez, Monsignor David Gallivan, and Thomas Quigley of the National Conference of Catholic Bishops, United States Catholic Conference, as well as members of national bishops' conferences and many observers in Latin America aided in the selection of documents. Valuable assistance was given by Rev. Robert Pelton, CSC, director, and colleagues of Latin America/North American Church Concerns, Institute for Pastoral and Social Ministry, University of Notre Dame, who aided in the administration of many details of this project.

A number of collegues helped in attempting to understand the contexts in which the bishops wrote the pastoral communications contained in this volume: James Malloy, Melvin Burke, Mark Rosenberg, Eduardo Gamarra, Catherine Conaghan, Daniel Levine, John Kirk, Dennis Ricker, Jaime Virreira, and Lawrence and Mary Hall. In addition, Rev. Msgr. John Kleinz offered invaluable editorial advice. Profound gratitude is also expressed to Rev. Msgr. Dennis Sheehan, president of Pontifical College Josephinum, for his encouragement.

Index